D1739173

Angelic Wisdom

STUDIES IN SPIRITUALITY AND THEOLOGY 2

Lawrence Cunningham, Bernard McGinn, and David Tracy
SERIES EDITORS

ANGELIC WISDOM

The Cherubim and the Grace of Contemplation
in Richard of St. Victor

STEVEN CHASE

University of Notre Dame Press
Notre Dame and London

Copyright © 1995
University of Notre Dame Press
Notre Dame, Indiana 46556
All Rights Reserved

Manufactured in the United States of America

Library of Congress Cataloging-in-Publication Data

Chase, Steven.
    Angelic wisdom : the cherubim and the grace of contemplation in
Richard of St. Victor / Steven Chase.
        p.   cm. — (Studies in spirituality and theology series : vol. 2)
    Includes bibliographical references and index.
    ISBN 0-268-00644-X (alk. paper)
    1. Contemplation—History of doctrines—Middle Ages, 600–
1500.   2. Richard, of St. Victor, d. 1173.   3. Angels—History of
doctrines—Middle Ages, 600–1500.   I. Title.   II. Series.
BV5091.C7C43   1995
248.3'4—dc20   94-47439
                                                                                    CIP

♾ *The paper used in this publication meets the minimum requirements of the*
American National Standard for Information Sciences—Permanence of
Paper for Printed Library Materials, ANSI Z39.48-1984

TO LEANNE AND RACHEL

. . . and of Richard,
who in contemplation was more than human.
—Dante, *Paradiso* X, 131–32

In several sources I have found the various characteristics of the dove
which, including them in this work, I took care to comment upon for
you. . . . Instead of a song the dove uses a sigh, because by wailing it
laments its willful acts. It is free of bile, that is, bitterness of anger.
It is eager for kisses, because it delights in an abundance of peace.
It flies in flocks, because it loves the community. It does not live by
predation, because it does not take from its neighbor. It collects the
finer grains, that is, moral teachings. It does not feed on corpses, that
is, carnal desires. It nests in the crevices of a rock, because it places
hope in the Passion of Christ. [The dove] lives near flowing water, so
that when it sees the shadow of the hawk it can more swiftly avoid its
approach, because it studies Scripture in order to avoid the deceit of
the approaching Devil. It raises twin chicks, that is, the love of God
and the love of neighbor. Whoever, therefore, has these traits, let him
put on the wings of contemplation by which he may fly to heaven.
—Hugh of Fouilloy, *Aviarium*, I.xi

your angels. . . .
Let them glorify your name and sing your praises,
for they have no need to understand [God's] word.
For ever they gaze upon your face and they read without
syllables that are spoken in time. . . .
They read; they choose; they love;
their reading is perpetual,
and what they read never passes away. . . .
Their book is never closed,
for you yourself are their book.
— Augustine, *Confessions* XIII.15

CONTENTS

ACKNOWLEDGMENTS   xiii
PROLOGUE   xv

INTRODUCTION   xvii

INTENT   xvii
METHODOLOGY   xvii
CONTEMPLATION   xix
"HOVERING"   xx
WHAT THIS BOOK "IS NOT"   xxiii
EXODUS 25   xxiv
ON EDITIONS, TRANSLATIONS, CITATIONS, AND TITLE   xxv

1. SETIM WOOD: 1
EXEGESIS OF THE ARK AND CHERUBIM

ON SANCTIFICATION AND WISDOM   2
HISTORIA, ALLEGORIA, TROPOLOGIA:
   THE INTERRELATION OF SENSES IN VICTORINE EXEGESIS   4
AN EMBODIED GROUND: RICHARD AND LITERAL EXEGESIS   8
ANTIQUI PATRES: RICHARD'S ALLEGORICAL FORMULATIONS   13
   The Christ Allegories   13
   The Greek Patristic Influence   14
   The Latin Patristic Influence   16
   Richard and the Patristic Influence   20
LIBER EXCEPTIONUM: EVIDENCE OF ALLEGORICAL CONTINUITY   21
SUMMARY   27

2. GILDING: 28
APOPHATIC AND CATAPHATIC THEOLOGY

RICHARD'S RECEPTION OF DENYS THE AREOPAGITE   28

CATAPHATIC AND APOPHATIC THEOLOGY IN DENYS THE
    AREOPAGITE   30
    Denys' Synthesis and Contemporary Commentary   30
    The Synthesis in the Dionysian CORPUS   33
CATAPHATIC AND APOPHATIC METHODOLOGY:
    RICHARD'S *DE ARCA MYSTICA*   37
SUMMARY   47

3. CROWN: SYMBOLIC THEOLOGY   48

A DEFINITION OF SYMBOL FROM RICHARD'S
    IN APOCALYPSIM JOANNIS   48
THE FUNCTION AND USE OF SYMBOL: THE WORK OF
    DENYS THE AREOPAGITE   51
THE FUNCTION AND USE OF SYMBOL: THE WORK OF
    HUGH OF ST. VICTOR   55
SUMMARY: SYMBOL AND METHODOLOGY   58

4. FIRST CHERUBIM: 61
CONTEMPLATION AND THE CHERUBIM AS SYMBOL

THE FUNCTION AND USE OF SYMBOL IN *DE ARCA MYSTICA*   61
    Patterns and "Thing"   62
    Nature Mysticism and Cataphatic Symbols   64
    Into the Self: Symbols and Soul Mysticism   67
THE SYMBOL OF THE CHERUBIM: CHRIST AND GOD MYSTICISM   70
    The Foundations of Richard's Angelic Spirituality   70
    The Symbol of the Cherubim in *DE ARCA MYSTICA*   75
SUMMARY   91
    A Reiteration and a Caution   91
    Cherubim, Symbol, and Contemplation   93

5. PROPITIATORY: APOPHATIC CHRISTOLOGY   97

BONAVENTURE AND CHRIST IN THE *ITINERARIUM*   98
A CONTEXT FOR RICHARD'S CHRISTOLOGY   100
    Denys the Areopagite   101
    Hugh of St. Victor   102
BECKONINGS AND HINTS: CHRISTOLOGY IN THE WORK OF
    RICHARD OF ST. VICTOR   104

INTERLUDE: IMAGE, THING, AND WORD   109
SUMMARY   111

6. SECOND CHERUBIM: ANGELIZATION   115
EXCUDENDA EST ANGELICA FORMA   116
ANGELIC CLOTHING   119
A SPIRITUAL BEING OF ANGELIC FORM   121
SUMMARY   126

VISIO   129

APPENDICES   137
    A. Book V of De arca mystica   137
    B. Hugh and Richard of St. Victor: Master and Student   142
    Table 1. Six Kinds of Contemplation in De arca mystica   147
    Table 2. Thinking, Meditation, Contemplation in
      De arca mystica   150

NOTES   151
BIBLIOGRAPHY   243
INDEX TO BIBLICAL CITATIONS IN DE ARCA MYSTICA   261
GENERAL INDEX   265
ABOUT THE AUTHOR   273

ACKNOWLEDGMENTS

This book represents the fruition and blooming of generous gardening. My teachers, editors, guides, and family have, indeed, been generous.

The book had its initial form as a Ph.D. dissertation done at Fordham University under Dr. Ewert Cousins who was, and continues to be, a model and inspiration for my own work in mysticism, contemporary spirituality, and interreligious dialogue. It is an honor to have been guided and taught by this man. Valuable insight into the Victorines and their milieu, as well as pastoral support, was provided by Professor Grover Zinn, Oberlin College. And Fr. William Dych, S.J. advanced my curiosity and interest in the possibilities of a history of spirituality founded, in part, on Christian doctrine. I would also like to thank Dr. Mary Calloway and Dr. Janet Ruffing without whose skillful intervention a healthy birth of the dissertation would not have been possible at Fordham. Thanks also to Professors Massa, Hudson, and Westphal. And gratitude also is due to Dr. Karlfried Froehlich at Princeton Theological Seminary who first introduced me to the marvels of the Christian mystical tradition.

The current book represents substantial revision of the original dissertation. A number of skilled professionals contributed to the final form; the book's comprehensibility is largely a matter of their talent; its faults are traceable to me alone. I am especially grateful to Dr. Lawrence Cunningham and Dr. Bernard McGinn, editors of the Theology and Spirituality Series, who showed early interest in my work and who both gave valuable suggestions for its improvement. Copyediting is becoming a lost art. But it is alive and well in John McCudden, whom I thank for his persistence and diligence with the manuscript. I would also like to acknowledge the staff at University of Notre Dame Press who kept the book on track: Director James R. Langford, my editor, Executive Editor Ann Rice, and all those working in promotions and production.

A book such as this does not see the light, let alone bloom without additional guidance in spiritual disciplines. The Rev. Robert Berger, C.F.C., first introduced me to insights of spiritual training. Father Ireneau Pop, a simple monk of the Romania Orthodox Church, who is himself a true flower of the vine, blessed me with his countenance. I also owe a debt of gratitude to the monks of Holy Cross Abby, Berryville, Virginia and the sister monks of Redwoods Monastery, Whitethorn, California.

This book is dedicated to my wife, Leanne Van Dyk, and to our daughter, Rachel Renée Chase. Leanne's wisdom and goodness were instrumental in nurturing this book to life. As the work progressed, Rachel became the incarnate heart born to us between the wings of the two cherubim.

PROLOGUE

This book is a contemplative and theological journey into the angelic wisdom at the heart of the symbol of the cherubim. Providing the guiding hand (*manuductio*) of this journey is Richard of St. Victor in his twelfth-century treatise on contemplation, *De arca mystica*. Richard's treatise encourages, as he says, a participation in the "wondrous sights of those who see marvelous things in the depths," and a journey with those who are "doing their work in deep waters."[1] The treatise illuminates by being a "narration of our night work."[2]

Richard's text comes to us from his own immersion in Exodus 25, God's instructions to Moses on the construction of the ark and the cherubim. The text from Exodus contains the word of God to Moses, and to us, that atop the ark, between the two cherubim, God will meet with and speak to God's people. God promises, "I will speak to you," *loquar ad te* (Exod. 25:22). In *De arca mystica* Richard of St. Victor reconstructs and weaves the ark and cherubim within the soul of the contemplative, so that therein God might speak and meet and dwell.

Contemplatives, "doing their work in deep waters," surface from and into an encounter with the "presence of God." This is the very God of the promises from Exodus, the God who dwells, as Richard says, in "the secret places of divine incomprehensibility" (*divinae incomprehensibilitatis arcana*).[3]

The encounter, though deep and wide, mysterious and incomprehensible, takes place nonetheless in the concreteness of our daily lives, in our body's flesh and breath and touch, in the earth and in the created world around and in us, in our reasoning, love, and relationships, in the symbols, signs, and sacraments of God's restoring work, in our imaginations and our prayers, in our birthing and our dying . . . on the ark, between the wings of the cherubim.

Those who encounter Richard's text, the contemplatives, those being shaped and instructed by wisdom, are putting on "spiritual wings." We are human souls clothing ourselves in angelic form.[4] We

xv

participate with the God of the promise in this work of restoration. For it is precisely you and I who are being sanctified today.[5]

In the midst of "sanctification today" the narration of our little work by candlelight begins.

INTRODUCTION

INTENT

In this work I will look closely at the use by an Augustinian canon, Richard of St. Victor (d. 1173), of the symbol of the cherubim as an object of contemplation in his twelfth-century treatise, *De arca mystica*. This book will examine the cherubim in exegesis, their function as symbols, how they represent Richard's theological methodology, how in contemplation they "mediate" an immediate consciousness of the presence of God, and how, as Wisdom, they perform as models of the process of sanctification. In examining these functions, I will focus on two related issues: first, the contemplative process of entering, by means of the symbol of the cherubim, into the presence of God, or what Richard of St. Victor calls "the secret places of divine incomprehensibility," and second, to pose the question of why, in *De arca mystica*, the crucified and the incarnate Christ is virtually absent from the propitiatory or mercy seat between the two cherubim. The former issue is related to what this work will call "angelization," the latter issue is discussed under the rubric of "apophatic Christology." We will find that, with regard to both issues, Richard's tropological interpretation of the cherubim as Wisdom leads to this inevitable silence concerning Christ. Woven among each of these functions and issues, the cherubim serve as a connecting thread.

METHODOLOGY

The methodology takes its cue from *De arca mystica* itself. As Richard uses the symbol of the ark and cherubim to structure, order, relate, and elucidate his six kinds of contemplation, I will in turn use the symbol of ark and cherubim as an organizing structure. Detailed analysis and utilization of that structure will become clear as the book

progresses, but as the wood, gilding, crown, and propitiatory of the
ark symbolize for Richard the first four kinds of contemplation and
the first cherubim (unity, oneness) and the second cherubim (diversity,
person, participation) symbolize the fifth and sixth kind of contemplation, so too will this work be ordered according to the ark and
cherubim. Thus the "wood" or foundation of the book is an encounter with Richard's exegetical method, particularly his tropological
interpretation of Exodus 25; the "gilding" is an encounter with the
historical influence on Richard of apophatic and cataphatic method;
the "crown" is an encounter with Richard's own symbolic method of
l'enseignement spirituel; the first "cherubim" is an encounter with the
symbolic meaning of the cherubim themselves in Richard's work; the
"propitiatory" is an encounter with the pivotal issue of Christological
absence in Richard's treatise; and finally, the second "cherubim" is
an encounter with the transformative construction of the ark and
cherubim within the heart, soul, and mind of the contemplative, what
I will call "angelization."[1]

As will be shown, this methodological structure runs at the deepest
levels in Richard's work and thought; the methodological structure of
ark and cherubim even determine internal methodological principles.
For instance, not only are the ark and cherubim used as an organizing
principle of contemplation, they also serve to systematize and construct his doctrinal theology.

In addition, initial interpretive work in many areas related to this
study has already been done. I will therefore survey the history of
these interpretations in order to organize and focus individual chapters
as needed. For example, the "crown," or Chapter 3, on Richard's
own symbolic method, will be prefaced and steered by contemporary
methodologies employed in the study of symbol and metaphor in
religious language.

Finally, one could choose to employ exclusively a modernist
methodology of positivism striving for "objective discrimination" and
"objective" and "value-free" research in an attempt to uncover the
"truth" about the past. But why should one want to do so? A larger
human capacity is the ability to distinguish (that is, to "objectively
discriminate") *and* to synthesize at the same time (that is, the capacity
to search out the "truth" in the context of one's own experience,
training, attitudes, politics, and spirituality).[2] Of course the study of
the history of Christian theology and spirituality is in part an academic

discipline, but such a study is not lessened by a scholar who meditates, nor is it forbidden to him, especially if the text is concerned with meditation and contemplation, as Richard's is. I do not believe such a practice either valorizes the art of the academic study of religion or subjects it to dangerous reductionistic tendencies; rather, the practice increases the risk of a life lived within an ethical center.

Thus as a final methodology, this book will incorporate the writer's own experience of meditating on and contemplating the ark and cherubim. In short, the work will commit the "sin of contemporaneity," attempting to find a "sense of connectedness [between the past and the present] that lends urgency"[3] to the project of exploring the twelfth-century spiritual horizon.

An initial insight into Richard of St. Victor's own methodology is the fact that while a symbol such as the ark and cherubim can be broken down into component parts in order to facilitate a demonstration of the six kinds of contemplation, the symbol does not function except as a whole. To use a favorite Victorine image for explaining the various levels of exegesis, the interpretation of scripture is like a house: the literal interpretation is the foundation, the allegorical interpretation the walls, the tropological the roof, the anagogical the ornaments or paint.[4] Made up of individual parts, the house itself nonetheless does not stand outside the whole. In like manner, in the twelfth-century Victorine universe, spirituality, exegesis, theology, contemplation, and symbol were not separate disciplines or subjects but were inextricably intertwined and related. A methodology which divides to understand must, especially in the context of the Victorine worldview, remember to unite in order to "transcend."

CONTEMPLATION

A subtitle of *De arca mystica*, given in Migne, is *De gratia contemplationis* (On The Grace of Contemplation). While the overall intent of Richard's treatise is the explication and practice of contemplation in its many forms and varieties, he does give two concise, preliminary definitions of contemplation:

> Contemplation is the free, sharp-sighted gaze of the mind hovering with awe in the visible showings of wisdom. Contemplation is an

insightful and free consideration of the soul extended in all directions in perceiving things.[5]

For more detailed analysis of contemplation as discussed by Richard, see table 1 on the six kinds of contemplation and table 2 on the relation of thinking and meditation to contemplation.[6]

Throughout the treatise, Richard uses images of birds, angels, and various forms of flight to further clarify the nature of contemplation. The flight patterns of birds are associated with ways of "thinking" in relation to objects: random flight is associated with thinking itself, circular flight with meditation, and hovering with contemplation. Foreshadowed by birds, angels too, and specifically the two cherubim which symbolize the two highest forms of contemplation, spread their wings and fly. In contemplation, at various times, the mind, the heart, the very soul fly, and the apex of flight, its highest from, is hovering.

"HOVERING"

"et volabo et requiescam" (I shall both fly and rest)
—Hugh of Fouilloy, *Aviarium*

"Hovering," the metaphor for the highest form of contemplation, is also the term I will use to describe the dialectic relation of the cherubim one to the other. But it is much more than that. The wide range of its meaning, its nuance and its polysemic complexity, will become clear only in the course of this work. To a certain degree, the flight into divine incomprehensibility is a flight of "hovering"; to a certain degree the symbol of the cherubim is a symbol of "hovering." A few preliminary points will help to orient the reader in Richard's system of contemplative flight.

First, Richard does give a definition that serves the concept of "hovering" well. He applies it to the pattern of bird flight which he associates with the highest forms of contemplation:

One may see others [i.e., other types of birds] suspending themselves in one and the same place for a long time with trembling and often rapidly vibrating wings and, through motion, maintain themselves motionless by their agitation.[7]

"Hovering" in this context is thus the relation of stillness and motion: this bird remains still in movement. Richard then applies this hovering action of birds to contemplation, drawing out the implications of the dialectic of stillness and motion throughout the treatise. But hovering is not limited to this single dialectic alone. To help orient us to Richard's deeper understanding of the nature of hovering, a second point needs to be made.

Stillness and motion reflect a metaphysical dialectic that is the basis for Richard's understanding of the relation of the two cherubim. This is the dialectic of the *coincidentia oppositorum*. Ewert Cousins has applied the Cusanian term of *coincidentia oppositorum* to the work of Bonaventure, finding in this application "at least three large metaphysical frameworks or models which include three different forms of the coincidence of opposites: (1) unity; (2) difference; (3) unity and difference." He calls these the "three architectonic models of the coincidence of opposites," which are extremely helpful for this work. Cousins adds:

> In the *first*, unity swallows up difference; opposites coincide to such an extent that they become one—in a unity where they no longer exist as opposites. This is a monistic view, in which opposites are judged either to be an illusion or to be transcended in an undifferentiated unity. . . . In the *second* class, that of difference, opposition remains; but there is no genuine coincidence. The opposites persist as opposites to such an extent that they achieve no real union. . . . In the *third* framework, that of unity and difference, opposites genuinely coincide while at the same time continuing to exist as opposites. They join in a real union, but one that does not obliterate differences; rather it is precisely the union that intensifies the difference. I call this a *coincidence of mutually affirming complementarity*.[8]

The following chapters will show that Richard of St. Victor works exclusively in this third framework. His exegetical method, his use of apophatic and cataphatic theology, his symbolic method, his contemplative teaching, his Trinitarian theology and Christology, even his refusal to speak the Word as only God has promised (*loquar ad te*), as well as the very nature of his use of the symbol of the cherubim themselves: all these indicate Richard's struggle in the difficult arena of Cousins' third framework. It is difficult, because at the heart of a coincidence of mutually affirming complementarity are elements beyond human knowledge, emotive control, or spiritual effort: mystery and incomprehensibility. Yet the contemplative wisdom of "hovering" in just such divine incomprehensibility is the aim and goal of Richard's work in *De arca mystica*. And as we shall see, this hovering in divine incomprehensibility is embodied; it is accomplished through participation in the created world and through participation of the human person in body and spirit; it is symbolized by the cherubim being firmly attached to the ark. For Richard, even ecstasy is personified,[9] and "wisdom is embodied in a human voice."[10] I call this embodied hovering "grounded flight."

The dialectic at the basis of Richard's metaphysics of hovering runs, as mentioned above, deeper than the single level of stillness and motion. Hovering in *De arca mystica* is applied to other coincidental opposites including unity and diversity, absence and presence, emptiness and fullness, emanation and return, active seeking and contemplative receiving, apophatic and cataphatic methods, and humanity and divinity. Ultimately, the two cherubim symbolize all of these coincidental opposites and more.

And yet, because of the nature of language in the context of the dialectical method used by Richard, while the dialectical relation symbolized by the two cherubim is "stillness and motion," it is also "not stillness and not motion"; it is "empty and full," but it is also "not empty and not full." I would thus expand Cousins' excellent definition of the third framework from "a coincidence of mutually affirming complementarity" to a *coincidence of mutually affirming and denying complementarity*. This is "logically" understandable. Its incomprehensible nature is that the wisdom about which Richard of St. Victor speaks is not contained even in the fullest nature of hovering. It is contained in the promise that *loquar ad te* (I will speak to you), which, finally, is a gift from beyond the borders of hovering.

Nonetheless, "hovering" must be our focus. I would say that hovering in Richard would most accurately be construed as the symbolic equivalent of what is metaphysically described as the *coincidentia oppositorum*. Because of Richard's emphasis on the symbol of the cherubim and its contemplative function of flight into the secret places of incomprehensibility, into—as I shall point out—the mystery of Trinity and Incarnation, I would say that in *De arca mystica* symbol consumes metaphysics. But the dialectic remains; its wings are affirmation and denial. And upon these wings, with the gift of grace, the cherubim fly to a place beyond affirmation and denial.

This book will serve, in part, to further refine and explicate Richard's concept and method of hovering. But what should be kept always in mind is that, finally, contemplative and metaphysical hovering in the presence of divine incomprehensibility is finally not to be named by Richard but is promised by God and received by you, the reader, exegete, and theologian, through participation in the grace of contemplation. This is so whether incomprehensibility is encountered in creation, in the human person, in the divine as Trinity, in Christ as crucified, or in the incarnate Word.

WHAT THIS BOOK "IS NOT"

Before proceeding with what the content and subject of what this book "is," I would like to point out what it "is not." This is an important step and justifiable for two reasons. First, the relationship of the "is" and the "is not" is itself an internal structuring device in *De arca mystica*. This relation of the "is" to the "is not" is also highlighted by the metaphor of hovering. In addition to having epistemological, metaphysical, psychological, and contemplative functions, this relation has also a basically narrative function. Thus to begin by claiming what this book "is not" effectively brackets the story of Richard's encounter with the symbol of the cherubim, which story is what this book "is." And second, Richard himself sets the precedent. Early in *De arca mystica*, before claiming what his treatise is, Richard claims what it is not by giving credit to scholars who have come before. He says:

> What this mystical ark designates by the allegorical sense, that is, how it signifies Christ, was spoken of by doctors before us, and by more penetrating study and detailed treatment. On that account, however, we do not suppose ourselves to run into the negligence of rashness, if we now speak of the same matter in the moral sense.[11]

Thus, in deference to "more penetrating study and detailed treatment" that has come before, making my study possible, this work "is not" concentrated on the life of Richard of St. Victor, on the abbey of St. Victor in Paris or the Victorines, on the twelfth century in general or twelfth-century theology in particular, or on the chronology of

Richard of St. Victor's works. Each of these topics will be drawn into the discussion when appropriate. But thanks to "more penetrating" scholarship that has come before, they are the firm foundation, not the primary focus, of what this project "is."

EXODUS 25

Richard's exegesis in *De arca mystica* is of Exodus 25:8–22. Though he explicitly cites only vv. 18–20 (at *De arca* IV.i) and a portion of v. 22 (at *De arca* IV.xxi), his discussion of vv. 8–17 is such that an intimate knowledge of that text must be assumed for his hearers. His citation of vv. 18–20, reconstructed from the text of *De arca mystica*, follows exactly that of the Latin Vulgate:[12]

> 18 duos quo que cherubim aureos et productiles facies ex utraqua parte oraculi
> 19 cherub unus sit in latere uno et alter in altero
> 20 utrumque latus propitiatorii tegant expandentes alas et operientes oraculum respiciantque se mutuo versis vultibus in propitiatirium quo operienda est arca.

Richard's citation of v. 22a differs slightly:

> Richard: Inde loquar ad te desuper propitiatorio et demedio duorem cherubin.
> Vulgate: inde praecipiam et loquar ad te supra propitiatorio scilicet ac medio duorum cherubim.

Exodus 25:22, one of the preeminent texts on the promise of the presence of God, is extremely important for this book. As such, it should be noted that a more accurate translation from the Hebrew is, "And *I will meet you there and will speak with you,* above the mercy seat," thus conveying the senses of both being in the presence of *and* speaking with God.[13] The RSV translation, also maintaining the senses of both presence and speaking, is, "There I will meet with you, and from above the mercy seat, from between the two cherubim that are upon the ark of the testimony, I will speak with you of all that I will give you in commandment for the people of Israel." I was able to find no Vulgate version conveying this double sense, and assume that Richard's version also contained only this aspect of "speaking."[14] I did, however, find one unfootnoted Latin translation which conveys both senses: "et ibi te conveniam et tecum loquar (I will meet you and I will speak with you) de loco qui erit supra operculum, et inter duos Cherubos."[15] I will explore both senses of God's approach as, I believe, did Richard of St. Victor.

ON EDITIONS, TRANSLATIONS, CITATIONS, AND TITLE

There is no critical edition of Richard of St. Victor's *De arca mystica*. The Latin text used for this book is from J.-P. Migne, *Patrologiae latinae* (*PL*), volume 196, *Richardi A Sancto Victore Opera Omnia*, columns 62B–192C. English translations include a complete translation by Grover A. Zinn[16] and a partial translation by Clare Kirchberger.[17] There is no complete translation in French, German, or other languages aside from the English.

My translations of *De arca mystica* as they appear in this book were done in consultation with the excellent work of Dr. Zinn and Dr. Kirchberger; having worked closely with Richard's text, I can only admire their persistence and felicity. Therefore, it is with the greatest of admiration of their work that I present these translations as my own, accepting for myself only the possibility of error, and granting to them the probability of inspiration, or even *revelatione*, as Richard might claim.

Citations from Richard's *De arca mystica* will be as follows: *De arca* I.i, 63B; 151. The first reference, from Migne, volume 196, refers to Book I, chapter i, column 63B. The second reference, following the semicolon, is to the page number of the same citation found in Zinn. If my translation differs from either Zinn or Kirchberger in such a way as to effect the argument, that difference will be cited.

Additional works of Richard of St. Victor, other Latin authors, and French secondary literature cited in the book are in my translations unless otherwise noted.

De arca mystica or, *The Mystical Ark* is the title by which this treatise was commonly referred to in manuscripts of medieval authors. In the modern period *De arca mystica* has more often been titled *Benjamin Maior*. This is the title by which it is named in Migne, followed by the subtitle, *De gratia contemplationis*, which actually indicates the intention of the treatise quite well. However, of these three possible titles, *De arca mystica* has been chosen because of its faithfulness to the medieval tradition, because it accurately reflects the dominant symbol in the work, and because it is the least likely of the three to cause confusion.[18]

1

SETIM WOOD:

EXEGESIS OF THE ARK AND CHERUBIM

> quicunque sanati sunt per sapientiam sa-
> nati sunt
> —De arca I.i

Richard of St. Victor's interpretation of the ark and cherubim of Exodus 25 in *De arca mystica* is a moral, or tropological, interpretation. As such, it is an interpretation intended to direct Richard's students and hearers into a life of virtue and a transformation of consciousness. Richard's tropological interpretation of the ark and cherubim as Wisdom thus influences every aspect of his contemplative and symbolic theology. It has a direct influence on the manner in which he describes the presence of God, that is, the "secret places of divine incomprehensibility"; it directly influences his teaching on angels, and it is the door, the way, and the goal of his silence concerning Christ.

In this chapter, then, I will look at Richard's use of tropological, or moral, exegesis. I will be particularly concerned with the relation of tropological exegesis to other methods employed by Richard, especially literal and allegorical exegesis. Beginning with a brief look at the significance of sanctification and Wisdom in tropological exegesis, I will then investigate the relation of *historia, allegoria,* and *tropologia* in Richard and other Victorines. Looking next at what Richard himself says about the nature and function of literal exegesis, I will then review patristic sources for evidence of allegorical interpretations of the ark and cherubim. Finally, in order to shed further light on Richard's tropological exegesis in *De arca mystica*, I will examine Richard's own allegorical interpretations of the ark and cherubim in other works.

ON SANCTIFICATION AND WISDOM

Richard of St. Victor proposes early in *De arca mystica* to investigate the meaning of the mystical ark and cherubim of Exodus 25:8–22 according to the moral sense. Previously, doctors of the church had investigated the same passage according to the allegorical sense and found that sense to point to Christ. Richard, however, proposes to speak of the same matter in the moral (*moraliter*) sense.[1] Through the moral, or tropological, sense Richard intends to investigate the ark as the ark of sanctification (*arca sanctificationis*). Moreover, he calls this ark an ark of sanctification "for you" (*dicitur arca sanctificationis vobis*). He asks this "you," his listeners, to pay careful attention to what the ark means for *them*:

> Do not neglect to attend to what it might mean for *you* that it is called the ark of sanctification . . . we know that whoever will touch it will be sanctified.[2]

Thus, from the very outset, the tropological interpretation of the ark and cherubim has explicit practical implications. Through grace, the ark and cherubim sanctify; whoever will touch the ark and cherubim will be transformed in practice and virtue.

Richard, then, is not interested primarily in the literal sense or even the allegorical sense as it conveys Christ, but rather in the tropological sense as it engages the listener in the process of sanctification and "teaches us what our Beloved wishes us to do."[3] What the shape of that process looks like and what we might be able to express regarding the goal of that process is the content of the remainder of Richard's treatise on the Mystical Ark.

But what is sanctification; for what are we sanctified? Richard's twelfth-century worldview concerning humanity's place in the order of creation is best exemplified by his near contemporary, Hugh of St. Victor:[4]

> The subject matter of all the Divine Scriptures is the works of man's restoration. For there are two works in which all that has been done is contained. The first is the work of foundation [*opus conditionis*]; the second is the work of restoration [*opus restaurationis*]. The work of foundation is that whereby those things which were not came into being. The work of restoration is that whereby those things which had been impaired were made better.[5]

Sanctification is the "work of restoration," it is healing, it is that by which "what has been impaired is made better." For Richard, the tropological interpretation of Divine Scripture is the interpretation that participates in this sanctification through the healing of creation. As Hugh of St. Victor makes clear in *De Sacramentis*, the relative order in history[6] of God's work and humankind's response follows a pattern of foundation, or the creation of the world and all its elements, followed by the fall, followed in turn, finally, by the Incarnation of the Word with all its sacraments.[7] Richard, in focusing on the ark as an ark of sanctification, searches Divine Scripture for insight applicable to the final portion of this order of history, that is, to God's *opus restaurationis*. What he finds and offers his listeners on the basis of his tropological interpretation is the *arca sanctificationis vobis*. What this means for "you" is the moral life, it is the healing of the human soul by discerning what Christ wishes us to do.

Richard's tropological interpretation is intended to facilitate heal-ing. And yet it is not an allegory of Christ. Instead, the healing sanc-tification that Richard does offer the listener by way of tropology is offered through the medium of Wisdom (*sapientia*):

> I wish very much to know what this ark is that is able to sanctify those approaching it. . . . Concerning Wisdom, I do not doubt but that it is Wisdom itself who conquers malice. I know nothing less than that whoever was healed was healed by Wisdom.[8]

Richard clothes the metaphorical context of sanctification in the image of healing. The medium of that healing is Wisdom, and through Wis-dom humanity is purged (*purgatur autem per sapientiam*). Wisdom is linked to truth, and "through contemplation of truth man is instructed for justice and perfected for glory."[9]

Two aspects of the purging medium of Wisdom, that is, of its role in the healing and restorative function of sanctification, are important to note. They will be discussed in detail in later chapters. One is the apparent substitution in *De arca mystica* of Wisdom for the Incarnation of the Word. This apparent substitution will be taken up in Chapter 5, and is itself dependent on Richard's tropological interpretation. A second point is that one of the primary meanings of the cherubim in exegetical literature of any kind, be it literal, allegorical, or tropological, is traditionally "fullness of knowledge" (*plenitudo scientiae*).[10] This "knowledge" is, for Richard, a category of Wisdom. In his text, the two cherubim themselves will become associated with Wisdom and the healing process. This point will be taken up in Chapter 4, on the symbolic function of the cherubim. As will be noted, these two points are not unrelated.

HISTORIA, ALLEGORIA, TROPOLOGIA: THE INTERRELATION OF SENSES IN VICTORINE EXEGESIS

Much work has been done, and still more needs to be done, on Victorine exegesis. Its continuity with exegetical tradition, its own contributions, and the reception by later exegetes of its methods and insights continue to intrigue and stimulate.[11] The following discussion will focus on the intimate weave between the various exegetical senses in Victorine interpretation in general and in Richard of St. Victor in particular.

In Richard's work, the exegetical thread leads finally to the tapestry of the ark and cherubim woven in the heart. To this end, the exegesis of scripture is present in almost all of his works, though the type of interpretation varies as a function of the objective Richard is pursuing at the time. A number of scholars have shown that Richard weaves the various exegetical senses into an integrated pattern. For one such scholar, Richard achieved a middle way, a "profound and intimate alliance of apparent contradictions," and in him a "synthesis is realized" among the various exegetical threads.[12] In a slightly different context, Jean Châtillon has pointed out that "it is very difficult to establish a rigorous boundary between the exegetical writings and the theological writings of Richard."[13] Richard's tropological writings deal with what we might call spirituality, but a spirituality of a special variety, focusing on morality and psychology rather than theology or spirituality proper.[14] This less than rigorous boundary, this synthesis in evidence throughout the Victorine corpus is, as we hope to show, represented symbolically in Richard by the cherubim and dialectically by "hovering."

With regard to this real and symbolic relation among the senses, recent scholarship has been, if not divided, often slightly prejudiced in favor of neat and inviolate categories. After surveying Hugh of St. Victor's work, B. Smalley examines two of his students, each of whom, she claims, concentrates on one aspect of his exegesis: Richard on the spiritual, and Andrew on the literal.[15] Smalley does not claim that Richard had no regard for the literal sense, in fact she is careful to provide evidence against such an un-Victorine idea.[16] However, her evidence is confined mainly to a disagreement Richard had with St. Gregory over the nature of literal exegesis of the visions of Ezekiel. Overall, Smalley's emphasis on a side issue relating to literal exegesis and her neat distinction between Richard the spiritualist and Andrew the literalist, as well as her own apparent and certainly justifiable preference for the literal sense, have *tended* to bias later scholarship.[17] The result is that Richard is often thought to be "merely" interested in the spiritual sense. Nothing could be further from the truth, as a closer look at Richard's own exegesis will show.[18] Nonetheless, Smalley does capture something of Richard's literary nature, if not his exegesis:

> What attracted him in the letter of Scripture was not the movement of human history but the jewels, the songs, and the flowers. . . . We must add to his sensitiveness to beauty a strong interest in architecture and then we shall understand his very individual type of exegesis.[19]

Among the spiritual interpretations, J. Châtillon points out that tropology "has for its object the realities of the moral life."[20] For Richard these realities include the *opus conditionis* as well as *opus restaurationis*: "A tropological interpretation is when we read through tropology what has been made and we understand what will be accomplished for us."[21] Tropology is a matter of conduct that influences present spiritual life and assists in understanding the eschatological future. Châtillon adds:

> Richard has found in biblical and liturgical symbolism, that is, in tropology, a method of interior investigation and means of expression which have not been surpassed. . . . It is the role of tropology to restore to daylight and to project from beyond the conscience one part at least of the interior complexes which each biblical image is capable of evoking. . . . In order to judge equitably the tropological exegesis of Richard it is necessary to remember that it is no longer a matter of philology or a critique which explains a text, but a "spiritual" who seeks to understand his soul or those of others and to come to discover by which roads he can approach his God.[22]

Châtillon, to be sure, equates the spiritual life with tropological work: it is moral conduct, finally, that brings a soul to God. Insightful and invaluable as Châtillon is here, he drives too strong a wedge between literal and spiritual exegesis, and between exegesis and theology. Richard simply insists on a "hovering" synthesis. Châtillon catches the relation between tropology and spirituality, but dissipates the unity between literal and spiritual meaning.[23]

Richard insists on a line of continuity between the first sense (always literal) and the last (sometimes tropological, sometimes anagogical),[24] but is often inconsistent with regard to both the order and number of senses.[25] In the *Liber exceptionum*, the order and number most frequently used occur: Scripture, Richard says, is to be interpreted *secundum historiam, secundum allegoriam, secundum tropologiam*.[26] This order is followed in several of Richard's sermons, and is the order and number initiated in *De arca mystica*. However, elsewhere the order and number are different: "After the historical understanding we ought to seek the moral; similarly, after this we proceed through an understanding of allegory to anagogy."[27] This is the order that seems to be followed later in *De arca mystica*:

> It often happens that one and the same [passage of] Scripture, when it is expounded multiply, says many things to us in one thing: expounded morally it teaches us what our Beloved wishes us to do; allegorically it reminds us what he will have done [*fecerit*] for us through himself; anagogically it promises what he arranged to make of us for the future.[28]

This also is the order and number followed in Richard's *Nonnullae allegoriae tabernaculi foederis*.[29]

In attempting to clarify Richard's use of tropology and its relation to the other senses, it is helpful to look at *Nonnullae allegoriae tabernaculi foederis*. Of interest is the allegorical comparison Richard makes there between the table of shewbread, composed of wood, and the lip and crown, composed of gold:

> By the work of wood we understand the historical sense; by the lip, the tropological; by the two crowns, the allegorical and anagogical. . . . That difference which is between wood and gold is the difference between the historical and spiritual senses of Scripture. History holds first place in Sacred Scripture. But mystical under-

standing is tripartite. Tropology holds the lowest place; allegory holds the middle; anagogy holds the highest.[30]

Richard further explicates the relation between the "golden" senses:

> For what is tropology except moral knowledge; what is allegory except the mystical teaching of secret things? . . . In the aforementioned two senses, we seek teaching concerning morals and hidden things. To anagogy belongs the foreseeing of hoped-for rewards.[31]

Richard, then, works with both the threefold and the fourfold senses of scripture,[32] and the order among these senses sometimes varies. These two points illustrate the Victorine tendency to sacrifice consistency in order to make an immediate point. That is, the Victorines often seem to attach no real importance to details of classification nor do they make an effort to unify terminology: their approach is eclectic and pragmatic rather than internally coherent or concordant.[33] Complete clarity according to our standards of logical consistency may not be possible. We can say that *De arca mystica* itself favors the threefold sense, tending, under tropology, to include morals as well as "hidden things" and "hoped for rewards."[34] Thus, while the tropological or moral sense that Richard employs in *De arca mystica* is certainly concerned with moral knowledge, our investigation into the contemplative function of the cherubim must not exclude Richard's tendency in this and other treatises to expand the tropological sense to include investigation into "hidden things" and "hoped for rewards."

De Lubac points out the frequent medieval exegetical expression that "the fruits of tropology can arrive only after the flowering of allegory." He quotes Hughes of Rouen to the effect that *historia et parabolis nutrimur; allegoria crescimus; moralitate perficimur* (we are perfected by the moral, or tropological, sense).[35]

In a very helpful article devoted mostly to a discussion of Victorine exegesis,[36] Jean Châtillon makes the connection between the teaching which will guide the Christian, that is, the tropological interpretation, and the interior way in Richard:

> It is this later [tropological] sense which will procure for the reader of Scripture the analytical instruments, means of expression, and language which will permit him to search the very depths of his soul, from there to observe the movements of nature and of grace

and to render an account, to himself and to others, of his interior experience.[37]

After the flowering, it is the fruit of tropology which explores the inner way, which, after faith, establishes and makes accountable, teachable, and repeatable the interior experience.[38] Châtillon could hardly have better defined Richard's sense of the working of tropology on the soul. Tropological teachings are those concerning the Wisdom of the *vie spirituelle*. They are what Christ wishes us to do.

In Richard's *De arca mystica*, the fruit of tropology, for the most part, follows the flowering of allegory; by means of the weaving of the ark and cherubim in the heart (the "goal" of Richard's tropology), we move toward perfection. The threads may vary, and the order and number of senses are inconsistent, but the weave or relation remains. The most important aspect of Victorine exegesis is this relation between the senses, the weave that binds all the senses in the journey of sanctification. The symbols of ark and cherubim function in part to depict the interrelation or weave of the various elements of the grace of sanctification.

It is with that relation in mind that we turn to Richard's own use of the literal, the allegorical, and the tropological senses and the sources behind them.

AN EMBODIED GROUND:
RICHARD AND LITERAL EXEGESIS

In this chapter on foundations, symbolized by setim wood, the important relation between literal, allegorical, and tropological exegesis has been highlighted. The importance of this relation cannot be overemphasized, for it has implications, as we have seen, not only for Richard's exegesis but also for the way he speaks about the soul's relation to God and the process by which he teaches that relation in *De arca mystica*. Richard's spirituality, as well as his theology and exegesis, are at all times personified; they are "embodied." That is, they begin and are delivered through the senses, the heart, and the mind. The cherubim, Richard's symbol of ascension and flight, are themselves upheld in that flight by being attached firmly to the ark and are thus blessed and "embodied" in wood.[39] Richard establishes the foundational, the "wood" of the historical and factual,

in the following works devoted in part either to the explication or
the utilization of the literal sense: *De Emmanuele, Expositio difficultatum suborientium in expositione tabernaculi foederis, Explicatio
aliquorum passuum difficilium Apostoli, In visionem Ezechielis,* and
the *Liber exceptionum.*[40] In looking briefly at a few of these works,
which serve as background to the "grounded" tropological exegesis
of *De arca mystica,* we will begin to get some sense of the importance
Richard places on the historical sense as the ground and body of his
contemplative flight.

In *Expositio difficultatum suborientium in expositione tabernaculi
foederis,*[41] Richard insists on the necessity of establishing the literal
sense in the context of both the allegorical and tropological senses.
Something of the power of each interpretation is lost if all three are
not "exposed to reason" and "studied with love" in equal proportions:

> Having been asked by friends to write something in explanation
> of the tabernacle, I was afraid, I confess, to satisfy their petition
> lest I should seem at the same time thereby to have diminished
> the authority of the Fathers (*Patrum auctoritati*). . . . Behold how
> confidently a person can propose something concerning the alle-
> gorical sense and nevertheless still bring out the exposition of the
> literal sense ambiguously. This person who confidently gives the
> testimony of his certitude denigrates the historical exposition and
> openly indicates that he himself can't even satisfy the allegorical
> exposition in these matters. . . . Let us direct our attention to how
> many, how great, how profoundly they have treated these things
> with great carefulness; how much history, how much allegory, how
> much tropology can be exposed by wondrous reason, and yet it
> ceases to be astonishing if in some situation these senses are reduced
> by a less sufficient exposition [of the other senses]. Therefore, it is
> not a great or wondrous thing if we are able to add some small
> something which is able to make progress toward major evidence
> or clearer understanding in only one of these senses.[42]

Insisting on the sufficient exposition of each sense, Richard thus
emphasizes the necessity of establishing the historical sense in order
to shed light and understanding on the allegorical and tropological
senses in turn.

Of particular interest to the themes of this book is what Richard
has to say by means of "literal" exposition concerning the cherubim:

Concerning the cherubim, it is said that they are turned facing each other [*mutuo se respiciant*].[43] Indeed, their bodies had been turned about to the more exterior parts of the tabernacle, but from where this ark stood in the middle under their wings, they stretched their faces toward that center part. Without doubt, those two cherubim who were in the temple of Solomon were made similar to these [cf. 1 Kings 6:23–30; 2 Chron. 3:10–13]. And so we read concerning those [i.e., the cherubim in the temple of Solomon] and we understand equally concerning these [i.e., the cherubim of the tabernacle] that the one cherubim touched its wing to one wall and the other cherubim touched its wing to the other wall; however, they themselves in turn touched wing to wing in the middle. And so those of the temple, just as these [of the tabernacle], were not able to stand over the ark and the propitiatory because the ark is only two and a half cubits long. But truly, for those cherubim [of the temple] the extension of the conjoined wings is ten cubits; in these [of the tabernacle] it is five cubits. Therefore what is said of these [i.e., of the tabernacle cherubim], that they are over the ark of the testimony, ought not to be understood as if they set foot upon the ark itself, but that they rise above the ark with their whole body.[44]

To be noticed immediately is that in this early "literal" interpretation of the cherubim, Richard makes an important distinction between the cherubim in the tabernacle of Solomon, from 1 Kings 6; 2 Chronicles 3, and those cherubim on the ark of Moses, from Exodus 25. Though Solomon's cherubim are in the tabernacle and so contained as such, they are not "grounded" in the way that they are in *De arca mystica*. That is, they do not "stand upon the ark" but "rise above it with their whole body." In *De arca mystica* the cherubim are grounded firmly on the ark.[45] It seems that early on Richard sensed this fundamental difference, later expanding on it and investing his "grounded" cherubim with implications for contemplation, sanctification, and Wisdom.

The *In visionem Ezechielis*,[46] along with *Liber exceptionum*, give effective witness to the importance that Richard, as a disciple of Hugh, gives to the literal sense. *In visionem Ezechielis* is devoted to a "literal" description of the temple of Solomon as shown to Ezekiel by "a man whose appearance shone like bronze, with a linen cord and measuring reed in his hand" (Exod. 40:3). Richard gives a very detailed description of the temple, with precise drawings, inside and out, from a variety of vantage points. Based on his literal reading of the text, the descriptions and drawings are so precise that one wonders if Richard, casting himself in the role of literal exegete, might be taking his cue from scripture itself, seeing himself as the man "with a linen cord and measuring reed in his hand."

In the prologue to *In visionem Ezechielis*, which is translated in part below, Richard declares that a spiritual (that is, allegorical or tropological) interpretation of scripture is valid only if it has been based on a solid, literal foundation. In fact the prologue is fairly vehement. He again pays honor to the Fathers,[47] while at the same time questioning their lack of attention to the literal sense. They looked into certain "places," he says (that is, historical, factual scriptural accounts), but they sometimes compelled the literal sense to conform absurdly to the spiritual and in so doing lost a clear exposition of the literal as a means of ascent to the spiritual. At the same time, Richard rails against the trifling (*frivolus*) foolishness (*fatuitas*) coming from the moderns (*ex modernis*).[48] They build the spiritual sense out of thin air, not based on the firm foundation[49] of the literal sense, and as such they succeed only in echoing a worthless nothing (*nihil frivolum resonat*).[50] In this very important prologue Richard says:

> Many people find divine scripture much more pleasing when they are able to perceive an understanding in it congruent with the literal sense. And then, so it seems to them, a firmer structure of spiritual understanding is established by being founded in the solidity of the historical sense. Indeed, who is able to strengthen any foundation or to firmly establish anything on a complete emptiness or void? When they are torn out [*eruantur*] and formed from the congruent similitude of these literal things, the mystical senses are put on view [*proponuntur*] in the literal sense. How then, they ask, does one construct a spiritual understanding when the spiritual understanding develops its own sense out of itself, or if it merely echoes a worthless nothing? And so persons of this sort are more often scandalized than edified when they run into such passages of scripture. On the other hand, the ancient Fathers freely accepted these things when they fell upon passages of scripture which according to the letter were not able to stand on their own. From these things certain persons, while they yet accepted Holy Scripture, ridiculed the allegorical sense by

compelling the absurdities of the letter to conform to the spiritual understanding, since they dared not deny that the Holy Spirit wrote nothing without meaning, however foolish the letter might seem. Hence I decided to touch on the fact that the ancient Fathers quietly allowed the exposition of the literal sense to escape their notice, especially in certain obscure passages—or more negligently, they drew out the literal sense only just a little. If they would have pursued this route more fully, they would doubtless have found a much more perfect explanation than anything from the moderns. But this I do not pass by silently: that certain people, out of reverence, as it were, for the Fathers, do not wish to attend to these omissions lest they should seem to presume things beyond their betters. These persons make, as it were, garments of their inertia; they are sluggish with leisure and they deride, ridicule, and run riot over the industry[51] of others in the investigation and discovery of the truth.[52]

Thus in this prologue, Richard gently chastises the Fathers. The moderns, in his mind, are not to be trusted; but the Fathers too need to be held accountable for not emphasizing the literal sense and for thus building the spiritual sense on a shaky, incongruous foundation. Later in the prologue, Richard suggests that it is only within the community, the environment in which one is held accountable by love, that one learns and grows from both the insights and mistakes of the Fathers.[53]

From these brief readings, it is apparent that, for Richard, the spiritual sense can create itself without the literal, but it ends as a worthless nothing and is foolishness. The allegorical, and especially the tropological, senses must be grounded in the literal sense in the same manner in which the spiritual ascent must be grounded in the body. Richard thus approaches his tropological work in *De arca mystica* having devoted a good number of texts to the literal interpretation of the temple, the tabernacle, and the ark. He is ready to move from the literal exegesis in which the ark and cherubim have been reconstructed from scripture to a tropological exegesis in which the ark and cherubim will now be constructed in the soul. And whereas in *In visionem Ezechielis* the cherubim are mentioned only in passing as part of the structure of the whole,[54] in the *De arca mystica* the cherubim are central. They become not only a symbol of ascent, but, in keeping with the image of hovering, they are paradoxically grounded in the ark (soul). Thus the ark (as *introvertere*) is pulled upward by the cherubim, while the cherubim (as *ascendere*) are pulled downward by the ark. In like manner, the literal sense is pulled upward by the tropological, while the tropological is grounded in the literal. It is within this tension that Richard will investigate the journey into the secret places of divine incomprehensibility.

To complete the preparation for our investigation, we will now turn to the influence of the allegorical tradition of interpreting Exodus 25 on Richard's thought and writing.

ANTIQUI PATRES:
RICHARD'S ALLEGORICAL FORMULATIONS

Though he sometimes chastens church Fathers for their too ready dismissal of the literal sense, Richard of St. Victor is nonetheless heavily in debt to the exegetical tradition, especially its allegorical formulations. In this section I will continue to examine the interwoven nature of Richard's exegetical writings, while paying careful attention to the formative influences on his allegorical interpretations. I will look especially at those sources dealing allegorically with the images of angels and edifices. The term "edifice" would include such structures as the temple, a city, a castle, the church, or the ark. These edifices, in the tradition, become allegorical figures used to describe the spiritual edifice of man: they are equated with the soul. Richard himself, in *De arca mystica*, shifts the emphasis from an allegorical to a tropological discussion. But the equation of the edifice with the human soul is present, whether the interpretation be allegorical or tropological.[55]

Richard was not in the habit of citing sources. While it would certainly be a curious misinterpretation of this fact to claim that Richard is more original than Hugh because he cites the sources less,[56] it is nonetheless an important habit to note. It is important because it makes what he does quote initially more significant, and because, finally, an investigation of his sources and influences must be made on some additional evidence.

The Christ Allegories

In looking at foundational sources of Richard's work I will shift the focus slightly from exegetical theory in general to the application of exegetical theory to biblical texts relating to the ark of the covenant and the cherubim, specifically for our use Exodus 25. I will look at the sources dealing with these texts both because they serve as additional evidence and because, though Richard cited his sources only rarely, he read deeply in this tradition.[57]

Yet he alters that tradition. He does this in two ways: first, as we have seen, he gently chides the Fathers for paying too little attention to the literal sense; and second, in *De arca mystica*, he emphasizes the tropological rather than the allegorical sense. Thus, as I have pointed out, his focus shifts from Christ to Wisdom.

The Greek Patristic Influence

Without making a claim for a direct influence on Richard, it is instructive to begin by looking briefly at the Greek patristic influence.[58] The Greek Christian writers used the text of Exodus 25 from an early date, finding in it a specific and precise statement of the habitation of divine presence.

Clement of Alexandria describes the face of each cherub as:

> A symbol of the rational soul, and the wings are the lofty ministers and energies of powers right and left; and the voice is delightsome glory in ceaseless contemplation.[59]

The Jewish exegete Philo of Alexandria, whose writings Clement knew "virtually by heart,"[60] was to influence Greek Fathers from Clement to Origen to Gregory of Nyssa. His allegorical exegesis would serve as a basis for the majority of Christian exegetes to follow, having given abundant interpretations of the mercy seat, the cherubim, and the Mosaic patterns of animal sacrifice. For Philo the cherubim represent "recognition and full knowledge"[61] separated by the logos.[62]

The first symbolic interpretation of the ark using explicitly Christian images is in a fragment from Hippolytus equating the ark and its incorruptible setim wood with the Savior, who is without sin according to his humanity, and equating the gold of the ark with the purity of the divine Word.[63] From this third-century fragment on, the ark takes on a clearly Christological context.

Origen, especially in his *Homilies on Numbers*, establishes and extends this Christological interpretation.[64] He uses the nature of setim wood and the purity of gold to equate the body of Jesus with the material of the ark. In Homily 5, Origen establishes the cherubim as fullness of knowledge:

> Those to whom God has confided his mysteries are called "The Ark of the Covenant of God." . . . Those who have merited the abundance of knowledge and the abundance of riches of the understanding of God can be taken for the cherubim, because the cherubim themselves are translated in our language as "fullness of knowledge."[65]

Then, as Richard himself would do a thousand years later, Origen equates the cherubim with the perfection of that knowledge as communicated in the Trinity:

> By the cherubim and the propitiatory it is necessary to understand the Wisdom of the Trinity, because Cherubim come to be called fullness, that is, perfection of Wisdom. And what other perfection of Wisdom can there be except knowledge of the Father, the Son, and the Holy Spirit?[66]

Revel-Neher traces the Christological interpretations of the ark, summarizing the patristic commentaries on the ark of the covenant between the third and sixth centuries and finding that they are primarily allegories of the ark as a type of the body of Christ. The propitiatory, maintaining also a fundamentally Christological sense, is a figure of redemption. And from Origen, the propitiatory and cherubim are together seen as "the Wisdom of the trinity."[67]

From the sixth century, the ark and cherubim become one of the essential components in an allegorical system of Marian prefigurations.[68] Romanos the Melodious compares the ark directly with the Virgin Mary: "And the ark? It is the Virgin who gave birth, and after having given birth, remains always virgin."[69] The theme of the Incarnation thus becomes associated with the Christological interpretations of the ark. In John Damascene a direct connection is made that compares the Virgin as the domicile of the Word on earth with the ark as the spiritual container of God's Word.[70] The ark and cherubim take on a "birthing" quality comparable to the same qualities in the Virgin, although the Virgin is superior, having had "a portion of the truth, not a shadow or figure."[71] However, both come to represent the "true presence" of God. In the Byzantine East, the liturgies of the

Theotokos often compare the Virgin to the ark. To give but one of a number of examples cited by Revel-Neher:

> O Most Completely Pure, we are thankful that in You is carried the spiritual ark, not the tables written by God, but the decrees of His Grace. . . . Moses, the greatest of prophets, wrote in advance of the ark, the table, the candles, and the vase: symbols and signs of the incarnation of the Most High in your womb, O Virgin and Mother.[72]

In summary, the Greek patristic tradition allegorized the ark and the cherubim as a Christological type of the body of Christ and as an incarnational prefiguration that was given Marian overtones. Thus the ark and the cherubim, always seen as a symbol of the presence of God, were given implicit connotations as bearer and birthing agent of the Word. The significance of this womb-like quality of the configuration of the ark and cherubim, as "receptor" of the Logos, is of great importance for how the symbols of the cherubim function in Richard and will be addressed in a later chapter.

The Latin Patristic Influence

The Latin West, though never developing an explicit Marian allegory for the ark and cherubim, developed a rich Christological interpretation of Exodus 25. Conscious of the ark and cherubim as a paramount symbol of the presence of God, they laid the foundation upon which Richard was able to build his own spirituality of presence.

Of the Latin sources which were known to Richard, the first to reflect on the theme of the ark was Augustine:

> It is customary to inquire what ought to be said concerning the propitiatory overhanging the ark. . . . Certainly the gold signifies Wisdom, the ark signifies the secret things of God. The law, the manna, and the rod of Aaron were commanded to be placed in the ark: the commandments are in the law, the rod signifies power, the manna grace, since unless one has grace, one has not the power to do the commandments.[73]

Each of the elements is interpreted by Augustine allegorically; the Christological reference is present only by allusion. Yet, clearly, the association of law and grace is present. This is an association Richard will explicitly make in *De arca mystica*: the ark, containing the law, is grace; the work of Richard's teaching is the contemplation of grace.

With Gregory the Great, the propitiatory becomes a figure of the Incarnation. The cherubim are associated with the two Testaments and at the same time represent figures between which Christ's Incarnation, life and teaching, Crucifixion and Resurrection are played out. The following is from Gregory's Homily 25 on John 20:11–18:

> We also understand by the two angels the two Testaments, first the one and then the one that follows. These angels, by their placing, have been united with the body of the Lord himself,[74] since both Testaments equally announce the message[75] of the incarnation, death, and resurrection of the Lord. Thus the earlier Testament sits at the head and the later Testament sits at the feet. The two cherubim who mutually touch the propitiatory look by turning their faces toward the propitiatory. Certainly, the word cherubim means fullness of knowledge [*scientiae*]. And what is signified by the two cherubim unless it be the two Testaments? And what is figured truly by the propitiatory unless it be the Incarnation of God? Concerning which, John said: "Christ is the propitiation for our sins" (1 John 2:2). When the Old Testament announces that something was to be done, which the New Testament claims God has done, it is as if both cherubim look at themselves reciprocally [*cherubim se invicem aspiciunt*][76] since they turn their faces toward the propitiatory. When they see that positioned between themselves is the Incarnate Lord, they do not disagree with what they see, but rather they narrate harmoniously the mystery of His dispensation.[77]

In the last lines of this text Gregory emphasizes the harmonious vision of the two cherubim regarding the mystery of the Incarnation. We will see that in Richard a tension of opposites (*coincidentia oppositorum*) is maintained in the midst of the apparent harmony of two mirror-imaged angels. This harmonious tension, not found in Gregory, is one aspect of Richard's dialectic of hovering. Also to be noted and emphasized is the fact that here, beginning with Gregory, the incarnational emphasis of ark and cherubim is so strong that it simply could not have been missed by Richard. Given Gregory's influence on the Victorines, and given the equally strong incarnational emphasis in the sources that follow below, Richard's shift in focus from the Incarnation to Wisdom is striking. The shift is necessarily conscious.

Whether the shift is toward the "absence" of Christ and apophatic theology, or whether it is toward an ethical basis of Christian action developed tropologically, is a question to be examined in this book. For the present, Gregory provides the ground of an incarnational context.

Isidore of Seville provides a system of allegory covering each detail of the Exodus text. Clearly following Augustine, Isidore also expands the allegorical interpretation so that the ark comes to signify the church and the various items placed within it come to signify aspects of the humanity, or flesh, of Christ. The basis of many latter commentaries, Isidore's allegory also directly influenced Richard in a number of his sermons from the *Liber exceptionum*, as will be shown below. And as with Gregory, the incarnational aspect of the propitiatory in Isidore is explicit. Isidore writes:

> Now, further, by means of the same placement as the propitiatory above the ark of the Testimony, Christ himself is insinuated; it is this same Christ who intervenes between God and humanity, mediating as propitiator, concerning whom the Apostle said, "whom God put forward as propitiation in his blood, through faith" (Rom 2:25). This propitiatory is placed above the ark, just as Christ, assisted to the left and the right by two cherubim, is the head of the church. However, the cherubim are understood as fullness of knowledge. Fullness of knowledge is charity, that is, love of God and neighbor by which the Lord is revealed. Indeed, no one is able to arrive at God except through charity; the fullness of the law is love. Others understand the same two cherubim as the two Testaments which by the multitudinous nature of their knowledge overshadow the propitiatory of God, that is, they overshadow the sacraments of Christ. So the Prophet bears witness: "You will understand in the middle of two animals" (Hab. 3:2). These cherubim look back at themselves with turned faces, when they are turned in the spiritual sense; thus indeed they are in the best harmony with themselves and most properly harmonized in all things. And just as they cover over the oracle or propitiatory from both sides, so indeed the Old and New Testaments conceal the sacraments of Christ which are the mysteries of the church under the enigma of a figure [*sub aenigmatum figuris*].[78]

Again, Richard could not have missed Isidore's phrase: "Christ himself . . . is introduced by the same placement as the propitiatory above the ark." Yet in *De arca mystica*, there is virtually no Christological presence. Also of interest is Isidore's fusion of "love and knowledge" in the symbol of the cherubim. He says, "fullness of knowledge [i.e., the Cherubim] is charity, that is, love of God." Isidore thus begins to articulate the emergence of love in the context of knowledge in a way that hints at the tropological interpretation which Richard will later pursue.[79]

Bede the Venerable, in two treatises, *De tabernaculo* and *De templo*,[80] continues an allegorical interpretation of the ark, the temple, and the cherubim as the figure of Christ:

> The ark, which was ordered to be made before everything else in the tabernacle, this ark is itself not incongruously designated as the incarnation of our Lord and savior, in whom all the treasures of Wisdom and knowledge are concealed.[81]

The uncovering and revealing of this concealed knowledge and Wisdom is Richard's project throughout the *De arca mystica*. However, Wisdom as tropology and ethic, not Christ himself, is again the process and the "end point" of the grace of Richard's contemplation.

The fragment from Bede points out the incarnational aspect of the ark; the following from Bede, while also emphasizing this incarnational aspect, suggests a crucified, resurrected, and glorified Christology as well as a Christ of full humanity:

> The ark is gilded inside and outside with purest gold since human nature has been assumed both inwardly and outwardly by the son of God. . . . certainly the golden crown of the ark is properly commanded to be circling above, since the son of God, who appears in the flesh and comes for the redemption of human kind, expected the time and the hour when, having undertaken death for us, he would conquer the author of death and so would ascend, victor, to the Father in heaven.[82]

Elsewhere, the Venerable Bede allegorizes the four rings at the corners of the ark as the full humanity and divinity of Christ, two representing the Incarnation and the Passion, and two representing the Resurrection and Ascension;[83] the urn is associated with Christ's full divinity, Aaron's rod with his Resurrection, and the tablets with Christ's Wisdom, power, and justice.[84] The cherubim signify the reign of heaven and are associated again with the two testaments, especially the inaccessible and incomprehensible (*inaccessabili atque incomprehensibili*) sections of Holy Scripture.[85]

Richard and the Patristic Influence

Before the seventh century, both the Greek and the Latin Fathers' allegorical interpretation of the ark was Christological. After the seventh century in the West, a strong Christological interpretation was maintained, while in certain fathers such as Isidore and Bede an interpretation of the ark as a figure of the church was also developed. In the East, the ark came to be seen as a system of Marian prefigurations. As the ark of the covenant received the divine word and presence, so the womb of Mary, as the new ark of the new covenant, similarly received and became the gestating and birthing place of the Word. While no such comparison with Mary existed in the West, the West did associate the propitiatory with the image of Christ. Latin Christological elements that became associated with the propitiatory included elements of the Incarnation, the full humanity and divinity of Christ, the Passion, Ascension, and Resurrection, and, as alpha and omega, the beginning and end of time. The cherubim were associated with fullness of knowledge as well as love or charity, based on their proximity to divinity. They were often allegories of the Old and New Testaments pointing to the internal unity of the Testaments. They were also often used to signify the obscure nature of certain passages of scripture and to "harmonize" or unite discord.[86] On rare occasions they were cited in association with the Trinity. Finally, whether seen as an element of the birthing presence of Mary, as in the East, or as a metaphor for "seeing" the space between them on the propitiatory, the cherubim functioned as the boundaries between which the Incarnate Lord is manifested.

Placing Richard within the context of these traditional sources, and without moving too far beyond the boundaries of the foundational intent of this chapter, what becomes most apparent following such a survey is the Christological absence in *De arca mystica*. In this text for Richard, the ark, the propitiatory, and the cherubim simply are not Jesus Christ; neither are they Jesus Christ in his humanity, his divinity, nor any of his Christological attributes. This omission can be explained in part by the fact that Richard's treatise is tropological, while the sources for the most part employ allegorical interpretation. It can be explained also in part by Richard's own disclaimer in the first chapter of his work: that the allegorical interpretation of the ark as Christ as expounded by Fathers before him is not the intent of his treatise, but rather that the tropological interpretation of the ark and cherubim as Wisdom is his aim. But there are other forces at work excluding a Christological interpretation. A preliminary explanation would include (1) the influence of a strain of apophatic theology constraining Richard from naming the Word that is spoken between the two cherubim, (2) the function of the cherubim themselves as symbols, and (3) the tropological or ethical nature of Richard's teaching forcing a kind of reconstruction or reweaving for the sake of the *opus restaurationis* of the ark and the cherubim on the stage of the heart of the contemplative. This latter teaching leads to sanctification not by means of Richard's speaking "Jesus Christ" but by means of the Word's own speaking on the individual, personal stage of the heart. These points will be investigated more fully in later chapters.

With regard to the function of the cherubim in the sources, Richard explicitly associates one cherubim with the unity within the Trinity and the other cherubim with the diversity in three persons within the Trinity. While he does not directly associate the ark and cherubim with Mary, he does provide an interpretation of the function of the cherubim which includes this "gestating" or "birthing," basically "feminine" element. Finally, as within the tradition, Richard describes the cherubim as defining the boundaries within which the divine presense is met: between the two cherubim, above the propitiatory, God meets and speaks with the contemplative. The difference between this and the promise of Exodus 25 is that the meeting now takes place within the contemplative, within a temple that is not made by human hands, as in the promise of Hebrews 9.

LIBER EXCEPTIONUM: EVIDENCE OF ALLEGORICAL CONTINUITY

Although Richard of St. Victor's *De arca mystica* explores the tropological interpretation of the ark and cherubim of Exodus 25, Richard's other writings do not ignore the tradition of the allegorical interpretation. The following discussion finds similarities between the traditional interpretations, as outlined above, and Richard's own allegorical interpretations in the *Liber exceptionum*. These similarities will serve both to link Richard with the tradition and to highlight important differences between the tradition and Richard's tropological, theological, and spiritual work in *De arca mystica*.[87]

In keeping with the Abbey of St. Victor's goal of "restoring in the soul the image of God tarnished by sin,"[88] through lessons, sermons, and public lectures, Richard's *Liber exceptionum* attempts to attain an understanding of scripture based on virtue and Wisdom. R. Rogues calls the work banal but important for an understanding of history and allegory in the twelfth century.[89] Châtillon sees it as a gold mine, in that "it reveals to us the principal readings of Richard, it indicates from what material the celebrated prior has constructed his work and what the primary sources are of his thought."[90] The following example, from *Liber exceptionum*, is a sermon of Richard's which allegorically interprets an "edifice," in this case the church. Many of his allegorical interpretations in this sermon equate portions of the church with Christ, and in so doing link Richard with the patristic tradition.

Also to be noted in this sermon are the interpretations of the walls as contemplatives, the roof as the actives (which, interestingly, projects downwards toward earth, its ground), the altar as Christ, and the church teaching outwardly through doctrine and ordered virtues while sanctifying inwardly through grace:

> The Lord sanctified his tabernacle. Dear brothers, the tabernacle of the Lord—that is, the holy Church—has its stones, it has mortar, it has a foundation, it has walls, it has a roof, it has length, width, height, it has a sanctuary, it has a choir, it has a nave, an atrium, an altar, a tower, it has celebrating gestures, it has glass windows, it has interior and exterior plaster, it has twelve candles, it has episcopal dedication. All of these things are full of sacraments and they carry spiritual teachings [*spiritualia preferunt documenta*]. Individual stones are individual faithful, foursquare and firm: foursquare in the stability of faith, firm in the virtue of patience. Mortar is charity which fits together, joins, and unifies single individuals, and, lest they mutually disagree through some discord, it measures them out uniformly. The foundations are the prophets and apostles, as it is written: "Raise up the building upon the foundation of the apostles and prophets, as Jesus Christ himself is the cornerstone." The walls are the contemplatives, the wall from its very foundation rises well beyond its beginnings, forsaking the earthly things, adhering to

heavenly things. The roof in this spiritual edifice [*spirituali edificio*] does not project upwards but downwards: in these things it turns in a different direction from the material building itself and, by such dissimilarity to the regular arrangements of the building, is withdrawn from the general direction of the building itself. The roof is the actives, neighbors by means of actions of earthly things, who, according to their imperfections, are less intending toward celestial things and so administering to earthly things such as necessities of neighbors. . . . The altar is Christ, upon which is not only the sacrifice of good works, but indeed, we offer prayers saying, "Through our Lord Jesus Christ your Son, etc. . . ." The tower is the name of the Lord, as it is written: "The highest tower is the name of the Lord"; in Him the just take refuge and will be saved. The gestures [*signa*] are the preachers who speak the word of God. The glass windows are the spiritual people, through whom divine understanding is illuminated for us. The interior plaster signifies the cleanliness of the heart, the exterior plaster signifies the cleanliness of the body. The twelve candles are the twelve apostles who preached the standard of the cross and the faith of the passion of Christ through the four corners of the world. . . . The bishop follows, who signifies Christ, who circles his church, first in the time of natural law [*in tempore naturalis legis*] admonishing through the patriarchs, then in the time of the written law [*in tempore scripte legis*] admonishing through the prophets, then in the time of grace [*in tempore gratie*] circling and entering it by means of Christ himself as he instructs it outwardly through doctrine and sanctifies it inwardly through grace.[91]

The following sermon, also from the *Liber exceptionum*, is particularly important for the light it sheds on *De arca mystica*. This sermon, portions of which employ tropological methodology, speaks not so much of Christ as of the soul in its preparation for the coming of Christ. In it, Richard weaves together the elements of the church in much the same way that the ark is woven or constructed in the heart of the contemplative in *De arca mystica*. In addition, Richard says explicitly what is only implied in *De arca mystica*: that the tabernacle (or ark), according to the tropological sense, is the soul:

Your tabernacle, Lord, is made holy. The tabernacle of the Lord according to the tropological sense is the soul [*Tabernaculum Domini secundum sensum tropologicum est anima*]. The soul itself possesses what is called the tabernacle of the Lord; its stones, mortar, etc., pertain to the construction of the Church, just as we arranged them in the preceeding sermon. The sides of the tabernacle are single virtues, well adorned by practice and made firm against corrupt things by immobility. The mortar is charity, through which the other virtues are held fast, united, and contained. The foundation is Christ; as the Apostle said, "No one can lay any foundation other than the one already laid, which is Jesus Christ." The tabernacle possesses walls for the contemplation of the good things of heaven, by which its foundation, which is Christ, is raised up from the earth, clinging most near to the heavens, by means of good will. And it has a roof through which good acts, even by means of unworthy temporal things, administer on behalf of eternity. It has length through faith [*fidem*], through which all that God made from the beginning through God's self, through angels, through man, or all that will be made continuously until the end is believed to be true. It has height because of hope [*spem*] which is raised from earth to heaven, from changeableness to eternity, from visible to invisible, from body to spirit. It has width through love [*caritatem*], by which it is extended to the right and to the left: to the right to friends, to the left to enemies; by loving [*diligendos*] friends in God, by loving enemies on account of God. It has a sacrarium through which one is made to the image of God [*facta est ad imaginem Dei*]: indeed, in the church edifice nothing is more worthy than the divine image, just as in the soul nothing is more holy, nothing is more noble or excellent than the divine image. It has a choir through which one is made to the likeness of God [*per hoc quod facta est ad similitudinem Dei*], so that just as in the church the chorus is found first after the sacrarium, so in the soul after the divine image, the divine likeness is understood to be most sublime. . . . Therefore, the church itself is the soul; the sides are by way of virtues, the mortar by way of love, the foundation by way of Christ, the walls by way of contemplation, the roof by way of good acts, the length by faith, the height by hope, the width by love, the sacrarium through those things which are made to the image of God, the choir through those things made in the likeness of God, the nave by way of the senses, the atrium by way of the flesh, the altar is the contrite heart. It has clear windows indicating spiritual senses, a tower indicating the name of the Lord, signs indicating preaching, interior plaster indicating the cleanliness of the heart, exterior plaster indicating the cleanliness of the body, twelve candles for the teaching of the twelve Apostles. Its Bishop is the holy Trinity. Therefore, make a great effort, dear brothers, every one of you, make a great effort so that, according to what has been said above, the tabernacle of God might come to be made within you so that there God deigns to dwell. Great indeed is the honor, worthiness, sublimity, security, glory, to have God dwell within you. And so it is certainly being provided to us that we are so made inwardly and outwardly; inwardly by faith, outwardly by good works, so that the Lord of Majesty comes to us and we are found worthy to have mansions made within us. But since we are not able to be such things without His grace, we ask incessantly for this necessary thing. And for just such works, grace will be given, and not only grace, but glory also.[92]

For Richard, then, tropologically, the church is equated with the soul. In *De arca mystica* the ark, an edifice similar in symbolic significance to the church and the tabernacle, also represents the soul. The last sentences of the second sermon thus function as an early outline of Richard's later work in the *De arca mystica*: the tropological "construction" in the soul of the contemplative is the process of weaving "the tabernacle of God made within you." It is there, within the soul, in the tabernacle not made by human hands, that God will come to dwell.[93] Richard's mystical ark prepares both the inner and outer self so that, as the sermon says, God might come, "making mansions" within. Above all, *De arca mystica* is a treatise on the grace of contemplation (its subtitle in Migne being *De gratia contemplationis*). The treatise focuses on the "contemplative work" of grace in the preparation of the soul for the inner dwelling of Wisdom. The sermon, too, speaks of the work of grace in God's *opus restaurationis*, it speaks of a preparation for a spirituality of presence. This sermon, dated somewhere between 1153 and 1162 by Châtillon,[94] thus appears as a concise outline and formative predecessor to *De arca mystica*.

Other points germinated in *Liber exceptionum* come to fruition in *De arca mystica*. For instance, Richard defines the three[95] manners of interpreting scripture as:

History [*historia*] is the narration of the birth of things which are contained in first things by means of literal signification. Allegory [*allegoria*] is when through it, what is said is made [*quod factum dicitur*] either in the past, the present or the future. Tropology [*tropologia*] is when by it we read what has been made and understand what is being made for us [*nobis sit*].[96]

Thus tropological understanding in the *Liber exceptionum* is the understanding of what is being made for us (*nobis sit*). This anticipates the tropological understanding proposed from the very first chapter of *De arca mystica*: that the ark of sanctification is fabricated for the contemplative, that is, "for you" (*sit vobis*). Another anticipation concerns Richard's rejection of the allegorical interpretation in *De arca mystica* of the ark and cherubim as Christ. This rejection is highlighted by the following interpretation of the same images from the *Liber exceptionum*:

Therefore the Paschal Lamb is Christ; the doves are Christ; the rock is Christ; the ark is Christ; the propitiatory is Christ; the table is Christ; the candelabrum is Christ; the altar is Christ.[97]

Again, Richard's tropological interpretation of the ark and cherubim as Wisdom does not occur in a vacuum; his interpretation must be understood in the context of his earlier, highly Christological interpretation. Another very brief section of allegorical interpretation in the *Liber exceptionum* has significance for Richard's later work on the cherubim in *De arca mystica*. In a statement that will be fully amplified in his later work, Richard says simply:

The two cherubim, which themselves are interpreted as fullness of knowledge, signify the two Testaments, since the Testaments themselves contain the fullness of knowledge.[98]

Finally, Richard assembles what might be called a team of "perfect exegetical masters." Along with the germinal ideas set forth in *Liber exceptionum*, these masters will prepare the soil for his interpretive work in *De arca mystica*:

In addition to what secular knowledge [*scientia*] taught, we also seek Wisdom [*sapientia*], most skillfully taught by divine scripture containing the Old and New Testaments to which belong history, allegory, tropology, anagogy. For example, Jerome teaches of the literal senses by means of three conversations, Augustine teaches by means of eloquent reasoning, Gregory teaches the moral sense, and finally, Solomon teaches Wisdom. Concerning such things, we would proclaim in every way: that is wondrous![99]

SUMMARY

Along with the other patristic sources discussed above and the germinal interpretive models from *Liber exceptionum*, these four exegetical masters, Jerome, Augustine, Gregory the Great, and Solomon, form the background of Richard's interpretation of Exodus 25. The patristic tradition provided Richard with a deep reservoir of literal and allegorical sources. He drew on these sources, yet he proposes something different in *De arca mystica*. There Richard proposes to contemplate the Ark of Moses and the cherubim tropologically as an "ark of sanctification." He proposes to interpret and teach, to act upon and contemplate "what our Beloved wishes us to do." In doing so, Richard of St. Victor weaves the threads of not only *historia* and *allegoria*, but also *tropologia* into, as it were, a rough cloth of contemplative virtue to be made whole and healed by Wisdom. Fit thus with the rudiments of angelic clothing, we may proceed with Richard into those secret places of divine incomprehensibility.

2

GILDING: APOPHATIC AND CATAPHATIC THEOLOGY

ultra Deum nihil est

—*De arca* I.i

Richard of St. Victor enters the secret places of divine incomprehensibility through the middle, the central and intermediate, the common, the center core, the *medium*. For Richard, God is met with and speaks precisely at that *medius* space, between the two cherubim (*medio duorum cherubim* [Exod. 25:22]). Denys the Areopagite's (*c.* 500) apophatic and cataphatic theology imprints an image of intervention, of center, on Richard's spirituality of participation and presence.[1] According to most commentators, the medieval period failed to develop a full Dionysian synthesis. It is my thesis that, with regard to the synthesis of positive and negative theology, Richard of St. Victor did manage a striking, imaginative, and fully integrated balance of Denys the Areopagite's fundamental dialectic. That balance is exemplified by the image of the center. That synthesis is manifested in the symbol of the cherubim. And the *medium* as entry into divine participation is actualized in the contemplation of the cherubim themselves.

RICHARD'S RECEPTION OF DENYS THE AREOPAGITE

In the general introduction to his four-volume study of Christian mysticism, Bernard McGinn has said:

> Precisely because of the incommensurability between finite and Infinite Subject, Christian mystics over the centuries have never been able to convey their message solely through the positive language of

presence. The paradoxical necessity of both presence and absence is one of the most important of all the verbal strategies by means of which mystical transformation has been symbolized. The relationship has been portrayed in many forms. . . . At other times, among the negative or apophatic mystics, presence and absence are more paradoxically and dialectically simultaneous.[2]

As I pointed out in the preceding chapter, Richard of St. Victor seeks a "mystical transformation" or restoration by means of the tropological interpretation of scripture and by means of the process of a particular type of contemplation. As a "negative or apophatic" writer, Richard can be portrayed as a mystic who, through cataphatic and apophatic methodology, establishes presence and absence as paradoxically and dialectically simultaneous.[3] This simultaneity is represented metaphorically by Richard's contemplative concept of "hovering." And as we shall see, this hovering simultaneity of presence and absence is not only a dialectical, or a psychological, or a metaphysical or epistemological paradox; in Richard it is a paradox at the deepest, symbolic and mythic level. This level of "mystical transformation" is symbolized by the cherubim, in the *medium* of whom divinity "speaks."

The general outlines of the history of the textual transmission of the Dionysian corpus to the twelfth century are known.[4] Yet the extent of the influence of Denys' writings on Richard of St. Victor continues to invite difficulty and controversy. Investigators must move with caution when a scholar of Etienne Gilson's caliber warns in a similar context, "The influence exerted on Cistercian mysticism by Dionysius is very difficult to estimate."[5] So too must they move with caution on the subject of the influence exerted on Richard by Denys.

One obvious influence of Denys is the transmission of his *Celestial Hierarchy* through John Scot Eriugena (*c.* 810–c. 877) and through Hugh of St. Victor (d. 1142) to Richard.[6] Less obvious is the overall impact on Richard of that transmission. G. Dumeige begins his investigation of the impact of Denys on Richard with a quotation from Bonaventure: "Anselm sought after Augustine in reasoning; Bernard followed Gregory in preaching; Richard aimed at Dionysius in contemplation."[7] But Dumeige himself concludes that:

> Richard knew Denys, but he more often used him as an illustration than as an inspiration of his own thought. [For Richard] the conception of a symbolic universe and of love as a kind of knowledge seem to be those things from Denys to which he became particularly

attached and which Richard transmitted to those upon whom he exercises influence.[8]

Did Richard "aim" at Denys, was he "inspired" by him, or did he merely "use him in illustration"? These are the questions which reverberate throughout the secondary literature.

Richard himself is enigmatic. He does cite Denys by name in his *In apocalypsim Joannis.*[9] And speculating that Richard comes to know Denys through Hugh's *Commentariorum hierarchiam coelestem S. Dionysii*, Châtillon notes that Richard reproduces a rather large section of Hugh's text in the same *In apocalypsim Joannis.*[10] But the *Celestial Hierarchy* of Denys, translated by Eriugena, commented on by Hugh, is in fact the only work of Denys that Richard cites. Elsewhere, and concerning other works of Denys, Richard is silent.

Overall, the assessment of contemporary scholarship on the effect and extent of Dionysian thought on Richard is indeed varied. Most scholars agree that Richard was directly influenced by Denys' symbolic theology.[11] A consensus is more difficult to establish with regard to Richard's use of Denys' apophatic theology. Though Kirchberger claims Richard did not accept the way of negation,[12] most other scholars claim that he did. Disagreement among these later scholars arises on two fronts: (1) whether Richard used Denys as a mere illustration or as a genuine inspiration of his thought,[13] and (2) whether Richard (and the twelfth century in general) emphasizes negative theology while deemphasizing affirmative theology in a manner that fails to do justice to the complete and complementary dynamic of Dionysian spirituality.[14]

CATAPHATIC AND APOPHATIC THEOLOGY IN DENYS THE AREOPAGITE

1. Denys' Synthesis and Contemporary Commentary

Richard's "symbolic" response to the relation of negative to positive theology does in fact do justice to this complementary dynamic of Dionysian spirituality. That response, of course, is the hovering symbol of the cherubim. To clarify Richard's own complementary dynamic, it is helpful to articulate the cataphatic and apophatic synthesis of

Denys himself before looking at the synthesis in Richard. We will do this by first looking at contemporary scholarship on the subject, then by looking directly at Denys.[15]

R. Roques, for instance, notes that the distinction between affirmative theology and negative theology corresponds to the distinction between similar and dissimilar symbols.[16] Affirmative theology, he claims, comes up against the same limitations as similar symbols:[17]

> Just as dissimilar symbolism has been necessary to redress the illusions of similar symbolism, it will be necessary, in a parallel way, that negative processions correct the intelligible representations of affirmative theology.[18]

Thus, Roques, noting the limitations of both similar symbols and affirmative theology, reminds us of the importance of parallel, reciprocal relations between similar and dissimilar symbols on the one hand, and negative and affirmative theology on the other. Used correctly, and used as Denys intended them to be used, negative theology and positive theology form a relation which functions as a dialectical coincidence of opposites; that is, they "hover."

The Dionysian view of God is grounded, according to B. McGinn, in the dialectic of negative and positive, and is in fact inseparable from their coincidental use.[19] Though Denys insists, at some points, on the superiority of negation over affirmation in the anagogic process leading to God,[20] his more consistent teaching is that "*both* negation and affirmation need to be surpassed to reach union with God."[21] This is so "Because within its undifferentiated unity the Trinity holds 'the assertion of all things, the denials of all things [and] *that which is beyond every assertion and denial*'" (DN 2.3–4) (my emphasis).

As noted in the previous section, P. Rorem has argued that the medieval period was often more interested in how Denys abandoned concepts than in how he attained them. Rorem insists, however, on Denys' own complementary use of the apophatic and cataphatic method:

> The Pseudo-Dionysian method is not simply a series of affirmations followed by their negation in reverse order. . . . Rather, just as procession and return in Neoplatonic metaphysics are not sequential moments, so affirmation and negation in Pseudo-Dionysius are not mutually exclusive options to be exercised separately. . . . The Areopagite carefully preserved the simultaneity of procession and

return, and thus of affirmation and negation. A given expression or symbol about God is denied because of its ultimate dissimilarity, but it is also, and at the same time, affirmed because of its relative similarity.[22]

R. Mortley also emphasizes the positive view of language in Denys' *via negativa*:

> Pseudo-Dionysius' negative theology does not damage this basic confidence in language: as indicated above, it is of the Proclian type. According to Proclus a negation secretes a positive transcendent statement, and implies it.[23]

Mortley takes Denys' phrase, "The most divine knowledge of God is one which knows through unknowing according to the unity beyond intellect,"[24] as an exact echo of Augustine's famous expression, *Deus scitur melius nesciendo*, and as an example of a negative concept masking a positive one.[25]

That unknowing is a form of knowing is but one of the examples Mortley gives of Denys' use of the method of contradiction.[26] For Mortley, the *via negativa* and the method of contradiction are similar: both attempt to swim upstream, to use the medium of language against itself.[27] We must keep in mind, however, that though these methods attempt to force language against itself, they are still based on language and its capacities. And so, dependent on language, negations secrete a positive transcendent statement: negatively, the transcendent is p and *not* p, and yet positively, it *is* neither of these.

Other scholars have tried to come to terms with the relation between Denys' negative and positive theological methods.[28] Throughout their work, and throughout Denys', one thing is clear: Denys the Areopogite intended these methodologies to be held in dialectical tension. And yet, even as he does so, Denys maintains that God is in some sense beyond all affirmation and negation. The claim that God is beyond all affirmation and denial is linked to language: as the flight of language soars, "language falters." There is a sense in which similar (positive) and dissimilar (negative) symbols serve to boost language precisely at its faltering point, providing the fuel, as it were, for a final anagogic leap. As we shall see, both Denys and Richard use symbols in this way. Yet even with this added symbolic fuel the new anagogic leap sputters and dies: the being, the "it," the dwelling of God is even beyond all symbolic affirmation and denial. This is particularly critical for Richard, who, as we saw in chapter 1, is interpreting a passage in which God has promised to be not silent, but speaking; to be not absent, but present. How is Richard to fly to that point where language falters and speak to God? How is he to weave a tapestry wherein the divine is never the "it" of a pattern but only "next to it," and yet still be in the spatial and temporal presence of God?

Spatially and linguistically, the cherubim provide a resting place and clue. They border the place where God will dwell; they hint the "within" wherein God will speak; they represent, symbolically, the boundaries of our anagogical leap.

2. The Synthesis in the Dionysian *Corpus*

The *Mystical Theology*, in setting out the nature of positive and negative theologies by first summarizing *The Divine Names* and then previewing the method of interpreting perceptible symbols, develops a pattern of descending affirmations and ascending negations. That is, following the Neoplatonic pattern of "procession" from the One down into plurality and the "return" of all things back to the One, Denys intimately and immediately links procession-affirmation to return-denial.[29] In this case, again, for Denys, apophatic theology does not function without its coincidental opposite, cataphatic theology.

Denys links the methods of apophatic and cataphatic theology many times in *The Mystical Theology*. He makes this interconnection very clear: to approach the ineffable One, one must have practiced both theologies. On the one hand he emphasizes cataphatic theology:

> In my *Theological Representations*,[30] I have praised the notions which are most appropriate to affirmative theology. . . . In *The Divine Names* I have shown the sense in which God is described as good, existent, life, wisdom, power, and whatever other things pertain to the conceptual names for God. In my *Symbolic Theology*,[31] I have discussed analogies of God drawn from what we perceive.[32]

On the other hand, he emphasizes apophatic theology, where the more one climbs the more language falters:

> The fact is that the more we take flight upward, the more our words are confined to the ideas we are capable of forming; so that now as

we plunge into that darkness which is beyond intellect, we shall find
ourselves not simply running short of words but actually speechless
and unknowing. . . . But my argument now rises from what is below
up to the transcendent, and the more it climbs the more language
falters.[33]

By the end of *The Mystical Theology*, after first considering and
negating the lowest or most obviously false statements about God,
even the most seemingly congruous statements about God must also be
denied.[34] Language, symbols, even Wisdom itself must be transcended
in the ascent from the perceptible to the inexpressible:

> Again, as we climb higher we say this. It is not soul or mind, nor
> is it speech per se, understanding per se. . . . There is no speaking
> of it, nor name nor knowledge of it. . . . It is beyond assertion and
> denial. We make assertions and denials of what is next to it.[35]

Denys thus employs the way of negation and affirmation in an intertwined pattern, but "as we climb higher" we reach a "something"
which is beyond both the way of affirmation and the way of denial.

Such emphasis and practice leads to a double paradox: first, we
make assertions and denials of "what is next to it" (that is, "God")
but not of the "it" itself; and second, the more one climbs the more
language appears to falter. Denys, though not intending to diminish
the dialectical tension within the paradox, attempts to clarify it in two
major ways.

First, the closest Denys comes to a "name" of God that captures
both the apophatic and cataphatic element and the closest he does
come to "it" is Trinity. Denys had begun *The Mystical Theology* with
a prayer exemplifying this relation between affirmation and denial:

> Trinity!! Higher than any being,
>   any divinity, any goodness!
> Guide of Christians
>   in the wisdom of heaven![36]

He begins with an affirmation: Trinity. And he moves immediately into
denial: the Trinity is not being, it is not divinity, it is not goodness. Yet,
affirmatively, it is a guide in the wisdom of heaven. And yet, while
Trinity is indeed the source of the processions and therefore source of
affirmations, it is also the goal of the return and therefore the goal of

denial. Trinity is a special case. As both source and goal of the ascent, it is a summation and "model" of the apophatic-cataphatic method. A second way in which Denys manipulates the ambiguity is by dealing with the spatial metaphor inherent in the image of "faltering." That is, the idea that in climbing toward the goal we can only make assertions about what is "next to it"; the "more one climbs," the more language falters. These spatial referents and the paradox implied within them are manipulated and addressed by the claim that it is not God's self who is encountered by language, but rather the *place where he dwells*. Referring to Moses, Denys says:

> When every purification is complete, he hears the many-voiced trumpets. He sees the many lights, pure and with rays streaming abundantly. Then, standing apart from the crowds and accompanied by chosen priests, he pushes ahead to the summit of the divine ascents. And yet he does not meet God himself, but contemplates, not him who is invisible, but rather *where he dwells*.[37]

Thus Denys does not try to diminish the dialectical tensions inherent in his apophatic paradox. He does, however, attempt to render them metaphysically plausible by employing the metaphors of "trinity" and "dwelling." Richard of St. Victor takes a remarkably similar approach to the paradoxical qualities inherent in the contemplative ascent. First, for Richard as for Denys, Trinity is the "name" of God reserved for the beginning as well as the goal of the ascent.[38] Second, by using the ark and cherubim as the place of God's presence, the language of *De arca mystica* is focused finally not on God's self, but on the place where God dwells. The connection with Denys is enhanced by the fact that in Denys' text it is Moses who enters the place of God's dwelling, and in Richard's text it is likewise Moses who enters that same dwelling. The dwelling place is developed, defined, and bounded by the ark and wings of the cherubim. In much the same way that Richard uses the symbol of the cherubim to participate in and define the space, he uses the cherubim to symbolize the Trinitarian unity of essence and multiplicity of persons. The cherubim are, as "Trinity," the word which comes closest to the "it" of what is "next to it." In *De arca mystica*, the "it" itself is neither named as Trinity, nor rendered within that space; language falters, we can only make assertions and denials about what is next to "it." Again, Richard does not name or speak it. As we shall see, the naming and the space are left "empty" for the contemplative to fill in as the gift of the grace of presence (or absence) arrives.

Richard's fifth and sixth levels of contemplation symbolized by the left and right cherubim thus link him to Denys by symbolizing, bordering, and defining that place where the contemplative "will be at one with him who is indescribable";[39] where, in Richard's words, the contemplative will "dare to attempt those angelic flights into the secret, difficult to reach places of divine incomprehensibility."[40]

With Denys' discussion of language and metaphor in mind, we can shift to the question of angels and their function as participative symbols in the contemplative ascent. Denys provides a brief discussion of angels in his *Divine Names*.[41]

For Denys, the highest positive name for God is the "Good." In discussing the Good in the context of the Neoplatonic structure of processions, and equating the rays that proceed from the archetypical Good with the angelic orders,[42] Denys describes how the angelic orders draw their being from the Good itself:

> Their longing for the Good makes them what they are and confers on them their well-being. Shaped by what they yearn for, they exemplify goodness and, as the Law of God requires them, they share with those below them the good gifts which have come their way.[43]

"Shaped by what they yearn for": this in itself could be a definition of tropology, and, in Richard, the particular shape of the cherubim themselves, who "exemplify" goodness and wisdom. If we picture the cherubim, standing atop the ark, overshadowing the ark with their wings as Richard describes them, and if we imagine a cataphatic descent through affirmations followed by an apophatic ascent through denials, then the cherubim serve as the symbol which "shares . . . good gifts which have come their way." The cherubim share and pass on processing assertions and returning denials. And at the point where language falters, where denial only indicates what is next to God, not God's self, at exactly that point, the contemplative is "shaped by what is yearned for": a gift shared, exemplified, and mediated by the cherubim. As Denys points out, the angels look at each other and the truth with a direct grasp of it, unmediated.[44] Richard's work, recognizing as it does that the final stage of God's visitation to us is that of a presence which is a gift beyond language, offers the cherubim as a tropological model of good gifts shared but not spoken. Sharing requires more than speaking. It requires the giving of the word spoken and the receiving of the gift, which at its highest good is shaped by Wisdom:[45]

> They, [angels] become shaped as close as possible to the transcendently wise mind and reason of God, and this happens through the workings of the divine Wisdom.[46]

It is this shape, in the form of "angelic clothing," that Richard will invite the contemplative to receive and wear.[47] This tropological aspect of interpretation of angelic clothing also falters; it approaches not God but only where he dwells. Yet as a symbol reflecting the presence of God, it comes as close as the skin.

CATAPHATIC AND APOPHATIC METHODOLOGY: RICHARD'S *DE ARCA MYSTICA*

Among negative or apophatic mystics, as Bernard McGinn has noted, presence and absence are paradoxically and dialectically simultaneous.[48] Richard of St. Victor must be considered, among other things, an apophatic mystic; he balances presence and absence. Having articulated the cataphatic and apophatic synthesis of Denys, Richard balances the negative and positive dynamic of Denys' spirituality as well. And this balance reflects a deeper dialectic,[49] that of the *coincidentia oppositorum*,[50] which lies at the basis of Richard's psychological, metaphysical, epistemological, and contemplative systems. The dialectic is also reflected in Richard's use of the image of hovering.

The dialectic of presence and absence is an appropriate one for Richard, yet the paradox and dialectic go much deeper. Richard has his own series of coincidence of opposites, including but not limited to presence and absence. Others include emptiness/fullness, light/dark, unity/diversity, hidden/manifest, and the relation of the apophatic to the cataphatic method. Richard, ever the metaphysical dialectician, plays with the coincidental nature of these opposites, but always and preeminently the symbolist, he manifests the coincidence of opposites most "concretely" in the symbol of the two golden cherubim. These two cherubim, wings outstretched, simultaneously and paradoxically grasp the ark, overshadowing the propitiatory, manifesting a duality *between which*, not within the synthesized or the either/or nature of which, Richard's spirituality of presence-absence takes place.

It is important to recognize the deep level at which the evocative power of Richard's symbol of the cherubim functions. As we begin to explore his simultaneous and paradoxical use of the apophatic and the cataphatic method, we begin to enter into his simultaneous and paradoxical use of symbols in general, of the coincidental nature of opposites, of his particular use of the symbol of the cherubim, of how and why it might be that the incarnational Christ as logos was not spoken in *De arca mystica*; we begin to enter into the very nature of the internalizing process or weaving of the ark and cherubim within the heart and mind of the contemplative. Thus, in speaking now of the coincidentally opposite relation of apophatic to cataphatic method in Richard, we begin to speak more generally of other simultaneous paradoxes. These are summarized by the cherubim.

Though the cherubim symbolize this "welling up" of simultaneous paradoxes at many levels, some of which are unnamed, Richard is explicit about the relation of the symbol of the cherubim to reason:

> Observe, I beseech you, how suitably they are placed opposite each other [the two cherubim] in having been turned toward each other and how they stand turned toward each other clearly as a figure of those things of which the one seems to consent to reason [*rationi consentire*], while the other seems contrary to reason [*rationi contraire*]. . . . See, therefore, it is not by means of chance that in that Cherubim who stands at the right, that kind of contemplation ought to be understood as above reason,[51] not, however, beyond reason [*est supra rationem, non tamen praeter rationem*]. However, in that one who stands at the left, the contemplation should be understood as above reason and it seems to be beyond reason[52] [*est supra rationem, et videtur esse praeter rationem*].[53]

This relation of one cherubim consenting to reason and the second seemingly contrary to reason is the ground of Richard's use of the apophatic and the cataphatic method. It allows him to use the same symbol of the two cherubim to invoke a wide variety of paradoxically simultaneous opposites,[54] while at the same time to deny (apophatically) and affirm (cataphatically) the spiritual presence of God between the same two angels. It also allows him to use paradoxically opposite images simultaneously in order to highlight the nature of his contemplative quest. One of many illustrations of this use of language is the relation Richard establishes between light and dark:

> This ultimate and highest heaven has its own day, however. And certainly it has its own night. . . . Surely God made the moon and stars in the power of the night, and on that account *this night is my illumination* in my delight.[55]

In order to establish the connection between the apophatic and cataphatic method and his use of the dialectic of "above" and "beyond" reason, Richard immediately links *rationi consentire* to more revealed or manifested things (*manifestiora*) and the *rationi contraire* to more hidden or concealed things (*occultiora*).[56] To revealed or manifested things Richard applies what he calls "the rational principle of similitudes" (*similitudinum ratione*),[57] which is, in part, his use of the cataphatic method. At the same time Richard employs the apophatic method, which "Consists in incorporeal things and invisible essences: that is, angelic spirits and human spirits."[58] In examining these hidden things of supermundane essences (*super mundanarum essentiarum occulta rimamur*),[59] Richard thus applies the apophatic terminology. It is important to remember, however, that, as we saw in chapter 1, there is always an underlying tropological emphasis to Richard's program of contemplation. In this case, for instance, angelic and human spirits are created in the image of God and, as such, are capable of cleansing, purification, or purging (*mundet, purgare intellectum*) in order to more closely examine "hidden things." Richard uses the image of the purification of gold to make this tropological point about purgation; thus even in the context of an apophatic progression towards "hidden things," the cataphatic or positive side provides balance by means of the very positive *imago Dei* and the image of purging symbolized by gold.

Richard also finds convenient metaphors for the necessary purgation involved in ascent in the metaphors of night and day or light and dark. Here too the "negative" or night side is related to the apophatic method, while the "positive" or day side is related to the cataphatic. While I have tried to establish the balance Richard maintains between the use of these two methods (symbolized most artfully by the cherubim), he is never completely consistent. The very nature of the language he uses often seems to betray the balance. In his discussion of the relation between night and day, night (or apophatic methodology) seems to win out:

> This ultimate and highest heaven has its own day, however. And certainly it has its own night. . . . Truly indeed this night will be illumined like the day, because the day of this inferior heaven is able to be conquered by the brilliance of this night. Surely God made the moon and stars in the power of the night, and on that account this night is my illumination.[60]

Heaven has its day and its night (a balance at the highest level), but it is emphatically the night or darkness which illuminates, which conquers the inferior heaven by its "brilliance" (a slight advantage to darkness, or apophatic method).[61] At the level of language, one metaphor (the positive or the negative) must win out over the other. It is only in silence and language, at that place formed upon the ark between the two cherubim, where paradox may be sustained in simultaneous synthesis, where opposites no longer "win" but coincide.

Richard uses the image of the propitiatory, whose length and width is given but whose height is unspoken, to reflect on the fourth level of contemplation, which he designates as "in reason according to reason" (*in ratione secundum rationem*).[62] The two given dimensions of the propitiatory reflect the positive abilities of reason; the unspoken dimension reflects the ability of reason to move from the visible world and begin to penetrate into the "invisible" things of God by means of similitudes.[63] Thus, in a very cataphatic move, Richard demonstrates that there are certain things, even very hidden things (words for hidden or concealed things abound in this passage), which understanding or "human natural ability" is able to make clear:

> See how the sharpness of understanding of that human natural ability [i.e., reason] is accustomed to investigate the deep things, to penetrate whatever is most inward and intimate, hidden within, perplexing, secret and placed in darkness, and to unfold, to make clear, to illuminate, and to call out into the light. With utmost intimacy, it daily visits the sinuous paths of concealed nature and the secret recesses of its liveliness; it bursts in and passes through, hastening and panting, always to penetrate into the deeper things and to ascend to higher things.[64]

There is thus a very cataphatic nature to reason's ascent to the invisible or hidden through the revealed and visible. That is to say, as with Denys, there are very positive attributes of reason.

But there are, equally, apophatic limits to reason. These are symbolized by the unspoken height of the propitiatory. Reason can grasp the propitiatory's width and length, but not its height:

> Who, I say, in this thus far fleshly position sees, or ever has been able to see, his own soul or even a spiritual substance in its own purity? Far from doubtful is the fact that in these things the human intellect [*intellectus*] has been blind from birth, making it necessary to cry out daily to the Lord: "Illumine my eyes" (Ps. 12:4). . . . Therefore, however much you will exercise your natural self in this consideration, however much you continue your zeal, however much you will enlarge your mental sense, you will not be able to extend your knowledge to a full cubit.[65]

A "vision" of the soul or spiritual substance is thus not available to human understanding. Also beyond reason at this point in Richard's contemplative methodology is "glorification":

> Certainly, therefore, no measure for the height of the aforementioned work (propitiatory) is proscribed since the manner of our glorification, as has been said, can be comprehended by no sense of ours.[66]

Glorification is beyond the capability of reason since no person has experienced or witnessed it. There is no "rational principle of similitude" by which one may symbolically transverse the world's landscape from sin to glorification.[67] To the eyes of reason there is a radical break, across which they cannot see, between the sin of this world and the glorification of the next. To emphasize this apophatic point of the limits of reason, Richard notes that scripture itself remains silent as to the nature of glorification, no person having known or witnessed it:

> By remaining silent it cries out that it considers itself wholly unworthy to instruct us concerning the measure of this work; in this life human infirmity is scarcely able to rise up to the beginning of the work.[68]

While the nature of glorification is beyond reason, glorification is made certain nonetheless by the attestation of faith (*glorificationis nostrae certitudinem fedei attestatione tenemus*).[69]

Keeping in mind that Richard reserves the highest levels of contemplation, above and beyond reason, for souls which are imprinted or reformed by grace,[70] we should note that reason both is and is not the organ for the "vision" or "presence" of God. It is not in the sense that, unreformed, it simply does not have the "optic" capacity to see God. It is in the sense that, reformed, it is mind or reason which is "rapt" to God, but a mind or reason in a reformed state that is alienated or "beyond" itself. These states are what Richard calls *excessus mentis* or *mentis alienatio*.[71]

This reformed or alienated reason is not, strictly speaking, Denys' apophatic reason: it moves beyond anthropological categories. For Denys, apophatic theology is always a matter of human understanding; it is evidential and foundational in the philosophical senses.[72] Richard moves beyond Denys' limitation on apophatic theology—that God is beyond all denial and affirmation and that we can deny and affirm what is next to God but not God's self—and he does it before Book V.[73] He does so in the context of his discussion on the symbol of the cherubim in contemplation. He does so in the context of a dialectic of the coincidence of opposites, not on the basis of a synthetic dialectic revolving around the relation of nature and grace. He does so in the context of not speaking the Word. He does so in the context of the cherubim as womb of Wisdom where the presence and participation of breath dwells in the place beyond denial. Richard is interested more in the dynamics, the guidance, the progression, the wonder and awe of that hidden thing beyond affirmations and denial than he is in the Dionysian dialectic. It is, for him, the very nature of the alternately hidden and revealed God to send us journeying and to confront us with the marvelous:

> But in the former [second kind of contemplation] we seek the rational principle of visible things, while in this [fourth kind of contemplation] we seek the dignity of invisible essences if they are hidden, or if they are uncovered we marvel.[74]

Book IV of *De arca mystica*, in speaking of the fifth and sixth kinds of contemplation, shifts the focus of the discussion to the cherubim themselves. In the context of the relation between apophatic and cataphatic methodology, Richard uses the symbol of the cherubim in two ways: first, as we have shown above and as he will continue to do throughout Book IV, the cherubim, in symbolizing the coincidence of opposites, represent the mirrored, simultaneous, and paradoxical nature of the apophatic and cataphatic methods; the cherubim stand equally and concordantly but opposite atop the ark; second, the cherubim come to symbolize that which, in Denys' words, is beyond every affirmation and denial; the cherubim represent the boundaries of that space within which God speaks and dwells, and they represent the positive value in the failure of language to speak only of where God dwells: they point, as symbols, to that which "transcends the smallness of our capacity by the greatness of its incomprehensibility." This second item, beyond affirmation and denial,[75] begins the process of the human person putting on angelic clothing:[76]

> It seems to pertain to these last two kinds of contemplation to be above a person and the manner of human reason and to exceed the capacity of human reason [*supra hominem esse, et humanae rationis modum*]. Whence it is proper to represent these things with an expression of similitude by means of an image that is angelic rather than human. Indeed, unless the material of these speculations goes out beyond the confines of human thinking, it is necessary that the example for forming our work have a form of human rather than angelic similitude. Therefore it is necessary to raise ourselves above ourselves [*nos supra nosmetipsos levare*] and to ascend to those things which are above reason by means of contemplation, if we desire to form the flight of our understanding in the image of the angelic similitude. And so we must seek what those things are which are above reason, those things which transcend the power of human reason and the mode of our thinking.[77]

Notwithstanding the significance of this passage for Richard's symbolic theology, Richard here reaps the harvest of Denys' methodology. The angels themselves represent the apophatic and cataphatic ways played out in perfect tandem. But more than that, they represent how we might "raise ourselves above ourselves," putting on the image of angelic similitude; that is, how we might rise above the limitations of apophatic denials and cataphatic affirmations. The process of "putting on angelic clothing" will be discussed in later chapters. It is, as hinted in chapter 1, a tropological process following the path of virtue modeled by Wisdom.

But the process of rising above oneself, the neat division between the apophatic and cataphatic, and the space shaded and protected by the wings of the cherubim which is above all affirmation and denial—these clear definitions do not mean that Richard's struggle with language is over. Apophatic language must not be allowed to run beyond the goal as if there were no "governor" in the machine:

> Surely, if you will have been lifted to the speculation of these things, you will not be able to find any other things to which you will have to ascend that are higher. Indeed, there is nothing higher than God [ultra Deum nihil est].[78]

That "nothing is higher than God" is a very apophatic-sounding cataphatic statement. An analogy would be a warning against shooting an arrow toward God but aiming beyond in the hope of getting "more" of God. It is senseless to aim beyond God with the mere arrow of reason. Richard seeks to adjust the contemplative's aim; the tendency of contemplation is to seek a manifestation which is always "higher." This cannot be found:

> Above God is nothing; nothing that exists, or nothing that is able to exist, or is able to be thought to exist. There is nothing by which knowledge [scientia] ascends higher, nor by which it might be able to ascend. And so to know [cognoscere] God is fullness of knowledge.[79]

For Richard, the figure of the work by which one is initiated to the fullness of all knowledge [plenitudo scientiae] is called "cherubim." The cherubim signify the method by which God is attained, they signify the place where God dwells beyond affirmation or denial, they signify the borders of an errant search by knowledge for what is beyond God. That is, they signify the limits, the outermost edges or extrema[80] within which divine presence is manifested. Beyond them, nihil est.[81]

Within the protection of the wings of the cherubim is the momentary forgetfulness of self. Exodus 25:20 says of the cherubim that "they cover both sides of the propitiatory, spreading their wings and covering the oracle." The wings of the cherubim, according to Richard's interpretation, thus provide a place for both hiding (absconsionem) and protection (protectionem) where the mind might temporarily forget itself:

> Oh that we might be snatched away with complete zeal and desire in looking at and in the admiration of them [the cherubim]; oh that we

might be led with complete "transfer of the property"[82] of the soul above our very self itself, so that for that time our very mind might not know itself [*mens nostra seipsam nesciret*] while it is struck senseless as it is hovering[83] in looking at the cherubim.[84]

Thus in sharpening the aim of the contemplative, Richard cautions both against the strategy of knowing anything "beyond" God and against making mind or knowledge itself God. The mark or bull's-eye is within the protection of the Cherubim, not beyond (though the Cherubim do define the most extreme outer boundaries), and the mark is not the self itself or the knowing of the self. Richard compares the latter point to St. Paul's experience, "whether in the body or whether outside the body I know not. God knows" (2 Cor. 12:2). Within the shadow of the wings of the cherubim, God lies hidden for that soul to view who is ignorant of itself.[85]

And yet there remains a problem of explaining the nature of the presence of God: the aim may have been true, but the return or the interpretation of the vision may or may not be accessible to reason and language. The presence of God may be a suddenly "revealed theophany" (*theorica revelatio*) and accessible to all by means of reason, or the Lord may "display the magnitude of His incomprehensibility by the remoteness of his vision,"[86] and thereby be contrary to all reason. Richard attempts to confront the problem of explaining the experience of the presence of God by linking the vision accessible to reason and the vision incomprehensible to reason to an allegorical interpretation of Abraham and Elijah awaiting the coming of the Lord and to an allegorical digression interpreting the Song of Songs.[87] Both allegories are in turn linked to Richard's discussion of the cherubim as symbols beyond the rational nature of language. The link is made precisely at the point where language begins to falter in *De arca mystica*. With the Song of Songs, Richard briefly indulges in affective bridal mysticism and the language of love in an attempt to recover the "rational" discussion of angels, and in so doing to regain the balance of their dialectical nature. At the same time the allegory on Abraham and Elijah focuses on the borders of language and our experience of God:

> And so we ought, according to the example of Abraham and Elijah,
> to expect the coming of our Lord by the "going out place" [*exitu*]
> of our habitations, and through the door, as it were.[88]

God, according to Richard, finds us at the boundaries of language, through the door, as it were, at the borders of that "dwelling" defined by the cherubim. We are found not within the habitations of our language but somewhere at the "going out" or "entering in" place at the borders of language. The cherubim symbolize and define those borders. And accordingly, Richard grounds his discussion of both the Song of Songs and Abraham and Elijah in the context of the symbol of the hovering wings of the cherubim. Only in the shadow of these wings is the "vision" or presence of God revealed by grace,[89] "brought down for the understanding of all,"[90] and returned to language.

And so it is that Richard can say that God is: "Essentially inside all things and outside all things, below all things and above all things."[91] This is a quintessential cataphatic statement framed in apophatic terms. It is another way of saying that God is beyond all affirmations and denials, that God awaits us at the border places of going out and going in. Richard even links the duality of this apophatic/cataphatic statement to other coincidental oppositions by following it immediately with the opposition of hidden/revealed:

> If he is inside all things, nothing is more secret [*secretius*] than he. If he is outside all things, nothing is more distant [*remotius*] than he. If he is below all things, nothing is more hidden [*occultius*] than he. If he is above all things, nothing is more sublime [*sublimius*] than he. Therefore, what is more incomprehensible than the thing than which there is nothing more secret, nothing more withdrawn, nothing more hidden, nothing more sublime?[92]

and of presence/absence:

> Also, if he is in every place there is nothing more present [*preae-sentius*] than he. If he is outside every place, there is nothing more absent [*absentius*] than he. But is anything more absent than that most present one of all, and is anyone more present than that most absent one of all who does not have to be one thing and another in order to be everything that is? But if nothing is more present than the most absent and nothing more absent than the most present, what is more incomprehensible than he?[93]

It is the hovering quality of the cherubim that allows these manifold opposites to coincide between the two gazing angels. The cherubim manifest these many pairs of opposition in a coincidental or concordant manner. And it is clear that these opposites do not represent the person, reality, or being of God, but rather where God dwells. Thus one could say that the problem of explaining the experience of the presence of God is only partially solved: the contemplative can dwell in the shadow of the wings of the cherubim; he or she can wait in the doorway of "going out" or "entering in," anticipating a glimpse of God. In neither case is language itself God. Language is simple shelter or waiting.

SUMMARY

Denys was explicit about the fact that negative and positive theology function simultaneously, and that divinity itself is beyond all affirmations and denials. One could say that such a claim is, in reality, a superaffirmation; or conversely and I think perversely, one could say with Eriugena that the being of all things is the Deity which is above being (*esse omnium est superesse diatas*) and that therefore the claim that God is above all affirmations and denials is in reality a superdenial. One could say these things, but at some point one has to cease from playing ontological games and take Denys and Richard at their "word." Both realize that the difficulty lies with language. Richard's use of negative and positive methods, his use of terms for the unknowability or incomprehensibility of God, the abundant use of eminent terminology and the explicit use of Dionysian terms of contemplation and ascent, place him firmly in the Dionysian strand of apophatic theology. That strand recognizes the barriers to a spirituality of presence inherent in language and symbol. Language seemed to Richard to be a kind of offspring of reason, and so reason itself, in the context of meditation and contemplation, was subjected to apophatic and cataphatic analysis. The result was the formation of the symbol of the cherubim: left and right, absent and present, above and beyond reason, hiding and revealing, manifesting unity and diversity while perched upon the propitiatory. The symbol of the cherubim thus defines opposites in concordant, coincidental patterns. The symbol establishes borders through the doors of which God has promised, "I will speak to you [*loquar ad te*]." It is there, *medio duorum cherubim*, that Richard seeks to dwell.

3

CROWN:

SYMBOLIC THEOLOGY

*est a visibilibus ad invisibilia similitudinem
trahere*

—*De arca* II.xiv

The distinctions between Richard of St. Victor's use of apophatic
methodology, his use of symbols, and his particular use of the symbol
of the cherubim are mostly arbitrary. All three are intimately related.
In turn, these three "interrelated distinctions" all regulate the curious
Christological absence in *De arca mystica* and also shape and define
Richard's overarching teaching on contemplation. It should not be a
surprise, therefore, that the questions raised by an investigation of
Richard's use of apophatic and cataphatic theology are in many ways
similar to questions raised by his use of symbols.

To illustrate this close relation, and to move into a general discussion of the function of symbol in contemplation, we turn to a work
of Richard's in which he quotes Denys the Areopagite directly on the
nature of symbol.

A DEFINITION OF SYMBOL
FROM RICHARD'S *IN APOCALYPSIM JOANNIS*

Richard of St. Victor uses his commentary on John's apocalyptic
visions to discuss the nature of visions and to explain the diverse
ways by which one might rise by means of symbols from sensible
things to an understanding of the divine realities. The commentary,
In apocalypsim Joannis, is also made notable by the fact that in it
there are several citations of Denys' *Celestial Hierarchy*.[1] As noted in
Chapter 2, Denys is only rarely cited in the rest of Richard's work.

Richard begins Book I by describing four kinds of visions. The first two visions are bodily, the second two are spiritual (*duo sunt corporales, duo sunt spirituales*). The first bodily vision takes place when:

We open the eye to exterior and visible things . . . yet since this vision is not sharp-sighted, it does not penetrate hidden things and therefore contains no mystical significance.[2]

The second bodily vision, using Moses and the burning bush (Exod. 3) as an example, takes place when: "A form or action is revealed to our sense of exterior sight while interiorly a virtue of great mystical significance is contained."[3] Richard notes that the first bodily vision is empty of the fullness of mystery while the second overflows or is full (*redundat*) of heavenly sacraments through the work of virtue.

The third and fourth spiritual visions are not through the eye of flesh, but through the eye of the heart (*non fit oculis carnis, sed oculis cordis*).[4] The third vision takes place when:

The soul is illuminated by the Holy Spirit by means of the similar forms of visible things and is thereby led to an understanding of invisible things by means of images of present things; that is, by means of certain figures and signs as it were.[5]

We note here an early example of the movement from the similitude of visible things to the invisible by means of symbols. The fourth kind of vision is initiated when:

The human spirit, by means of subtle and sweet internal aspirations, and having touched nothing in the way of mediating figures or qualities of visible things, is spiritually raised to the contemplation of celestial things.[6]

In these last two forms of vision which Richard calls "spiritual," we find two examples of his method of spiritual ascent, both of which will later be employed in *De arca mystica*. The first is the ascent to invisible things through visible things by means of symbol or similitude, that is, by means of present and visible images, figures, and signs. The second is ascent through contemplation which eschews the mediatory quality of symbols, relying instead on "revelation" or "showing" (*revelatione*).

Richard links these last two types of vision to Denys the Areopagite's work on symbol and anagogy:

Beyond the illuminating rays of the most sacred eloquence, when it is possible, we look upon the manifestation of heavenly souls by means of symbol and anagogy.[7]

Richard defines symbol and anagogy as:

The symbol is the gathering together of visible forms to demonstrate invisible things. Anagogy is the ascension or elevation of the mind contemplating the highest things.[8]

Richard thus distinguishes symbol from anagogy, but he also unites them. He notes that symbol and anagogy are both what the Greeks call "theophanies" (*theophanias*), the one demonstrating the invisible through symbols having likeness to the senses, the other demonstrating the invisible through contemplation ascending into the highest purity.[9] Richard adds that:

In the third vision the truth of hidden things is overshadowed by forms and figures and similitudes. The fourth vision is expressed by naked and pure things without covering [*integumento*]. And so the *symbol* is demonstrated when what is hidden is revealed by a form or sign or similitude. While *anagogy* is demonstrated when naked and pure things are revealed by revelation or when that which is plain and open is taught by reason.[10]

In Richard's *In Apocalypsim Joannis*, symbol and anagogy seem to be united in the same way that the apophatic and cataphatic methods are united, as explained in the previous chapter. That is, they are opposites, but they coincide, they hover. There is a way of ascent or making present that reveals what is hidden by means of symbol; while at the same time there is a way in which naked things are revealed by means of revelation and without the use of symbol. It should be noted however that Richard, again following Denys, notes that it is impossible to ascend from material things to the celestial hierarchy, whether using symbols or anagogic contemplation, without the use of the "guiding hand" (*manuductionem*). The material or content of that "guiding hand" are the images of corporeal things themselves (*materialem manuductionem vocat rerum corporalium imagines*). Thus even anagogy or contemplation must begin in corporeal images.

In order to obtain a deeper understanding of Richard's use of symbol, we will now turn to the work of Denys the Areopagite and Hugh of

St. Victor. In doing so, we will focus our attention on *De arca mystica* by following the lead of a few stubborn questions. First, is there in the relation between symbol and contemplative ascent a "place," as there was in the relation between language and the apophatic method, where symbol simply falters? Second, what becomes of corporeal images in both the symbolic and anagogic ascent as the hidden becomes revealed? And third, and perhaps more important, is there in Richard's *De arca mystica* some symbolic function which the cherubim perform other than those functions defined as "symbolic" and "anagogic" in his *In Apocalypsim Joannis?*

THE FUNCTION AND USE OF SYMBOL: THE WORK OF DENYS THE AREOPAGITE

Near the end of chapter 2 of *The Celestial Hierarchy*, Denys the Areopagite allows a brief autobiographical glimpse that is both an insight into his own spiritual character and a short outline of his anagogic theory of symbols:[11]

> And I myself might not have been stirred from this difficulty to my current inquiry, to an uplifting through a precise explanation of these sacred truths, had I not been troubled by the deformed imagery used by scripture in regard to the angels. My mind was not permitted to dwell on imagery so inadequate, but was provoked to get behind the material show, to get accustomed to the idea of going beyond appearances to those upliftings which are not of this world.[12]

As interesting as this passage is with regard to Denys' character, more importantly it raises several questions about his symbolic theology. What is "deformed imagery," for instance? How does one "get behind the material show" to things which are "not of this world"? And why should inadequate imagery, particularly imagery of angels, provoke him to his "upliftings"? The answers to these questions are found in Denys' writing on the function and use of symbols, and they are answers that will help us decipher the manner in which Richard puts symbols to good use in *De arca mystica*.

Denys distinguishes between like and unlike symbols (*homoia* and *anomoia symbola*).[13] Thus, in looking at the nature of symbol in Denys, we must keep in mind that we are working with a dialectic which we have previously named the coincidence of opposites. Both Denys and Richard ground their discussion of the spiritual ascent in this dialectic. We have seen the dialectic applied by Richard and Denys to the relation of apophatic and cataphatic theology, and have noted that Richard's symbolic expression of this dialectic is represented by the two cherubim.[14]

We have also noted a number of pairs of coincidental opposites including, for instance, motion and rest[15] and hidden and revealed.[16] It is this last dialectic, that of hidden and revealed, that is of great importance in Denys' discussion of symbol. Throughout his work Denys alludes to the function of symbol to both obscure or hide and yet at the same time to reveal or open. And most importantly, all things both reveal and conceal God. Thus the "divine ray"[17] can enlighten us by "being concealed in a variety of sacred veils," which the Father adopts to "our nature as human beings." These veils then become "gifts which are granted to us in a symbolic mode,"[18] revealing in that they conceal.

Denys uses the incongruity between the images used by scripture to describe angels and the reality of those sacred forms as a way of beginning his discussion of this revealing/concealing nature of symbols. The dissimilarity between scriptural images and their sacred forms are, he says, "a concession to the nature of our own mind."[19]

This concession makes allowance for what Denys calls "dissimilar similarities" that create forms for the formless, or types for the type-less. He gives two reasons for scripture creating types for the typeless (for example, angels as lions or eagles or thrones). First, we lack the ability to be directly raised up to conceptual contemplations without these types; and second: "It is most fitting . . . that the hidden truth about celestial intelligences be concealed through the inexpressible and the sacred."[20]

Denys then points out the twofold manner by which scripture works through incongruous imagery.[21] First, scripture works through sacred images in which like represents like. Instances of like representing like would include God represented as "word" or "being" or "light." Yet Denys warns that Deity is incomparably distant to even the most similar manifestation of itself. Every symbol of similarity falls far short of similarity to Deity.[22] The second approach, then, is to "praise the deity by presenting it in utterly dissimilar relations" (i.e., unlike symbols). Examples of dissimilar relations would include *in*visible, *in*finite, *in*comprehensible. Denys is clear as to his preference between these two approaches:

> Since the way of negation appears to be more suitable to the realm of the divine and since positive affirmations are always unfitting to the hiddenness of the inexpressible, a manifestation through dissimilar shapes is more correctly to be applied to the invisible . . . incongruities are more suitable for lifting our minds up into the domain of the spiritual than similarities are.[23]

Denys thus develops two types of symbols: similar and dissimilar. Similar symbols are applicable to the natural world, even the soul. Dissimilar symbols are most applicable to the transcendent world. It may seem inconsistent, given the effort to develop the coincidentally opposite nature of the relation of negative to positive theology in the previous chapter, that Denys here seems obviously to prefer dissimilar symbols. However, he is talking here about the uplifting or anagogic function of symbols.[24] The emphasis on dissimilarity with regard to the celestial realms has the effect of lifting the contemplative "closer" to those realms. But finally, even dissimilarity as an "attribute" of Deity must be jettisoned and abandoned.[25] "The very same things are both similar and dissimilar to God," Denys says in the *Divine Names*, and likewise God is neither similar nor dissimilar to those things.

Thus, "everything can be a help to contemplation; and dissimilar similarities . . . can be applied to beings which are both intelligible and intelligent [i.e., the angels]".[26] But finally, as with apophatic theology and language, even dissimilar symbols must be dropped at the highest point of contemplation:

> They [the wise men of God] therefore honor the dissimilar shape so that the divine things remain inaccessible . . . and so that all those with a real wish to see the sacred imagery may not dwell on the types [i.e., the symbols] as true. . . . For this reason there is nothing ridiculous about representing heavenly beings with similarities which are dissimilar and incongruous.[27]

The relation of similar to dissimilar symbols applied to celestial or invisible things is very reminiscent of the relation between negative and positive theology discussed in the previous chapter.[28] "It is beyond assertion and denial," Denys had claimed in *The Mystical Theology*. "We make assertions and denials of what is next to it but never of it."

As with negative theology, so too with dissimilar symbols: they are helpful but they are not "it," they are not the divine, they too must be denied.

This section on Denys began with a quote which raised some questions to which we should now return. The "deformed imagery" which so "troubled" Denys is what he calls dissimilar similarities or dissimilar symbols. They have, he finds, great value in lifting the contemplative up beyond the material world and "behind the things not of this world."[29] Such deformed or dissimilar symbols serve as an anagogic path to the divine by shocking the mind, so to speak, and providing uplift beyond material similarities. The anagogic value of dissimilar symbols becomes apparent precisely as they trouble, stir, shock:

> The dissimilar images . . . their failure is a stimulant for the spirit which prevents it from becoming sluggish or hypnotized by figures through which the natural enchantment might perhaps otherwise jeopardize one's motion toward God.[30]

All things both reveal and conceal God:[31] only by cataphatic immersion in the beauty of the universe can we obtain the negative representations necessary for discovering that God is always beyond what we can conceive.[32] But dissimilar symbols perform the additional anagogic function of stimulating the mind beyond the material show and moving it beyond appearances.

If we recall Richard's discussion of symbols in *In Apocalypsim Joannis*, a number of distinctions between Denys and Richard can now be made: (1) Richard's definition of symbol as a collection of visible forms to demonstrate invisible things is a narrow, incomplete definition compared to Denys', unless Richard's definition of anagogy is added to it;[33] (2) Denys' focus is on dissimilar, deformed, or jarring forms that in a sense catapult the mind into the transcendent realm; (3) in this sense Richard's definition of anagogy as ascension of the mind into contemplation of the highest things is contained within Denys' definition of dissimilar symbols; that is, Denys did not separate anagogy and symbol: the deformed symbol was the anagogic process;[34] (4) in both, as with negative and positive theology, similar and dissimilar symbols are inadequate and must, eventually, be denied. However, with regard to this last point, Denys seems to prejudice dissimilar symbols in a way that he did not prejudice negative theology. As was pointed out in the previous chapter, Denys' dialectic in *The*

Mystical Theology managed to hold negative and positive together in coincidental tension. But ultimately, God was "in" neither the negative nor positive way, and finally both "ways" were to be denied and transcended. In *The Celestial Hierarchy*, the dialectic does not function so reciprocally. Statements such as "the Deity is far beyond every manifestation of being and of life [i.e., beyond similar symbols]," coupled with statements favorably prejudicing the dissimilar such as "this second way of talking about him [in utterly dissimilar revelations] seems much more appropriate," and "the way of negation appears to be more suitable to the realm of the divine," seem to overturn the carefully structured balance of opposites portrayed in *The Mystical Theology*. This may be a matter of emphasis, or it may be that Denys employs a slightly different dialectic with symbols than he does with method or theology. We will watch for a similar shift in Richard.

THE FUNCTION AND USE OF SYMBOL: THE WORK OF HUGH OF ST. VICTOR

Hugh of St. Victor inherits from Denys both the anagogic use of symbols and the basic structure of symbols as moving *per visibilia ad invisibilia*.[35] Hugh defines a symbol as "A juxtaposition, that is, a joining together of visible forms set forth to demonstrate invisible things."[36]

To support this definition of symbol, Hugh makes a number of distinctions. First, he makes a distinction between mundane theology (*mundana theologia*), or philosophy, and divine theology (*divina theologia*) which he uses to support the additional distinction between the work of creation (*opus conditionis*) and the work of restoration (*opus restaurationis*).[37] And second, Hugh makes a distinction between the images of nature (*simulacrum naturae*) and the images of grace (*simulacrum gratiae*).[38] He thus establishes two foci or sets of symbols: mundane or divine theology and images of nature or grace.

Images of nature are associated with the works of creation and, though available to mundane theology, have the power to point only to the manifestation of God, not to God in God's true being. Much as Richard was to do later in his *In visionem Ezechielis*, Hugh takes the opportunity of explaining mundane theology and the *simulacra* of nature to rail against the presumption of worldly philosophers (*moderni*). The presumption of the worldly philosophers is that the wisdom of this world is itself God. Hugh says:[39]

> And taking what it had found, the world said that it would proceed farther to the highest wisdom, having complete trust in its own wisdom, as if that might be the road. Indeed, the world ascended, and it was lifted up so that it might arrive at a high heart. And the world, this mundane philosophy, made itself a ladder from the outward appearance of creatures, thus climbing up to the invisible things of the Creator. . . . For those things which were being seen were indeed known, and yet there were other things which were not known. Through those things which have been clearly shown, they thought to go into those things which were hidden. Yet in the falsehood of the images which they employed, where the fullest things are not found, their minds were ruined for the highest possible truth. On that account God made the wisdom of this world foolish, since the wisdom of God is not able to be found in the world. . . . Christ crucified has been preached so that truth might be sought through humility. But the world despised the healer and thus was not able to know truth.[40]

Thus the "images of nature" allow a certain knowledge, but fall short of the truth. Nature demonstrates the creator, but does not allow full understanding and participation. The mundane philosophers end in error who, wishing to raise themselves to the highest truth, lack the exemplars formed for healing of the interior vision through grace [*per gratiam exemplaria formabantur ad sanitatem visionis internae*], lack the ark of Wisdom made new by the flesh of the eternal word in the humanity of Jesus [*neque arcam sapientiae noverat . . . carnem Verbi aeterni in Jesu humanitate*], and have only the pattern of natural things.[41] The healing, the work of restoration, initiated with the humility of the crucified Christ—it is through this humility that we may really seek truth (*humilitate veritas quaereretur*).[42]

The "images of grace" and divine theology, on the other hand, participate in the illumination of truth:

> The image of nature was the outward appearance of the things of the world. However, the image of grace is the humanity of the Word. And in both means God was shown, but God was not understood in both ways since though nature certainly demonstrated an art by

means of its outward appearance, it is not able to illuminate the eye of contemplation. Truly then, the humanity of the Savior was the healing through whom the blind received light and teaching, so that seeing they might know truth.[43]

Symbols function in basically the same way according to nature and to grace, but: "Therefore, first [Jesus] illuminated, then [Jesus] demonstrated. Nature is able to demonstrate, it is not able to illuminate."[44] Symbols both demonstrate and illuminate. But only divine theology that has access to the humility of the word, has access to the illuminating capacity of symbols. Put another way, natural symbols demonstrate that God is; the symbols of grace illuminate and participate in God's presence:

> Therefore, through the images [simulacra] of nature the Creator signified many things, in the images of grace God is revealed present now: the images of nature were created so that God might be understood to be [ut intelligeretur esse], while in the images of grace those things were created so that God might be known to be present [ut agnoscreretur praesens esse]. This is the distance of this theology of the world from that which is called divine theology. Indeed, the invisible world is impossible unless it be demonstrated by visible things. On that account all theology must necessarily contain visible demonstrations for the open expression of invisible things. . . . Divine theology has chosen the work of restoration according to the humanity of Jesus and his sacraments.[45]

Hugh of St. Victor's mundane theology is similar in many ways to Denys' anagogic symbology.[46] In addition, through his emphasis on the participation of the humility of Christ in the opus restaurationis, Hugh pursues a symbology of participation in which the contemplative not only knows of God, but participates in God's presence.[47] This latter is made possible through the exemplar of grace (exemplaria gratiae) in which the form of grace was itself humility. Both the anagogic and participatory or "presence" symbolism will be of great interest and value to Richard as he turns to the symbolism of the ark and cherubim to evoke the presence of God. In addition, in both anagogic and presence symbolism, symbols not only provide a starting point in the quest for God, they also provide an aid or a "guiding hand" (manuductio) in conducting the contemplative toward those things which cannot be conceived.[48]

One other aspect of symbol and language in Hugh is of value to Richard. This is Richard's use of symbol and the construction or weaving of the interior icon in the heart of the contemplative. Hugh makes a distinction between seeing "into a mirror in a dark manner" and seeing "face to face" (1 Cor. 13:12). He relates these two kinds of seeing to faith and contemplation: "Now when we see through faith, we see through a mirror enigmatically; however, when we see through contemplation, we see face to face."[49]Hugh then asks what it is to see through a mirror. It is, he says, to see the image (*imaginem videre*). What is it to see face to face? It is to see the thing (*rem videre*). Thus, it seems to be that the "thing" is the goal of the dynamic, contemplative process leading to God.[50] Hugh makes a similar distinction between word and thing: "the unsubstantial word is the sign of man's perceptions; the thing is a resemblance of a divine idea."[51] Word and symbol, of course, contain evocative and anagogic qualities, but they remain always, in some sense, veils or coverings concealing the reality of things:

> For what are the coverings of words [*involucra verborum*][52] except certain coverings [*involumenta*] of the intelligence. And as long as the human sense is covered [*involumenta*] with these, never is the eye of the heart opened perfectly to the light of truth.[53]

In *De arca mystica*, Richard uses images, words, symbols in a contemplative process leading to God. His goal, participation in the presence of God, is the thing (*res*) of God. God's presence is that "thing" believed to be truly and substantially there (*res ibi veraciter it substantialiter praesens creditur*).[54]

It remains to be seen to what extent Richard peels back and discards words and symbols, and to what extent they remain as an integral part of the "presence" of God. The life and breath and drama of the contemplative as the "thing" of God remains to be seen.

SUMMARY: SYMBOL AND METHODOLOGY

M.D. Chenu has remarked that, "In the whole range of its culture, the medieval period was an era of the symbol as much, indeed more than, an era of dialectic."[55] We now turn to a very few of the myriad analyses of the use and function of symbols, attempting to look not at the "whole range" of medieval culture, but rather at twelfth-century symbolic theology in particular. The intent is to examine some of the contemporary analyses of symbolic method that have a bearing on Richard of St. Victor's own use of symbols.[56]

Theories of twelfth-century religious symbols are abundant and complex. Insights of particular relevance to Richard's use of symbol include the following: (1) that symbols are "polysemic"; they have the quality of possessing manifold meanings;[57] (2) that they point beyond themselves, giving meaning to ordinary experience;[58] (3) that they are agents of transformation and as such they often guide the contemplative along the path of the spiritual quest;[59] (4) and that they have the "capacity for expressing paradoxical situations or certain patterns of ultimate reality that can be expressed in no other way."[60]

If we keep these attributes of symbols in mind, a number of typologies of symbols may be developed, all of which Richard of St. Victor employs. These typologies include (1) theories of symbols employing the logic of identity and the logic of participation;[61] (2) theories of a symbolism of analogy vs. a symbolism of participation;[62] (3) theories employing the logical principle of contradiction vs. the logical principle of noncontradiction;[63] (4) models describing the symbols of center (introversion) and symbols of ascent (extroversion);[64] (5) and finally models of the symbolism of the sacred ground and the symbolism of magic flight.[65]

All of these typologies are crucial to Richard's understanding and use of symbols.[66] They, along with the basic Dionysian typology of similar and dissimilar symbols, are, in the presencing symbols of ark and cherubim, supremely characteristic of Richard's symbolic methodology. But, as will be shown in the following chapters, they are not the whole story. For Richard uses anagogy and symbols which at the same time utilize the hierarchical cosmology of Denys and the medieval period and yet manage to "break through" that cosmology and move into a symbolism of presencing, participation, and synthesis. As will be shown, Richard's use of the twin cherubim allows a simultaneous opposition and muting of opposition, a simultaneous contradiction and noncontradiction, a simultaneous experience and inversion of experience, a simultaneous ascent along the hierarchies and birth into the womb of Wisdom formed by the wings of the cherubim. For finally, the cherubim make present a Christological "Word" that is not for the language of symbol to speak. The cherubim make present a "Word" which is not a literary conceit concealing inner meaning beneath a fabulous surface (*involucrum* or *integumentum*). This "Word" presents itself in spite of the veil. This "Word" is a grand and startling gift, not an achievement. It is a "Word" which, though unspoken, breathes within the flesh of each incarnate heart.

4

First Cherubim:
Contemplation and the
Cherubim as Symbol

Cherubin cherubin respicit . . . loquar ad te
—*De arca* IV.xix, xxi

Richard of St. Victor uses the same word or its derivatives to describe both the flight pattern of birds I have been referring to as "hovering" and a key component of contemplation.[1] The word is *suspendo*. In addition to the use of hovering in this book as a metaphor of the *coincidentia oppositorum*, this word also has the meaning of "to keep in suspense," and, in the best sense, to "leave undecided." As a participle it carries the added nuances of "ambiguity," "uncertainty," and "doubt." In contemplation, the highest form of thinking, the mind hovers. The contemplative, kept in suspense, ambiguity, and even doubt as to the appropriateness or adequacy of his or her own groping toward God, is left free for the implosive gift of grace. It may strike us as odd that to think is to enter the ambiguity of doubt or indecision; for Richard, however, the work of contemplation is the peace of paradox. The cherubim are *suspensa*, and to touch them is to hover.

THE FUNCTION AND USE OF SYMBOL
IN *DE ARCA MYSTICA*

I will now turn to Richard of St. Victor's use of the symbol of the cherubim as an object of contemplationin *De arca mystica*.[2] Prudence

61

warns, however, of two related, preliminary precautions. First, that to separate the qualities and aspects of contemplation, spirituality, theology, exegesis, tropology, and symbolic method from each other in the work of Richard of St. Victor is not only difficult and arbitrary but weakens the value and intent of each. Such a separation is here undertaken with the explicit caveat that the sum of the parts is less than the whole and that detachment, isolation, and dissection done in the name of contemporary sensibility and methodology must in the end give way to reunification, participation, and interwovenness in the name of historical accuracy *and* contemporary edification. And second, that in a similar manner, the function of symbol per se in Richard's *De arca mystica* is continuous with the function of the symbol of the cherubim. We look at the context of one to better understand the other; but the contexts and functions blend.

This interparticipation is nowhere better illustrated than in the root metaphor or symbol of hovering itself. Richard gives concrete examples of hovering in the birds of the air, which are used to illustrate modes of contemplation. Like the birds, the cherubim are creatures that fly; hovering atop the ark, they provide both the tension and the resolution for Richard's dialectic of the presence of God. The first cherubim as unity of essence and the second cherubim as trinity of persons describe a Trinity participating in a relationship of hovering. The coincidence of opposites symbolized by hovering at every layer of Richard's work, whether psychological, dialectical, contemplative, metaphysical, or spiritual, caution a stillness in our movement, a silence in our words, a synthesis in our dissociations.

And yet with that caution given and absorbed, we continue to harken to the *ordo* and *sacra historia* of scripture followed by Richard himself. That is, we follow the route of wood, gilding, crown, propitiatory, cherubim: we dissociate to synthesize.

Patterns and "Thing"

In the opening chapter of *De arca mystica*, Richard of St. Victor claims that the ark and cherubim "are named after the thing [*re*] itself" or "that it receives its name from its own reality."[3] While it is likely that this statement stems from Hugh of St. Victor's distinction between *res* and *imago* in *De Sacramentis*,[4] it is nonetheless curious that the ark and cherubim are called *res* and not *imago*. It is curious, and yet somehow elegant when we remember that the ark of sanctification is called "an ark of sanctification for you."[5] That is, the contemplative who touches this symbol will be sanctified. As we investigate the nature of symbol in Richard's work, we would do well to keep in mind this physical (*res*) power of that "thing" which Richard calls symbol.

In I.v, Richard sets out the patterns of various types of bird flight, claiming that, "According to this pattern of designed similitudes, the flight of our contemplation is varied in many ways."[6] Thus from the beginning of the treatise, examples from the natural world are used to symbolize varieties of contemplation. Here, for instance, birds form a pattern (*exemplar*) that is a symbol (*prepositarum similitudinum*); in fact they are the very "form of the thing" (*rei formam*) of contemplation.[7] As Richard advances in sophistication and explication of his use of symbols, images not only of nature but of soul and of the transcendent will "form a pattern that is a symbol." They will form a pattern and they will describe a "way" of being with God.

De arca mystica, I.xii serves both as a summary of Richard's method and intent and as a grounding or launching pad for his work in the later chapters. Indeed, the chapter's opening paragraph provides a summary of his symbolic method:

> However, the last two kinds of contemplation are expressed by an angelic form [*figura*]. And indeed rightly so; that labor to be performed [*operis factura*] has not a human but an angelic form [*formam*]. It is proper for those kinds of contemplations, whose object goes beyond all human reason, to be represented [*repraesentare*] by a similitude [*similitudinem*].[8]

Thus that which goes beyond human reason is represented in the form and figure of a symbol or similitude. The angels, themselves the form of a symbol, stand apart, yet turned toward each other, "As a figure of those things [*rerum figuram*] of which the one seems to consent to reason [*rationi consentire*] and the other seems contrary to reason [*rationi contraire*]."[9] Here, symbols form a pattern that functions both according to reason as well as contrary to reason. Thus while the "contemplations whose object goes beyond reason" are represented by angelic form, the contemplations whose object may be reason or according to reason are also represented by the angelic figure. This represents one aspect of Richard's deepest level of separating-synthesizing consciousness which in turn reflects his use of the coincidence of opposites. Again, the image of hovering best manifests this consciousness. The tropological and ethical result of this contemplative work, that is, of this hovering in Wisdom, is also mentioned in I.xii. As might be expected, this result is mentioned in the context of the tension between opposites: in this case that of the relation between human activity and divine grace. Richard says:

> But in these final contemplations, everything depends on grace. They are exceedingly remote from any human activity, except in the way that each person receives from heaven the clothing of angelic similitude, and by divine guidance they clothe themselves.[10]

The tropological implications of the contemplative putting on the clothing of "angelic similitude" will be taken up in Chapter 6. For now, it is apparent that for Richard the pattern of symbols alter the very aspect, appearance, and being of the contemplative who "hovers" over them in awe as the manifestations of God's Wisdom.[11] The form and figure of symbols are the garments of angels.

Nature Mysticism and Cataphatic Symbols

With the first and second kinds of contemplation, and especially the third, symbolized for Richard by the crown of the ark (*coronam arcae designatur*), we begin to grasp the invisible things of God by means of the similitude of visible things of the world.[12] This is an important concept of symbol at the level of the natural world and even at the level of the soul.[13] The concept is based on Romans 1:20:

> Since the invisible things of God, from the creation of the world, have been clearly seen, having been understood by means of those things which have been made.[14]

The concept is aptly symbolized by the crown of the ark in that it is fastened, or begins, in the literal, corporeal wood of the ark and yet rises above the wood, displaying the invisible qualities symbolized by gold. This third kind of contemplation, then, employs symbols in an anagogic fashion, raising the contemplative to the transcendent things of God, but at the same time it is also cataphatic in its methodology in that it is by means of *rerum visibilium similitudinem* that we catch hold of or seize *invisibilium qualitatem*. It is this very cataphatic aspect of Richard's use of symbols in the third kind of contemplation that allows for a contemplative spirituality grounded in the body and the natural world. Richard says:

> Rightly, however, this contemplation, in order that it might ascend to invisible things, supports itself by means of a *staff of corporeal similitudes* and, so to speak, raises itself to the heights by means of a ladder of the properties of *bodily things*.[15]

Supported by the staff of corporeal similitudes (*baculo se corporeae similitudinis sustentat*), Richard makes a connection between the natural world and "invisible things," ascending to the latter by means of natural symbols. This, then, is the foundation of Richard's spirituality of grounded flight: his symbolic method necessitates an ongoing integration of physicality into the contemplative ascent.[16] The cherubim, their wings out-stretched and hovering, nonetheless grasp the wood, the crown, the propitiatory, with the ferocity of physical, bodily things. Their flight is on the wings of corporeal symbols.

Chapter II.xii provides a kind of synopsis of the symbolic function of the cataphatic ascent. In this third kind of contemplation: "The soul of the contemplative is supported not a little towards an understanding of invisible things from a similtude (or likeness) of visible things."[17] But there is a range of relations between visible similitudes or symbols and invisible things.[18] Later in this same chapter, Richard investigates this range of relations by employing a series of spatial metaphors indicating the nearness or distance of the visible to the invisible. He does this by noting the relative similarity or dissimilarity to invisible things of symbols drawn from the natural world. He says:

> Nevertheless, every bodily thing has good similitude to invisible things; but some have a slight similitude and are greatly distant and exceedingly strange, while others are exceedingly near and have a more manifest similitude.[19]

Richard establishes a hierarchy of the nearness of the visible to the invisible by using spatial terms and metaphors.[20] These spatial terms, making their claim of the "nearness" of the visible to the invisible on the basis of the *imago Dei*, allow Richard to substitute "experience" for things which we do "not know":

> Thus, by means of these things which draw near and give birth to a more evident image of the invisible, we ought certainly to draw a

similitude, so that our understanding can ascend through that which we know to that which we do not know through experience.[21]

This link of experience between the known and the unknown may seem odd if we forget that Richard insists on grounding contemplative "flight" in the literal, corporeal, natural world. The third contemplation progresses in reason according to imagination. Its intent or principal property is to draw out, even in some cases to "tear out" (*eruere*),[22] a "rational principle of similitude" (*similitudinum rationem trahere*) to investigate invisible things.[23] At this point in Richard's teaching on contemplation, "experience" is as viable a grounding as the literal, corporeal, or natural world. It is an element of coherence in the symbolic ascent of the soul from the visible to the invisible.[24]

Emphasizing the extreme philosophical and spiritual importance of sensual physicality and experience in the contemplative ascent, Richard devotes a full chapter to the leading or guiding hand of corporeal similitudes (*corporeae similitudinis manuductione utimur*).[25] This chapter not only emphasizes the importance of the body and senses as an entry into and beyond self, it also focuses on the corporeal similitudes as the very guide of reason.[26] By means of corporeal similitude, imagination conducts reason to a "place" it could not attain on its own:

> For indeed, while imagination represents the form of visible things to reason, and shapes itself by a similitude of these same things for the investigation of invisible things, in a certain way imagination conducts reason to that place where it does not know how to go on its own.[27]

And more important at this stage in his use of symbol, the "guiding hand" is unable to make the journey, even with the aid of reason, without the aid of this "novitiate of the senses":

> Therefore, as often as it is considered to grasp through the bodily senses the experience of understanding things, just as often our inner person seems to follow its leader. Without doubt, the sense of the flesh precedes the sense of the heart in the understanding of things, because unless the soul first might grasp sensible things through the bodily senses, it would completely fail to discover what it might be able to understand concerning them.[28]

There is no doubt that in the last stages of contemplation, as described and taught by Richard, the contemplative is purged of some aspects of his or her bodily senses. And the encounter on the ark between the two cherubim seems at first somehow disembodied. But as we follow Richard in his use of symbols, and especially as we keep in mind the incarnate nature of the divinity that is met with and spoken to upon the ark, these lower levels of contemplation begin to reassert themselves. For eyes and ears, experience, hands and breath are the instruments by which God's presence is ascertained. They are the spiritual senses grounded in the literal, bodily senses.[29] They make possible the rational symbols which lead through imagination to the angelic symbols, which lead back by means of the ark of sanctification to the virtual embodiment of Wisdom.

Into the Self: Symbols and Soul Mysticism

Book III of Richard's *De arca mystica* begins a kind of anthropology of symbol the intent of which is that the contemplative find access to symbols which facilitate entry into the self or soul. With soul mysticism, it is knowledge of self (rather than knowledge of nature through the senses) which leads to an understanding of heavenly things. As Richard notes, this form of contemplation and use of symbol "consists in incorporeal things and invisible essences: that is, angelic spirits and human spirits," made accessible to us as creatures because we were "created according to the image of God."[30] Since symbols used in this kind of contemplation deal with invisible human and angelic spirits, Richard details an anthropology that finds God at the core or center of self. Symbols, at this level of contemplation, assist as both ways *and* means to that center or core.

The propitiatory, itself placed at the center of the transcendent cherubim, symbolizes this stage of contemplation and the function and use of symbol at this point. The art and craftsmanship of working the gold of the propitiatory serve as a representation of the *process* of the work of symbols, whereas the wood, gilding, and crown serve as representations of the *structure* of symbol.[31] Richard thus develops the anthropological process of participation or "ascension" by introversion as symbolized by the propitiatory atop the ark.[32] Much of Book III is spent in developing a psychology or anthropology of the soul which in turn might be labeled a "psychology of symbol." For it is through these symbols that the self is entered, the self is known, and God is encountered:

> Therefore, the first thing in this consideration is that you should return to yourself, you should enter your heart. . . . Learn what you are. . . . Learn therefore to understand from your own spirit what you ought to appraise concerning other spirits. This is the gate. This is the ladder. This is the entrance. This is the ascent. By this we enter into the inmost parts, by this we are raised to the heights. This is the art of the propitiatory.[33]

Richard also uses the rising sun as a symbol of the process of entry into the soul,[34] and thus as a symbol of movement through the self to the transcendent:

> However, the reborn [*renascens*] sun little by little rises up to the higher places when through an understanding of itself it rises by contemplation into the heavens. . . . Do you see how much a full understanding of himself is of value for man? For from this understanding he advances to an understanding of all heavenly, earthly, and infernal things.[35]

Functioning in this way, the soul serves as a microcosmic symbol of the macrocosmic heaven and earth. Containing as it does the *imago Dei* which serves as a mirror of the divine nature, knowledge of self provides an entry point, a gate to "heavenly, earthly, and infernal things."

Richard has a carefully worked out doctrine of the *imago Dei* in *De arca mystica*. This doctrine also has important implications for Richard's assumptions concerning the nature and function of symbols. For instance, through the doctrine of the *imago Dei* the human spirit can be likened to heavenly spirits, and in this way through contemplation of likenesses through similar symbols, humanity can become spiritual:

> And in this way, to rise up through a consideration of your spirit to a contemplation of spiritual things and to couple together [*comparare*] spiritual with spiritual things, you begin in a similar way to be spiritual.[36]

The important word *comparare* (cf. 1 Cor. 2:13, *spiritualibus spiritualia comparantes*) indicates "couple together, form into pairs, liken," so that through it a definite twin relation between human and spiritual things is established, very much in the manner of the relation between the two identical cherubim themselves. Coupled together with spiritual things, the soul, then, is itself a kind of temple: it is fit for the immediate acquisition and storage of the internal icon that Richard is painting. The soul of the spiritual person (*spiritualis*), which has "its own earth and its own kind of heaven,"[37] is a microcosmic gate and abode of divine presence.

Symbols of the soul thus function by means of similitudes, and as such (as is the case with symbols from the natural world) are still in the purview of cataphatic methodology.[38] Richard says: "From much consideration and recognition of your spirit you will be lifted up to an understanding and contemplation of the spirit of angels and the Spirit of the divine."[39] But it is precisely at this point that the power of cataphatic method and of similar symbols begins to wane, and apophatic method along with dissimilar symbols begins to prevail. The point is not distinctly marked in Richard; he does not simply shift from similar to dissimilar symbols, their interrelation is too complex and coincidentally opposite. Rather he uses, so to speak, a metaphor to signal a shift in metaphor; he uses an image to signal a metaphysical reversal of image;[40] he uses a symbol to hint at the path of the eventual destruction of symbol:

> However, this ultimate and highest heaven has its own day. And certainly it has its own night. And if we attend to this heaven, as long as we are in this life, what other than night do we have or are we able to have until night will have completed its course and the reddening dawn of light will have frightened away the night. . . . Surely God made the moon and stars in the power of the night, and on that account his night is my illumination.[41]

Richard's methodology of symbol here begins to move into an apophatic context and into a symbolism based on paradox and ambiguity rather than likeness or coupling. This new symbolic method is necessary because, as he says, "what of our glorification is human sense able to acquire? What of our glorification is reason able to comprehend?"[42] The final chapters of Book III of De arca mystica begin to grapple with the necessarily paradoxical nature of symbol used contemplatively to grasp what is "beyond human sense."

One of the patterns at the end of Book III used by Richard to anticipate the core symbol of dissimilarity and ambiguity represented by the cherubim is that of scripture shouting by means of its silence. He says:

Certainly, this is what holy scripture symbolizes [*innuit*] by remaining silent, since it said nothing at all concerning the height of our propitiatory. It is as if it might shout more loudly and penetrate longer and better through silence. . . . Remaining silent, it shouts out [*Tacendo clamat*].[43]

Here is a clear example of hovering applied to the function of symbol. Scripture makes a sign by shouting its silence (that is, it uses the symbol of the propitiatory but is silent concerning its height). To claim that scripture "shouts loudly to penetrate through silence" is to assert that symbols manifest a mechanism of paradox; using our core metaphor, they hover.[44]

But for Richard, this is not to be wondered at; the soul often "clothes" (*induit*) itself in contrary natures. The human soul is easily led over from one affection to a contrary affection (*contrariis affectibus contrarios affectus superducit*).[45] The soul, immersed in the quality and nature of hovering, points the way to a necessary symbolism of dissimilarity and paradox; necessary, because at the heart of divinity is paradox, mystery. The final chapter of Book III in fact hints at the *imago Dei* reflected in the human soul as participating in the paradox of trinitarian nature. The soul, like the Trinity, is "one heart in a plurality and multiplicity of affections";[46] the soul thus supports the coincidental opposites of trinitarian unity and plurality.

Richard's discussion of symbolism does not so much end as begin to merge into his discussion of the cherubim. By the end of Book III, it is clear that the discussion of the soul as an entry point to the divine, based on the pattern of scripture and symbolized by the propitiatory, is, if not completed, at least temporarily exhausted.[47] The analysis of the use and function of symbol in Richard's *De arca mystica* is thus best continued by turning our gaze directly to the cherubim themselves.

THE SYMBOL OF THE CHERUBIM:
CHRIST AND GOD MYSTICISM

The Foundations of Richard's Angelic Spirituality

Medieval angelology was dependent on scriptural references[48] and the patristic tradition.[49] Traditional interpretations of the functions of angels are vast and encompass in one way or another every conceivable aspect and nuance of the relationship between God and humanity. Though certainly not limited to these, angels have traditionally served the functions of messengers, protectors, mediators, praisers, helpers and savers, ministers, heralds of peace, avengers, guardians, guides, symbols of ascent into heaven, and many more.[50] Certain of these, and some as yet not mentioned, were used by Richard of St. Victor as typologies of the symbol of the cherubim. The remainder of this chapter will trace the influences on Richard's use of the cherubim and then, in outlining Richard's own use in *De arca mystica*, attempt to develop typologies of Richard's use of the cherubim as a symbol.

As in the areas of apophatic and cataphatic methodology, and in the area of symbols generally, Richard was influenced by the angelology of Denys the Areopagite, who elaborated the doctrine of the nine choirs of angels in his short work *The Celestial Hierarchy*.[51] In Chapter 3 we noted Denys' use of deformed imagery, like and unlike symbols, the hidden truth concealed in symbols, and the uplifting or anagogic function of symbols. We also noted that, while dissimilar symbols are a superior means of "uplift" to God, they themselves are not God. These aspects of symbol can be applied equally to the symbol of angels.

An example of the fact that symbols (and angels) function anagogically to lift a contemplative to God, but are never themselves God, is Denys' use of hierarchy. Denys defines hierarchy as: "A sacred order, a state of understanding and an activity approximating as closely as possible the divine."[52] Hierarchy is thus order, understanding, and activity, and like symbols or angels it closely approximates but is not itself the divine.[53] In the same way angels approximate and look upon the divine intelligences, but are not themselves divinity:

> Their [angels] thinking process imitates the divine. They look on the divine likeness with a transcendent eye. They model their intellects on him. . . . They have the first and most diverse participation in the divine and they, in turn, provide the first and the most diverse revelations of the divine hiddenness. That is why they have a preeminent right to the title of angel or messenger, since it is they who first are granted the divine enlightenment and it is they who pass on to us these revelations which are so far beyond us.[54]

Angels thus imitate, look upon, model, have first participation in, are first granted enlightenment of, and pass on revelations concerning the divine. As with symbols and hierarchies, angels are the eyes which gaze upon the secret places of divine incomprehensibility. But they are not the divine.

And yet Denys uses hierarchy, symbol, and angel to talk about an "immediate" relation to God. For instance, with regard to angels in particular, Denys says: "The first group [i.e., seraphim, cherubim, thrones] is forever around God and is said to be permanently united with him ahead of any of the others and with no intermediary."[55] R. Roques, in an introduction to a French translation of *The Celestial Hierarchy*, makes this relation between the angels or hierarchy and divinity in Denys very clear:

> From this point of view, that which essentially characterizes the first hierarchy is its *immediate* proximity to the Divine principle. Nothing separates it from that principle. Being on the highest rung, they receive the first of the thearchic illuminations in all their original clarity and according to all their original vigor. . . . we must say that all these relationships with God operate without any kind of intermediary: they are direct, *unmediated*.[56]

The slight dissonance resulting from the juxtaposition of concepts such as "permanently united" and "no intermediary" to the concept of "imitation" or "activity as close as possible to the divine" yet not actually *being* the divine should perhaps not be surprising. Denys, in holding the classic Christian tension between the created order and the Creator while at the same time manipulating a Neoplatonic metaphysics, is bound to perpetuate dissonance: Neoplatonic union with the One (*hen*) beyond Mind (*nous*) is founded on the presupposition of disintegration of differences, while the Christian tension seeks metaphors and symbols for separateness in union.[57] Metaphors of seeing, marriage, likeness, and symbols such as the angels, aid in describing this activity that is "as close as possible to the divine" yet at the same time clearly is not equivalent to the divine.

Denys uses the symbols of cherubim, seraphim, and thrones to describe this activity that is close to the divine. The seraphim, for instance, signifying an affective proximity to the divine, mean "fire-makers," that is to say, "carriers of warmth."[58] The cherubim, signifying an intellective proximity to the divine, mean "fullness of knowledge" or "outpouring of Wisdom."[59] Denys expands on the nature of the cherubim in a manner that is of direct importance for Richard's own work:

> The name cherubim signifies the power to know and to see God, to receive the greatest gifts of his light, to contemplate the divine splendor in primordial power, to be filled with the gifts that bring Wisdom and to share these generously with subordinates as a part of the beneficent outpouring of Wisdom.[60]

All of these images, which Richard himself will use, begin to shift the emphasis in the use of the symbol of the cherubim from one of ascent and "uplift" to one of centering and participation. In this sense, as symbols, images, or likenesses, the cherubim shift from a relation of ever closer proximity to one of partnership and communion. This shift (and the fragility of symbols) becomes particularly noticeable when communion or participation is with the divine as Jesus:

> They [the first angelic beings] are contemplative also because they have been allowed to enter into communion with Jesus *not by means of holy images*, reflecting the likeness of God's working in forms, *but by truly coming close to him in primary participation* in the knowledge of the divine lights working out of him.[61]

As we shall see, this fragile delicacy of symbol, this disintegration of the capacity of symbol precisely at the apex of its functional trajectory, is one of the primary reasons Richard does not, against all reasonable expectations, propose a Christological object, work, or name in his own contemplative teaching. To do so would be to transgress the contemplative's "primary participation" in Christ as Wisdom.

Yet, though symbols are fragile and in some sense disintegrate, Denys leaves us with an imperative: "We have therefore to run counter to mass prejudice and we must make the holy journey to the heart of the sacred symbols."[62] For symbols "are the descendants and bear the mark of the divine stamp." They "take on the imprint of God."[63] The paradox again is striking: a truly immediate relation to God would require no "imprint" or "mark," because an imprint or mark mediates. Yet we take a journey to the heart of symbol, to the unmediated source, and what we find is still another imprint, still another mark, yet another veil. The paradox prevails: much as a human approaching the speed of light becomes ever more like light as the goal is approached, so the angels as symbols "evolve" from simple anagogy to complex participation as the immediacy of the divine goal is approached. In the same way, Denys begins to talk of angels in terms of participation in the divine.[64] The angels as symbols, finally, get caught in the shift from ascent (or speed of light, in the case of the human approaching) to participation. Still, the spirituality of presence is a journey, and so, as Denys insists, "we must make the holy journey to the heart of the sacred symbols."

For Hugh of St. Victor, too, this journey to the heart of the sacred symbols leads to deformity or dissimilarity which forces the understanding to exit from the figure or symbol in order to rejoin truth.[65] That is, again, symbols outline the path of the journey but are not the goal. As we saw in Chapter 3 on Hugh's discussion of looking into "a mirror enigmatically" as *imaginem videre* and seeing "face to face" as *rem videre*, and his association of faith with *imago* and contemplation with *res*,[66] it is the image which must be abandoned in the contemplation of the thing (i.e., the exit of understanding from symbol in order to join truth). This is true, as we will see in Richard also, whether the image is dissimilar or similar. Similar symbols may in fact be received and employed dissimilarly, as Hugh points out:

> The very similitudes, which seem similarly to be displayed on both sides, are however received dissimilarly; and they are understood at the one time as similar symbols, and at another time as dissimilar symbols.[67]

But, as we have seen with Denys, even dissimilar symbols must also be abandoned.

Another way of looking at the necessary "abandoned" nature of symbols in Hugh is to look closely at his choice of words as he discusses the nature of symbol, thing, and angel. Again, seeing into an unpolished mirror is seeing an image; seeing face to face is seeing the thing. Imagine, says Hugh, that someone is behind or above you, and you are turned away (*aversus*) and do not see him face to face. You do not see that person face to face because your face is turned away (*aversa*); even if the person looks back at you (*respicit*), you will not see him or her face to face. Even if you place a mirror before both of you, you do not see as you are seen (*nondum vides, sicut videris*). The person may look back (*respicit*) at you, but you are still turned (*aversus*) from him. So, Hugh says, "Turn toward (*converte*) him and place your face before his face and you will see not an image but the thing itself."[68]

We will note, then, that in *De arca mystica* both cherubim look back (*respicit*), they are not turned away (*aversa*),[69] exactly as Hugh advises. Richard, of course, uses the gazing cherubim as a symbol of contemplation (they *rem vident*). In fact the complete ark along with the cherubim is interpreted as the grace of contemplation (*gratia contemplationis*). Richard, then, in some very real sense associates mutual looking back (*mutuo se respiciant*) with contemplation, not with faith, as Hugh seems to do. Though this is in part a break with Hugh, Richard also bases his association of *respiciant* (and thus *converte*) with contemplation, and therefore with the thing (*res*), on the work of Hugh. For we find in Hugh's inquiry into the nature of angels in I.v of *De Sacramentis* that there were those angels who were converted (*convertebantur*) to good, and those angels who were averted (*avertebantur*) from good.[70] It is this positive aspect of conversion or "turning toward" that Richard links with the terminology of *respiciant* by associating *mutuo se respiciant* with the cherubim in *De arca mystica*. And the very thing that Richard's cherubim turn to see, as promised in Exodus 25, is the presence and word of God. This presence and word is the thing (*res*) and not the image (*imago*). Thus it would seem in Richard that the cherubim as symbols, being linked so closely to contemplation, actually do see the "thing" or "face to face."

In Hugh, "we make the holy journey to the heart of sacred symbols" to come face to face with the "thing."[71] But one comes face to face with this "thing" only in the play between the similar and the dissimilar, in which the understanding finally abandons symbol and image and finally abandons all mirrors, turning, as the angels turned, in contemplation toward the ark where stands the *opus restaurationis* which *est incarnatio Verbi*.[72] In Richard, fullness of understanding, knowledge, and Wisdom is symbolized by the cherubim,[73] who look mutually back upon the ark and one another and come face to face with the "thing" only to utter silence. The grace of contemplation leads through the heart of sacred symbols to the unuttered "thing."[74] For any word but the Word is itself an image.

The Symbol of the Cherubim in *De arca mystica*

Richard of St. Victor begins his explicit treatment of the cherubim, as described by God to Moses in Exodus 25, in Book IV of *De arca mystica*. The three previous books provide the framework or foundation for Richard's treatment of the cherubim; the final book,

Book V, while expanding on ecstatic contemplation touched on at the end of Book IV, does not continue explicit treatment of the cherubim. Book IV can be outlined as follows:

Chap. i. Summary of the nature of the fifth and sixth kinds of contemplation based on tropological exegesis of the cherubim in Exodus 25:18–20, 22.

Chaps. ii–vii. Tropological exegesis of Exodus 25:18, "Make two cherubim of gold and beaten work for both sides of the oracle."[75] Primarily a process of purification through faith (Chap. iii), reason (Chap. iv), knowledge of God (Chap. v), grace and revelation (Chaps. vi–vii).

Chap. viii. Tropological exegesis of Exodus 25:19, "Let one cherubim be on one side and the other cherubim on the other."[76] Discussion of *imago Dei* in humanity and angels; discussion of the nature of similar and dissimilar symbols.

Chaps. ix–xvi. Tropological exegesis of Exodus 25:20a, "Let them, stretching out their wings and covering the oracle, conceal both sides of the propitiatory."[77] Discussion of knowledge of self and love of God; movement toward sanctification through the last two kinds of contemplation which strengthen against evil and assist to virtue.

Chaps. xvii–xx. Tropological exegesis of Exodus 25:20b, "Let them look back at each other, with their countenances swept toward the propitiatory."[79] Cherubim explicitly symbolize the Trinity: one cherubim representing unity of supreme and simple essence is said to be beyond but not contrary to reason, one cherubim representing trinity of persons is said to be above and contrary to reason.

Chaps. xxi–xxxiii. Tropological exegesis of Exodus 25:22, "From there I will speak to you from above the propitiatory, from between the two cherubim."[79] Explication of a spirituality of presence based on the doctrines of revelation and grace.

ONE CHERUBIM ON ONE SIDE, ONE ON THE OTHER. The difference between the similar and dissimilar aspects of the cherubim as symbols is explicitly stated: the first cherubim, representing the fifth kind of contemplation, "permits the rational principle of similitude," but the second cherubim, representing the sixth kind of contemplation, "totally exceeds the property of similitude."[80]

We have already encountered this concept in the discussion on apophatic and cataphatic theology. As we saw, Richard uses the cherubim to symbolize contemplation according to reason and contemplation seemingly contrary to all reason.[81] The cherubim also symbolize similarity and dissimilarity to God. To claim similarity, Richard asserts an image and similitude of God for all rational creatures, angelic as well as human. His claim for this *imago Dei* for humanity is, of course, based on Genesis 1:27. His not very convincing argument for an angelic *imago Dei* is based on Ezekiel 28:12–13.[82] His argument for dissimilarities between God and angelic beings and humanity is much more convincing.[83] Richard thus concludes that:

> Therefore, what else are we able to gather from such diverse sentences, unless that truly and without a doubt on account of one thing we consider similarities to our Author and on account of another thing, dissimilarities?[84]

He then connects the first cherubim symbolically to similarity and the second cherubim symbolically to dissimilarity.[85] For one cherubim, "any adaptation of similitude is easily accommodated." Contemplation symbolized by the second cherubim is of that to which "no shadow of similitude fully joins itself."[86]

MAKE TWO CHERUBIM. Richard opens Book IV with the cherubim serving not only as symbols but also as images of how symbols function and might be used. The opening paragraph of Chapter i is peppered with words indicating symbol or image which in turn are linked to the name "cherubim" or "angel."[87] Something represented to us under the form of an angel "must be something great, excellent, and certainly more than human," Richard says. They are, in fact, a "link" between the human and divine which deepens and strengthens with each forging, and as such, they are an excellent representation of how symbols, linking *imago* with *res*, function.

As a symbol of a symbol "cherubim" means "fullness of knowledge" (*plenitudo scientiae*). And the cherubim are not just any angels, but, echoing what we encountered in the celestial hierarchy of Denys, they are only:

> the highest and those joined immediately to God. And so the form of this manner of work calls us out to supermundane, not to supercelestial things—and under this proposition, it invites us to a speculation of the highest, divine things.[88]

Thus, in that the cherubim are *summos et Deo immediate conjunctos*, the form of the tropological symbol of the cherubim becomes the very form of our work of contemplation. The effect of this work (or *gratia contemplationis*) is that the cherubim themselves become the form of our work. They represent the fact that the struggle for a way of finding a symbolic correspondence of angels to God or of ourselves to angels or of ourselves to God, being finally *supra rationem*,[89] is also finally above reason's understanding of symbol.[90] Nevertheless the symbol of the cherubim, unlike language, does not falter upon contact with God.

They do not falter, as Denys' language falters, because in Chapters ii–vii Richard traces the symbol of the cherubim through a trajectory that finally must include grace and revelation. Revelation, for Richard, is *supra rationem*, but is seen with the eye of faith (*fidei oculo*),[91] and so does not preclude the active function of symbol. The symbol of the cherubim does not falter upon contact with God because it is a symbol based both on similitude and on dissimilitude. At the level of dissimilitude, symbols no longer "represent" or are "images" or "forms," they *are*, to the extent that they are capable of supporting the content of revelation, what they represent.[92]

But, having made the claim that, with regard to participating in the transcendent level similitude is an inadequate symbolic method,[93] Richard shows that as dissimilar symbols the cherubim function as a symbol of contemplation beyond which one cannot go but through which God *is*. They serve as a "figurative copy" (*figuraliter exprimunter*) of the highest knowledge.[94] To arrive at this conclusion, Richard reiterates in Chapter v his description of the cherubim in Chapter i as "fullness of knowledge." As we saw in Chapter 2 of this work, Richard's Chapter v describes God as that than which there is nothing higher (*ultra Deum nihil est*) and that for that reason our knowledge (*scientia*)[95] is not able to ascend higher or farther than God. But if to know (*cognoscere*) God *is* fullness of knowledge (*plenitudo scientia*) then:

> If "cherubim" is said to mean fullness of knowledge, see how correctly the outermost portions of our ongoing work, in which the supreme levels of all knowledge [*scientia*] are represented figuratively, are named "cherubim. . . . So the figure of this work, in which we are initiated to the fullness of all knowledge, is rightly called "cherubim."[96]

Thus, says Richard, these last two contemplations push us little by little to the shadow of full knowledge.[97] From our perspective the "figure of this work" is dissimilar to God. From God's perspective fullness of knowledge is similar to God's self. The cherubim, as symbol, mediate these perspectives and, from our side, allow a shadow of transcendent knowing.[98]

Chapter vii, the final chapter interpreting Exodus 25:18 ("make the cherubim of gold and beaten work") as an injunction to undertake the process of purification, asks "how shall I represent a form that I am not capable of seeing?"[99] The answer for Moses was to represent the form on the basis of revelation (*revelationem*). For the contemplative:

> It is when [the soul] draws into itself a similitude through the imitation of those orders of celestial beings which adhere without mediation to the highest light and which see face to face and without a mirror and without enigma.[100]

The key for representing an unseen form, then, is imitation. When imitation takes the form of Wisdom (*sapientia*), described by Richard in I.i of *De arca mystica* as the goal and method of his work, the human soul clothes itself in angelic form (*humanum animum, angelicam formam induere*).[101] It is thus through imitation of Wisdom that the soul sees God face to face and without mediation. This is the goal of Richard's tropological interpretation of the ark and cherubim. But with the "imitation of celestial orders," it appears that, contrary to how the angels were used as dissimilar symbols, the cherubim represent a kind of similitude the imitation of which serves to draw us to an unmediated vision of God. Here we must be careful with Richard's terminology, especially in trying to represent a form that one cannot see. On the one hand, the cherubim function as dissimilar symbols "forging" the place where God will dwell (though never "forging" God's presence or speech); on the other hand, the cherubim function as a similitude drawing the contemplative to a vision face to face with God (though the "force" or "power" that draws is God's own revelation, not humanity's action). The key to this difference is stated succinctly by Richard: "In short, it is one thing to make the ark, it is another thing to form the cherubim."[102] The difference is how each functions as a symbol: the ark utilizes similar or dissimilar symbols to facilitate entry into the self and to provide glimpses of invisible things; the cherubim utilize similar and dissimilar attributes to prepare and draw the contemplative into a "vision" of God or the "place" where God dwells. As such, the cherubim function not only as symbols of ascent leading to the unseen, but as symbols, themselves unseen, which draw one, through imitation of Wisdom, into the presence of God. It is this unseen, guiding, patterning, containing, mutually reciprocal, and finally birthing and presencing nature of the cherubim which renders them symbolic of symbol; they are a symbol containing symbol; they are a womb of revelation.

SPREADING WINGS, CONCEALING THE PROPITIATORY. The last two kinds of contemplation symbolized by the cherubim contribute to the work of imitating Wisdom by "either strengthening us against evil or assisting us to virtue."[103] Strength and assistance is the tropological interpretation Richard gives to Exodus 25:20: "Spreading wings and covering the oracle, let them [the cherubim] cover both sides of the propitiatory." Richard interprets the fact that the cherubim's wings cover (*tegant*) the propitiatory to mean that they provide both a place of hiding (*absconsionem*) and protection (*protectionem*), and thus strength and assistance.[104]

The contemplative, preparing for entrance into the presence of God, has need of both a place of hiding and of protection. When, through the very transformation of the property of the soul (*animi abalienatione*),[105] the contemplative rises above his or her very self (*nosmetipsos*); when the mind of the contemplative does not even know its very self (*mens nostra seipsam nesciret*); and when for a time the contemplative lies numbed and amazed as the soul is hovering in the sight of the cherubim (*dum in ejusmodi cherubin aspectum suspensa stuperet*), then the contemplative has recourse to necessary assistance found in deep retreat under the cherubim's wings.[106] When the golden gleam of the propitiatory (*aureum propitiatorii fulgorem*) competes with a greater and more supereminent brightness (*majoris et supereminentioris claritatis*) from the dazzling face of God, then the contemplative has urgent need of the strength afforded by the protection of the spreading of the cherubim's wings and of the shadow thus formed to cover her (*superducta obumbratione obnubilatur*).[107] The shadow of the wings of the cherubim thus provides a protective veil between the soul and God.[108] It is as if the very symbol itself provides shelter and protection from things too awesome to see or contemplate alone:

What wonder is it therefore, if in this way both sides of our propitiatory are covered by shadow? For, as has been said above, whatever in
us that is perceived as similar or dissimilar to the divine is darkened
by comparison to divine things. . . . I said truly therefore that the
cherubim can be said to conceal/protect [*tegere*] both sides of our
propitiatory, since nothing at all is found in us that is not foreign in
quality or incomparable in quantity to supreme and divine things.[109]

Without the symbol, without the wings and the shadow of their
protection, the contemplative would be continually stupefied, above
himself, struck permanently dumb by the dissimilarity between the
vision and the self. Paul returned to himself yet, needfully protected,
could not recall the particulars of his vision: "I do not know, God
knows" (2 Cor. 12:2). And Moses spoke with God in a cloud that
the Children of Israel saw as a consuming fire (Exod. 24:15–18). For
Richard also, the shadow of the wings mercifully hide and protect.

And yet, after the strengthening and protecting, after the construction of the ark and cherubim in the heart, there is still vision "beyond
symbol." The difference is that the vision beyond symbol, the vision of
God face to face, is beyond human construction or formation. This is
a vision solely dependent on grace. The contemplative, Richard says,
having been led through ecstasy of mind (*per mentis excessum*) outside
of himself,

Contemplates the light of highest Wisdom without any cover [*involucro*] or shadow [*adumbratione*] of images, in short, as I have
said, not in a mirror and enigma, but in simple truth.[110]

And while the vision itself is beyond images and without cover, it is
drawn forth for the understanding of others by means of the adaptation of symbols (*similitudinum adaptatione, ad communem intelligentiam deducit*). Thus in the vision of the transcendent, symbols
function in a threefold pattern: (1) symbols lead to the vision by
means of strengthening, protecting, and covering; (2) the vision itself is
without symbol (*sine involucro, figurarumve adumbratione*); (3) symbols (*similitudinum adaptatione*) are needed once again to explain
the vision to others. I believe that Richard intended the cherubim to
function in each step in this pattern: (1) as symbols of strength and
assistance; (2) as outlines or borders of that space wherein God would
speak to us face to face, present, but during the moment of the vision,

unobserved;[111] (3) as symbols explaining or interpreting the divine meeting by which we might "cling to the traces of revealing grace" (*vestigiis revelantis gratiae inhaerentes*)[112] and thereby reveal the meeting to others. And in each of the three patterns the cherubim serve as tropological aides: (1) by preparing or forming the soul through the Wisdom of virtue; (2) by presencing God through the Wisdom of grace; (3) by communicating grace by the Wisdom of love.[113] Thus, says Richard: "We ought, according to the divine pattern, to spread out the wings of our cherubim and to hasten in rapid steps of desire to meet the grace of a showing."[114]

Spread wings, for Richard, indicate longing, desire, waiting on the Beloved.[115] The more the wings are stretched for flight, the more the heart swells with desiring. And the more the heart swells with desiring, the more we are able to forge the cherubim, and our beaten work (*opus nostrum ductile*) begins to make progress. Thus, the wings of our desire (*desideriorum nostrorum pennas*) shelter and strengthen the ethical life:

> It is at this time, I think, that our beaten work begins to make progress and not moderately to draw near to consummation, since now our cherubim begin to spread their wings widely and to hover at every hour prepared for flying.[116]

THE TWIN GAZE. Chapter xvii of Book Four begins Richard's important interpretation of why the cherubim look back upon the propitiatory and upon each other. Richard is careful in this section to emphasize the shared mutuality and mirrored identity of the cherubim, but at the same time to insist upon their opposition or difference. The interpretation is of Exodus 25:20b: "Let the cherubim look back upon each other [*respiciant se*] mutually turning their faces toward the propitiatory."[117]

On the basis of the distinction between the two cherubim and reason, Richard explicitly links the cherubim as symbols to the Trinity. The first cherubim pertains to the unity of divine essence within the Trinity (which is accessible to reason); the second cherubim pertains to the persons within the Trinity (which is beyond the grasp of reason):

> And so according to this distinction you must see that it is not by chance that the first cherubim pertains especially to all those things which are considered concerning the unity of the supreme and simple

divine essence; to the second cherubim however pertain those things which are considered concerning the Trinity of persons.[118]

Richard then devotes one chapter to a philosophical consideration of the unity of divine essence,[119] and one chapter to consideration of divine revelation and the multiplicity of persons within the Trinity.[120]

He moves from a consideration of the cherubim as opposites symbolizing the unity and diversity within the Trinity, to a consideration focused on the relation of these opposites. This new consideration has important implications for Richard's symbolic method. Recalling that Exodus 25:20 mentions both that the cherubim face back toward each other and that they look back together at the propitiatory, Richard begins by establishing the relation of their mutual gaze.

Of primary importance to Richard in the gaze of twin consideration (*gemina consideratione*) of the cherubim is that what we affirm about one cherubim does not destroy what we affirm about the other. Warning over and over that we ought not to dismantle, break up, or empty out (*destraumus, dissipemus, evacuemus*) the symbolic significance of one cherubim by asserting its opposite value in the second cherubim, Richard seeks to establish a truly coincidental dialectic of opposites:

> One ought to observe carefully and one ought to be diligently on one's guard in observation so that as we join ourselves to those things which pertain to the one, we might not dismantle that which pertains to the other. . . . And so cherubim reflects upon cherubim when what one says does not contradict the other. Cherubim looks back at cherubim when the fifth kind of contemplation joins itself to those considerations of its own in such a way that it wishes to empty out nothing that belongs to the other cherubim.[121]

Richard draws examples of opposite content from both the Trinity and the Incarnation. That is, the cherubim represent unity and diversity, or the divine and the human, and in doing so, as they look back across at each other, neither empties the content of the other. To make his point, Richard gives examples of theologians of the Trinity who have not been successful in maintaining the balance between unity and diversity so harmoniously symbolized by the cherubim. Arius, for example, dissolves the unity of divinity (*divinitatis unitatem dissolvit*), while Sabellius tries to empty out faith in a trinity of persons (*Trinitatis fidem evacuare conatur*).[122]

The cherubim, while identical, thus signify a dialectical relation of opposites. Richard tries to capture this mutual regard through constant reiteration of the Exodus passage (*respiciantque se mutuo*) with slight variations: the cherubim come together mutually (*mutua collatione*), they mutually regard each other (*seipsos mutuo respicare*) by a mutual consent of concord (*mutuo concordiae consensu*), they look at each other mutually (*respiciant se cherubin mutuo*) and according to a mutual regard (*mutuum respectum*), and they look at each other mutually (*se mutuo respiciant*) even as cherubim regards cherubim (*cherubin cherubin respicit*).[123] At the same time, he captures the opposite attributes of the cherubim by focusing on the opposites within the Trinity, on the incarnate Christ, on the nature of contemplation as rest in activity, and by maintaining that because of the very nature of their opposition on the ark, the cherubim often turn their faces and "by a contrary assertion often direct their thoughts towards diverse opinions and themselves rest in opposites."[124]

The symbol of the cherubim represents a way or path of being in relation; they join themselves to considerations that are their own without emptying any consideration of the other. And the cherubim also, in a sense, face away from looking at only half of a mutual relationship: in facing each other they face away from the narcissism of looking only at their own faces; and in gazing upon the propitiatory they face away from the destructive projection or self-dispersal (*dissipare*) of looking only at the face of the other. Finally, in describing the "hovering" nature of the cherubim, Richard also hints at how the cherubim work as a symbol. Symbols depicting divinity manifest, uphold, and even require the maintenance of opposites. To the degree that symbols and language fail in this delicate balance, they empty themselves of the very divinity to which they are capable of giving birth. The cherubim, wings encircling and protecting the propitiatory, balancing the alpha and omega of creation, signifying harmony and diversity: these cherubim evacuate a space for the birth of the divine. They become womb.

The cherubim also turn their faces to the propitiatory (*versis vultibus in propitiatorium* [Exod. 25:20b]) from whence comes the seed of the Word. Chapter xx, which considers the faces of the cherubim turned toward the propitiatory, is important both for its insight into the nature of symbol and for the way it continues to add depth to the symbolic functions of the cherubim. Having looked at each other, and in continuing to look at one another, the cherubim now also slowly turn their faces to the propitiatory (*vultum in propitiatorium vertere*).[125]

For Richard, the two cherubim turn their faces toward the propitiatory after having contemplated the Trinitarian things of God (symbolized in turn by the cherubim themselves) thus:

> The last two kinds of contemplation harmoniously agree [*concorditer sentiunt*] in those things which concern supreme and divine things and from assertions of their own testimony they draw a similitude of reason [*rationis similitudinem*] from those things which are subject to the fourth kind of contemplation.[126]

As we recall, the fourth kind of contemplation of the propitiatory symbolizes contemplation of the rational, human soul. Richard uses the return to this fourth kind of contemplation to reintroduce the *imago Dei* concept, finding that the image of God in the human soul now carries the trace (*vestigia*) of the Trinity: "In this rational creature itself, if we diligently pay attention, we will find some vestige of the supreme Trinity—so we believe."[127] Thus there is an almost circular functioning of the symbol of the cherubim at this point: Richard moves from a consideration of the divine Trinity in its unity and multiplicity to a consideration of the image-Trinity (*imaginaria Trinitate*) as a vestige of the divine Trinity in the human soul.[128] It is from this "vestige of Trinity" that he is able to draw a similitude of reason that in turn draws him back into the divine Trinity. He thus moves from consideration of supreme things downward to consideration of lower things and from thence back upward to a consideration of supreme things.[129] This movement had been anticipated earlier in Chapter xix:

> One cherubim regards the other when (as usually happens) our speculation begins with a penultimate thing and concludes with a last thing. Or again on the contrary, it begins from the last thing and descends to the penultimate.[130]

Thus, in an important passage, Richard clarifies that, while the cherubim turn their faces toward the propitiatory in order to draw a similitude of reason from the vestige of the Trinity in the human soul, they do so in order to speculate, ultimately, upon divine things:

> So what does it mean that the Cherubim turn their faces to the propitiatory other than, in speculation and investigation of divine

things, to advance higher toward an understanding of divinity from having looked into a similitude?[131]

The vestige of the Trinity (*Trinitatis vestigium*) within the human soul, by which, as contemplated by the cherubim, we move to the things of supreme truth,[132] is characterized in Chapter xx by Richard as mind, Wisdom, and love. Mind (*mens*) is the Father, Wisdom (*sapientia*) is the Son, and love (alternately and apparently interchangeably *dilectio* or *amor*) is the Holy Spirit. In keeping with the Latin formulation of the procession of the Holy Spirit, Richard says:

> For indeed, every mind loves its Wisdom [*mens sapientiam suam diligit*] and on that account love [*amor*] of Wisdom proceeds from them both. Wisdom, indeed, is only from the mind, love [*amor*] is equally a part from mind and a part from Wisdom.[133]

Richard refers to this vestige of the divine Trinity in the human soul as the image-Trinity of the mind (*imaginaria Trinitate mentis*). It is because of this vestige of the Trinity in the human soul that the first cherubim, and even the second cherubim as the twin of the first, is able to turn its face to the propitiatory, seeking and finding a symbol that functions anagogically in the contemplation of divine things.[134]

Earlier in this same chapter, Richard had stated that the fourth contemplation "hovers" (*versatur*) especially in those things which are considered concerning the rational but created spirit (*circa spiritum rationalem, sed creatum*), while the fifth and sixth contemplations "hover" (*versantur*)[135] concerning the divine and uncreated Spirit (*circa Spiritum divinum et increatum*).[136] The cherubim, then, symbolize two things with regard to the Trinity: (1) as Richard discusses in Chapters xviii–xix, they symbolize the unity and Three Persons of the divine Trinity itself, that is, the divine and uncreated Spirit, and (2) as he discusses in Chapter xx, they symbolize the ability of the contemplative to "step back," as it were, and participate in hovering speculation of the image-Trinity of the contemplative's own self, that is, the rational but created spirit.

Richard, however, makes a distinction between the image-Trinity and the divine Trinity itself: "Surely it ought to be noted that these three things that come together in the consideration of the soul do not make a Trinity of persons."[137] In fact, using the methodology of similitude, as similar as the image-Trinity of the soul is to the supreme divine Trinity, it is still more dissimilar than it is similar:

> You see therefore, those things which have been drawn into the soul by means of a rational similitude are much more dissimilar than [*major est dissimilitudo quam*] similar to the highest Trinity.[138]

It is this "more dissimilar than" which prohibits a complete fusion or identification of the soul with God.[139] And it is the second cherubim that, even while it looks across to the side of similitude, represents symbolically the dissimilarity between the soul and God: "Do not wonder that the second cherubim touches more closely the side of dissimilarity on our propitiatory. However, it regards [*respicit*] the side of similarity as though from afar.[140]

In regarding each other, and in gazing mutually upon the propitiatory, the cherubim function as symbols of both similitude and dissimilitude. On the one hand, as similar symbols, respectively, of divine unity in simplicity and Trinity of persons, they participate in maintaining a harmonious and hovering balance between the opposites of unity and diversity by remaining gently and mutually in the vision of the other. On the other hand, the first cherubim functions to establish the similarity of the image-Trinity to the supreme Trinity while the second cherubim establishes the dissimilarity between the two, looking, nonetheless, across the scene to the cherubim of similarity. The net effect of this is twofold: (1) with regard to the divine and uncreated spirit spoken of most clearly as the divine Trinity, the cherubim symbolically maintain a mutually coincidental relation of opposites between simple unity and multiple personhood, and (2) with regard to the rational but created spirit described as the image-Trinity of the soul, the cherubim function both as symbol of the similarity of the soul to God and as a symbol of the fact that God is more than, or dissimilar to, the soul. In both cases God is made manifest by means of revelation, not as a part of the divine attributes which the two cherubim represent (the mystery of the divine Trinity being beyond human reason) but "between" them as Wisdom.[141]

As symbols and as mutual opposites, the cherubim shelter the soul while at the same time they manifest the two natures of Wisdom.[142] That is, they represent similarity and dissimilarity to the human soul, while at the same time they manifest the rational but created spirit and the divine and uncreated spirit. And thus, says Richard, according to the example or pattern of the Lord (*juxta Dominicum documentum*), we know why it is that the cherubim ought to reflect mutually upon each other (*se invicem respicere habeant*) and at the same time how they ought to turn their countenance to the propitiatory (*vultus suos in propitiatorium vertere debeant*).[143]

"*LOQUAR AD TE.*" The cherubim ought to turn their countenance to the propitiatory, because it is upon this propitiatory and between the two cherubim that God promised, "I will speak to you [*loquar ad te*]."[144] It is significant that, in the context of God speaking above the propitiatory and between the two cherubim, Richard points out that, of the triune image and similitude of God in the soul (mind, Wisdom, love), "Only Wisdom is embodied in a human voice and comes forth by means of a bodily voice."[145] Thus to the contemplative hovering in wonder above the propitiatory and between the two cherubim, it is God as Wisdom that will speak and it is God as the voice of Wisdom that the (embodied) contemplative will hear. Recalling Richard's early claim that *De arca mystica* is a tropological exegesis equating the ark and cherubim symbolically with Wisdom and not an allegorical exegesis interpreting them as Christ, we will have to investigate the ambiguous tension of this embodied voice of Wisdom. Because on the one hand while it is God as Wisdom which speaks, on the other hand it is the Son, namely the Wisdom of the Father, about whom Richard himself is silent. I will take up this issue in more detail in Chapter 5, but it should be mentioned at this point that the two cherubim, which at every level have manifested and supported a dialectic of the coincidence of opposites, symbolize at the very deepest level of the psyche the coincidental opposites of speaking and silence. As symbols, the first cherubim represents speaking, the second silence. Taken together, *they* are not the word which God speaks, but they encompass, define, and bound the possibility of that speaking. The embodied voice requires the embodied ear. The contemplative, symbolically, must be between speaking and silence, but actually and in practice and fact, the contemplative must be embodied and clothed in the angelic form; the soul must receive spiritual wings (*humanum animum, angelicam formam induere . . . spiritales pennas accipere*).[146]

How the soul does, in fact, put on angelic clothing is the subject of Chapter 6. However, such "angelization" of the contemplative may be a requirement, both for seeing and understanding the deep level at which Richard uses the cherubim to symbolize the coincidental or mutual opposition within the very nature of God (for instance the mystery of the Trinity), and for seeing and harmonizing the deep contradictions inherent in the very experience of the presence of God. Angelization may, in fact, be a requirement for flight into those secret places of divine incomprehensibility.

For example, Richard uses the last three chapters of Book IV to discuss the procedure or method by which the contemplative might be spoken to by God. One method, symbolized by Bezeleel, is accomplished by Bezeleel's craftsmanship and by looking at the cherubim continually with the eye of understanding (*opus operaretur et intueretur . . . intelligentiae oculo assidue*).[147] A second method, as symbolized by Moses, is accomplished through seeing by means of ecstasy of mind (*per mentis excessum saepe videndo*).[148] Immediately, Richard illustrates Moses' method by employing symbolic opposites to illustrate the "illumination" or "seeing" by ecstasy of mind. These include "entering into the middle of a cloud" and being "engrossed by the boundlessness of divine light."[149] Heaping up a series of coincidental opposites to illustrate seeing in darkness and speaking in silence, Richard adds:

> And so you might marvel, and you ought justly to marvel, how there the cloud is in harmony with the fire and the fire in harmony with the cloud: the cloud of ignorance is in harmony with the fire of illuminated understanding; the unknowing and forgetting of things known and experienced is in harmony with the revelation and understanding of things unknown and not experienced. For at one and the same time human understanding is illuminated with respect to divine things and darkened with respect to human things. This peace of the uplifted soul, this darkness and illumination,[150] is comprehended by a few words by the Psalmist when he says, "In peace in the selfsame I will sleep and rest."(Ps. 4:9)[151]

To see, to comprehend, to experience God in God's true self, the contemplative must be clothed in angelic clothing.[152] Only the cherubim, as they look mutually at the propitiatory and across at each other, can symbolize the presence of *loquar ad te*; only the cherubim internalized by the contemplative can represent both the mysterious paradox of God and the frightening ambiguity of God's presence; only the cherubim can harmonize the cloud of ignorance with the fire of illumination; only the cherubim can symbolize the illumination with respect to divine things and the darkening with respect to human things. Only between the two cherubim does God promise that *loquar ad te.*[153]

Richard's coincidental opposites here echo the opposites of speaking and silence noted earlier. The fact that these mutual opposites are described in the context of God's promise that *loquar ad te . . . de medio duorum cherubin,* and in fact are intended to manifest Wisdom between the two cherubim, indicates the deep symbolic nature of the cherubim: the cherubim symbolize the necessary coincidence of opposites *between which* God as Wisdom will speak. As such, we can say at this point that the cherubim symbolize the mystery and incomprehensibility of God, but not the voice as that voice is heard. Put another way,

> When the human mind itself exceeds itself and passes into alienation so that it might be able to distinguish things more penetratingly and more clearly, it is necessary to express this very thing mystically and in an angelic form rather than a human representation.[154]

But this "angelic form," again, is not itself the voice of Wisdom. It is not the voice of Wisdom even when exercised by ecstasy of mind, for as noted above, "human understanding is illuminated with respect to divine things and darkened with respect to human things." The voice of God is heard not in the eye of understanding, nor in the vision of alienation of mind, but rather in divine revelation. Because illumination darkens human understanding, the angelic form merely "expresses" the thing mystically.

The cherubim, then, as they border, define, and in a sense contain the voice of God, function symbolically as both receptors[155] and transmitters: as receptors they prepare the "angelized" soul for illumination by divine showings (*divina revelatione*), an illumination grounded in mutual opposites (i.e., *cherubin se mutuo respiciunt*); as transmitters they provide an angelic form which recalls the contemplative, darkened with respect to human things, back to herself, back to the voice embodied by Wisdom, back to corporeal seeing[156] and the interpretation of a vision seen in a cloud.[157]

Thus, Richard employs the cherubim symbolically as mutual opposites between which God's presence is embraced and as symbols of the veil-like border between ourselves and God across which God calls us to the Wisdom of virtue in this life. Richard says: "One went secretly into that secret conversation of divine showing from only the calling of the Lord; the other went from his own deliberation."[158] One cherubim symbolizes the Lord's calling forth to Wisdom of virtue by revelation, the other cherubim symbolizes the Wisdom of action or "deliberation" itself. The cherubim remind us of Richard's earlier claim from Book I: "We are at rest and speak to people at rest."[159] The cherubim model the contemplative posture of hovering. In the motion of rapidly vibrating wings there is rest: there is rest in action and there is action in rest; there is a speaking in the silence and in the silence there is the memory of the promised Word.

Finally, the cherubim symbolize the different paths by which different individuals, embodied as they are in the particularity of flesh and blood, view and speak to the same God. Specifically, Richard compares Moses and Aaron according to the different paths by which they reach God.[160] Moses enters into the presence of God by ascending the mountain and entering the cloud, Aaron enters into the same presence by entering the *sancta sanctorum* and passing through the veil. Richard says: "And indeed it is no less the same to penetrate into the cloud itself as it is to enter the midst of the veil itself."[161] Both Moses and Aaron "entered secretly into that secret place of divine revelation with consolation,"[162] but along highly personalized and distinctive routes. Symbolizing distinctive routes, both of the cherubim nonetheless gaze toward the same secret place of divine revelation. Both "identical differences" gaze toward that place where God has promised to be revealed in the flesh of the speaking Word.

SUMMARY

A Reiteration and a Caution

To reiterate, Richard's use of symbols in the first through third contemplations is an anagogic use wedded to the cataphatic method of movement from the visible things of nature to invisible substances. Symbols in these first contemplations are grounded on the "staff of corporeal similitudes," that is, they are embodied and perceived by imagination and reason through the bodily senses. As such, they can be classified as participating in the sacramental aspects of the natural world. Based primarily on Romans 1:20, Richard's use of symbols at this level moves to "God's invisible qualities" (*invisibilia Dei*) from what "since the creation of the world . . . has been clearly seen, being understood from what has been made" (*quia . . . a creatura mundi per ea quae facta sunt intellecta conspiciuntur*). I have pointed out that, following his interpretation of Exodus 25, Richard's primary symbols for this level of contemplation are setim wood, the gilding of the ark, and the crown of the ark. But these materials from the created world also serve in turn as models for the possibility of any item of the created world serving as a symbol of God's invisible qualities. Following Richard's lead, I have classified the function and use of symbol at this level as participating in nature mysticism or spirituality.

Richard's use of symbols in the fourth contemplation is in part cataphatic and in part apophatic in nature. This dual nature is aptly symbolized by Richard's primary symbol for this level of contemplation, that of the propitiatory. The propitiatory, again according to Exodus 25, is given dimensions for its length and width (cataphatic), but is given no dimension for its height (apophatic). This level of symbolic function is based on the doctrine of the *imago Dei* finding its scriptural base in Genesis 1:26, "And God said, let us make humanity in our image and likeness (*ad imaginem et similitudinem nostram*)."[163] From the soul's internal image and likeness to the invisible things of God, Richard develops a psychology of symbol based on a spiritual anthropology of the contemplative. "Know thyself" (that is, "know" God's image and likeness within) becomes the second entry point to the divine. Here symbols (and in particular the propitiatory) function as entry points or gates into the self, opening the soul to deeper and deeper levels of self-understanding and healing, and leading finally, at the "pinnacle" of the self, to God. These symbols, grounded on the staff of the soul, evoke Richard's soul mysticism or spirituality.

As a caution, we must keep in mind that while Richard draws sharp distinctions between symbolic categories, he does so only to lend clarity to a subject whose boundaries, in fact, are permeable. The cherubim, for instance, are symbols of the transcendent. As symbols of the image-Trinity and the divine Trinity as well as symbols of the rational but created spirit and the uncreated and divine Spirit representing the two natures of the Incarnate Christ, they function as entry points into the transcendent mystery of God and have represented, in turn, Richard's God mysticism and Christ mysticism. They are explained and examined by Richard from a variety of theological, epistemological, and methodological perspectives. But the cherubim also function metaphysically to raise the contemplative from the visible to the invisible world, just as do symbols drawn from the created world; they also function psychologically to make known, transform, and integrate the self just as do symbols of the soul. Thus we must proceed with care in drawing distinctions between the different functions of symbols. The distinctions are appropriate, but they must not mask the more important multivalent nature of symbols. This point can be clarified and illustrated by drawing on one of Richard's own images. This is the image of the patterns of bird flight as models for the numerous ways of contemplating an object. As Richard observes, birds fly in straight, hurried lines, they fly in darting, zigzag motions, they fly in seemingly random ways, they glide in circular paths, and they hover. Richard links all of these patterns to patterns of thinking, meditation, and contemplation.[164] As such, all are valid, valued, and taught by Richard. Yet hovering, even as an independent pattern, is dependent upon and, finally, incorporates all: thus contemplation is dependent upon and incorporates thinking and meditation. In a similar way, the cherubim function as a symbol which is dependent upon yet incorporates all symbols: it is a symbol encompassing symbol.

Cherubim, Symbol, and Contemplation

In general, Richard uses contemplative symbols as aids in revealing the hidden truth concealed in the inexpressible. They serve the anagogic function of "lifting" the contemplative into God. As such, they are polysemic, taking as their broadest function the ability to weave finer and finer patterns into the mosaic of our understanding and consciousness of, and participation in, the presence of the Triune God.

As angels, Richard's cherubim function as do any angelic symbol of contemplation. That is, in addition to the particular functions listed below, as angels the cherubim function as symbols of flight and ascent, as messengers or announcers from the divine to the human, as protectors, and as participants in songs of praise to God. We can follow Denys in saying that the angels function in the role of mediator between God and humanity within the divine hierarchies.

The cherubim themselves are polysemic and, like any symbol, give concrete expression to many levels of meaning. Richard's metaphysics, cosmology, and theology employ the cherubim as symbols of a dialectic based on the *coincidentia oppositorum*; his psychology or "spiritual anthropology" uses the cherubim as symbols more consonant with a dialectic based on mutual consent in harmony (*mutuo concordiae consensu*). This latter use of symbol moves the contemplative into the larger context of the healing *opus restaurationis*.

The cherubim also function as a symbol of symbol: that is, they indicate both the deep resonating quality of symbols and the relation of symbols as images (*imago, similitudo*) to the "thing" (*res*) they symbolize. They are thus a kind of symbol of Richard's symbolic theology, and as such function as a kind of "core symbol" representing the dissimilarity, ambiguity, and paradox of the relation of the soul to God and the mystery of the divine itself as well as the similarity and likeness of the soul and the natural world to that *res* which is the divine.

As "fullness of knowledge" (*plentitudo scientia*) they symbolize an immediate and unmediated access to the summit of the knowledge of God, the contemplative's work according to and above reason, and the ability to gaze upon and enter into the most hidden knowledge (*secretioris scientiae*) adhering immediately to the supreme clarity, seeing face to face without mirror or enigma.

The cherubim function as symbols of what is similar and of what is dissimilar to God. They symbolize the contemplation of God according to reason and beyond reason (i.e., *revelatione*), and they symbolize the methods of apophatic and cataphatic theology. In addition, they symbolize the coincidental opposition of a wide range of related images. To name only the two that have the greatest impact on Richard's adaptation of symbols to theology, the cherubim symbolize the simple unity and diversity of persons within the Trinity and the humanity and divinity within the Incarnate Christ.

Taken as a whole, with the propitiatory and the ark to which they are intimately attached and which themselves symbolize the created world and the soul, the cherubim symbolize "grounded flight" wherein the contemplative ascent is securely based in the objects of the world and the self. Also taken as a whole, the symbols of ark and cherubim function as a mandala. The same whole also indicates a womb-like structure in the center of which the word, as Wisdom, is born. And taken as a whole again, the cherubim form the sheltering boundaries between which God will meet with and speak to the contemplative. The cherubim thus symbolize an embodied spirituality, presence, birth

and fecundity, renewal, introversion, the mandalic qualities of individ-
uation, contemplation itself, and participation in the divine drama.
They look toward and envision for the contemplative's seeing the
center, the *medium*, the place of God's being and speaking.

The cherubim symbolize as well a number of contemplative attributes as described in Exodus 25 and interpreted by Richard. The
spread wings of the cherubim symbolize cover and protection. The
wings also symbolize openness to the gifts of Wisdom, longing, preparation, and desire for the ascent to the divine, and readiness to receive
the breath of aspired grace (*aura aspirantis gratiae affleverit*). The dialectic of the coincidence of opposites is most symbolically represented
in the cherubim as they look back mutually upon each other (*cherubin
se mutuo respiciunt*) and in turn gaze back upon the propitiatory. In
this mutual regarding and as they direct their gaze back toward the
propitiatory, the cherubim symbolize looking at God "face to face."
They also symbolize the boundaries between which God will speak
(*loquar ad te*). Thus symbolizing the presence of God, the cherubim
most explicitly symbolize the necessary and coincidental opposites of
darkness and illumination, hiddeness and revelation, activity and rest,
speaking and silence. All of these opposites are most imaginatively and
precisely illustrated by the image of hovering.

The cherubim symbolize the wings, as it were, of a stage formed
by the propitiatory, upon which the contemplative acts out his or her
spiritual drama in harmony with the divine drama. The play upon
the stage of the propitiatory allows for new insight and action; thus
the cherubim symbolize the possibility of transformation, even "angelization." As the spiritual drama is externalized, the play undergoes
the infusion of the contemplative's breath and flesh and blood, and
so begins the active component of transformation. Another metaphor
describing this same process is that of the "internal icon": the contemplative internalizes the ark and cherubim as icon, providing an internal
"space" for the divine drama, thus activating the same component of
transformation.

As images of vision and flight, the cherubim serve to provide continuity between preparation for the presence of God, the presence
itself, and the interpretation of that presence. That is, they serve as
similar symbols preparing and leading the contemplative to the vision
of God; as dissimilar symbols they remind us that the vision or presence
itself is without symbol, and in fact is dependent on the destruction or

collapse of symbols; and again as similar symbols they provide access to interpreting and describing the vision or meeting. The cherubim symbolize intimacy, friendship, and love of the kind possible only among equals.[165] It is in the midst of the fullness of Wisdom that the love of God promises to speak.

The cherubim symbolize the variety of contemplative paths to the same God. As one cherubim stands on the left side of the propitiatory and the second cherubim stands on the right side of the propitiatory, we see that light and dark look upon the same God, we see that entry via the cloud or entry via the veil look upon the same God, we see that unity and diversity look upon and are the same God, we see that through the imitation of Wisdom this person and that person look upon the same God.

More broadly, the ark and cherubim are a journey symbol.[166] As such, they express the process of spiritual growth through stages and, in a microcosm, they contain the entire mystical life, not only the types of mystical consciousness, but the process by which they are acquired. As the ark and propitiatory represent a journey through the natural world or the self and the cherubim symbolically represent the continuation and perpetual return of that journey into God, so Richard develops a cosmology, anthropology, and theology to express and describe that journey. The journey progresses through the symbols of the ark, into the symbol of the cherubim, and beyond into the midst of the cherubim where by promise and gift God, as divine companion, as Incarnate Word, or as Trinity, is encountered and spoken with by you, the contemplative. There the journey has the potential to begin again, "ending" in an ever-deepening consciousness of the presence of God.

5

PROPITIATORY:

APOPHATIC CHRISTOLOGY

In principio erat sermo
—John 1:1, trans. Erasmus

Our conversation is in heaven
—Phil. 3:20; *De arca* II.xiii

We interpose a phenomenal veil of constructs between ourselves and God, a veil, we might say, between ourselves, the cherubim, and God's living presence.[1] And yet there is a necessary intervention of divinity between the two cherubim.[2] Exodus 25, of course, had promised such an intervention, such a gift, and Richard of St. Victor's work in *De arca mystica* is an exegesis of the mystical meaning (*mystice designet*) of this promise. Richard was heir to a tradition rich in interpretations of divine intervention allegorically described as Christ.[3] Yet from the very first chapter of *De arca mystica*, Richard made it clear that he himself would not pursue the allegorical sense of the ark as it represents Christ (*vel quomodo Christum significet*), but rather the moral or tropological sense (*materiam moraliter*) of the ark as it represents Wisdom (*sapientia*).[4]

I will now ask, why is it that Richard focuses more on tropological Wisdom as the name of divinity that rends the veil and intervenes than on Christ in any of his Christological manifestations?[5] Noting that the cherubim explicitly symbolize divinity in its triune form and only implicitly symbolize Christ in his two natures, I will inquire as to Richard's reluctance to announce the presence or intervention of the flesh of the eternal Word.[6] In effect, I will ask why, in a culture saturated with Christological images of the Word, Richard's contemplative path "into the secret places of divine incomprehensibility" follows

97

the route of silence. I will thus explore what I would like to call the "apophatic Christology" of Richard of St. Victor.

I will begin to ask these questions by looking briefly at the Christology of the *Itinerarium mentis in Deum*, by Bonaventure, a later treatise than Richard's but in its use and kinds of symbols a similar one.

BONAVENTURE AND CHRIST IN THE *ITINERARIUM*

In the years around 1260, a short century after the completion of *De arca mystica*, Bonaventure was completing his *Itinerarium mentis in Deum*.[7] In both works, the cherubim are used as framing devices which, gazing toward the propitiatory, look upon transcendence itself. Other similarities between Richard and Bonaventure's work are equally compelling.[8] Nonetheless, where Richard's *De arca mystica* is pregnant with the absence of Christ, Bonaventure's *Itinerarium* gives birth to the explicit presence of Christ.

From the beginning, Bonaventure's Christological consciousness is made very clear in the *Itinerarium*. He states emphatically: "There is no other path but through the burning love of the Crucified."[9] This opening reflection on the path to the intimate presence of God is echoed and expanded in Chapter VII, the final chapter of the *Itinerarium*. Christ is thus the beginning and the end of the journey. A rather large section of Chapter VII is here quoted, in order to give a sense of the centrality of the mediatory nature of the crucified Christ in contrast to Richard's relative Christological emptiness in *De arca mystica*:

> 1. . . . when finally in the sixth stage
> our mind reaches that point
> where it contemplates
> in the First and Supreme Principle
> and in the *mediator of God and men*,
> Jesus Christ.
> . . . .
> In this passing over,
> Christ is the *way and the door*;
> Christ is the Ladder and the vehicle,
> like the Mercy Seat placed above the ark of God
> and the *mystery hidden from eternity*.

2. Whoever turns his face fully to the Mercy Seat

. . . .

beholds him hanging upon the cross,
such a one makes the Pasch, that is, the passover,
with Christ.

6. . . . This fire is God,
and *his furnace is in Jerusalem*;
and Christ enkindles it
in the heat of his burning passion,

. . . .

With Christ crucified
let us pass *out of this world to the Father*.[10]

Fourteen years after the appearance of the *Itinerarium*, Bonaventure would title the first chapter of his mature and final work, *Collationes in Hexaemeron, Christus medium omnium scientiarum*, or *Christ the Center of All Sciences*. Ewert Cousins has pointed out how the seed of Bonaventure's mature Christology of Christ as *medium* is planted in the *Itinerarium* and comes to full blossom in *Collationes in Hexaemeron*, adding:

> In this development of the doctrine of Christ the center, Bonaventure's understanding of the coincidence of opposites reaches its fullest realization. Not only is Christ seen as the greatest coincidence of opposites, as in the *Itinerarium*; but he is viewed as the center through whom all the opposites in reality are differentiated and held together. Thus all coincidences of opposites in the Trinity, in the world, and in the relation of God and the world are mediated through Christ the universal center.[11]

As Cousins makes clear in his work, the full notion of Christ the Center is not explicitly stated in the *Itinerarium*, though its symbolic structure expresses the notion in a germinal way. In addition, in the idea of Christ as "mediator of God and men" cited above, Christ as mediator of all coincidences of opposites is certainly present in the *Itinerarium* in an embryonic form.[12] In Bonaventure's Christology of Christ as mediator, the intervention of deity between the framing cherubim is the intervention of the work of Christ crucified effected in paschal sacrifice and in the soul's repose with Christ.[13]

This Christic intervention mediates all imagination and knowledge (i.e., *medium metaphysicum, medium physicum, mathematicum, logicum, ethicum, politicum, theologicum*). Bonaventure's Christological "eruption" is thus made all the more distinct and conspicuous in comparison to Richard's by his obvious parallel use of the framing device of the cherubim and propitiatory detailed above. It is distinct in comparison to Richard in that it consciously names and elevates Christ to the position of mediating center of all opposites, beheld hanging on the cross. It is conspicuous in comparison to Richard by its very presence: in *De arca mystica* Christ is virtually absent.

Finally, though Richard associates Trinity and Christology on the basis of their shared mystery,[14] he does not, as Bonaventure does, terminate the sixth level of contemplation in an exemplaristic meditation on Christ. Bonaventure's notion of Christ as *via et ostium*,[15] road and door to the Father, which opens into the "mystery hidden from eternity," indicates a conscious centrality of the specific and isolated incomprehensibility of Christ which was not brought to bear in Richard's *De arca mystica*.[16]

The remainder of this chapter will investigate the dam behind which Richard's Christology is apparently retained in the reservoir of his consciousness. A short century later Bonaventure would open the floodgates of that dam—floodgates which perhaps Richard himself had installed though had not opened—sending a new Christological flood over the landscape of Latin contemplative theology.

A CONTEXT FOR RICHARD'S CHRISTOLOGY

As with Bonaventure, who followed Richard, those preceeding him upon whose Christological formulations he depended were, in various ways, flooded in Christological light.[17] An extremely brief but telling survey of Richard's Christology, one which would highlight the audacity of his Christological darkness or absence and at the same time provide hints as to why he would choose to be silent about the God-man, would include orienting his work in the Christological context of Denys the Areopagite and Richard's twelfth-century mentor, Hugh of St. Victor.

Denys the Areopagite

The role of Christ in Dionysian mysticism continues to evoke controversy and debate.[18] Regardless of this debate, certain of Denys' Christological formulations affect Richard and begin to provide insight into the question of Christological absence in *De arca mystica*. For instance, Denys insists on the hiddenness of the divine nature of God,[19] and further insists on the importance of "honor(ing) in respectful silence the hidden things which are beyond me."[20] Christ is elsewhere explicitly equated with the divine.[21] The hiddenness of the divine, the insistence on silence concerning hidden things, and the equation of Christ with the divine thus logically combine to imply the necessity of at least a certain kind of silence concerning Christ.

Additionally, Denys insists over and over on the Incarnation as a work of divine love,[22] and more importantly that "every affirmation regarding Jesus' love for humanity has the force of negation pointing toward transcendence."[23] Silence concerning Christ and the *affirmation* of love forcing a *denial* of the divine are both examples of the thesis developed in chapters 2 and 3 of this work on the necessary relation between affirmation and denial in Denys' apophatic theology and in his symbolic methodology. We thus see, in Deny's very "silence" concerning the divinity of Christ and in the "negating" quality of affirmations regarding Christ's humanity, examples of Deny's theology and method applied to his Christology.

With regard to anagogic theology, Jesus is obviously a centerpoint in Denys' apophatic and cataphatic ascent; in fact Christ contains and incorporates both affirmation and denial in a manner not unlike Bonaventure's Christ as *medium*. With regard to symbols, the silence concerning the divinity of Christ and the apophatic methodology associated with the ascent to divinity reinforce the notion of the fragility of symbols. Thus, while it is through symbols as "protective garb" that we reach the "marvelous, transcendent," and while we must "make the journey to the heart of sacred symbols,"[24] transcendent Wisdom is beyond language and every symbolic assertion and denial.[25]

We see then in Denys that the contemplative is led from Christ the incarnate symbol to Christ the unspoken Word through Deny's apophatic method, his symbolic theology, and silence. Thus, for instance, except for symbolic images drawn from scripture one will find that the *Divine Names* and the *Celestial Hierarchy* maintain a "respectful silence" with regard to Christ as divine Word.

Christ is, however, located by Denys in liturgical space and time. He is symbolically present in the sacramental ritual of baptism where Christ arranges for the initiate to share mystically in the death of Christ himself;[26] he is present in the rite of anointing where the oil is a symbol of Christ;[27] and he is, of course, present in the Eucharist or "rite of synaxis."[28]

Christ is also closely associated with the hierarchies. Denys calls on "Jesus, the source and perfection of every hierarchy" which, given the importance of hierarchy in the anagogic ascent, indicates an important role for Jesus, though Denys does not expand on this role.[29] Though the divine aspect of the Word is hidden, within this hierarchical perspective the divine Word functions as an illuminating principle of the celestial order, while Denys' less developed humanity of the Word[30] illuminates the human order.[31]

Taken in sum, Denys' relatively docetic (and perhaps Monophysite) Christ, his apophatic and symbolic methods which caution silence concerning Christ's divinity, the relatively undeveloped role of Christ as mediator between God and humanity, and even the highly symbolic Christological presence in the liturgical context would, taken as a whole, lend themselves to a methodology of silence concerning the flesh of the eternal Word.

Hugh of St. Victor

But also of primary importance for Richard's unspoken, existential Christology is Denys' emphasis not on humanity's metaphysical identity with Christ but on communion and participation with him:

> They are contemplative also because they have been allowed to enter *communion* with Jesus *not by means of the holy images*, reflecting the likeness of God's working in forms, but *by truly coming close to him in primary participation* in knowledge of divine lights working out of him.[32]

Yet with regard to hierarchy, cosmology, and Christology, Denys' point of view would still be interpreted as "objective" and distancing compared to the even more consciously "participatory" Christology of

Richard's contemporary, Hugh of St. Victor. While Denys speaks tangentially and objectively about communion and participation, Hugh prefers the psychological, moral, practical, and affective content of "participation" in the flesh of the Word. In R. Roques' words, Hugh: "More willingly describes divinization of understanding as an intimate experience. . . . [Hugh] thus marks the essentials of Denys' system with a practical and affective understanding."[33] This more practical and affective understanding, in which Richard of St. Victor was to participate deeply, shapes Hugh's Christology in such a way that human participation in and restoration through the flesh of the Word in the humanity of Jesus is the center of Hugh's divine theology.

What is particularly striking about theologians of the twelfth century is the examination of Christ's role in the work of the restoration of humanity. As noted in Chapter 3 of this work, for Hugh of St. Victor the healing work of restoration is initiated with the humility of the crucified Christ and the humanity of the Word. Hugh says, in short, "*Opus restaurationis est incarnatio Verbi . . . Verbum enim incarnatum rex noster est.*"[34] The relation of the work of creation or foundation (*opus conditionis*) and restoration is crucial in Hugh.[35] In the person of Christ, foundation and restoration are linked;[36] in the work of Christ, restoration is accomplished in the incarnation of the Word.[37] For Hugh all construction/creation, even the tropological construction of ark and cherubim in the soul of the contemplative, are useless in the ascent from the visible to the invisible without the entry into the world of time and being of the flesh of the Word. No created, constructed, or woven thing participates in restoration this side of the Incarnation without the ongoing presence of Christ. In fact, even the exegesis of scripture participates in this redemptive work of Christ: "All divine scripture is one book, and that one book is Christ since all of divine scripture speaks about Christ and all divine scripture is filled with Christ."[38] Thus though the Old Testament would speak silently concerning Christ, the presence of the person and work of the incarnate Word in the restoration of creation is so central (and even obvious) in Hugh, that for Richard consciously not to speak the Word from between the very cherubim of sanctification would have been unconscionable unless fully conscious.

Hugh makes additional references to participation with the flesh of the eternal Word that would not likely have passed Richard's notice. Christ, Hugh says, "according to humanity is now in heaven, according to divinity is everywhere";[39] Christ is "the mediator of God and man";[40] Christ is the mediator of reconciliation, and "the Word, which was one with God the Father through ineffable unity, was made one with man through a wonderful union."[41] Hugh also notes that "the altar signifies the cross,"[42] and all sanctification flows from the "sacrament of the body and blood of Christ."[43] To Richard, the ark and cherubim signified the grace of sanctification. He could not have missed the association of the cross with the propitiatory nor the blood of Christ with sanctification which his teacher and mentor Hugh so firmly established. Yet Richard chose a different Christological route. The traces of that route, by which *Christus de ore ad cor transit*,[44] we will now attempt to follow.

BECKONINGS AND HINTS:
CHRISTOLOGY IN THE WORK OF RICHARD OF ST. VICTOR

Richard's complete corpus, situated as it is in the twelfth century, is of course saturated with references to Christ. My intent in proposing an "apophatic" Christology in *De arca mystica* is in no way meant to deny or degrade this saturation. The intent is rather to highlight the Christological absence in *De arca mystica* by placing it in the context of a culture, and indeed in the context of Richard's own writings, which themselves establish a high degree of emphasis on Christ.

From Richard's own work, we find that Christ is explicitly linked with "truth" and is the "way" as well as the "guide" in contemplative ascent:[45]

> I think therefore that only those who follow Christ, only those who are led by truth run without error and arrive without hindrance. Anyone who hastens to the high places goes in security if truth goes before you: without truth you labor in deception. As truth does not wish to lead astray, so it is not able to be led astray. Therefore, follow Christ if you do not wish to err.[46]

Elsewhere, at least partially inspired by Anselm of Canterbury, Richard writes on the necessity of the Incarnation and on the reasons for which it was necessary that the second person of the Trinity become incarnate.[47] He devotes four Books in his *Liber exceptionum* to commentary on the Gospels and, as noted in Chapter 1 of this work, several sermons allegorizing the tabernacle, altar, and portions of the church as Christ.[48] One of Richard's later works develops a theology of charity in which the fourth and final degree of love (*caritas*) consumes the soul in perfect consummation and conformity to Christ. Thus conformed to Christ—and the language of conformity to Christ is really quite explicit and often repeated—the soul participates in perfect love of God and humanity.[49] Richard's *De Trinitate*, while not explicitly concerned with Christology, nonetheless focuses on the coincidence of opposites within the divine Trinity and so reflects the same dialectic of the coincidence of mutually affirming and denying complementarity (hovering) as is found in the two-natures doctrine of Christ. Even in regard to the Trinity in *De Trinitate*, the dialectic between human and divine nature pushes Richard's discussion from the Trinity into the borders of Christology:

> Behold how human nature and divine nature seem to regard each other mutually and yet from places of opposition; the one is oriented towards the other through contrary means. They are mutually related and should be mutually contrasted.[50]

This mutual gazing/contrasting one to another (*videntur se mutuo*) is obviously reminiscent of Richard's description of the cherubim in *De arca mystica*, where the Cherubim also regard each other mutually. There also appears to be something seen or manifested between the gaze of the hovering opposites: "However, where there is fullness of all goodness, true and highest charity is not able not to be [*deesse non potest*]."[51] Likewise, in *De arca mystica*, where the cherubim are an explicit symbol of the Trinity, the fact that the cherubim are only two tends to force a shift in their symbolic function both toward an implicit Christology and toward a "third" which is also unable not to be. However, in *De Trinitate*, that which is not able not to be is charity erupting from *plenitudo amoris* and associated with the person of the Holy Spirit.[52] While in Richard's *De arca mystica*, which gives symbolic testimony to the dynamic nature of *plenitudo scientiae* of that same Trinitarian dialectic, the necessary "third" is an encounter with the flesh of the incarnate Word.

Yet, in *De arca mystica*, the nature of that flesh of the eternal Word which is not able not to be is left muted and unspoken.

A survey of the few, muted Christological references in *De arca mystica* shows that none of the references are on the order of

Bonaventure's *Christus medium omnium scientiarum*, and none are on the order of Hugh's *opus restaurationis est incarnatio Verbi*.[53] Instead, the references are opaque, buried in the tropological interpretation of the ark and cherubim as Wisdom, and generally subordinate to Richard's more conscious symbolic and doctrinal Trinitarian interests. But as the general twelfth-century context and Richard's other writings betray, the flesh of the eternal Word is there, waiting to (speak) be (met) heard.

Several points of interest emerge from a survey of Christological references or omissions in *De arca mystica*. First, some functions normally associated with the work of Christ are associated not directly with him but with Christ "surrogates." For instance, Wisdom (rather than Christ) restores the soul to health, Wisdom pleases God, Wisdom purifies, and contemplation of truth purifies and sanctifies.[54] Richard makes it clear that Christ is Wisdom and truth, but the association of restoration, purification, and sanctification with Wisdom and truth rather than with Christ himself is striking.[55] In a related omission, Richard associates the propitiatory (rather than Christ) with the creation, restoration, and glorification of the soul (*animae creatione, reparatione, glorificatione*).[56] The length, width, and height of the propitiatory symbolize respectively the goods of creation, justification or restoration, and glorification. And as with the propitiatory:

> First the spiritual nature is created so that it might be [*ut sit*]. Second it is made just so that it might be good [*ut bona sit*]. Third it is glorified so that it might be blessed [*ut beata sit*]. And so through creation it is started toward the good, through justification it is expanded into the good, and through glorification it is consummated in the good.[57]

Thus again, it is the "surrogate" propitiatory (upon which we would expect to see Christ) which initiates the works leading to glorification.

A second point from a survey of Christological references or omissions is the linking of the Trinity and the Incarnation on the basis of (1) their shared mystery and incomprehensibility, and (2) the dialectical language of mutuality and hovering applied to the cherubim to describe the Trinity but which seems to shift to accommodate the Incarnation as well. Concerning their shared incomprehensibility, Richard says:

You will find many things like this—and an innumerable amount more—concerning the Trinity of persons which are not only incomprehensible but also discordant to reason. . . . you will also find many things of this kind concerning the union of substances in the incarnation of the Word.[58]

This link between the Trinity and Incarnation based on mystery and incomprehensibility is keyed to the symbol of the second cherubim, which signifies mystery, or that which is *supra rationem*. Thus, though those things concerning the body of Christ are incomprehensible, and those things concerning the soul of Christ are more incomprehensible, and those things concerning the Trinity of persons are most sublime and incomprehensible of all,[59] all are rightly said to pertain to the second cherubim (*recte dicuntur ad secundum cherubin pertinere*), and are therefore identified with the notion of incomprehensibility. A parallel yet silent discussion of the incomprehensibility of the Incarnation is thus advanced in the context of Richard's explicit discussion of the incomprehensibility of the Trinity.

As a strategy of both clarification and emphasis of this notion of linkage on the basis of incomprehensibility, Richard moves immediately in the following chapter to his discussion of the dialectical relation between the two cherubim. This chapter attempts to encompass the mystery in a symbolic way (rather than in a logical or rational way), teaching Wisdom by means of participation rather than argument. Symbolically, incomprehensibility is embodied in the two cherubim, whose relation allows the "twin consideration" of opposites. This dialectic is variously described,[60] with hints of various options for the contemplative's own relation to mystery encountered in the divine. It is in this context, using the symbol of the two cherubim to demonstrate the incomprehensible hovering relation within the divine Trinity, that Richard is reminded of and briefly uses the cherubim to describe the birth of the flesh of the eternal Word: "We truly profess, however, according to mutual regard that the Son alone has truly been incarnated."[61] But then, after this brief sentence, he returns immediately to the cherubim as Trinity. Unlike Bonaventure's nearly identical use of the framing cherubim in which the meditation obviously moves from Trinity to the crucified Word, we receive Richard's suppression of this shift as silence.[62] This silence is Richard's final "Wisdom": the veil protecting mystery lifts only in the context of the contemplative's dramatic participation. No word Richard utters will rend the veil for you, the contemplative. Thus Richard's meditation on the symbol of the cherubim as the trinitarian route of ascent to God seems to open silently into the heart of the Incarnation: the incomprehensibility of the flesh of the eternal Word and the mutuality of his two natures erupt beneath Richard's discussion of the Trinity, finding ready accommodation in the polysemic symbol of the cherubim.

A third notion to be drawn from a survey of Christological references is the idea that "Wisdom is embodied in a human voice" and the critical point that Wisdom is then equated with Christ. Richard says:

> If it is a wonder to you how the Son (clearly the Wisdom of the Father) alone has become incarnate, how he comes to us in flesh and yet did not leave the Father, reflect upon the fact that in the image-Trinity [what Richard defines as *mens, sapientia, amor*] of the mind, only Wisdom [*sapientia*] is embodied by a human voice and hence comes forth by means of the bodily voice.[63]

As Wisdom is embodied in a human voice, so the Son, as the Wisdom of the Father, is tropologically linked to the Wisdom that is found upon the ark. Thus while Richard does not name Christ here, it is the flesh of the eternal Word as the human, embodied voice of Wisdom that comes to meet the contemplative between the two framing and sustaining cherubim. Tropologically, then, imitation of that Wisdom becomes our vision of God.

In the midst of Richard's meditation on the Trinity, the human voice of the incarnate Word interjects itself more than once as Wisdom. In a sense, Richard speaks Trinity, and we hear God's promise of Exodus 25:22 (*loquar ad te*) as the voice of Christ. It is as if Richard cannot speak the "truth of things reserved for God,"[64] he can only point, as the symbol of the cherubim point, to the sacred place where the incarnate Word speaks with bodily voice. And so it is not by accident that Richard, in the beginning of the very next chapter, harkens immediately to his exegesis of the voice of the Lord:

> We ought not to neglect nor let pass by without diligent consideration that which was promised by the voice of the Lord when he spoke to Moses: "From there I will speak to you from above the propitiatory, clearly from between the two cherubim."[65]

The connection between the human and bodily voice of the previous chapter and the "voice of the Lord" here is intentional and explicit: the cherubim turn their faces toward the propitiatory and see the voice of the flesh of the eternal Word that you, who are being sanctified by the ark of sanctification, hear and in whose presence you participate, communicate, live and breathe.

In summary, by the middle of the thirteenth century, Bonaventure would shift the gaze of the cherubim from Richard's *unspoken* flesh of the eternal and glorified Word to the humble, crucified Lord. In both, a distinct slippage or oscillation occurs as a natural part of their contemplation of divinity: in Richard the contemplation of Trinity forces a shift (based on the linkage of incomprehensibility and the metaphysics of hovering) to a narratively silent contemplation of the flesh of the eternal Word; in Bonaventure the contemplation of Christ crucified, the *medium* of all opposites, leads to a contemplation of the Trinity as "being in itself" and "goodness in itself" and thence back to the only path to peace, the "burning love of the crucified."[66] In both writers, the vision in contemplation is framed by the eyes and wings of the cherubim. In both, this slippage between meditations on Christology and Trinity illustrates a feature common to much Christian mystical contemplation. But Richard's silence concerning the flesh of the eternal Word, a silence leaving us unencumbered by twelfth-century desires, allows a new Christ, appropriate to the contemplative's own enfleshed drama, to be born continuously and contemporaneously between the two cherubim. Framed between the cherubim, the contemplative even participates in this slippage: this very oscillation is an energy of birth;[67] it is an oscillation of evident givenness: that *God is*.

And, of course, there is the hint that the unspoken word between the two cherubim is the eucharistic body and blood of Jesus Christ: "See in how many places the same body of Christ is consecrated and held daily."[68] But this is no more than a hint, another piece of silence.

INTERLUDE: IMAGE, THING, AND WORD

As noted in Chapter 3 of this work, Hugh of St. Victor makes a distinction based on 1 Corinthians 13:12 between faith which is able to see the image (*imaginem videre*) as in a mirror, and contemplation which is able to see the thing (*rem videre*) as though face to face.[69] Words, images, and symbols cover the core truth or thing as if by a veil.[70] Thus, also as noted earlier, the "image" must be abandoned in contemplation of the "thing." Elsewhere Hugh had said:

> There came, therefore, the Son of God, and he put on our nature, was born of the Virgin, was crucified, buried; he rose again, ascended to the skies, and by fulfilling the things which had been promised, he opened up what lay hidden. . . . unless you know beforehand the nativity of Christ, his teaching, his suffering, his resurrection and ascension, and all the other things which he did in the flesh and through the flesh, you will not be able to penetrate the mysteries of the old figures.[71]

Again, it is inconceivable that Richard of St. Victor would have been unaware either of Christ as exegetical key to the "old figures" of the Old Testament mysteries or of Hugh's Christological application to the distinction between "image" and "thing." The grace of contemplation leads through the sacred symbols to the unuttered "thing." Any word except the flesh of the eternal Word is itself an image, a figure, a symbol. And so, I believe, Richard does not use an image, symbol, or word for the Christ who penetrates the old figures; Richard chooses rather to remain silent so that the supreme truth of things (*rerum veritatem, quae summa veritas est*) might speak its own word in the heart of each particular contemplative. Richard says:

> In these things you will discover a very notable thing: that the truth of things—of which God is the highest truth—he reserved for himself, but he conceded to his image the power of forming images of things at any time.[72]

We ourselves fashion, by means of imagination, any shape or figure of things (*rerum figuras per imaginationem fingere*)[73] we please. We can in fact fashion images of things (*rerum imagines*) continually if we please. The problem is that to name Christ upon the ark between the two cherubim would be but another image of things (*rerum imagines*). No human word can speak the truth of things (*rerum veritatem*) which God reserves alone for God's self. God reserves for God's self the gift of the "thing" of the flesh of the eternal Word. For this "thing," for the personal, participative communion in existence and deed with Christ, the contemplative must turn inward[74] to the internal icon of ark and cherubim *ubi non verbis sed rebus ipsis veritas probatur.*[75] Yet even after this turn, there is no affirmation, no word that Richard or Hugh can speak; once again, they must follow the Wisdom of Denys the Areopagite:

> Every affirmation regarding Jesus' love for humanity has the force of a negation pointing toward transcendence.[76] . . . But he [Jesus] is hidden even after this revelation. . . . For this mystery of Jesus remains hidden and can be drawn out by no word or mind. What is to be said of it remains unsayable; what is to be understood of it remains unknowable.[77]

As the cherubim, woven in the heart of the contemplative, sweep their all-seeing gaze across the propitiatory, Richard of St. Victor speaks no word concerning their vision of the flesh of the Word, Jesus Christ. With regard to that incommunicable "thing," Richard chooses silence.

The key is that, for Richard and Hugh, the "thing" is unuttered. The cherubim look back on desert emptiness, they see silence. For Richard, the assent to God through the created world, including the self, is a balance of the cataphatic and the apophatic. The ascent to God through symbols begins in this balance but finally must assent to the apophatic power of negation. The grace of contemplation leads into the power of this silence, awaiting the revelation of the "thing" as promised in Exodus 25. Hugh invokes the affirmative power of history to name the angel's vision as *opus restaurationis est incarnatio Verbi.* Richard teaches reliance on the power of revelation to cross the negative or apophatic boundaries of silence and emptiness and utter a final cataphatic Word.

SUMMARY

In the secret places of divine incomprehensibility Christ comes to participate comprehensibly in the acts of our lives. Richard of St. Victor's use of the symbol of the cherubim prepares the ground and space for this participation; we can but speculate, reconstruct, and weave the reasons for his apophatic Christology, the evocations of his silence. Richard's silence is but one of the modes of God's presence— not an argument, but a mode of presence and a mode of "speaking" of that presence.

We might begin to participate in Richard of St. Victor's contemplative weave of silence by making a distinction between the divinity of Christ and the humanity of Christ. Such a distinction would model the dialectic of the coincidence of opposites, or hovering, so crucial to Richard's symbolic and contemplative system. In this weave, Richard's understanding of the divinity of Christ would be expressed in "hiddenness" and in "absence" language and based on the apophatic methodology of Denys the Areopagite. Denys' insistence on the hiddenness of the divinity of Christ coupled with his insistence on silence concerning hidden things might easily lead to Richard's practice of weaving silence concerning Christ. Richard's silence would in turn be reinforced by Hugh of St. Victor's insistence on the inability of words and concepts to express the "thing." The "thing" of course is the Christ of history and our participation at the intersection of history and eternity with him. Apophatic method and dissimilar symbols then become appropriate approaches to that which, as Denys says, is "beyond all language." (If you doubt this, just look in Christ's eyes, touch his divine hand). Thus, in this first distinction, Christ's divinity would be imageless, hidden, absent, empty, beyond reason, and likely to follow the Old Testament tradition of not naming the highest good. Christ's divinity would generally be associated with the glorified Christ and be symbolized by the second cherubim (remembering always the second cherubim's relation to the first) and, in a word, be silent.[78]

In the second distinction the humanity of Christ, symbolized most appropriately by the first cherubim (again, remembering the first cherubim's relation to the second), would be associated with "light,"[79] "fullness," and "present" language. In this weave of silence the elements of reason, fullness, images, the cataphatic method, similar symbols, and presence might best express Richard's evocation of Christ's humanity which, associated with Wisdom, has the healing force of restoration. (If you doubt this, just look in Christ's eyes, touch his human hand.) This restoration would of course be tied in turn to the crucified Christ, but always with the implication of justification as *via et ostium*. Thus the humanity of Christ expressed in the image of participation (i.e., "putting on angelic clothing") is "Wisdom" in the tropological sense; it is Wisdom "embodied in a human voice." This Wisdom embodied in a human voice (the healing humanity of Christ) takes Richard's silence and uses it to speak (*loquar ad te*) in the heart of the contemplative.

The Wisdom of imitation, of Christ-modeled action based on the humanity of Christ, is reinterpreted, relived, and rebreathed with each new human generation. Richard of St. Victor helped set the stage and the space of creativity upon which transcendence in the human shape of Christ intervenes. The divinity of that intervention requires emptiness and silence; the humanity of that intervention requires fullness and participation.[80] In neither case would a mere human word embrace the healing and renewing birth of that "thing" of flesh and blood. The cherubim can look, but our presence is required in the womb of their gaze to breath the present act of the flesh of the Word.

Other omissions or Christological eruptions, just barely submerged, indicate Richard's silent and parallel narrative and hinting weave of silence. For instance, the two cherubim as a symbol of the Trinity lack a "third." In *De arca mystica*, a treatise on the *plenitudo scientiae*, the third which is not able not to be emerges explicitly as Wisdom. In the *De Trinitate* Richard speaks of the purifying work of the Holy Spirit in a way that echoes the restorative work of Wisdom:

> For at the infusion of this fire, the human soul lays aside little by little all darkness, dullness, and severity and it changes over completely into the resemblance [*similitudinem*] of that One by which it is inflamed.[81]

This changeover (*transit*) hints in turn at the restorative work of the flesh of the Word. Wisdom, already linked allegorically to Christ, is further implicitly associated with the incarnate Word by the dynamic demands of the two persons of the Trinity seeking a third. This seeking on the part of divinity gently forces the presence of the restoration-oriented Christ. Yet while Richard could not avoid the flame of this third, he weaves only silence around the name of the incomprehensible nature of that very fire by which and into which the contemplative is restored.[82]

Also hinting Richard's parallel, but silent, weave of the flesh of the eternal Word is the notion of the death of reason on the propitiatory. As the cherubim watch, the contemplative moves above and beyond reason into that area of the *excessus mentis*. Language and naming, presumably categories of reason, are useless where reason has died; they are as useless in naming what might be born from this death of reason as it is useless to name the fire by which and into which we are restored.

Strengthening the weave of silence that speaks Christ is the additional fact that God does not actually "speak" the promise in the Exodus 25 passage. God speaks describing the method of construction of the ark and cherubim, and God speaks a promise to speak, but God does not actually "speak" the promise; the promise itself does not "speak." Here again, Richard's exegetical, contemplative, and metaphysical honesty required that he too remain silent where the Old Testament God had not yet spoken. God's speech of course was the flesh of the Word, but in interpreting and constructing the ark and cherubim for the contemplative, God's speech is not Richard's to utter.[83]

In short, Richard's tropological interpretation of the ark and cherubim as Wisdom does not permit his own speaking of the Word.

The effect of Richard's clear focus on an apophatic Christology is that, unlike Bonaventure, who a century later would speak and unleash Christ with a "Passion," Richard weaves a contemplative cloth of silence around the Word, thus in effect insuring its incessant and irresistible "speaking" with all the force of Wisdom seeking its incarnate act.

In Richard's *De arca mystica*, the path of the journey to Christ, the unspoken word, takes the symbolic shape of the ark and cherubim, and is a journey to the center, the *medium*. As we have seen, that path leads through Trinity as well as Christology, both being separate but linked by incomprehensible mystery; that path leads through "image" and "thing" where symbols and language fall short of the flesh, blood, and the breathing "thing" that is our promise; that path leads through the apophatic, absent, and silent nature of Christ's divinity and through the cataphatic and present nature of Christ's humanity; that path leads to the space where Wisdom speaks with a human voice; that path leads through the dialectic of hovering itself; that path leads through Wisdom as imitation and act, not word alone; that path leads to that space provided and sustained by the two cherubim wherein the contemplative does meet and speak with God and where our participation and drama in flesh and blood occurs once, twice, again and again.

And thus is silence woven around and through our person: on the human side Richard recognizes, demonstrates, and contemplates the validity of an apophatic Christology; in that center space and eternal present where God is, Richard awaits the gift of a cataphatic Word crossing the borders of silence.

6

SECOND CHERUBIM:

ANGELIZATION

Beatrice stood with her eyes fixed only on the eternal wheels, and on her I fixed mine, withdrawn from above. At her aspect I was changed within, as was Glaucus when he tasted of the herb that made him one among the other gods in the sea. The passing beyond humanity cannot be set forth in words; let the example suffice, therefore, for those to whom grace reserves the experience.

—Dante, *Paradiso* I.64–72

Today, the search for cosmological myths supporting a general theory which would embrace all physical and spiritual laws and beyond which no angel would dare to tread is being abandoned. Once again fissures of mystery are erupting, and we are intrigued as Wisdom speaks. We can peer into these new eruptive "heavens," in part, by paying renewed attention to the old masters of incomprehensibility. Richard of St. Victor listened to mystery through metaphors of "angelization,"[1] in which "the human soul transforms itself into the symbolic expression of heavenly and winged animals and transfigures itself into their image."[2] Much of the material discussed in the previous chapters, in fact, is related to the methods and goals of the contemplative's transformation into the image of the cherubim.[3] Such angelization is no more than the ability to "dare those angelic ecstasies into the lofty, secret, difficult to reach places of divine incomprehensibility,"[4] and to thus listen, witness, and participate in angelic announcements of angelic birthings of the very structure of incomprehensibility and of the many "heavens" of mystery. Contemplation as angelization is joy, *gaudium*; the joy of participation *with God*, of consummation through and in our humanness. Rebbe Nachman of Breslov says, "Always

115

remember: Joy is not merely incidental to the spiritual quest, it is vital." Human *gaudium* takes all the forms of angelic symbolism, from praise to protection, from ascent to centering, from announcements of hope and understanding to mediating divinity. In examining the various metaphors of angelization, this chapter will also be describing sanctification. Indeed, Richard himself uses the doctrinal category of sanctification as he describes the ark and cherubim as an ark of sanctification for you (*dicitur arca sanctificationis vobis*). Angelization, or sanctification, is thus the process of the contemplative's preparation for, reception of, and participation in the *gaudium* of the incomprehensible presence of God. This joy is Wisdom speaking.

EXCUDENDA EST ANGELICA FORMA

One of the fundamental images Richard of St. Victor uses to describe the process of angelization is of the obligation of the contemplative to hatch or to forge or to hammer out the angelic form (*excudenda est angelica forma*).[5] Explicitly identifying himself with Bezeleel as the builder of the ark,[6] Richard bases the obligation to construct the ark on Exodus 25 and on his own contemplative principle that the ark and cherubim must be hatched or formed in the core of the soul of the contemplative. They ought to be so formed, and Richard as the master builder will aid in their formation, because, between these two cherubim, God has promised to be present and to speak: *loquar ad te supra propitiatorio ac medio duorum cherubin* (Exod. 25:22).

Richard begins to explain the idea that the cherubim *excudenda est* in the course of his exegesis of the command to Moses to "make two cherubim of the gold that nurtures one into wholeness."[7] The first image Richard uses to describe the formation of the cherubim is that of the verb *excudere*, which, as noted, may mean to hatch, to strike, beat out, hammer, or to forge. In many cases, *excudere* is linked to verbs expressing molding, pressing out, and copying such as *exprimo* and *imitor*, to form and to represent such as *formare* and *repraesentere*, and nouns or adjectives of image or likeness such as *similitude, effigies,* and *instar*.[8] Thus the image must be hatched according to the image and form of the cherubim:

> It certainly pleases us to turn to this description, both to affirm
> the rule of our doctrine from the similitude set forth [*proposita*

similitudine] and in like manner with the description of this formula to hatch out the form and way of our work [*formulam operis nostri formam . . . excudere*]. . . . What is proper to represent [*repraesentari*] to us under angelic form [*angelica forma*] ought truly to be something great, excellent, and certainly more than human. . . . Whence it is proper to represent [*repraesentare*] these things with an expression of similitude [*similitudinis*] by means of an image [*effigie*] that is angelic rather than human . . . if we desire to form [*formare*] the flight of our understanding in the image of [*instar*] the angelic similitude.[9]

In the following chapter, Richard uses the same verb, *excudere*, to ask how the cherubim ought to be hatched in the contemplative. He answers, in effect, they ought to be hatched by contemplating:

> Therefore, so that we are able to hatch [*excudere*] the form of an angelic similitude within ourselves, it is necessary to suspend our soul in perpetual quickness by wonder at such things and to grow accustomed to the wings of our contemplation and to sublime and angelic flights.[10]

Richard uses a variation on his definition of contemplation ("to suspend our soul in perpetual quickness by wonder at such things") to describe the nature of angelic construction and reinforces that definition by explicitly stating that in such a way are the wings of our contemplation strengthened for angelic flight. And yet they are only strengthened; even after additional forging, the strength to fly into divine incomprehensibility is not yet granted:

> But clearly thus far our cherubim do not have wings, or if they have, they have not yet stretched them out. Perhaps we have not yet fully formed [*formavimus*] our work, nor yet completed that angelic form [*formam*] in its full integrity according to the meaning of the Lord.[11]

The cherubim must be hatched, and yet the wings, through practice in virtue, need added strength. Here, metaphors are piled upon metaphors to explain, on the one hand, that contemplation is beyond explanation by metaphor, and that, on the other hand and as an added illustration, that just as metaphor and language are inadequate to the task of naming God, so too is our own effort inadequate to the task of angelic flight. In both cases God must act by the gift of God's own speaking. And that is exactly what God has promised (*loquar ad te*), and what Richard, in contemplation, awaits.

For Richard, the best "material" out of which the soul can begin to hatch the angelic form is contemplation itself, and specifically the contemplation of the secrets of faith:

> Certainly, this is that fully worthy material from which the angelic form and the winged creatures ought to be hatched [*excudenda est*]. We form the cherubim for ourselves from this material when we train ourselves to draw into contemplation the secrets of our faith which we have learned either by revelation or have received from a theologian. And we also form the cherubim for ourselves when our souls hover in these secrets in admiration and when our souls feed, humble, and sharply inflame themselves in the desire for divine things.[12]

The "secrets of our faith" that Richard is alluding to here are explicitly the Trinity and implicitly the flesh of the eternal Word in the humanity of Jesus. And here again, Richard uses a variation on his definition of contemplation ("when our souls hover in these secrets in admiration") to describe the process of the scriptural injunction to forge the angelic form. He is careful to emphasize the importance of the "grace of revelation" even in the context of ardent contemplative hovering over the "secrets" of faith. For it is at the height of watchful desiring and waiting[13] that the grace is given and the hatching of the cherubim begins to make progress:

> It is at this time, I think, that our beaten work [*opus nostrum ductile*] begins to make progress and to draw near not moderately to completion, since now our cherubim begin to spread their wings and at every hour, in preparation for flying, to hover.[14]

Of course, it is "one thing to make the ark, it is another to form the cherubim."[15] To form the cherubim, the contemplatives clothe themselves in the tropological interpretation; the contemplative hatches the cherubim by practicing the "teaching of what our beloved wishes us to do" (*docens quid dilectus noster facere nos velit*).[16] Tropologically, we are able "to form and to hatch an angelic form" (*formare et angelicam formam excudere*)[17] by means of the imitation of Wisdom and Wisdom's path in virtue. In this sense, the cherubim having been tropologically "hatched" and formed, God speaks (*loquar ad te*) between them the flesh of the eternal Word (*carnem aeterni Verbi*), a speaking which the contemplative, imitating, hears.[18]

ANGELIC CLOTHING

A second metaphor descriptive of the process of angelization is that of "putting on angelic clothing." A favorite of Richard's, the clothing metaphor is used to elucidate the dialectic of hidden and revealed.[19] Clothing is also related to Aaron and the vestments of the priestly office. Human clothing indicates what can be seen and known by all, while the vestments of the priest are appropriately worn only upon entering the most secret areas of the temple. The temple being associated with the self in Richard,[20] it is not difficult to understand the connection he makes between the priestly robes of Aaron and the garments of the contemplative: both must be properly clothed to enter the *Sancta sanctorum*.[21] Metaphors of clothing the soul in angelic robes thus give angelization the added nuance of one of Richard's most evocative dialectics (that of hidden/revealed) and of the liturgical ritual of entering into holy communion with God.

Richard's overarching concern, that of interpreting Exodus 25 tropologically as the Wisdom of construction or weaving of the ark and cherubim in the heart, might be described metaphorically as the process of putting on angelic clothing. Thus all of Book IV of *De arca mystica* which describes the forming of the cherubim, the spreading of their wings, their complementary regard relating as mutually affirming and denying opposites across the propitiatory, their shadowing or covering of the oracle, and their function of providing a birthing and breathing space for the presence of God can be described as explaining the process, requirements, privileges, and expectations of putting on angelic clothing. But lest the emphasis of this angelic construction appear to constrict the gratuitous nature of divine providence, Richard makes an early distinction between receiving angelic clothing and putting it on:

> But in these last two kinds of contemplation everything depends on grace. And they are all distant and exceedingly remote from all human industry, except that each person receives the clothing of

angelic similitude [*angelicae similitudinis habitum*] from heaven and by divine providence puts it on herself. And certainly not without cause did these last two works that the contemplative is about to do [*operis factura*][22] receive the name cherubim.[23]

Human industry amounts to little in constructing the cherubim, the human soul is the recipient: each person receives (*accipit*) angelic clothing from heaven and even the very work of construction itself receives (*accipit*) the name cherubim; the contemplative puts the clothing on himself, but only with the aid of divine providence. The putting on of angelic clothing is thus a gift of the grace of sanctification.

In the context of a discussion on the necessity of compunction and contrition in the processes by which the soul "melts down the gold of understanding,"[24] Richard links this gift of angelic clothing to the metaphor of hatching or forging the angelic form discussed above:

> Without doubt and without any contradiction, it is not a light or an easy thing for the human soul to clothe itself [*induere se*] in angelic form, and to go above a certain earthly state to a truly more than human state and to receive [*accipere*] spiritual wings and to raise itself to the heights. It is necessary daily to place your gold into the fire, and to turn it this way and that and to hammer it with frequent blows before one forges the angelic form and produces the cherubim [*angelicam formam excudat cherubinque producat*]! . . . Certainly it is necessary that one first grow accustomed to walks in heavenly places with heavenly creatures never descending to earthly creatures and the care of external things (unless only for the duty of obedience or the office of charity) before one dares to try those angelic ecstasies into the secret, difficult to reach places of divine incomprehensibility.[25]

By forging (*excudat*) the angelic form and producing the cherubim, and having clothed the contemplative in angelic clothing, Richard can begin to suggest "walks in heavenly places," which further prepare the contemplative for the more secret, difficult to reach places of divine incomprehensibility. Putting on angelic clothing in this context is the preparation for *and* the encounter with God in those secret places. Those secret places, though beyond comprehensibility, are nonetheless, in part, the "secrets of our faith": the doctrine of the Trinity and the person and work of Jesus Christ.

Thus the answer to the question of why the soul should clothe itself in angelic cloth is that thus "in-vested," the contemplative can "hear" what God has promised to "speak"—*loquar ad te . . . de medio duorum cherubin.* The language of that speech is the secret language of incomprehensibility available not to the knowledgeable but to the wise, not to the well instructed but to the graced. It is "heard" by those who to speculation, investigation, observation, work, knowledge, and understanding add devotion, wonder, piety, love, humility, and joy.

As woven by Richard, clothing as the imitation of Wisdom places the contemplative at the center of the ark and cherubim, where in turn, at the very center, *in medio,* of the contemplative, God is present as grace wills. Thus clothed in angelic Wisdom, through an *internal icon*[26] as it were, we have access to God's promise at any hour.

The metaphor of clothing as the imitation of Wisdom is the contemplative equivalent of the command to Moses to construct the cherubim. In both cases, in contemplative clothing or material construction, it is "there" that God will speak. Angelic clothing is therefore also a way of describing that "there" as an internal icon. To this icon, as Richard helps us construct it, we may go at any hour; when we are thus clothed, God may speak as necessity and grace might will:

> Think what a great thing this is and what it means to consider God at every hour whenever it might be necessary and in whatever necessity to seek and to receive counsel as is proper.[27] In this way you are able, whenever it might be necessary or useful, to turn the mind in a familiar manner to these last three modes of contemplation where God has said, "From whence I will speak to you."[28]

A SPIRITUAL BEING OF ANGELIC FORM

Another metaphor which Richard uses to express the process of angelization is that of the human person transformed into a spiritual being of angelic form. This metaphor is less concrete than the previous but more inclusive; forging the angelic form, putting on angelic clothing, and the work which the contemplative is about to do (*operis factura*) are all subcategories of the more inclusive metaphor of spiritual transformation. This metaphor, perhaps more than the others, indicates the restorative character of transformation and is more often immediately associated with preparation most befitting entry into divine incomprehensibility.[29]

The contemplative begins to become a spiritual being or celestial animal (*coeleste animal*) through the angelic clothing of the six wings of contemplation (*sex contemplationum alis*).[30] The first pair of wings used to cover and protect the body indicate that you (*tu*—the contemplative) are still an earthly animal and in no way a heavenly one (*terrenum et nondum coeleste animal tu esse*). The second pair of wings, used in flying to the furthest limits of earth and knowledge, indicate that you have become a heavenly animal and have given birth to a heavenly body (*te coeleste animal esse et corpus coeleste gerere*). The third pair of wings are given to fly up to the secrets of the third heaven and the hidden things of divinity (*ad tertii coeli secreta Divinitatisque arcana volare*).[31] With these wings, associated with the six kinds of contemplation, the contemplative, clothed in angelic clothing, becomes a spiritual being with a spiritual body capable of flights into heavenly mystery.

In his chapters on knowledge of self associated with the symbols of the gilding of setim wood and of the crown of the ark, Richard indicates that the contemplative begins to become an angelic spirit by first gaining a thorough knowledge of the human spirit. This is accomplished, he says,

> When you begin to dwell upon spiritual contemplations and to rise up through a consideration of your spirit to a contemplation of spirits and to couple together [*comparare*] in this way spiritual things with spiritual things, you begin in like manner to be spiritual.[32]

The human spirit is thus a loop in the path to angelization. In Richard, clothing oneself in the gold of a spiritual being is always grounded in the gilded wood of the human spirit. The important verb *comparare* here indicates the nature of the link between human spirit and angelic spirit: it is one of coupling together based on likeness, one of forming into like pairs, one of likeness itself on which Richard's symbolic theory of similitude and dissimilitude is based.[33]

That the human spirit is a portion of the route of the path to transformation into a spiritual being of angelic form is so important to Richard that he repeats it in a variety of ways:

> And so this kind of contemplation consists in incorporeal things and invisible essences: that is, angelic spirits and human spirits.[34]

He knows nothing who does not first reflect on his own spirit; he does not know what to feel about angelic spirits or the divine Spirit. First return to yourself, then you might presume to search those things that are above you.[35] If you desire to fly up to the second or even third heaven . . . if you prepare to search the depths of God, first examine the depths of your own spirit.[36] From much consideration and recognition of your spirit you will be lifted up to an understanding and contemplation of the spirit of angels and the Spirit of the divine.[37]

Thus by first turning inward (*in te redi*, as Augustine advocates) to find a likeness of self to angelic spirits, and perhaps more importantly, to find a likeness to those "other" human spirits in our own spirit, we begin to form the basis of Wisdom as charity. Through such knowledge of self, always associated with images of flight or lifting up, the contemplative begins to take wing.

But while the human spirit is the route into the hiddenness of God through the process of angelization, the process is nonetheless one of transformation and restoration of that spirit. Unpurified gold is still gold, but refined and purified gold out of which the cherubim are forged is something "more": "What is proper to represent to us under angelic form ought truly to be something great, excellent, even above earthly things and certainly more than human."[38] Something more than human is this transfigured human spirit:

But who can worthily describe what skill and what anxiety and disquiet are needed until the human soul transforms itself into the symbolic expression of heavenly and winged animals and transfigures itself into their image.[39]

Ultimately this transformation is dependent on grace and revelation, as Richard often makes clear. But penultimately, human effort and divine grace together play a role in two ways: first, in the purification and transformation of affections into virtues (*labor cum fructu*) and, second, through the imitation of angels by the contemplation of spiritual creatures (*sine labore cum fructu*). Both are related, but while the first concentrates on the transformation of the human spirit, the second focuses on the imitation of angelic spirit.

Purification and transformation of affections into virtues is further brought to mind in recalling that, from the beginning, *De arca mystica* is consciously a tropological (*moraliter*) treatise devoted to an interpretation of ark and cherubim as an ark of sanctification for you (*arca sanctificationis vobis*).[40] The interpretation of the cherubim, their fabrication and weaving, and their special status as an internal icon defining a place of divine speaking all converge in the ongoing process of purification, sanctification, and beatification of the contemplative.[41] The ark of sanctification, a sacred structure (*sacrario*), means for Richard the grace of contemplation. And this contemplation which sanctifies also contains a Wisdom which purifies:

> These are the things that defile a person [i.e., impurities-*immunditia*]. However, a person is purged by Wisdom when Wisdom, attacking more bravely, conquers malice, that is, touching completely from one end of the earth to the other and distributing all things in order delightfully. And I think, to be purified in this way is to be sanctified.[42]

Thus this tropological treatise on Wisdom finds that the ark of sanctification means the grace of contemplation of truth, and that whoever receives this grace is not only purified but sanctified. "Whoever was made whole [*sanati sunt*] was restored to health by Wisdom," Richard says.[43] *Sanati sunt*, restored health, is the goal of purification and also a first step in the contemplative's angelization; it is the contemplative's first feathers one might say, the undergarment of angelic clothing.

The actual work of purification is not a primary concern of *De arca mystica*. Richard's *De praeparatione animi ad contemplationem* or the *Benjamin Minor* more properly deals with purification and the Wisdom of virtue through ordered affections as preparation to the grace of contemplation.[44] However, since purification is so intimately linked with angelization and the presence of God, which *are* the primary concerns of *De arca mystica*, the process of purification is discussed in a number of instances.[45]

The issue of purification is raised in the context of its relation to the transformation of human into angelic spirit. In the process of this transformation, the angelic spirit is to become something "more than human." The issue and the question of just how this transformation is to be accomplished are always difficult and delicate ones. Richard himself asks, "what . . . does it mean to fabricate the ark, to cloth it with gold and encircle it with a crown, to cover it with the propitiatory and to connect the cherubim?"[46] His answer, in part, is an answer of purgation and restoration.[47] The project of purgation and transformation into angelic spirit thus becomes a project of Wisdom and virtue. Hugh of St. Victor had earlier made the connection between reformed human nature, virtue, Wisdom, and angelic spirits. In making this connection, Hugh provides a perfect definition of angelization:

> This is our entire task—the restoration of our nature and the removal of our deficiency. The integrity of human nature, however, is attained in two things—knowledge and virtue, and in these lie our sole likeness to the supernal [angels] and divine substances.[48]

Through knowledge (the fullness of which is symbolized by the cherubim) and virtue we attend to the presence of God. This is the work of contemplation.[49] For Richard as for Hugh, this work "imitates the archangelic sublimity" (*archangelicam sublimitatem imitatur*), and these "contemplative ecstasies of supercelestial souls" (*super coelestium animorum theoricos excessus*) encounter God finally not in *imago* but in *res*, that is, face to face:

> Think, I beg you, of how excellent it is when, through the imitation of those orders of celestial beings which adhere without mediation to the highest light, contemplation draws a similitude into itself and sees face to face and without a mirror and without enigma.[50]

In hovering contemplation, the contemplative encounters the sanctifying process of angelization. Angelized, without mediation, we participate in God's presence born in the soul. But, "without doubt, it is above human nature to have wings and to fly to the heights,"[51] Richard says, and so he asks, following Psalm 54, "who will give me wings like the dove that I may fly away and be at rest?"[52] The gift of grace, a showing, *revelatio*, he answers; specifically, the grace of contemplation provides the wings. It provides the air beneath the wings, and the very pattern of flight into the veil, into the cloud, into the open secrets of incomprehensibility, into the center, *in medio*, into the very face of the holy things of God. Who but angels would dare receive such wings?

But when received and accepted and dared, angelization is a simple thing, really. It is no more than the imitation of Wisdom. It is no more than charity. It is no more than joy. It is no more than the Wisdom of charity for, and joy in the revealed mystery of, every face. The critical link between apophatic Christology and angelization is the human breath, human touching face to face.

SUMMARY

Book IV of *De arca mystica* gives instruction in the contemplative imitation of the cherubim. "Angelization" is our name for this imitation. Angelization, though potentially a misunderstood term, is nonetheless appropriate for describing the ongoing process of purification, reformation and restoration, illumination, ascension, consummation: in short, sanctification, joy. It thus includes both work and rest, both the active and the contemplative life. Angelization is that hovering ground between humanization and divinization; it is thus important to keep in mind the grounding of angelization in the created world and in the soul clothed in self-understanding as well as the seemingly more glorious flight of the soul into the incomprehensible manifestations of God's gracious Wisdom. As a process, angelization is a journey, a transformation in consciousness, a path through progress in virtue to the center, the dwelling place of God. It employs symbols, but the height of angelic flight depends on rebirth through symbols into the nonsymbolic flesh of the Word: "The highest Wisdom of God which, having been hidden in the flesh, cannot be seen by the eyes of flesh."[53] The cherubim function both as symbols of that flight and as markers of that birth beyond symbol.

This chapter has shown that Richard uses different metaphors of "angelization" in his attempt to instruct the contemplative in this grounded flight beyond symbol.

The primary metaphors are those drawn from Exodus itself which Richard interprets tropologically and which we have been investigating throughout the course of this book. These include the construction of the ark, crown, and propitiatory, which become symbols themselves of the first four kinds of contemplation, and especially metaphors relating to the cherubim themselves, which describe the final two forms of contemplation. These latter images and metaphors include contemplative teaching on the cherubim's construction, their material, and their dimensions, their location, what they see, how their wings cover the ark, the nature of their hovering flight, and how between them, as each cherubim keeps its complementary opposite in view,

God moves beyond the boundaries of silence to speak a cataphatic Word. How this Word is heard and acted is the contemplative's own drama; it is each person's unique participation in God.

Richard himself uses secondary metaphors of his own devising to describe our imitation of the cherubim through which, by grace, our angelization takes place. These are the metaphors examined in this chapter. They include, first, the metaphor of hatching or forging (*excudare*) the cherubim. Second, they include the visual and evocative metaphor of putting on angelic clothing that is linked to Aaron's priestly vestments. A third image of angelization is the *operis factura*, or the "work about to be done or made," which insists on the tension between the *opus restaurationis* of the present in which the contemplative continues the internal construction of the cherubim and the *opus restaurationis* of the eschatological future in which the process of angelic weaving will be complete. A fourth image is the complex metaphor of the human spirit transformed into a spiritual being, or angelic or celestial spirit. This metaphor of transformation into a spiritual being contains within it the notions of the process of purgation or purification, and illumination or transformation of consciousness. This final image or metaphor is the imitation of Wisdom itself which has as its fruit the active life and progress in virtue, based on the ability to hear and act upon God's word. The "highest" Wisdom put forth for contemplative (and active) imitation is the flesh of the eternal Word in the humanity of Jesus (*carnem aeterni Verbi in humanitate Jesu*). Though this is the "highest" Wisdom, as we have seen, Richard, because of the constraints as well as the liberating qualities of his symbolic theology and methodology, does not speak the Wisdom of this Word, it being beyond the capacity of symbol to touch (or of the *oculis carnis videre*). He speaks, rather, of the necessity of silence beyond the angelic form; into this weave of silence God alone will speak.

Finally, we must keep in mind that "imitation" is itself a metaphor. Richard uses many verbs to express the contemplative "relation" we are to have to the cherubim as we participate in the process of internalization of ark and cherubim for grounded flight.[54] These include, besides "to imitate" itself, verbs which indicate how we are to "be" in relation to the cherubim. That is, how we are to form, or to fabricate, or to hatch the cherubim, and how we are to transform or transfigure ourselves (with grace) into the figure of angelic spirits.

For the contemplative, flight into the secret places of incompre-hensibility means "imitation" of the cherubim, or "angelization," for "flight" into the mystery of Trinity and the flesh of the eternal Word in the humanity of Jesus; it means spreading the wings, looking at the propitiatory, gazing into the eyes of all that is the mutual complement of affirmation and denial; it means knowledge of self and action in the world modeled on Wisdom; it means ascent through symbols and denial of symbols; it means hovering in the presence of silence and it means hovering in the presence of *loquar ad te*; it means awaiting that gift from beyond the word hidden at the center, *in medio*, in the flesh (*in carne latitantem*). Angelization means being willing to participate in both the weaving and the rending of the veil. And being willing to hear and act and see what the weave and the rend present.

VISIO

An evening, unlike an argument, does not lead to a conclusion. That is why a reflection on the living presence of God
must remain open-ended, leading at most to a confession,
not to a conclusion or a denominational preference. Clues,
though, do arise within it. Perhaps the most basic among
them is that *God is.*

—Erazim Kohák
The Embers and the Stars

This book has not sought to argue, "but to see and evoke a vision."[1]
My hope is that this "narration of our night work" (*lucubratiunculae
nostrae expositione*), as I called this undertaking in the book's opening
section, this dark, evening work, is also an illumination. Night work
does not lead to a conclusion. But perhaps it can illuminate. In my
case, the evening work emerges from years spent close to the center
between the two cherubim, years lived in the radical brackets of the
cherubim's vision. The hint, the clue, is that, with the cherubim's eyes,
we can see that *God is.* Not only that, but we can see ourselves and
our world as they are too. And not only that, but there in that center
the fire[2] illuminates the mystery that we are *with* God. I see us dancing
around this fire in joy and praise. Richard says: "And this nature of
ours forms the applause of its great rejoicing according to the joyful
dance of angelic likeness."[3] The following is no conclusion. It simply
asks the contemplative reader for a pausing and a stillness, a moment's
wonder, a glimpse through your own nature (*nostram naturam*) of the
joy the cherubim see.

In Richard of St. Victor's flight into contemplative mystery, the symbol of the cherubim points beyond itself, giving meaning to ordinary
and nonordinary experience; it is transformative, and it is capable

129

of dwelling in paradox. Polysemic, the symbol of the cherubim also manifests the logic or path of participation; the cherubim serve as guides for contemplative journeys of introversion and extroversion, as sacramental images of anagogic daring, and as models of sacred ground and magic flight. Symbolizing the dialectical and contemplative method of hovering, the cherubim function according to the basic Dionysian typology of similar and dissimilar symbols. As angels, the cherubim are messengers, warriors, protectors and guardians, and symbols of flight, light, praise, and ascent. In Richard's contemplative teaching, the cherubim also symbolize the presence of divine mystery, participation in divine drama, and hovering in divine manifestations of joy and wisdom. In addition, for the contemplative, the cherubim and ark present an icon in the shape and form of a sacred womb that represents the process of the rebirthing of self and the birth of the promise of divine speaking. Explicitly the cherubim symbolize the unity of substance and trinity of persons within the Trinity, and implicitly they symbolize the two natures, God and human, of Christ. In their hovering the cherubim symbolize and illuminate Richard's use of the coincidence of mutually affirming and denying complementarity, including reason and beyond reason, empty and full, presence and absence, rest and motion, and many more. "Angelization," within the context of the grace of contemplation, is the contemplative's acquisition of and clothing in this full, polysemic knowledge and manifold wisdom found in the symbol of the cherubim. But the cherubim also transcend all these aspects of symbol, manifesting, finally, that which is beyond symbol, the flesh of the Word. The cherubim manifest the unity of thing (*res*), that is, flesh, and image (*imago*), that is, Word. This unity, this Word, is constant prayer.

Richard of St. Victor's *De arca mystica* is a tropological exegesis of Exodus 25. While previous exegesis on this text had focused on literal interpretations or allegorical interpretations of the ark and cherubim as Christ, Richard's tropological exegesis is of the ark and cherubim as Wisdom. The Exodus text is a text of divine presence. Richard's contemplative teaching based on the symbolic structure of the ark and cherubim attempts to paint, weave, construct, and hatch an internal icon of ark and cherubim in the soul of the contemplative for the purpose of manifesting the divine presence.

The tropological wisdom explicitly referred to by Richard is an ethical wisdom of discernment, transformation of consciousness, and active progress in virtue. It is the wisdom of the Old Testament, but it is also the wisdom of the flesh of the eternal Word of the New Testament. But while in Exodus 25 God has promised that *loquar ad te*, in *De arca mystica* Richard does not speak the Word of the humanity or divinity of Jesus Christ; tropological wisdom of the New Testament is not word (as language) but rather Word (as incarnate being) in act. Intimate imitation of Word in act is accomplished in contemplative hovering modeled on the wisdom of the Old Testament and the life of Christ. Such intimacy with Christ, such imitation of wisdom is a circle of rest and action. This circle is constant prayer.

The literal, allegorical, anagogical and tropological senses of scripture in Victorine exegesis are mutually dependent and related. In fact, an emphasis on integration can be seen in all of Victorine thought and practice. Thus in Richard's exegesis, theology, and what we would call "spirituality," a separation between reflective analysis of experience and the practice, process, and consciousness of that experience is made only to reintegrate and fuse these elements at a higher level. This reintegration is constant prayer.

Dialectical integration of a particular type has been variously and interchangeably described in this book as the *coincidentia oppositorum* and contemplative hovering. The coincidence of opposites, or more precisely in Richard's case, the coincidence of mutually affirming and denying complementarity, has generally been used to describe the metaphysics of dialectical integration while hovering has generally been used to describe the symbolics of dialectical integration. Both, through the grace of contemplation, draw the contemplative "in" toward divine incomprehensibility and "out" toward angelization, "in" toward wisdom and "out" toward virtue, "in" toward transformation of consciousness and "out" toward sanctification. Both the coincidence of opposites and "hovering" sanction and animate a participatory relation between "in" and "out": *cherubin cherubin respicit.*[4]

Richard uses the imagery of flight throughout *De arca mystica*. Hovering itself, *suspensa*, both as a type of flight and as an image of a certain type of dialectical integration, actually serves as one of the primary threads within the treatise, providing narrative continuity, teaching models, and theological coherence. Thus in the created order birds hover and the soul in process of restoration hovers even as heart, mind, and wisdom fly. The body itself becomes spiritual and flies as the contemplative is given six wings with which to hover in the secret places of incomprehensibility. And, of course, the cherubim themselves fly. Bird flight, in addition, is used to represent ways of thinking (including meditation and contemplation), while angelic flight is used to represent the final forms of contemplation, and contemplative flight itself is used to represent the ascent of the soul into God. Hence "hovering" is a particularly apt symbol of the relational dialectic Richard has in mind. As a pattern of flight it represents the highest form of thinking, that is, contemplation; it is even used to define the activity of contemplation itself as the contemplative "hovers in the manifestations of God's wisdom" and mystery.

The two cherubim, while hovering atop the ark, are nonetheless securely attached to the ark, which represents the created world and the soul. Thus this hovering can be described as "grounded flight." All Richard's teaching and theology of contemplation is of flight well-grounded. We would say today that it is "embodied" flight. For Richard, the paths to God lead through the bodily senses, through the self known well, and through the created world. Ungrounded flight is possible, but it has no charity, it makes no progress in virtue, it does not act in the world and so it has no wisdom. It may not even return to earth.

Hovering, at its most concrete level, represents stillness in motion. The cherubim themselves, as a symbol, represent this dialectic of the coincidence of opposites, or hovering stillness in motion. As the cherubim hover in absolute rest, they become the eternal ground for motion. As they hover, their mutual opposites remain in coincidental tension on either side of the ark while their coincidental tension does not resolve. While neither cherubim diminishes the fullness of the other, each stands as the other's complementary opposite. One is stillness, one is motion. One is fullness, one is emptiness. One is presence, one is absence. One is unity, one is diversity. When divinity speaks, it does not speak through either cherubim as symbolic of, say, stillness or motion, but rather from their center, *in medio*, in the internal space stillness and motion create. The hovering cherubim, then, represent the coincidence of mutually affirming and denying complementarity. Stillness and motion coincide mutually, both affirming and denying the other in complementarity; divinity speaks in this center "space of complementarity." Hovering is constant prayer.

Paradoxically, the cherubim most explicitly symbolize the core of that incomprehensibility, Trinity itself. The Trinity as unity and plurality is at the heart of divine incomprehensibility, but God will not speak even through unity and/or plurality. And since God will not speak where God does not dwell, Richard himself can attempt no more: he cannot speak the dwelling of the flesh of the eternal Word, that is, the incomprehensibility of eternal/flesh or God/human. Richard will not and cannot speak this word: the cherubim hover as well between speech and Word as between unity and plurality and between language and language's faltering, but God is not precisely "there." On the human side, Denys' method thus leads to apophatic Christology—at each moment the contemplative awaits the divine, Christic presence in silence; on the divine side, the cataphatic Word is delivered as gift—at each moment God may speak.

The tropological Word is not Richard's to speak. Richard's theurgy, we might say, is silence, *tacitus*. The Word is God's to speak. Where words and symbols fall short, revelation, grace, and gift saturate the boundaries of the "heavens of mystery" (see chapter 5). Richard's teaching is on the *labor* of contemplation to *receive* the grace of sanctification as the union of thing (*res*) and symbol (*imago*), that is, the Word. Bonaventure, a century later, would look toward the mercy seat and see and speak the Word of the God-man crucified. Richard, in waiting, looks yet dares not speak. And the cherubim look, but rather than daring not speak, they become a symbol of the inability of symbols to name the full Christological sense of the Word.[5] The cherubim symbolize the inability of symbols to convey the Incarnation, the *res* of flesh, breath, and blood; they symbolize the inability of symbols to convey the Crucifixion, the *res* of death. But they also symbolize the vision of the Incarnation and Passion of Jesus Christ, which are not simply symbols. Divinity does not simply speak a symbol, an *imago*, it speaks also the *res* of flesh, breath, blood, and death. *God is.* Specifically, as Wisdom to the world, God is *carnem aeterni Verbi in humanitate Jesu.* This Word, as flesh, this Word as eternity, this Word as humanity, this Word as Jesus, this Word as the union of *imago* and *res* is breath and blood, hope and death, it is all we have to go on, it arrives in waiting, an act before language. It arrives within the radical brackets of the cherubim, it arrives at the contemplative's center, *in medio*. It is constant prayer.

As an internal icon of grounded flight, woven in the soul, the ark and cherubim function as a kind of stage for the ongoing production of and participation in our own contemplative drama. This spiritual drama is in turn enacted in our own flesh and breath and hope, enacted on the stage of the propitiatory between the wings of the cherubim. As contemplative, I "act" a drama of meeting with the *res* and *imago* of Word on that stage. I act my birth; I act the continual breath and birth of the *loquar ad te* which, being born and breathed on this stage, is continually born in my soul.[6] I act my life. I act the drama of my many meetings and lettings-go of various personal persona and the *dramatis persona* of my own embodied, inspirited journey. I act my death. There are many such acts on the stage of the ark between the two cherubim—the acts of a lifetime and the acts of a deathtime. These acts are constant prayer.

The process of preparation, restoration, and consummation, and of ongoing sanctification for this "act" and "birth," is the process of "angelization." Angelization requires active participation on the part of the contemplative. Angelization includes all that the cherubim are, symbolize, participate in, and see. One cannot do justice to Richard's work on the use of the cherubim in contemplation without participating in his teaching.[7] Grounded flight, angelization, birth, divine drama, all insist on participation of body, heart, and mind in the world. Tropological encounters with wisdom persist in shaping humility, charity, and peace in a womb of participation. Born from this womb is the fruit of a divine promise: *loquar ad te*, I will speak to you. The cherubim model, teach, and look upon participation in this promise. Participation, action, is constant prayer.

Chapter 5 of this work lays the groundwork of Richard's investigation of divine mystery. Incomprehensibility, by its very nature, is beyond logic, reason, comprehensibility. While incomprehensibility might be encountered in the contemplation of any object, created or uncreated, it is most perfectly manifested in contemplation of the Trinity, named by Richard, and in contemplation and imitation of the person and work of Jesus Christ, unnamed by Richard and left for the contemplative's own participation.

What might be called an internal structure is encountered in the contemplation of divine incomprehensibility. Within this structure is a "slippage" or oscillation between contemplation of Trinity and contemplation of the dual-natured flesh of the eternal Word: Trinity "slips" into Christology and Christology "slips" back to Trinity on the basis of their shared incomprehensibility. This "slippage," I believe, gives us a hint as to the internal structure of incomprehensibility or mystery.

That structure might be called "relation," and given the formal relation of hovering between the two cherubim, which is the basis of the whole of De arca mystica; "a hovering relation" would be an accurate description of the structure of mystery.

But let us return to the "slippage" between the shared mystery of Trinity and Christology. At the highest point of Richard of St. Victor's angelic flight the contemplative mind and heart soar beyond words and supposedly beyond structure, only to "slip" from incomprehensibility to incomprehensibility. This "slippage" between Trinity and Christology along the path of the incomprehensibility of the coincidence of mutually affirming and denying complementarity begins to hint the "structure" beyond description. Contemplation on the doctrinal nature of the Trinity (the contemplative concern of De arca mystica) leads to contemplation of the secret places of divine incomprehensibility, leading in turn to contemplation of the incomprehensible nature of the flesh of the eternal Word (the contemplative concern toward which De arca mystica hints). The doctrinal nature of the Trinity is pushed to the extreme limits of logic and reason; beyond this boundary the Trinity does not dissolve, but the fullness of logic and of knowledge is transcended. Logic and knowledge are appropriated in this process, but they are also transcended as the doctrinal nature of the Trinity meets the incomprehensible, contemplative nature of the Trinity. And in this incomprehensible contemplative Trinitarian nature a hovering relation remains.

The incomprehensible contemplative Trinitarian nature is not "emptiness," it is not "silence," it is not "nothing." Likewise it is not "fullness," it is not "word," it is not "something." Likewise also, as we saw in Chapters 2 and 3 of this work, it is not the metaphysics of negation: it is beyond the language of affirmation and denial. And because of this internal structure of incomprehensibility which is not emptiness, not fullness, not nothing, the incomprehensible contemplative Trinitarian nature slips without effort or image into and back from the incomprehensible contemplative Christological nature. Contemplation on the theology of Trinity and Christology leads into a hovering relation with divine incomprehensibility, there to dwell, as Richard says, with a "free, penetrating gaze of a mind hovering with wonder, participating in manifestations of wisdom."[8] Angelized, the human soul flies from the doctrinal structure of Trinitarian hovering to the contemplative structure of Trinitarian incomprehensibility. There, at the heart of darkness, structure as a hovering relation is illuminated. This structure is the mystery of constant prayer.

As Richard of St. Victor was to explore later in *De Trinitate* and also in *De quatuor gradibus violentae charitatis*, this structure may take the shape of *caritas*, charity. There are hints, even in *De arca mystica*, that Richard thought this to be the case.[9] But they are just hints. In *De arca mystica*, his treatise on the cherubim whose name means "fullness of knowledge," the focus of vision is on wisdom and the spiritual journeys along the ways of knowledge, language, and symbol. In this vision, the wisdom of incomprehensibility utters not a Word, not even "charity." In this vision, the contemplative adorns herself in Angelic Wisdom and, well grounded, flys to meet *God's speaking*. Angelic Wisdom is constant prayer.

Appendices

A. BOOK V OF *DE ARCA MYSTICA*

At the end of *De arca mystica*, in the final chapter of Book V, Richard of St. Victor writes:

> In this matter [that is, the matter of Book V and of its core verse, 2 Cor. 12:2] we are better instructed by the skill of those persons who have advanced to the fullness of this knowledge, not so much by the teaching of another person as from their own experience.[1]

I have purposefully avoided a detailed discussion of Book V for a number of reasons, not the least of which is Richard's own insight that its intent (if not its content) is best absorbed through experience tinged with a healthy dose of grace.[2] That is, its wisdom is acquired not through activity or teaching but through direct experience. To use Richard's own allegories, the subject matter of Book V is the wisdom of Moses, who saw the ark and cherubim on the mountain and in a cloud. It is not the wisdom of Bezeleel, who from human activity and labor was able to see it; nor is it the wisdom of Aaron, who from the work and instruction of another was able to enter it.

Book V is Richard of St. Victor's own experience (*propria experientia*) of the ark and cherubim and of God's promise to speak with him there (*loquar ad te*). Thus, having given instruction for the construction of the ark and cherubim in the soul of the contemplative and on how the mind and heart might enter that inmost place of hidden secrets in Books I–IV, Book V becomes a record of Richard's own experience contemplating this internal icon. The book is an example of God's cataphatic word transgressing the boundaries of Richard's own, human, apophatic Christology; as such it is not the word God speaks to me, and it is not the word God speaks to you. As an example, it is the word God speaks to Richard. It is a hint. Our next step is the teaching of our own experience.

Another reason I have limited discussion to Books I–IV is that the cherubim themselves are not mentioned in Book V. In fact, except for one brief acknowledgement of Books I–IV at the end,[3] Book V could be a related, but altogether separate, treatise from the rest of *De arca mystica*. Still, there is continuity. For instance, Richard uses Book V to discuss what he calls modes of contemplation. These include *dilatatio mentis, sublevatio mentis, and alienatio/excessus mentis*. J. Châtillon concludes a discussion of these three modes by saying that the "three modes of contemplation" deal with love, while the "six kinds of contemplation" (outlined by Richard in Books I–IV) deal with knowledge.[4] A brief look at Book V of *De arca mystica* will show that the distinction is not that easy to make. In Book V both the *sapientia* tradition and the *caritas* tradition are represented.[5] The cherubim, as pointed out, are not mentioned in Book V, but as the way of *sapientia* or knowledge, they are present in a silent way. The seraphim also are not mentioned, but as the way of *caritas* or love, they too are quietly present.

Though Book V does move into the language and imagery of *caritas*, the cherubim as wisdom are still present. In support of this is the fact that the "three modes of contemplation" themselves, that is, dilation, raising up, and ecstasy or alienation, are all "of the mind" (*mentis*). As are the cherubim, they are categories of mind. One of the many examples of the category of mind in the contemplative ascent in Book V can be found in Chapter iv. Here words in the general category of mind abound: knowledge (*scientia*), verbs of learning (*cognoscit*), understanding (*intelligentia*), and human understanding divinely illuminated (*humana intelligentia divinitus illuminatur*), to mention a very few. These categories are reminiscent of Richard's discussion of the cherubim as fullness of knowledge. The cherubim's silent presence can also be ascertained in this same chapter by means of images normally associated with knowledge. These include the broad group of symbols and metaphors of flight encountered in Richard's work on the cherubim in Books I–IV (for instance, *expandit alas suas, per aera iter habere, ad alta volare*).[6] In the very next chapter, Richard switches the category and the imagery; now he speaks silently of the seraphim; that is, the category is now *caritas*. Words of love now abound, including love (*amor*), devotion (*devotione*), if you love fully and perfectly (*si . . . plene perfecteque diligeris*), inebriate the longing of your heart (*cordis tui desiderium inebriaret*), and many

more. These categories, of course, are reminiscent of Hugh's interpretation of Denys' discussion of the seraphim as love. As if to reinforce
these opaque references to seraphim, the imagery associated with the
category of love is not flight, but rather fire, burning, smoke, and
longing.[7] Thus the imagery of flight is used to depict the ascent of
the cherubim as knowledge or mind, while imagery of fire is used
to depict the ascent of seraphim as love. In both cases the names of
the particular angelic hierarchies are not given, but their presence is
quietly insistent.

Richard does use the word "angel" in Book V, and again, while a
particular order is never named, it becomes apparent that the celestial
hierarchy is at work in his anagogic concept of angels. That angels are
messengers he states clearly: "Indeed an angel is called a messenger."[8]
And that angels serve as an anagogic, guiding hand he also states
clearly and openly: "The other, by angelic leading, is raised by alienation of mind above the common state of human possibility."[9] And
that the process of "angelization" continues is also explicit: "into the
secret place of divinity . . . by means of a marvelous transfiguration;
she is completely immersed in angelic manifestations."[10] What is not
explicit, but apparent in the context of Denys and Hugh's work on the
celestial hierarchy, is how Richard uses this image of the angel. Again,
though he does not use the terms seraphim, cherubim, thrones, he does
not hesitate to use their attributes in describing his own participation
in God's presence. For instance, that angel who is called a messenger
is the same angel through whom "we are illuminated for knowing
eternal things [i.e., cherubim] and inflamed with longing for them
[i.e., seraphim]." This angelic messenger also "leads the human soul to
all truth" and "imparts knowledge [*cognitionem*, i.e., cherubim] and
love [*amorem*, i.e., seraphim] of celestial and eternal things."[11] This
same angel, in whose angelic footprints (*angelica vestigia*) Richard
walks, also echoes the work of the angelic thrones, the guides of
discernment: "(he) sets an oppressed soul free from the involvements of
its concupiscence and leads it from the darkness of its ignorance."[12]
In continuing to follow angelic footprints, and while in exultation
according to the "dancing of angelic similitude," Richard discusses
the "highest orders of angels," that is, the seraphim, cherubim, and
thrones, and the "lower order of angels" without naming them but in a
way that is again reminiscent of Denys and Hugh.[13] Richard concludes
by associating the higher orders of angels with unmediated proximity

to God, face to face, and the lower orders with mediated proximity as in a mirror, thus echoing 1 Corinthians 13:12:

> But, in contrast, mountains exult as it were in resemblance to rams [earlier interpreted as the highest orders of angels] when in the ecstasies of their joy the greater ones see in pure and simple truth what the lesser [interpreted as the lower orders of angels] are scarcely able to see by a mirror and in an enigma. (xiv)

Book V, then, expands the concept of angelization to include the seraphim as the pathway to God of love, and even to include other orders of the celestial hierarchy. But it would be too convenient, and not really accurate, to claim that Richard moves from the *sapientia* tradition to the *caritas* tradition in Book V. As has been shown, both are present. A clearer interpretation of Book V is that, unlike Books I–IV which clearly do focus on the way of wisdom and knowledge through the symbol of the cherubim, Book V begins to incorporate the celestial hierarchy itself as a spiritual path. In doing so, the hierarchy, as it incorporates the ways of love, knowledge, discernment, and other angelic "footprints," assimilates a fuller, mandelic, and circular path which manifests (but in our language, does not speak directly of) Christ as its center. Richard moves from a detailed discussion of the way of knowledge to an *exemplum* of his own personal participation, in so doing laboring over (Bezeleel) and instructing on (Aaron) the weave of silence surrounding God's Word. At rest (Moses) he breathes God's presence; at rest we hear and at peace we act.

Our own best act is charity. It would be tempting to claim that Richard's final account in Book V shifts from tropology based on wisdom to anagogy based on wisdom, love, and discernment. This is in part true. But only in part; Richard says, "the consummation [i.e., of anagogy] of virtues [i.e., of tropology] is charity." This charity in the soul is enkindled or "rises up like smoke from the desert"[14] through affection in longing for the "**celestial** bridegroom."[15] But this charity for "you," the you of "the ark of sanctification for you," is not named by the cherubim of knowledge. It is named by the bridegroom of the Passion, not by the resurrected celestial bridegroom. Richard's center is celestial. Bonaventure's center will be the Passion. Charity arises from both. But for reasons elucidated in chapter 5 of this work, Richard will not name the center. He will name that *experience* "charity." Your own experience of participation in God as charity awaits you outside the instruction of Richard's teaching or of this book. It awaits God's "speaking" to you, it awaits the grace of your contemplation, it awaits your own experience of the presence of God.

In summary, in Book V of *De arca mystica*, Richard of St. Victor continues the process of angelization in the context of apophatic Christology. The process of angelization, however, takes place in the fullest range of the angelic hierarchy; the contemplative/active pursues and participates in the wisdom of love, knowledge, discernment, protection, and message, each in its turn symbolized by an angelic order and each in its turn reflecting the wisdom of the other orders. Book V is Richard of St. Victor's own personal experience upon the ark and between the two cherubim; it is the grace of contemplation for Richard. Richard's invitation is for you to likewise experience. On the ark, between the cherubim, safely, love and mind meet in shadow.

In privileged moments, we receive the gift of sight. Then we know: we are *with* God.[16] Beyond Richard's teaching for the weaving of the ark and cherubim in the heart, there is still your own personal experience, your own vision of God, your own touching, thinking, reason, meditation, contemplation, even ecstasy beyond symbol.

B. HUGH AND RICHARD OF ST. VICTOR:
MASTER AND STUDENT

Historia est rerum gestarum narratio, quae in prima significatione litterae continetur; allegoria est cum per id quod
factum dicitur, aliquid aliud factum sive in praeterito sive in
praesenti, sive in futuro significatur; tropologia est cum per
id quod factum dicitur, aliquid faciendum esse significatur.
Hugh of St. Victor, *De sacramentis Christiannae fidei*,
Prol. IV

Historia est rerum gestarum narratio que in prima significatione littere continetur. Allegoria est cum per id quod factum
dicitur, aliud factum sive in preterito, sive in presenti, sive in
futuro significatur. Tropologia est cum per id quod factum
legimus, quid nobis sit faciendum agnoscimus.
Richard of St. Victor, *Liber exceptionum*, II.III

These two quotations connote the obvious influence of the teachings
of Hugh of St. Victor on his student, Richard. Scholars have argued
for many years over the exact nature of that influence, and of their
relationship. This postscript will attempt to sort out some of those
arguments.

A very informative and valuable study could be made comparing
Hugh's *Didascalicon* and *De Sacramentis* with Richard's *De arca
mystica*. This could be done not only for the obvious exegetical
foundation to Richard's work in the *Didascalicon* and equally important foundational work on symbol and the work of restoration
in *De Sacramentis*, but, I believe, for the way that Richard takes
these foundational teachings and expands them toward their logical
spiritual conclusion; spirituality, for Richard, of course, being the near
equivalent of tropology. I will give two examples.

In *Didascalicon* VI.V, in a section on tropology, Hugh says:

By contemplating what God has made we realize what we ourselves
ought to do. Every nature tells of God; every nature teaches man; every nature reproduces its essential form, and nothing in the universe
is infecund [*et nihil in universitate infecundum est*]. (Translation by
J. Taylor)

Richard's own instruction in *De arca mystica* is a teaching on "contemplating what God has made." It teaches that every nature tells

us of and manifests God. *De arca mystica*, thus grounded in Hugh's earlier work, teaches contemplation so that we might know what "we ourselves ought to do."

In *De Sacramentis*, Prol. VI, in a section on the relation of all arts to divine wisdom and on the relation of words to things, Hugh says:

> Besides these, there is above all that divine science to which the Divine Scripture leads, whether in allegory or in tropology; one division of this which is in allegory, teaches right faith, the other, which is in tropology, teaches good work. In these consist knowledge of truth and love of virtue; and this is the true restoration of man. (Translation by R. J. Deferrari)

De arca mystica, a tropological interpretation, teaches good work arising from the knowledge of truth and the love of virtue. In these things Richard takes up the human effort side of the restoration of humanity to which Hugh refers. In both these quotes Hugh points the way along a path which Richard follows even to a point beyond Hugh. Between outright plagiarism, suggested by the quotations at the beginning of this appendix, and the acceptance of a task by Richard to find what humanity ought to do towards its own restoration, a task defined and hinted at by Hugh above, we begin to glimpse the complex relation between master and student. The following survey looks at attempts by earlier scholars to decipher that relationship.

The influence on Richard of Hugh's work with Denys the Areopagite's *Celestial Hierarchy* is given below only briefly. Chapter 2 of this book deals with that subject in more detail.

J. Châtillon supports de Toulouse on the question of whether Richard actually knew or studied with Hugh. De Toulouse claims (*Liber antiquitatum, PL*, 196, p. ix) that Richard arrived at St. Victor before Hugh's death (1141) and therefore would have been a disciple of Hugh and would have followed his lessons (*magistri Hugonis de Sancto Victore dicti discipulus sub ejus magisterio studiis incubuit*). This point is contested by C. Ottaviano (*Riccardo di S. Vittore*, p. 414), who believes that nothing in Richard's writings permits us to believe that he had a personal, direct knowledge of Hugh. Châtillon does not find this argument convincing, noting that in any case Richard *a professé une grande admiration pour son illustre prédécesseur et qu'il a profondément subi son influence* (Châtillon, "Richard de Saint-Victor" in *Dictionnaire de spiritualité* 13:594).

C. Kirchberger sides with Ottaviano. She claims that Richard entered the Abbey of St. Victor after 1141, and concludes that, "It was formerly thought that he knew Hugh as master, but this appears unlikely and his discipleship must have been one of study, imbibing the master's spirit" (C. Kirchberger, trans., *Richard of St. Victor: Selected Writings on Contemplation*, p. 15).

Finally, on this point, G. Dumeige takes what is probably the best course. Noting that Richard calls Hugh "the primary theologian of our time" but never calls him master and that many of Richard's literal citations of Hugh could have been copied in the cloister, Dumeige concludes that the evidence is inconclusive. On whether Richard heard Hugh's teaching orally or whether he read his texts, Dumeige says flatly, "*Rien ne permet de le dire.*" He concludes that Hugh's influence on Richard remains in any case "considerable" (Dumeige, *Richard de Saint-Vidtor et l'idée chrétienne de l'amour*, p. 166).

Richard's works contain only two laudatory mentions of Hugh, one of which does not name him but praises him then quotes him: *vel certe sicut praecipuo illi nostri temporis theologo placuit, qui eam in haec verba definivit* (*De arca mystica*, I.iv, 67D). The second quotation names him parenthetically as the greatest theologian of the day: "*magistrum Hugonem loquor*" (*De Spiritu Blasphemiae*, 1189B).

On Hugh as an exegete, later influencing the exegetical principles of Richard, J. Châtillon, "La Bible dans les écoles du XIIe siècle," pp. 178–83, shows that Richard's biblical work is inspired by Hugh. Hugh's *Didascalicon*, edited, translated, and with fine notes by Jerome Taylor, and *De Sacramentis* are also of formative importance: cf., G. Paré et al., *La renaissance du XIIe siècle: les écoles et l'enseignement*, pp. 21–265, which offers a fine comparison of these two works, and Richard's *Liber exceptionum* edited by J. Châtillon. In addition, of particular importance for exegetical principles, symbolic theology, and contemplation are Hugh's three "ark" treatises, especially *De arca Noe* and *Libellus de formatione arche*. On the latter, especially, see P. Sicard's recent work, *Diagrammes médiévaux et exégèse visuelle, le "Libellus de formatione arche" de Hugues de Saint-Victor*.

J. Leclercq argues for the deep influence of Hugh on Richard, not from a historical standpoint, but on the basis of finding philosophical and metaphysical similarities, including the fact that neither separate the natural from the supernatural order, that both find continuity between intellectual life and love of God, and that for both the object of contemplation is truth: cf., J. Leclercq et al., *La spiritualité de moyen age*, pp. 293–94.

E. Cousins notes the general influence of Hugh on Richard based on their mutual twelfth-century environment in "The Notion of the Person," pp. 65–67. G. Zinn, in *"De Gradibus Ascensionum*: The Stages of Contemplative Assent," pp. 61–67, delineates the exegetical, theological, and contemplative elements in Hugh which are followed by Richard. Zinn also points out Hugh's distinction between mundane and divine theology (*mundana theologia, divina theologia*) and the *simulacra* of these two theologies later adapted by Richard in G. Zinn, "Book and Word," p. 150.

On the influence of Denys the Areopagite on Richard through the work of Hugh, primarily via Hugh's *Commentariorum hierarchiam coelestem S. Dionyssi Areopagite*, see G. Ladner, "Medieval and Modern Understanding of Symbolism," pp. 224–25; G. Dumeige, "Richard de Saint-Victor," in *Dictionnaire de spiritualité* 3:324–29; B. McGinn, *Foundations of Mysticism*, 157–85; J. Leclercq, "Influence and Non-influence of Dionysius in the Western Middle Ages," pp. 25–32; H. F. Dondaine, *Le Corpus Dionysien de l'université de Paris*; R. Mortley, *From Word to Silence*, pp. 221–41; B. McGinn, "Pseudo-Dionysius and the Early Cistercians," in *One Yet Two*, pp. 201–41; D. Moran, "Eriugena's Influence on Later Medieval Philosophy," in *Philosophy of John Scottus Eriugena*, pp. 272–76.

For specific aspects of Hugh's commentary on Denys' *Celestial Hierarchy*, see R. Roques, "Connaissance de Dieu et théologie symbolique d'aprés l' *In hierarchiam coelestem Sancti Dionysii*," in *Structures théologiques*, pp. 294–364; J. Châtillon, "Hugues de Saint-Victor critique de Jean Scot," in *Jean Scot Erigène et l'histoire de la philosophie*, pp. 415–31; R. Baron, in *Etudes sur Hugues de Saint-Victor*, "Le Commentaire de la *Hiérarchie Céleste* par Hugues de Saint-Victor," pp. 133–216.

I make a final comment on the influence of Hugh on Richard, through Hugh's commentary on Denys, by noting a kind of "plagiarism" similar to that exhibited in the two quotations at the beginning of this appendix. Because Richard rarely cites anyone, J. Châtillon points out the significance of Richard's rare use of Denys by name: cf. Richard's *In Apocalypsim* (*PL*, 196, cols. 687a, 688ad, 689c, 759a). Châtillon, in *DS*, p. 604, also speculates that Richard comes to know

Denys through Hugh's *Commentariorum hierarchiam coelestem*, since Richard had reproduced a rather larger section of Hugh's text in the same *In Apocalypsim* (see *In Apoc.* I.1, 687ac, citing Hugh from *PL*, 175, 941cd). It is thus apparent that at the very least Richard was a careful, admiring, and enthusiastic student of the master. Richard, we can conclude, was one of the delightful fragrances of the Hugonian flower.

TABLE 1. SIX KINDS OF CONTEMPLATION IN *DE ARCA MYSTICA*

	First	Second	Third	Fourth	Fifth	Sixth
Symbol	Ark				Cherubim	
	Wood	Gilding	Crown	Propitiatory	1st Cherubim	2d Cherubim
	wood		wood and gold		gold	
Location in *De arca.*	II.i-II.vi	II.vii-II.xi	II.xii-II.xxvii	III	IV	IV
Creator/ Creature	natural world (mundana theologia)			soul (psychology)	transcendent (divina theologia)	
	created things (rebus creatis)				uncreated and invisible things	
	visible and created things		invisible and created things			
	human effort (Bezeleel)			human effort & divine grace (Aaron)	divine grace only— ex divina revelatione (Moses)	
Grade (I.vi)	in imagination and according to imagination	in imagination according to reason	in reason according to reason	in reason and according to reason	above, but not contrary to reason	above reason and seemingly contrary to reason

TABLE 1. *(Continued)*

	First	Second	Third	Fourth	Fifth	Sixth
Object (I.vi)	the form and image of visible things	the rational principle of visible things	contemplation of invisible things through the similitude of visible things	the invisible things of ourselves and the spirit of celestial souls	the unity of that highest and simple divine essence	the Trinity of persons
Character of: (I.viii)	to cling to wonder of visible things	to pursue rational principle of visible things	to rise from visible to invisible things	to gather invisible things from visible things	to allow reason into understanding of intellectible things	to transcend reasoning in the understanding of intellectible things
Level/Aspect (I.vii)	in imagination, directed toward sensible things		in reason, applied to intelligible things		in understanding, directed to intellectible things	
Wings (I.x)	1st pair of wings: you are an earthly animal, and in no way a heavenly one		2d pair of wings: you are a heavenly animal and have given birth to a heavenly body		3d pair of wings: to fly up to the secrets of the third heaven and the hidden things of divinity	
Eyes (III.ix, IV.xxi)	eye of flesh		eye of reason/intellectual eye	eye of understanding	seeing by means of ecstasy of mind	eye of faith from divine showings

TABLE 1. *(Continued)*

	First	Second	Third	Fourth	Fifth	Sixth
Heavens (III.viii)	imaginative heaven/imagination		rational heaven/reason		intellectual heaven/understanding	
Flight of: (I.v)	in every contemplation the mode (defined according to flight) may vary accordingly: random—goes out and comes back with marvelous quickness circular—turns in a circle, suddenly and often repeating the same circle hovering—immobilize with tremulous, rapidly vibrating wings; hovering motionless in motion					
Mind of: (V.ii–xvi)	in every contemplation the mode (defined according to mind) may vary according to: dilatio mentis—expansion, broadening of the mind sublevatio mentis—raising up of the mind alienatio mentis—alienation or ecstasy of mind excessus mentis					
Nature of Spirit	none		rational but created spirit		divine and uncreated Spirit	
Trinity (IV.xx)	none		image-Trinity		divine Trinity	
Cherubim as Symbol	not applicable				allows a rational likeness	passes beyond the property of likeness
					we consider ourselves like our Creator	we consider ourselves unlike our Creator

TABLE 2. THINKING, MEDITATION, CONTEMPLATION IN *DE ARCA MYSTICA*

	Thinking (Cogitatio)	Meditation (Meditatio)	Contemplation (Contemplatio)
Definition	improvident looking about of a soul inclined to wandering	prudent gaze of the soul ardently occupied in search for truth	free, more insightful gaze of the mind hovering with awe in the visible showings of wisdom
Property	turns aside here and there with a rambling walk	always aims to higher things	clings with wonder to manifestations of joy
Path and Mode	wanders without arriving, crawls	presses forward to the end, marches/runs	circles impulsively with quickness, flies around, "hovers"
Labor and Fruit	without labor and fruit	labor with fruit	without labor but with fruit
Mode of Gaze	strays away	investigation	wonder
Grade	from imagination	from reason	from understanding
Object is:	grasped by imagination	grasped by imagination and reason	grasped by imagination and reason, perceived by understanding (contemplation diffuses itself to innumerable things under one ray of vision— contemplatio sub uno visionis radio ad innumera se diffundit)
	All differ in mode and grade but have the same object. Everything subject to a lesser sense is also necessarily subject to a higher sense. Thus meditation encompasses thinking and contemplation encompasses thinking and meditation.		

NOTES

PROLOGUE

1. *De arca* II.viii, 86B; 184. (On the style of citations for Richard's *De arca mystica*, see "Editions, Translations, Citations, and Title" in the Introduction.) Cf. Ps. 35:7, "iudicia tua abyssus multa"; Richard bases his discussion of working in deep waters and seeing marvelous things at great depths on this passage.

2. *De arca* I.i, 63B; 151. Literally, "the narration of our little candle-light," or "little lamplight" (lucubratiunculae nostrae expositione).

3. *De arca* IV.vi, 140D; 267.

4. Ibid.

5. *De arca* I.i, 63D; 151.

INTRODUCTION

1. In the course of writing, and for reasons elaborated in the book itself, it became apparent that it would be more appropriate to shift the order of the final three chapters just slightly. Thus Chapter 4 is informed by the first cherubim, Chapter 5 by the propitiatory, and Chapter 6 by the second cherubim (rather than propitiatory, first cherubim, second cherubim, as in Richard).

2. Justification, description, and philosophy for a methodology of synthesis and context which would integrate "objective" research with experience and participation and which are important as "background noise" for this book include the following sources. The sources are important for the overall "flavor", but since this is not a book on methodology per se, and more important, since Richard of St. Victor's own methodology is not unlike that of these contemporary sources, these sources will be mentioned only here and assumed throughout the remainder of this work. Beyond these works, the emphasis is on the hermeneutics of the presence of God (or hermeneutics of participation) and integrative methodology of Richard of St. Victor. Cf. John D. Caputo, *Radical Hermeneutics: Repetition, Deconstruction, and the Hermeneutic Project* (Bloomington:

Indiana University Press, 1987); Ernst Cassirer, *Philosophy of Symbolic Forms*, 3 vols., trans. Ralph Manheim (New Haven: Yale University Press, 1953); Hans-Georg Gadamer, *Truth and Method*, 2d rev. ed., trans. Joel Weinsheimer and Donald G. Marshall (New York: Cross-road, 1989); Hans-Georg Gadamer, *Philosophical Hermeneutics*, trans. David E. Linge (Berkeley: University of California Press, 1976); Martin Heidegger, *Basic Writings*, ed. David Farrell Krell (New York: Harper & Row, 1977); Martin Heidegger, *On The Way to Language*, trans. Peter D. Hertz (New York: Harper & Row, 1971); Martin Heidegger, *Poetry, Language, Thought*, trans. Albert Hofstadter (New York: Harper & Row, 1971); Erazim Kohák, *The Embers and the Stars: A Philosophical Inquiry into the Moral Sense of Nature* (Chicago: University of Chicago Press, 1984); Sallie McFague, *Metaphorical Theology: Models of God in Religious Language* (London: SCM Press, 1983); Paul Ricoeur, *Hermeneutics and the Human Sciences*, ed. and trans. John B. Thompson (Cambridge: Cambridge University Press, 1981); Paul Ricoeur, *The Rule of Metaphor*, trans. Robert Czerny et al. (Toronto: University of Toronto Press, 1977); Philip Sheldrake, *Spirituality and History: Questions of Interpretation and Method* (New York: Crossroad, 1992).

3. Judith M. Bennett, "Medievalism and Feminism," *Speculum* 68, 2 (April 1993): 322, citing E. N. Johnson, "American Mediaevalists Today," *Speculum* 28 (1953): 844, and Lee Patterson, "On the Margin: Postmodernism, Ironic History, and Medieval Studies," *Speculum* 65 (1990): 107. In making an explicit case for a postmodern, antipositivist methodology for feminist medieval studies, Bennett also formulates an implicit methodology for the study of spirituality.

4. I have found the metaphor of "weaving" to be of equal value to that of "construction" and will use it often. I believe that Richard and the Victorines would have no objection.

5. *De arca* I.iv, 67D; 157. "Contemplatio est libera mentis perspicacia in sapientiae spectacula cum admiratione suspensa. Contemplatio est per-spicax et liber animi contuitus in res perspiciendas usquequaque diffusus."

6. For a summary of Richard's ideas on contemplation, see Richard of St. Victor, *Richard of St. Victor: Selected Writings on Contemplation*, trans. Clare Kirchberger (London: Faber and Faber, 1957), pp. 37–47. For an excellent summary of contemplation, including sources for critical biographies on the subject, see Gervais Dumeige, *Richard de Saint-Victor et l'idée chrétienne de l'amour* (Paris: Presses Universitaires de France, 1952), p. 7, n. 2. For a bioliography of studies on the six kinds of contemplation in Richard, see Jean Châtillon, "Les trois modes de la contemplation selon Richard de Saint-Victor," *Bulletin de littérature ecclésiastique* 41. (1940), p. 3, n. 2. For a thorough bibliography of studies on Richard's "modes" and "kinds" of contemplation, see Gaston

Salet, "Les chemins de Dieu d'apres Richard de Saint-Victor," in *L'homme devant Dieu: Mélanges offerts au Père Henri de Lubac* (Paris: Aubier, 1963), p. 83, n.69. For a good overview of "kinds" of contemplation, see J. A. Robilliard, "Les six genres de contemplation chez Richard de Saint-Victor et leur origine platonicienne," in *Revue des sciences philosophiques et théologiques* 28 (1939), pp. 229–33. For a bibliography of works giving analysis of six "kinds" of contemplation, objects of contemplation of each, and faculties for perceiving these objects, see Grover Zinn, "Personification Allegory and Visions of Light in Richard of St. Victor's Teaching on Contemplation," in *University of Toronto Quarterly* 46 (1977), p. 213, n.74. For a bibliography on studies of Victorine contemplation, see Richard of St. Victor, *Richard of St. Victor: The Twelve Patriarchs, the Mystical Ark, Book Three of the Trinity*, trans. Grover Zinn (New York: Paulist Press, 1979), p. 24, n.17.

7. *De arca* I.v, 69A; 159. "Videre licet alia quomodo tremulis alis saepeque reverberatis se in uno eodemque loco diutius suspendunt, et mobili se agitatione quasi immobiliter figunt."

8. Ewert H. Cousins, *Bonaventure and the Coincidence of Opposites* (Chicago: Franciscan Herald Press, 1978), pp. 18–20. Emphasis mine. Richard, of course, does not himself employ the term *coincidentia oppositorum*. But, as did Bonaventure after him, he does utilize its methodology implicitly without explicitly naming the later Cusanian term.

9. As, for instance, Moses or Aaron or Bezeleel. See *Appendices*.

10. *De arca* IV.xx, 163A; 299. "sapientia voci humanae incorporatur."

11. *De arca* I.i, 63C; 151. "Quid juxta allegoricum sensum haec arca mystice designet, vel quomodo Christum significet, a doctoribus fuit jam ante nos dictum et a perspicacioribus pertractatum. Nec idcirco tamen temeritatis incuriam incurrere nos suspicamur, si aliud in eamdem adhuc materiam moraliter loquamur."

12. *Biblia sacra iuxta latinam vulgatam versionem*, ed. B. Fischer et al., 3d edition (Stuttgart: Deutsche Bibelgesellschaft, 1983).

13. Cf. *The Hexaglot Bible of the Old and New Testaments*, vol. 1, ed. E. R. de Levante (New York: Funk and Wagnalls, 1901), pp. 228–29.

14. On the Vulgate edition available to Richard, see Raphael Loewe, "The Medieval History of the Latin Vulgate," in *The Cambridge History of The Bible: The West From the Fathers to the Reformation*, ed. G. W. H. Lampe (Cambridge: Cambridge University Press, 1969), pp. 102–54.

15. See Eduardo C. Aug. Riehm, *De natura et notione symbolica cheruborum* (Basileae et Ludoviciburgi, 1864), p. 13.

16. Richard of St. Victor, *Richard of St. Victor: The Twelve Patriarchs, the Mystical Ark, Book Three of the Trinity*, trans. Grover A. Zinn (New York: Paulist Press, 1979), pp. 149–343.

17. Richard of St. Victor, *Richard of St. Victor: Selected Writings on Contemplation*, trans. Clare Kirchberger (London: Faber and Faber, 1957), pp. 131–212.

18. Jean Châtillon notes that the titles of Richard's works in Migne were often intended to make known the doctrinal content of the treatises, but that this content was often misconstrued. Châtillon prefers titles that take into account the "internal significance" over the ancient manuscript tradition. The title *De arca mystica* seems best to include both internal criteria and the tradition. See Jean Châtillon, "Richard de Saint-Victor," pp. 593–654, *Dictionnaire de spiritualité: ascétique et mystique, doctrine et histoire* (Paris, 1988), 13: 599.

CHAPTER 1

1. *De arca* I.i, 63C; 151. See section on "What This Book Is Not," in Introduction for Latin citation of this text.

2. *De arca* I.i, 63D; 151. "Nolite negligenter attendere quid *sibi* velit quod dicitur arca sanctificationis . . . scimus quod quicunque tetigerit eam sanctificabitur." Emphasis is mine.

3. *De arca* IV.xiv, 151C; 283. Continuing in this passage, Richard adds that the allegorical sense reminds us what the "Beloved" has done for us and the anagogical sense proposes his plans for the future: "*moraliter* nos docens quid dilectus noster facere nos velit, *allegoriter* admonens quid pro nobis per semetipsum facerit, *anagogice* propones quid adhuc de nobis facere disponit." Emphasis mine.

4. For a discussion of the relation between Richard and Hugh of St. Victor (1096–1141), see Appendix B.

5. *Hugh of St. Victor on the Sacraments of the Christian Faith (De Sacramentis)*, trans. Roy J. Deferrari (Cambridge, Mass.: Medieval Academy of America, 1951), Prologue, II, p. 3. "Materia divinarum Scripturarum omnium, sunt opera restaurationis humanae. Duo enim sunt opera in quibus universa continentur quae facta sunt. Primum est opus conditionis. Secundum est opus restaurationis. Opus conditionis est quo factum est, ut essent quae non erant. Opus restaurationis est quo factum est ut melius essent quae perierant." *PL*, 176, col. 183a.

6. For a discussion of Hugh's incorporation of history into the process of restoration, see Grover A. Zinn, "History and Contemplation. The Dimensions of the Restoration of Man in Two Treatises on the Ark of Noah by Hugh of St. Victor" (Ph.D. diss., Duke University, 1969).

7. Cf. *De Sacramentis*, *PL*, 176, 183B: "Opus restaurationis est incarnatio Verbi cum omnibus sacramentis suis." Hugh goes on to say

that the Incarnation of the Word with all its sacraments include those sacraments which have proceeded from the beginning of creation in time ("sive iis quae praecesserunt ab initio saeculi") as well as those which extend even to the end of the world ("ad finem mundi"). Thus while the Incarnation of the Word can be considered as the final step in the process of restoration, the work of restoration has been proceeding through the sacraments since the Fall.

8. *De arca* I.i, 64C; 152. "Multum vellem scire quae sit haec arca quae possit sanctificare accedentes. . . . De sapientia . . . non dubito quin ipsa sit quae vincit malitiam (Sap. vii). Scio nihilominus quia quicunque sanati sunt ab initio per sapientiam sanati sunt (Sap. ix)."

9. *De arca* I.i, 65B; 152. "Per veritatis sane contemplationem homo et eruditur ad justitiam et consummatur ad gloriam."

10. See Henri de Lubac, *Exégèse médiévale: Les quatre sens de l'Ecriture* (Paris: Aubier, 1954–64), vol. 2, p. 363, n.13, on the tradition of referring to cherubim as fullness of Wisdom.

11. For overview and introduction issues in Victorine exegesis, see Beryl Smalley, *The Study of the Bible in the Middle Ages* (Notre Dame: University of Notre Dame Press, 1978), pp. 83–195; Jean Châtillon, "La Bible dans les écoles du XIIe siècle," in *Le moyen age et la Bible* (Paris: Beauchesne, 1984), pp. 177–97; René Roques, *Structures théologique: de la gnose à Richard de Saint-Victor* (Paris: Presses Universitaires de France, 1962), pp. 374–91; Clare Kirchberger, trans., *Richard of Saint-Victor: Selected Writings on Contemplation* (London: Faber and Faber, 1957), pp. 31–36; Jean Châtillon, "Richard de Saint-Victor," in *Dictionnaire de spiritualité: ascétique et mystique, doctrine et histoire* (Paris, 1988), 13: 593–654 (hereafter DS 13); *Richard de Saint-Victor: sermons et opuscules spirituels inédits*, vol. 1, *L'édit d'Alexandre ou les trois processions*, Latin text, intro., notes by Jean Châtillon and William-Joseph Tulloch, French trans. by Joseph Barthélmy (Paris: Desclée de Brouwer, 1949), pp. xliv–liii. On exegesis in Andrew of St. Victor, student of Hugh and later contemporary of Richard, see Rainer Berndt, *André de Saint-Victor, exégète et théologien*, Bibliotheca Victorina II (Turnhout: Brepols, 1991). For discussion of the theory of multiple meaning in Victorine exegesis, see G. Paré, A. Bunet, P. Tremblay, *La renaissance du XIIe siècle: les écoles et l'enseignement* (Paris: Vrin, 1933), p. 221; Gervais Dumeige, *Richard de Saint-Victor et l'idée chrétienne de l'amour* (Paris, 1952), p. 24; R. Roques, "Une encyclopédie du savoir médiévale: le *Liber exceptionum* de Richard de Saint-Victor," in *Structures théologiques*, p. 379, n.3. On the influence of Jewish exegesis on twelfth-century and Victorine exegesis, see J. W. M. Van Zwieten, "Jewish Exegesis within Christian Bounds: Richard of St. Victor's *De Emmanuele* and Victorine

Hermeneutics," *Bijdragen* 48 (1987): 327–35; Grover A. Zinn, "History and Interpretation: 'Hebrew Truth,' Judaism, and the Victorine Exegetical Tradition," in *Jews and Christians: Exploring the Past, Present, and Future*, ed. James H. Charlesworth (New York: Crossroad, 1990), pp. 100–123.

12. Gervais Dumeige, *Richard de Saint-Victor et l'idée chrétienne de l'amour* (Paris: Presses Universitaires de France, 1952), p. 164. The "middle way" in Victorine study is also expressed by other scholars. Cf. G. Pare et al., *La Renaissance du XIIe siécle*, p. 213. R. Roques, *Structures théologiques*, p. 375, claims that in ancient and medieval theology, exegesis is not auxiliary to theology, but theology itself. J. Châtillon, *Richard de Saint-Victor: sermons et opuscules spirituels Inédits*, pp. xlvi–l; Robert Javelet, "La dignité de l'homme dans la pensée du XIIe siècle," in *De dignitate hominis: festschrift für Carlos- Josaphat Pinto de Oliveira*, ed. Holderegger, Imbach, de Miguel (Fribourg: Institut de Théologie Moral de l'Université de Fribourg, 1987), p. 40, claims that the moral Christian equals the spiritual Christian. Châtillon also points out the "middle way" in another context, that of the fertile relation between contemplation and action. For Richard contemplation is, of course, important, but he never neglects moral action (the pragmatic intent of tropological exegesis) which procures the fruit of contemplation. Cf. Jean Châtillon, "Contemplation, action et prédication d'après un sermon inédit de Richard de Saint-Victor en l'honneur de saint Grégoire-le-Grand," in *L'homme devant Dieu: mélanges offerts au Père Henri de Lubac* (Paris: Aubier, 1963), pp. 96–98. Caroline Walker Bynum, "Spirituality of the Regular Canons in the Twelfth Century," *Jesus as Mother: Studies in the Spirituality of the High Middle Ages* (Berkeley: University of California Press, 1982), pp. 22–58, distinguishes canons from monks by focusing on "works of practical spiritual advice" (p. 35), that is, works on the soul's spiritual and moral progress. Her conclusion, that "canonical authors see canons as teachers and learners, whereas monastic authors see monks only as learners . . . a canon's sense of responsibility is to edify his fellow men both by what he says and by what he does" (p. 36), has important implications for Richard's own tropology in which he attempts to edify by saying and doing. Richard's language thus links the moral education offered by word to that offered by example and emphasizes both. This linking of word and deed is an example of the Victorine linking of tropological exegesis (word) and spirituality (in this case, deed). On the distinction of spirituality from exegesis and theology in the twelfth century, see Henri de Lubac, *Exégèse médiévale*, vol. 2, pp. 423–29, 478–88. Châtillon, *DS* 13: 628–46, suggests reading B. Smalley and H. de Lubac on Richard's exegesis, and L. Ott, A.-M. Ethier, G. Salet, and J. Ribaillier on Richard's

theology, then goes on to discuss the difficulty of separating exegesis and theology from his subject, spirituality. Elsewhere, Châtillon, *DS* 13: 601, 604, 612, shows the spiritual life to be intimately related to the moral life. As all these scholars have tried to show, and as the concept of hovering tries to depict, the Victorines are not trying to make "categorical" sense, but rather an intuitive, symbolic, hovering sense, that is, a sense that is epistemologically both/and rather than either/or.

13. Châtillon, *DS* 13: 604. "Il est bien difficile, on l'a dit, d'établir une frontiére rigoureuse entre les écrits exégétiques et les écrits théologiques de Richard."

14. Châtillon, *DS* 13: 612.

15. Smalley, *The Study of the Bible*, pp. 83–111 on Victorines, pp. 106–11 on Richard.

16. Ibid., pp. 107–10.

17. I emphasize "tended" because I do not believe that the tendency was her overall intent.

18. Another problem with the too-neat division between "spiritual" and "literal" exegetes is that the categories themselves are often ambiguous. See Grover A. Zinn, "History and Interpretation," pp. 115–17, who in the midst of a discussion of a disagreement between Richard and Andrew on the exegesis of a passage in Isaiah 7–8 points out that the conflict emerges as a result of two differing conceptions of literal exegesis.

19. Smalley, *Study of the Bible*, p. 107. Châtillon, *DS* 13: 628, has this to say about Richard's style: "What is more, and this is another difficulty, the vocabulary of Richard is of a great elasticity. Different words can designate a single reality, and a single word can correspond to dissimilar objects. Richard enlarges or restricts the terms that he employs, according to the circumstances or according to the requirements of his rhetoric. This is, however, a manner of style of which he is perfectly conscious: 'The penury of words forces us now to enlarge, now to restrict their signification according to the necessity of the exegesis.' (*Benj. maj.* III, 18, col. 127b)."

20. Châtillon, *Sermons et opuscules spirituels*, p. xlvii.

21. Richard of St. Victor, *Liber. except.*, P.I,1.II,3, *PL*, 177, 205B. "Troplogia est cum per id quod factum legimus, quid nobis sit faciendum agnoscimus." Quoted in Châtillon, *Sermons et opuscules spirituels*, p. xlvii, note 2 from the Migne edition before Châtillon's later critical edition.

22. Châtillon, *Sermons et opuscules spirituels*, pp. xlviii–l. "Richard a trouvé dans le symbolisme biblique et liturgique, c'est-à-dire dans la tropologie, cette méthode d'investigation intérieure et ces moyens d'expression dont il ne pouvait se passer. . . . C'est le rôle de la tropologie

158 / NOTES TO PAGES 6–7

que de ramener au jour et de projeter hors de la conscience une part au moins de ces complexes intérieurs que chaque image biblique est susceptible d'évoquer. . . . Pour juger équitablement de l'exégèse tropologique de Richard, il faut se souvenir que ce n'est point ici un philologue ou un critique qui explique un texte, mais un spirituel qui cherche à connaître son âme ou celle des autres et veut découvrir par quels chemins il peut approcher de son Dieu."

23. Châtillon's distinction between "spiritual" and "mundane" is, I think, telling. These *are* Victorine categories, but only within a field, such as philosophy or theology. As terms of cross-reference between fields, such as exegesis and theology, or literal and tropological, or identity and participation, they are irrelevant and have no meaning. Thus it would make no sense for a Victorine to say "mundane" literal sense and "spiritual" tropology, or "mundane" exegesis and "spiritual" theology. Here, I believe, Châtillon affixes some of his own categories to Richard. On *mundana scriptura* and *divina scriptura* see *Liber except.* I,2.

24. Cf. de Lubac, *Exégèse médiévale*, vol. 1, pp. 167–68.

25. Inconsistent logic and contradictory schemata seem not to bother the twelfth century; Hugh and Richard are no exceptions. They are eclectic in drawing from the tradition, and intent on making the point at hand.

26. *Liber except.*, P.1, 1.II, c.iii. Cited in de Lubac, vol. 1, p. 165.

27. From *Adnotatio mystica in psalmum CXXXIV*, cited in de Lubac, vol. 1, p. 166. "Post historiam cognitam debemus quarere moralitatem; similiter post istam, per allegoriae cognitionem proficimus ad anagogen."

28. *De arca* IV.xiv, 151C–D; 283. "Et saepe fit ut una eademque Scriptura, dum multipliciter exponitur, multa nobis in unum loquatur, moraliter nos docens quid dilectus noster facere nos velit, allegoriter admonens quid pro nobis per semetipsum fecerit, anagogice proponens quid adhuc de nobis facere disponit." Note the hovering nature of "expounded multiply says many things to us in one thing." I take *fecerit* as future perfect indicative rather than perfect subjunctive.

29. This work, "Some Allegories of the Tabernacle of the Covenant," is in Migne, 196, following *De arca mystica*, pp. 191D–202B. See *Richard of St. Victor*, trans. Zinn, pp. 344–70, for English.

30. *Nonnullae allegoriae tabernaculi foederis*, PL, 199D; 364–65. "Per opus ligneum intelligimus sensum historicum; per labium tropologicum, per geminam coronam allegoricum et anagogicum. . . . Quod est inter lignum et aurum, hoc est inter historicum et mysticum sensum. In Scriptura sacra primum locum tenet historia. Mystica vero intelligentia pro certo est tripertita. Troplogica tenet locum unum, allegorica medium anagogica summum." Translation by Zinn.

31. *Nonnullae, PL,* 200C,200D; 366,367. "Quid est enim tropologia nisi moralis scientia, et quid allegoria nisi mystica mysteriorum doctrina . . . In praedictis duobus quaeritur doctrina morum et mysteriorum. Ad anagogen spectat sperandorum praevidentia praemiorum."

32. Jerome Taylor gives a helpful history of the sources of the threefold and fourfold senses. The threefold understanding derives from Gregory the Great, being also taught by Jerome, Origen, and Philo. The fourfold understanding is found in Augustine, Bede, and Rhabanus Marus. See, *The Didascalicon of Hugh of St. Victor,* trans., intro., and notes by Jerome Taylor (New York: Columbia University Press, 1961), p. 219, n.1.

33. Gaston Salet has noticed the same Victorine tendency in another context. After surveying the current state of scholarship on Richard's classification of contemplation, he speculates that Richard himself may not be as interested as the scholars are to harmonize their various classifications and terminologies: "Nous ne savons pas quelle importance réelle notre auteur attachait au détail de ces classifications. En tous cas il s'est peu soucié d'établir des concordances entre les diverses manières dont il décrit les étapes de la montée vers Dieu, moins encore d'unifier les terminologies par lesquelles il les exprime." Gaston Salet, S.J., "Les chemins de Dieu d'aprés Richard de Saint-Victor," in *L'homme devant Dieu: mélanges offerts au Père Henri De Lubac* (Paris: Aubier, 1963), p. 83.

34. I believe that *Nonnullae allegoriae tabernaculi foederis* is not as intimately connected to *De arca mystica* as it might seem simply by its placement in Migne. For one thing, the different emphasis on the senses of scripture and the attendant meanings of those senses is telling:

De arca		*Nonnullae*	
sense	*meaning*	*sense*	*meaning*
literal	history, things	literal	history, things
allegory	Christ	tropology	moral knowledge
tropology	moral knowledge	allegory	hidden things
	hidden things	anagogy	rewards
	rewards		

A second hint is Richard's use of words for a category that is very important in *De arca mystica*: that of "hidden/secret things." In the passage quoted above from *Nonnullae,* the word is *mysteria,* a word used seldom in *De arca,* which employs *occultus, arcanus, secretus* with great regularity. *Nonnullae* is helpful in explicating *De arca,* but it should be used with caution. (Châtillon, *DS* 13: 616 cites *Nonnullae* as authentic but does not date it.)

35. De Lubac, *Exégèse médiévale*, vol. 1, pp. 550, 556; J. W. M. Van Zwieten, who claims that Richard's main concern is to show the interdependence of the literal and spiritual sense of prophecy, also sees the importance of order and relation in Richard. Zwieten points out that Andrew of St. Victor follows Hugh's guidelines for *lectio historica*, while Richard follows Hugh's guidelines for *sensus historicus* as a part of multiple interpretations leading to spiritual meanings. Zwieten puts it nicely: "Thus Richard's rejection of unbounded literal exegesis complimented Hugh's criticism of unfounded spiritual exegesis." See J. W. M. Van Zwieten, "Jewish Exegesis within Christian Bounds: Richard of St. Victor's *De Emmanuel* and Victorine Hermeneutics," *Bijdragen* 48 (1987): 327–35. See Châtillon, *DS* 13: 601, for discussion of how Richard often mixes theological (allegorical) with spiritual (tropological) teachings. The sequential link between *historia* and the moral life is never broken; it is always hovering.

36. J. Châtillon, "La Bible dans les écoles du XII siècle," pp. 177–97.

37. Ibid., p. 181. "C'est ce dernier sens, également, qui procurera au lecteur de l'Ecriture les instruments d'analyse, les moyens d'expression et le langage qui lui permettront de scruter les profondeurs de son âme, d'y observer les mouvements de la nature et de la grâce et de rendre compte, a lui-même et aux autres, de son expérience intérieure."

38. With regard to the interior and fecund nature of the tropological sense, R. Roques finds two kinds of tropology, one in which tropology is placed after literal and before allegorical (thereby serving as a link between the two), and a second which has a relation to the spiritual sense of scripture; it does not precede the spiritual edifice but completes it. Coming after allegory, this second kind of tropology constitutes a "subjective" aspect following the "objective" allegory. Allegory proposes *facta mystica* or *mysterium fidei*, while tropology defines the *facienda mystica* or *opera fidei* which is necessarily connected to the understanding of mystery and to the manifestation of spiritual fecundity. See R. Roques, *Structures théologiques*, pp. 382–83.

39. One way of approaching the importance of the literal as the body of tropological flight is through the work of Jean Houston. Dr. Houston has developed what she calls "sacred psychology," and finds that such psychology tends to map three major realms of experience: (1) the realm of the historic and factual (This is Me); (2) the realm of the mythic and symbolic (We Are); (3) the realm of the unitive, the source level of being (I Am). The realms of the mythic and unitive are largely what this book examines by centering on Richard's contemplative use of the angels. But the realm of the historic and factual, the realm bounded by geographical space and calendrical time, a realm structured by gender,

physical characteristics, name, local identity, profession, family, place, relationships, this realm is also important to our study because Richard makes it so. It is the realm of the body, the senses; it is the realm, for Richard, of literal exegesis. But these realms are related: the literal to the symbolic to the transcendent; the "Me" to the "We" to the "I Am." Or as Richard would translate it, the relation is equally strong between the natural world (contemplations 1 and 2), the soul (contemplations 3 and 4), and God (contemplations 5 and 6). Cf. Jean Houston, *The Hero and the Goddess: The Odyssey as Mystery and Initiation* (New York: Balantine Books, 1992), pp. 17–19.

40. All are found in Migne, volume 196. The critical edition of the *Liber exceptionum*, edited by Châtillon, is also available and is used for this book.

41. *PL*, 196, 211–22. See Châtillon, *DS* 13: 603, for a brief account of this text. In this text, along with *De templo Salomonis ad litteram* (*PL*, 223–42), which is also a literal exegesis of Solomon's temple as described in 2 Kings, and *De concordia temporum conregnantium super Judam et Israel* (PL, 241–46), Châtillon believes the editions, including Migne, have united three very distinct works.

42. *Expositio diff.*, Prologus, *PL*, 196, 211B–212B. "Rogatus ab amicis aliqua in explanationem tabernaculi scribere, timui, fateor, eorum petitioni satisfacere, ne viderer in eo ipso Patrum auctoritati derogasse. . . . Ecce quam fidenter de allegoriae sensu proponit, qui tamen litterae expositionem sub ambiguitate praemisit. Qui igitur certitudinis suae testimonium allegoricae expositioni tam fidenter dat, historicae denegat, patenter innuit, quod in illa sua expositione nec sibi ipsi satisfecerit. . . . Attendamus quam multa, quam magna, quam profunda cum omni diligentia pertractaverunt, quam multa historice, quam multa allegorice, quam multa tropologice miranda ratione exposuerunt, et tunc desinet esse mirum si alicui loco minus sufficientem expositionem reliquerunt. Non est ergo magnum, vel mirum si in uno aliquo aliquid possumus addere, quod ad majorem evidentiam, vel planiorem intelligentiam possit proficere."

43. The Vulgate text for Exodus 25:20 reads "*respiciantque se mutuo versis vultibus in propitiatorium.*" This text will be of major importance for later chapters.

44. *Expositio diff.*, caput II, *PL*, 196, 213B–C. "De cherubin dicit quod mutuo se respiciant. Corpore quidem ad exterius tabernaculum versi erant; sed versis vultibus in eam partem intendebant qua arca de sub alis eorum in medio stabat. Illi duo cherubin qui in templo Salomonis erant, ad horum absque dubio similitudinem facti fuerant. Quod itaque de illis legimus, de istis et aeque intelligimus, quod cherubin unus tangebat ala sua parietem unum, et alius ala sua tangebat parietem alium; aliis autem

alis in medio tangebant se vicissim. Sicut itaque illi de templo, sic nec isti super arcam et propitiatorium stare poterant, quia nonnisi bicubitum et semissem longetudinis arca habebat. In illis vero cherubin extensio conjunctarum alarum decem cubitos, in istis quinque cubitos tenebant. Quod igitur de istis dicitur quod essent super arcam testimonii, non sic debet intelligi quasi ipsi arcae insisterent, sed quod ipsi arcae toto corpore supereminerent."

45. In *De arca*, as we shall see, Richard "grounds" the cherubim in a number of ways: most obviously they stand (*stare*) on the ark (IV.viii); they look toward the propitiatory, thus "touching" it both by a metaphor of vision and as they draw a similitude of reason (*rationis similitudinem trahunt*), by orienting themselves back toward the fourth contemplation which is symbolized by the propitiatory (IV.xx); and they cover the ark by the shadow of their wings, thus providing cover, shelter, and divine darkness for the tropological mystery to unfold (IV.ix).

46. *PL*, 196, 527–600; see Châtillon, *DS* 13: 604, and de Lubac, *Exégèse médiévale*, vol 3, pp. 387–93 for discussions of this text.

47. In this case, primarily Gregory's mystical interpretations of the visions of Ezekiel in *Hom. in Ezechielem*.

48. *In visionem Ezechielis*, *PL*, 196, 527D.

49. To emphasize his point concerning the constructive, foundational nature of the literal, Richard employs a large number of words here having to do with building, strengthening, construction, and foundation, all within a short section of this prologue. These include *structura, firmus, statuo, apte, fundo, solidum, formo, instruo*. These are set against the images of foolishness, emptiness, uselessness, and sluggishness used to condemn those "moderns" and even some of the ancient Fathers who construct a spiritual interpretation without having established a firm foundation, that is, without having established the foundation of the literal sense. These terms include *inanis, inaniter, frivolus, subsannare, fatuitas, torpeo*.

50. *In visionem Ezechielis*, 527B.

51. Industry (*industria*) and leisure (*otium*), especially with regard to their respective relation to contemplation and action, are very loaded words, especially in the canonical environment in which Richard dwells. In *De arca*, where he begins and ends by saying he is speaking as a person at leisure to persons at leisure (*otiosi otiosis locuti summus*), Richard reverses the assessment of these words that he had given in *In visionem*. In *De arca*, industry becomes the expression of tropology, the process of construction of the ark and cherubim, which themselves arise out of contemplation or leisure. The two terms are intimately related and circular. For an excellent discussion of the relation of these terms in medieval contemplation, see

Jean Leclercq, *Otia Monastica: Etudes sur le vocabulaire de la contem-plation au moyen age*, Studia Anselmiana philosophica theologica, fasc. 51 (Rome: Orbis Catholicus, 1963). Châtillon, *DS* 13: 597, suggests that Richard's emphasis on the relation of industry and leisure may have been a forced emphasis arising out of the disastrous abbacy of Ernisius from 1162 to 1172.

52. *In visionem Ezechielis*, prologus, 527B–D. "Multis divinae Scrip-turae multo amplius dulcescunt, quando congruum in eis aliquem se-cundum litteram intellectum percipere possunt. Et tunc, ut eis videtur, spiritualis intelligentiae structura firmius statuitur quando in historici sensus solido apte fundatur. Super vacuum enim et inane quis possit solidum alliquid fundare, vel firmiter statuere? Cum enim mystici sensus ex earum congrua rerum similitudine eruantur atque formentur, quae in littera proponuntur, quomodo nos ad spiritualem intelligentiam instruat in his duntaxat locis, ubi ipsa sibi expugnat, vel nihil nisi frivolum resonat? Scandalizantur itaque saepe potius quam aedificentur, qui ejusmodi sunt, cum hujus modi Scripturarum loca incurrunt. Econtra autem antiqui Patres libenter accipiebant cum in hujus modi Scripturarum loca incider-ent, quae juxta litteram stare non poterant. Ex his namque quosdam, quae Scripturam sanctam recipiebant, sensus tamen allegoricos subsanna-bant, ex his, inquam, absurdis litterae locis compellebant ad spiritalem intelligentiam confugere, cum negare non auderent. Spiritum sanctum in quantalibet fatuitate litterae nihil inaniter scripsisse. Hinc contigisse arbitror, ut litterae expositionem in obscurioribus quibusdam locis antiqui Patres tacite praeterirent, vel paulo negligentius tracterent, qui si plenius insisterent multo perfectius procul dubio, quam aliquis ex modernis id po-tuissent. Sed nec illud tacite praetereo, quod quidam quasi ob reverentiam Patrum nolunt ab illis omissa attentare, ne videantur aliquid ultra majores praesumere. Sed inertiae suae ejusmodi velamen habentes, otio torpent et aliorum industriam in veritatis investigatione et inventione derident, subsannant, exsufflant."

B. Smalley, *Study of the Bible*, p. 108, also translates this passage. As Smalley points out, Richard is referring to Gregory the Great as one of the Fathers who sometimes fails to acknowledge the literal sense. According to Richard, Gregory finds no literal meaning to the second vision of Ezechial: "De secunda visione dicit, quod juxta litteram stare non possit." *In visionem Ezechielis*, 527D.

53. *In visionem Ezechielis*, 527D–528A.

54. Ibid., 589A–590C.

55. See F. L. Battles, "Hugo of St. Victor as a Moral Allegorist," *Church History* 18 (1949): 227–33, for discussion of "edifice" as descriptive of the spiritual edifice of the human soul. Battles focuses mainly on Origen's

influence on Hugh. On the symbols of arks and tabernacles in exegesis, see H. de Lubac, *Exégèse médiévale*, vol. 2, pp. 403–18. Though not concerned primarily with exegesis, one of the best discussions on the function of a symbol (the temple) as a metaphor for the soul can be found in Sr. Lillian Turney, "The Symbolism of the Temple in *Itinerarium in mentis deum* of Bonaventure," (Ph.D. diss. Fordham University, 1968). See also P. Sicard, *Diagrammes médiévaux et exégèse visuelle, le Libellus de formatione arche de Hugues de Saint-Victor*, Bibliotheca Victorina IV (Turnhout: Brepols, 1993), Apendix 6, pp. 269–71.

56. As does Leclercq, *Histoire de la spiritualité chrétienne* II, p. 289: "Mais Richard fait figure d'esprit plus original (than Hugh), en ce sens qu'il cite beeaucoup moins ses prédécesseurs." A more accurate assessment of Richard would probably be similar to that which F. L. Battles, "Hugh as a Moral Allegorist," p. 229, made of Hugh: "he was in no sense of the word an innovator, rather a skilled exploiter of traditional materials." However, we can at least say that Richard was "independent", and sought the proof of "personal diligence" when convincing reasons could not be found in the Fathers; see Dumeige, *L'idée chrétienne de l'amour*, p. 12.

57. The lack of citations in Richard notwithstanding, the claim that Richard read deeply in this tradition is substantiated by the obvious similarity of some of his interpretations, the outright "plagiarism" of others, and of course Richard's own statement at the beginning of *De arca* that the meaning of the ark and the cherubim had already been "articulated by learned persons and investigated by more penetrating minds before" (I.i). A bibliography of sources for tracing the possible contents of Richard of St. Victor's library can be found in S. Chase, "Into the Secret Places of Divine Incomprehensibility: The Symbol of the Cherubim in *De arca mystica* of Richard of St. Victor" (Ph.D. diss., Fordham University, 1994), Appendix C, pp. 299–302. For additional sources and influences for Richard, see the following: on the traditional exegetical interpretations of Augustine, Hugh, Gregory, Isidore, Bede, Rhabanus Maurus and the *Glossa ordinaria* that influenced Richard, see Châtillon, *DS* 13: 601–2, and Châtillon, ed., *Liber Exceptionum*, pp. 68–71, 539ff.; see J. Châtillon, *Théologie, spiritualité, et métaphysique dans l'oeuvre oratoire d'Achard de Saint Victor* (Paris: J. Vrin, 1969) on the influence of Boethius, p. 309, on the influence of Augustine, Dionysius, Eriugena, pp. 312ff., and on Richard's own citations of exegetical influence, p. 372; see Dumeige, *L'idée chrétienne de l'amour*, on the location of Richard's few citations, p. 12, on possible sources for reconstruction of the library at the abbey of St. Victor, p. 19, n.2, on pagan and Christian sources, pp. 161–62; see R. Javelet, "Sens et réalité ultime selon Richard de Saint-Victor," *Ultimate*

Reality and Meaning (1982–83), on patristic sources, pp. 224–27, and Javelet, "Thomas Gallus ou les ecritures dans une dialectique mystique," in *L'homme devant Dieu* (Paris: Aubier, 1963), on sources of Richard's negative theology, pp. 206–7; see Richard of St. Victor, *Selected Writings*, trans. Kirchberger, on general sources of Richard's work, pp. 38–56; see Leclercq, *Histoire de la spiritualité chrétienne* II, p. 289ff., on the exegetical influence of Gregory, Isidore, and Bede; see *Richard de Saint-Victor: opuscules théologiques*, critical text by J. Ribaillier (Paris: J. Vrin, 1967) for a table of sources, pp. 345f.; see G. Zinn, "History and Contemplation," on patristic exegetical influence, pp. 42–51/282–84. See also Chapters 2 and 3 of this work for a survey of Dionysian influences on Richard. Finally, Hugh of St. Victor's *Didascalicon* contains what would have been the most thorough lists available to Richard of both "Authors of the Arts" (see especially 3.2) and writers on sacred scripture, including those whose "Writings Are Authentic" (see 4.14) and "Apocryphal" (see 4.15). Combined with "Pagans" and "Fathers," also useful to the study of the Arts (see 1), these authors can be assumed to be, if not in Richard's library, at least well known to him. See J. Taylor's translation, with excellent notes.

58. In the context of his work on the Trinity, de Régnon has made the claim that Richard knew certain of the Greek Fathers and had largely submitted to their influence; see his *Etudes de théologie positive sur la sainte Trinité*, 2d series (Paris, 1892), pp. 235–335. More recent commentators have strongly nuanced this judgment, cf. Dumeige, *L'idée chrétienne de l'amour*, pp. 100–101; Jean Ribaillier, *Richard de Saint-Victor: De Trinitate*, critical text with intro., notes, and tables (Paris: J. Vrin, 1958), pp. 20–33; Gaston Salet, *Richard de Saint-Victor: La trinité*, Latin text, with introduction and notes (Paris: Editions du Cerf, 1959), pp. 10–13. Although this recent scholarship may be correct with regard to Richard's work on the Trinity, a different approach, that of focusing on his exegetical work with particular reference to the function of the angels and ark, may prove a fruitful avenue for exploring Greek patristic influence on Richard.

59. *The Writings of Clement of Alexandria*, trans. William Wilson, in Ante-Nicene Christian Library (Edinburgh, 1869), vol. 2, p. 243.

60. R. C. Lilla, *Clement of Alexandria: A Study in Christian Platonism and Gnosticism* (Oxford: Oxford University Press, 1971), p. 5.

61. Philo, *De Vita Mosis*, xx.97; cited in Budick, p. 24, n.17.

62. On influence of Philo, see Sanford Budick, *The Dividing Muse* (New Haven: Yale University Press, 1985), pp. 24–26. See also Elisabeth Revel-Neher, *L'arche d'alliance dans l'art Juif et Chrétien du second au dixième siècles: le signe de la recontre* (Paris: Association Des Amis Des Etudes Archéologiques, 1984), p. 49, n.53. Revel-Neher's section on

Greek patristic exegesis of the texts on the Ark of the Covenant, pp. 47–61, is excellent, and I am in debt to her work. Her translations of the Greek Fathers are given in French; the English translations are mine.

63. Revel-Neher, *L'arche d'alliance*, p. 48.

64. On Origen's exegesis of Exodus 25, see ibid., pp. 49–52. Origen's homilies are found in Origen, *Homélies sur les Nombres*, ed., intr., and tran. by André Mehat, Sources Chrétiennes (Paris: 1957).

65. Revel-Neher, *L'arche d'alliance*, p. 51.

66. Ibid.

67. Ibid., pp. 52–53, 61.

68. Ibid., pp. 53–61.

69. Ibid., p. 53.

70. See especially Damascene's *Homélies sur la Nativité et la Dormition*, trans. Pierre Voulet, Sources Chrétiennes (Paris, 1963), cited in Revel-Neher, *L'arche d'alliance*, pp. 55–56.

71. Revel-Neher, *L'arche d'alliance*, p. 56.

72. Cited in ibid., pp. 58 and 59.

73. Augustine, *Quaestiones in Heptateuchum*, *Quaest. Exodi*, Corpus Christianorum 33 (Turnholt: Brepols, 1975), p. 121. "Propitiatorium quid dicat superinponendum super arcam quaeri solet. . . . Arum quippe significat sapientiam, arca significat secretum Dei. In arca iussa sunt poni lex et manna et uirga Aaron: in lege praecepta sunt, uirga potestas significatur, manna gratia, quia nisi cum gratia non est potestas praecepta faciendi."

74. John 20:12 reads, "She saw two angels in white sitting, one at the head and one at the feet where the body of Jesus had been laid."

75. Gregory here makes a play on the word *nuntius*, or messenger. Earlier in this homily he had said, in the "Latin language angel means messenger" (*Latina lingua angelus nuntius dicitur*). See *PL*, 76, 1191B, cited below. Here, equating the two cherubim with the two testaments, he says that both testaments "announce the message" (*nuntiant*). Thus both testament and cherubim "announce the message."

76. The Vulgate reads *respiciunt* at Exodus 25:20, thus making the reciprocal nature of the gaze that much stronger. Richard plays on this reciprocity. Gregory may have "remembered" *aspiciunt* for *respiciunt*.

77. Gregory the Great, *XL Homiliarum in Evangelia, Liber II*, Homil. XXV, *PL*, 76, 1191B–D. "Possumus etiam per duos angelos duo Testamenta cognoscere, unum prius, et aliud sequens. Qui videlicet angeli per locum dominici corporis sibimet sunt conjuncti, quia nimirum utraque Testamenta, dum pari sensu incarnatum et mortuum ac resurrexisse Dominum nuntiant, quasi Testamentum prius ad caput, et Testamentum posterius ad pedes sedet. Unde et duo cherubim quae propitiatorium

tegunt sese invicem aspiciunt versis vultibus in propitiatorium (Exod. XXV, 20). Cherubim quippe plenitudo scientiae dicitur. Et quid per duo cherubim nisi utraque Testamenta signantur? Quid vero per propitiatorium nisi incarnatus Dominus figuratur? De quo Joannes ait: "Ipse est enim propitiatio pro peccatis nostris" (I Joan. II, 2). Et dum Testamentum Vetus hoc faciendum denuntiat quod Testamentum Novum de Domino factum clamat, quasi utraque cherubim se invicem aspiciunt, dum vultus in propitiatorium vertunt, quia dum inter se positum incarnatum Dominum vident, a suo aspectu non discrepant, quae dispensationis ejus mysterium concorditer narrant."

78. S. Isidore of Seville, *Quaestiones in Vetus Testamentum, In Exodum*, chap. xlvi, *PL*, 83, 311B–312B. "Jam porro per propitiatorium super arcam Testamenti positum idem ipse Christus insinuatur, qui inter Deum et hominem medius propitiator intervenit; de quo dicit Apostolus: "Quem proposuit Deus propitiationem per fidem in sanguine ipsius (Rom. III, 25). Hoc propitiatorium arcae superponitur, sicut et Christus caput est Ecclesiae, cujus a dextris et a sinistris duo cherubim assistunt. Cherubim autem plenitudo scientiae interpretatur, plenitudo scientiae est charitas, id est, dilectio Dei et proximi, qua Dominus ostenditur; nemo enim potest pervenire ad Deum, nisi per charitatem; plenitudo enim legis dilectio est. Alii eadem duo cherubim duo intelligunt Testamenta quae multitudinis suae scientia propitiatorium Dei, id est, Christi sacramenta obumbrant, testante propheta: "In medio duorum animalium cognosceris" (Habacus III, 2). Hi versis vultibus se respiciunt, dum in spiritualem sensum vertuntur; tunc enim alterutrum sibi melius concordant, et in omnibus rectius consonant. Siquidem ex utroque latere oraculum, vel propitiatorium, tegunt, quia Vetus et Novum Testamentum tam Christi sacramenta quam Ecclesiae mysteria sub aenigmatum figuris operiunt."

79. Though the relation of love to knowledge is not a direct concern of this book, it should be pointed out that Richard, in *De arca mystica*, never really moves from the way of knowledge to a metaphysics of love as he does, for instance, in *De quatuor gradibus violentae charitatis*. Even Book V of *De arca mystica*, which moves "beyond" mind with the concept of *excessus mentis*, nonetheless remains focused on the category of mind. On Book V of *De arca mystica* and the relation of the *caritas* to the *scientia* traditions, see above, Appendix A.

80. Found in Bede the Venerable, *De tabernaculo*, Corpus Christianorum, Latin series, 119A, ed. D. Hurst, O.S.B. (Turnholt: Brepols, 1964).

81. *De tabernaculo*, p. 13. "Archa quae prima omnium in tabernaculo fieri iubetur non incongrue ipsam domini et saluatoris nostri incarnationem designat in quo sunt omnes thesauri sapientiae et scientiae absconditi."

82. Ibid., p. 15. "Archa intus et foris auro mundissimo deauratur quia assumpta a filio Dei humana natura et intus . . . et foris . . . nimirum archae bene corona aurea supra circumdari praecipitur quia apparens in carne atque ad redemptionem humani generis ueniens filius Dei certum expectabat tempus et horam quando susceptam pro nobis mortem cum ipso mortis auctore superaret atque ad patrem uictor in caelos ascenderet."

83. Cf. ibid., p. 16.

84. Ibid., p. 17.

85. Cf. Bede, *De templo*, p. 181.

86. For instance, in Gregory, *XL homiliarum in Evangelia, mysterium concorditer narrant*, the cherubim "harmoniously narrate the mysteries," that is, they make the discordant mysteries concordant. In Isidore, *Mysticorum expositiones,* they *melius concordant, et in omnibus rectius consonant*, that is, they make a better unity and correctly harmonize all things. This use of the cherubim collapses the tension which Richard maintains in his use of the cherubim as a coincidence of opposites. Richard would never use the cherubim simply as a force for the harmonizing of opposites.

87. The difficulty of creating a chronology of Richard's works has often been noted. In his critical edition of Richard's *Liber exceptionum*, Châtillon, pp. 77–81, places this work in Richard's early period, between 1153 (the death of Bernard of Clairvaux) and 1159 or 1162 (the dates, respectively, of Richard's election as subprior and prior). *De arca mystica* is generally considered to date from Richard's later period, that is, between 1162 and his death in 1173; cf. Dumeige, *L'idée chrétienne de l'amour*, pp. 165–70; Châtillon, *DS* 13: 612–16; Kirchberger, *RSV: Selected Writings*, pp. 20–24; and Ewert Cousins, "Notion of the Person in the *De Trinitate* of Richard of St. Victor" (Ph.D. diss., Fordham University, 1966), pp. 69–71. This book will assume this relative chronology, that is, that *Liber exceptionum* is earlier than *De arca mystica*. The internal criticism that follows would seem to confirm this chronology.

88. *Liber exceptionum*, J. Châtillon, ed., p. 8: "restaurer dans les âmes l'image de Dieu ternie par péché." See the introduction to this excellent edition for background on sources, content, intent ("to attain to a clear understanding of scripture"), and influence on later generations. On issues of dating, sources, relation to other texts attributed to Richard, and for a brief description of contents, including the later books of the first part which "have for their principal interest to show the importance attached by Richard to establish the literal or historical sense," see Châtillon, *DS* 13: 599–602.

89. R. Roques, *Structures théologiques*, p. 374.

90. *Liber except.*, Châtillon, ed., p. 10. "De plus, en nous révélant les lectures principales de Richard, il nous indique à partir de quels matériaux

le célèbre prieur a construit son oeuvre et quelles sont les sources premières de sa pensée."

91. *Liber except.*, II.x, sermo primus, Châtillon, ed., pp. 375–77. "*Sanctificavit* Dominus *tabernaculum suum.* Habet, fratres carissimi, tabernaculum Domini, id est sancta Ecclesia, lapides suos, habet cementum, habet fundamentum, habet parietes, habet tectum, habet longitudinem, habet latitudinem, habet altitudinem, habet sanctuarium, habet chorum, habet navem, habet atrium, habet altere, habet turrim, habet signa sonantia, habet vitreas fenestras, habet dealbaturam interiorem et exteriorem, habet cereos duodecim, habet pontificem dedicantem. Omnia que dicta sunt, plena sunt sacrementis et spiritualia preferunt documenta. Singuli lapides sunt singuli fideles, quadri et firmi: quadri stabilitate fidei, firmi virtute patiendi. Cementum est caritas, que singulos coaptat, conjungit et unifacat, et ne per aliquam discordiam invicem discrepent, uniformiter edquat. Fundamentum sunt prophete et apostoli, sicut scriptum est: *Superedificati superfundamentum apostolorum et prophetarum, ipso summo angulari lapide Christo Jesu.* Parietes sunt contemplativi, ipsi fundamento quod superius est vicini, terrena deserentes, celestibus adherentes. Tectum, in hoc spirituali edificio, non sursum eminet, sed deorsum dependet, in hoc ab edificio materiali diversum, et ab ipso talis dispositionis dissimili modo remotum. Tectum sunt activi, terrenis actionibus proximi, propter suam imperfectionem minus celestibus intendentes et necessitati proximorum res terrenas administrantes. . . . Altare Christus est, super quem non solum sacrificia bonorum operum, sed itiam orationum offerimus, dicentes: *Per Dominum nostrum Jesum Christum Filium tuum, etc.* . . . Turris est nomen Domini, sicut scriptum est: *Turris fortissima nomen Domini; ad* eam confugiet *justus, et* salvabitur. Signa sunt predicatores, qui verba Dei loquuntur. Fenestre vitree sunt viri spirituales, per quos nobis divina cognitio illucet. Interior dealbatura significat munditiam cordium, exterior munditiam corporum. Duodecim cerei XII sunt apostoli, qui vexillum crucis et fidem passionis Christi predicaverunt per quatuor partes mundi. . . . Sequitur pontifex, qui significat Christum, qui circuivit Ecclesiam suam, primum in tempore naturalis legis ammonendo eam per patriarchas, deinde in tempore scripte legis ammonendo eam per prophetas; deinde in tempore gratie per semetipsum eam circuivit et introivit, foris eam erudiendo per doctrinam, intus sanctificando per gratiam."

92. *Liber except.*, II.x, sermo secundus, Châtillon ed., pp. 377–79. "*Sanctificavit* Dominus *tabernaculum suum.* Tabernaculum Domini secundum sensu tropologicum est anima. Habet autem ipsa anima, que tabernaculum Domini dicitur, lapides suos, cementum suum, et cetera

que ad constructionem ecclesie pertinent, sicut ea in precedenti sermon disposuimus. Lapides istius tabernaculi sunt singule virtutes, per exercitationem bene polite et per immobilitatem contra vitia stabiles. Cementum est caritas, per quam cetere virtutes complectuntur, uniuntur, equantur et continentur. Fundamentum Christus est, sicut ait Apostolus: *Fundamentum aliud nemo potest ponere preter id quod poitum est, quod est Christus Jesus.* Habet parietes per contemplationem celestium bonorum, per quam fundamento suo, id est Christo, terrenis affectibus elongata, vicinius inheret. Habet et tectum per bonam actionem, per quam indigentibus temporalia pro eternis administrat. Habet longitudinem per fidem, per quam cuncta que Deus per se, per angelos, per homines fecit ab initio, vel facturus est usque in finem, vera esse credit. Habet altitudinem per spem, per quam erigitur a terrenis ad celestia, a transituris ad eterna, a visibilibus ad invisibilia, a corporalibus ad spiritualia. Habet latitudinem per caritatem, per quam dilatatur dextrorsum et sinistrorsum: dextrorsum ad amicos, sinistrorsum ad inimicos; ad amicos diligendos in Deo, ad inimicos diligendos propter Deum. Habet sacrarium per hoc quod facta est ad imaginem Dei: sicut enim in edificio ecclesie sacrario nichil est dignius, sic in anima divina imagine nichil est sanctius, nichil nobilius aut excellentius. Habet chorum per hoc quod facta est ad similitudinem Dei: sicut namque in ecclesia post sacrarium chorus primus invenitur, sic in anima post divinam imaginem divina similitudo sublimior intelligitur. . . . Habet ergo ecclesia ista, id est anima, lapides per virtutes, cementum per caritatem, fundamentum per Christum, parietes per contemplationem, tectum per bonam actionem, longitudinem per fidem, altitudinem per spem, latitudenem per dilectionem, sacrarium per hoc quod facta est ad Dei imaginem, chorum per hoc quod facta est ad Dei similitudinem, navem per sensualitatem, atrium per carnem, altare per cor contritum. Habet et vitreas fenestras per sensus spirituales, turrim per nomen Domini, signa per predicationem, interiorem dealbaturam per munditiam cordis, exteriorem per munditiam corporis, duodecim cereos per duodecim apostolorum doctrinam. Pontifex ejus sancta Trinitas est. Conetur igitur, fratres carissimi, unusquisque vestrum, conetur, inquam ut, secundum ea que supra dicta sunt, tabernaculum Dei fiat ut in ipso dignetur Deus habitare. Magnus est enim honor, magna dignitas magna sublimitas, magna securitas, magna gloria Deum in se habere habitatorem. Providendum itaque nobis summopere est ut tales simus intus et foris, intus per fidem, foris per bonam operationem, ut Dominus majestatis ad nos venire et apud nos dignetur facere mansionem. Sed quia tales sine ejus gratia esse non possumus, ipsam necesse est incessanter imploremus. Ipse namque dabit gratiam, et non solum gratiam, sed et gloriam."

93. *De arca mystica*, since it is a tropological exegesis of the deeper significance of the ark and cherubim of Exodus 25, concentrates on exactly that place where God will come to dwell; that is, on the ark, between the two cherubim, and, as the internalized ark and cherubim imply, within the soul of the contemplative. Cf. Exodus 25:22 (*Vulgate*): "et ibi te conveniam et tecum loquar de loca qui erit supra operculum et inter duos Cherubos."

94. *Liber except.* Châtillon, ed., pp. 77–81.

95. Elsewhere in *Liber except.* Richard discusses four senses, though this is rare. Cf. *Liber except.* II.III.xi, p. 258: "quatuor sunt sensu Scripture: historia, allegoria, tropologia, anagoge." But these four senses are discussed in the context of an allegorical interpretation of the table of the propitiatory as Holy Scripture. Since the table has four legs, so must the senses of scripture be four. As noted earlier, it is more important for Richard to maintain allegorical consistency based on the "things" of scripture, that is, a consistency within the symbolic narration, than it is to be consistent about a small matter such as the number of the senses of scripture.

96. *Liber except.*, Châtillon, ed., I,III, iii, pp. 115–16. "Historia est rerum gestarum narratio que in prima significatione littere continetur. Allegoria est cum per id quod factum dicitur, aliud factum sive in preterito, sive in presenti, sive in futuro significatur. Tropologia est cum per id quod factum legimus, quid nobis sit faciendum agnoscimus."

97. *Liber except.*, II.III., ii, Châtillon, ed., p. 251. "Agnus igitur paschalis, Christus; columpna, Christus; petra, Christus; archa, Christus; propitiatorium, Christus; mensa, Christus; candelabrum, Christus; altare, Christus; hircus, Christus; vitula, Christus."

98. *Liber except.*, II.III, Cap. xiv, Châtillon, ed., p. 259. "Duo cherubin, eo quod Cherubim interpretatur plenitudo scientie [*sic*], duo significant Testamenta, quia in ipsis plenitudo scientie [*sic*] continetur."

99. *Liber except.*, II.X, x, Châtillon, ed., p. 395. "Si quoque videremus istum taliter seculari scientia doctum, sapientia divine Scripture peritissimum, doctum scilicet Veteri et Novo Testamento, historia, allegoria, tropologia, anagoge, litterarum triplici sermone sicut Jeronimum, in ratiocinatione disertum sicut Augustinum, in moralitate sicut Gregorium, sapientem denique sicut Salomonem, omnibus modis proclamaremus: magnus iste." Richard, following Hugh, rehabilitates all human disciplines, which he gives the name *scientia*. Thus *sapientia* is an understanding of heavenly and divine things ("sapientia dicitur cogitio de celestibus et divinis), while *scientia* concerns things of earth and of man (scientia de terrenis et humanis). *Liber except.*, II.X, x, p. 395.

CHAPTER 2

1. On the life and possible identity of Denys the Areopagite, or Pseudo-Dionysius, and a survey of the current picture of Dionysian studies, see René Roques et al., "Denys L'Aréopagite (Le pseudo-)," in *Dictionnaire de spiritualité: ascétique et mystique, doctrine et histoire*, vol. 3 (Paris, 1957), pp. 244–429 (hereafter *DS* 3); Bernard McGinn, "Pseudo-Dionysius and the Early Cistercians," in *One Yet Two: Monastic Tradition East and West* (Kalamazoo: Cistercian Publications, 1976), pp. 201–7; René Roques, "La question dionysienne, " in *Structures théologiques de la gnose à Richard de Saint-Victor* (Paris: Presses universitaires de France, 1962), pp. 74–91; David Knowles, O.S.B., "The Influence of Pseudo-Dionysius on Western Mysticism," in *Christian Spirituality: Essays in Honor of Gordon Rupp*, ed. Peter Brooks (London: SCM Press, 1975), pp. 81–94; Jaroslav Pelikan, "The Odyssey of Dionysian Spirituality," in *Pseudo-Dionysius: The Complete Works*, trans. Colm Luibheid (New York: Paulist Press, 1987), pp. 11–24; Raoul Mortley, *From Word to Silence: The Way of Negation, Christian, and Greek* (Bonn: Hanstein, 1986), p. 219–23.

2. Bernard McGinn, *The Foundations of Mysticism*. Volume 1 of *The Presence of God: A History of Western Christian Mysticism* (New York: Crossroad, 1991), p. xviii.

3. The Dionysian categories of hierarchy, or "theophany," and mediation, while important, are not of such immediate concern to this book. Richard's definition of contemplation as the mind "hovering with wonder in manifestations of wisdom" (*in sapientiae spectacula cum admiratione suspensa, De arca* I.iv, 67D) turns on Deny's idea of theophany; and one of Richard's uses of symbol is as a mediating agent in the contemplative's ascent through the hierarchies. But the overall emphasis will be on the symbol of the cherubim, which, as we shall see, takes into account a spirituality of both ascent and presence.

4. The best survey to date of the textual transmission can be found in Paul Rorem, *Pseudo-Dionysius: A Commentary on the Texts and an Introduction to Their Influence* (New York: Oxford University Press, 1993).

See also Jean Leclercq, "Influence and Noninfluence of Dionysius in the Western Middle Ages," pp. 25–32 in *Pseudo-Dionysius: The Complete Works*, trans. Colm Luibheid (New York: Paulist Press, 1987), pp. 26–29; Grover Zinn, "Suger, Theology, and the Pseudo-Dionysian Tradition," in *Abbot Suger and Saint-Denis*, ed. Paula Lieber Gerson (New York: Metropolitan Museum of Art, 1986), pp. 33–40, esp. p. 34, n. 11; Philippe Chevallier, "Du 6e au 12e siècle: Origine de l'influence

Dionysienne," in *DS* 3: 318–23; Henri Weisweiler, "Du 6e au 12e siècle: Hughues de Saint-Victor," *DS* 3: 323–24; Gervais Dumeige, "Du 6e au 12e siècle: Richard de Saint-Victor," *DS* 3: 324–29; David Knowles, "The Influence of Pseudo-Dionysius on Western Mysticism"; Andrew Louth, *Denys the Areopagite* (Wilton, Conn.: Morehouse-Barlow, 1989), pp. 120–29; Grover Zinn, "Book and Word: The Victorine Background of Bonaventure's Use of Symbols," *S. Bonaventura 1274–1974* (Rome: Grottaferrata, 1973), vol. 2, pp. 145–48; Jean Châtillon, *Théologie, spiritualité, et métaphysique dans l'oeuvre oratoire d'Achard de Saint Victor*, Etudes de philosophie médiévale, no. 58 (Paris, J. Vrin, 1969), pp. 307–13. On the particular influence of John Scottus Eriugena on the transmission of Dionysian texts and ideas to the twelfth century, see J. Châtillon, "Hugues de Saint-Victor critique de Jean Scot," in *Le mouvement canonial au moyen age, réforme de l'église, spiritualité et culture* (Turnhout: Brepols, 1992), pp. 419–45; Bernard McGinn, "The Negative Element in the Anthropology of John the Scot," in *Jean Scot Erigène et l'histoire de la philosophie* (Paris: Editions du centre national de la recherche scientifique, 1977), pp. 315–25; N. Haring, "John Scottus in Twelfth-Century Angelology," in *The Mind of Eriugena*, ed. O'Meara and Beiler (Irish University Press, 1973), pp. 158–69; Dermot Moran, *The Philosophy of John Scottus Eriugena: A Study of Idealism in the Middle Ages* (Cambridge: Cambridge University Press, 1989), pp. 269–81; John J. O'Meara, *Eriugena* (Oxford: Clarendon Press, 1988), pp. 57–69 and 216–19; Edouard Jeauneau, "Le renouveau érigénien du XIIe siècle," in *Eriugena redivivus*, ed. W. Beierwaltes (Heidelberg, 1987), pp. 26–46. On the manuscripts of the Dionysian corpus available by the thirteenth century at the University of Paris, including comments on Hilduin, Eriugena, Sarrazin, Gallus, Grossetete, and Hugh, see H. F. Dondaine, *Le corpus Dionysien de l'université de Paris au XIIIe siècle* (Rome: Edizioni de Storia e Letteratura, 1953).

On the transmission of Denys' works through Hugh, see Appendix B.

5. Etienne Gilson, *The Mystical Theology of St. Bernard* (Kalamazoo: Cistercian Publications, 1990), p. 25.

6. The general outline of the history of transmission of the *Celestial Hierarchy* from Denys to Richard, available in Rorem, Leclerq, Zinn, Dumeige, Weisweiler, and Châtillon in note 4 above, is as follows. Pope Gregory the Great refers to Denys as "ancient and venerable Father" and quotes him on the subject of angels (*In Evang.* Homily 34, 12, *PL* 76, 1254). After Gregory the Great there are few references to Denys until the beginning of the Carolingian Age. In 827 a gift of a codex of the Dionysian writings was sent by the Byzantine Emperor Michael the Stammerer to Louis the Pious. At the monastery of St. Denys, Hilduin made a translation

that was so bad it was generally considered to be unintelligible. Charles the Bald requested John Scotus Eriugena to make a new translation, which he finished in 862. This new translation made the *Corpus Areopagiticum* generally available to the West. Eriugena, the primary transmitter of Dionysian thought to the later medieval period (J. O'Meara, *Eriugena*, pp. 57–69), influenced the ninth and tenth centuries in the area of commentary, explication, and analysis of the meaning of dialectic. Yet his negative dialectics and his speculative division of nature seem to have been generally ignored or misunderstood (D. Moran, *Philosophy of Eriugena*, pp. 271ff.). The twelfth century, however, was a period of revival for Eriugena, including his negative dialectics. Hugh of St. Victor gave Eriugena the title of "theologus" (Moran, p. 274, O'Meara, pp. 216–19, and Châtillon, "Hugues de Saint-Victor," pp. 419f.). For a somewhat less enthusiastic interpretation of the influence of Eriugena on Hugh, taking into account the 1225 condemnation of Eriugena by Pope Honorius III, see J. Jeauneau, "L'renouveau érigènien du XIIe siècle," pp. 44–46). Hugh of St. Victor edited two commentaries on Denys' *Celestial Hierarchy*, both titled *Commentariorum Hierarchiam coelestem S. Dionysii Areopagite*, between 1125 and 1137, later revising them as one. Hugh's commentary was based on the translation of Eriugena. Commenting on the Dionysian corpus as a whole, P. Rorem outlines "several well-known clusters of Dionysians" as they are transmitted to the Latin West. These include, first, the authors of the early *Scholia*; second, the ninth-century Carolingian translators and commentators including Hilduin and Eriugena; third, the twelfth-century Parisians Suger, Hugh, and Sarracenus; and fourth, later thirteenth-century commentators (including the Victorine, Thomas Gallus) after which the "narrative" divides. See Rorem, *Pseudo-Dionysius*, p. 238f.

7. *De reductione artium ad theologiam* (*Opera*, vol. 5, Quaracchi, 1891, p. 321). Cited in Dumeige, *DS* 3: 324. "Anselmus sequitur Augustinum, Bernardus sequitur Gregorium, Richardus sequitur Dionysium, quia Anselmus in ratiocinatione, Bernardus in praedicatione, Richardus in contemplatione."

8. Dumeige, *DS* 3: 328–29. "Richard a connu Denys, mais il l'a plus souvent utilise comme une illustration que comme une inspiration de sa propre pensée. La conception d'un univers symbolique et de l'amour comme de la connaissance semblent être celles auzquelles il s'est particulièrement attaché et qu'il a transmises à ceux sur qui, son tour, son influence s'est exercée."

9. *PL*, 196, cols. 687A, 688AD, 689C, 759A.

10. *In Apoc.* I.1, 687ac, citing Hugh from *PL*, 175, 941cd. Cited in Châtillon, *DS* 13: 604. Dumeige, *DS* 3: 325, notes that this citation of Denys follows a poorly read, or poorly transcribed, version of Eriugena.

11. Cf. Dumeige, *DS* 3: pp. 325–28, and R. Javelet, "Gallus et Richard de Saint-Victor," p. 103, n. 143.

12. While admiting Richard's debt to Denys, Kirchberger claims, oddly, that Richard does not accept the way of negation, "for his whole training had been towards an affirmative apprehension of God." Cf. Clare Kirchberger, *Richard of Saint-Victor: Selected Writings on Contemplation* (London: Faber and Faber, 1957), pp. 48–56.

13. Cf. Dumeige cited above at n. 8, and B. McGinn, "Pseudo-Dionysius and the Early Cistercians," p. 212, supporting the contention that Denys was mostly used as an illustration. R. Javelet, too, comparing Richard's assimilation of Denys with that of Thomas Gallus, the late twelfth-century Victorine, concludes that while Richard and Hugh were merely influenced (*infléchi*) by Denys' thought, Thomas adopted (*adoptée*) it (Javelet, "Gallus et Richard," p. 102).

14. M.-D. Chenu, for instance, consistently displays a basic distrust of Denys and the Eriugenist transmission of his thought to the twelfth century and repeatedly and vehemently condemns Dionysian strains of Platonism in favor of more orthodox Augustinian strains. Nonetheless, he does endorse Denys' way of negation both as orthodox and genuinely influential for the twelfth century, seeing in the *via negativa* Denys' "most admirable Christian adaptation of Neoplatonistic method." Cf. M.-D. Chenu, *Nature, Man and Society in the Twelfth Century: Essays on the New Theological Perspectives in the Latin West*, selected, ed., trans., Jerome Taylor and Lester K. Little (Chicago: University of Chicago Press, 1968), p. 85. See also, in Chenu, pp. 25, 52–53, 82–86. Robert Javelet has traced Richard's apophaticism in the following articles: "Thomas Gallus ou les Ecritures dans une dialectique mystique," in *L'homme devant Dieu: mélanges offerts au Père Henri de Lubac* (Paris: Aubier, 1963), pp. 99–110; "Thomas Gallus et Richard de Saint-Victor, mystiques," *Recherches de théologie ancienne et mediévale* 29 (1962) and 30 (1963): 206–33 and 88–121; and "Sens et réalité ultime selon Richard de Saint-Victor," *Ultimate Reality and Meaning* 5–6 (1982–83): 221–43. In the latter work Javelet calls only Richard's metaphysics "Dionysian" and claims that Richard's apophaticism is not as defined as Thomas Gallus's. Javelet here feels Richard, to the end, relies on a mysticism of intellect and equates apophaticism with a move from intellect to love. But Javelet's "love" is in fact an element foreign to Denys' apophaticism, and Richard does, as we shall see, explore the depths of apophatic mysteries in the most radical way. Nonetheless, Javelet does present a nuanced assessment of Richard's and Thomas's apophaticism, cradling Richard's form in immanent terms and Thomas's in radically transcendent terms. Javelet says: "Richard écrit: 'Summe potens, summe sapiens, summe bonus,' sans plus, pour signifier que rien ne dépasse Dieu, mais non pas que Deiu dépasse radicalement ce

qui est, est étranger à toute idée que nous pouvons avoir de lui" ("Gallus et Richard de Saint-Victor, mystiques," pp. 102–3.) Paul Rorem claims that, in many cases, the medieval transmission of the Dionysian corpus was less than comprehensive and thus, compared to the Dionysian synthesis, flawed or aberrant, and more interested in how Denys abandoned than attained concepts. Cf. P. Rorem, *Biblical and Liturgical Symbols*, pp. 142–49. Simon Tugwell also laments the medieval emphasis on the dynamic of return (*reditus*) and not on its complementary dynamic of procession (*exitus*), and says that the need to combine negative and affirmative theology was also not appreciated. See his *Albert & Thomas: Selected Writings*, trans., ed., introd. Simon Tugwell, O.P. (New York: Paulist Press, 1989), pp. 42–44, 46, 48.

15. The translation of Denys' works used for this discussion is *Pseudo-Dionysius: The Complete Works*, trans. Colm Luibheid and foreword, notes, trans. collaboration Paul Rorem (New York: Paulist, 1987). Luibheid's translation is based on the Greek text of the Migne edition (*PG vol. 3*). Treatises are abbreviated as follows: *DN* = *The Divine Names*, *MT* = *The Mystical Theology*, *CH* = *The Celestial Hierarchy*, *Ep.* = one of the *Letters*. Citations are taken from the Luibheid translation, giving title, chapter, and page number. Thus *CH* 2, p. 184, indicates *The Celestial Hierarchy*, chapter two, page 184, in Luibheid. Notes in this Luibheid edition are by Paul Rorem.

16. R. Roques, *Structures théologiques*, p. 142.

17. These limitations will be discussed in detail in Chapter 3. They stem from the fact that, "manifestation de Dieu est inférieure à Dieu lui-meme, comme l'image est inférieure au modèle." Cf. Roques, *Structures théologiques*, p. 138.

18. Ibid., p. 143. "De même que le symbolisme dissemblable a dû redresser les illusions du symbolisme ressemblant, il faudra, pareillement, que la démarche négative corrige les représentations intelligibles de la théologie affirmative."

19. Cf. B. McGinn, *Foundations of Mysticism*, p. 58, where McGinn describes the revolution that took place in the Christian Neoplatonism of Denys as an application to a single trinitarian God of these negative and positive theological expressions.

20. This is true especially on the symbolic level, where "incongruities are more suitable for lifting our minds up into the domain of the spiritual than similarities are" (*CH* 2.3). See also McGinn, *Foundations of Mysticism*, p. 173.

21. Ibid., pp. 174, 176.

22. P. Rorem, *Biblical and Liturgical Symbols*, pp. 89, 90.

23. Mortley, *From Word to Silence*, p. 229.

24. DN 7.3, p. 108.

25. Mortley, *From Word to Silence*, p. 231.

26. Denys has no patience with the complicated principles of noncontradiction which were previously applied to discussions of the Trinity, for instance the arguments about *hypostasis* and *ousia*: he simply asserts both propositions simultaneously: p and not p. Mortley also notes that the West does move toward this principle of contradiction in philosophical mysticism. See ibid., pp. 238–39.

27. Mortley says, for instance, "It [contradiction] is designed to force language to include rather than exclude. Language, the only available instrument, is induced to play a new tune, a tune for which it was not designed." Ibid., p. 240.

28. On the paradox of the dialectic of negative and positive theology culminating in superaffirmation see B. McGinn, "The Negative Element in the Anthropology of John the Scot," pp. 321–23; for a clear, concise explanation of the necessary relation of negative to positive theology and of the "third" moment of moving beyond affirmation and denial (saying that God *est qui plus quam esse est* is not saying what God is), and the related notion that God is both pantheistic and totally transcendent, see Etienne Gilson, *History of Christian Philosophy in the Middle Ages* (New York: Random House, 1955), pp. 117, 121; on affirmative theology suggesting only that the infinite is the highest within the same order as created beings and the necessary corrective of negative theology to suggest a being beyond the finite order, and on the relation of negative and affirmative theology to divine unity and plurality, see Werner Beierwaltes, "*Negati Affirmatio*: Or the World as Metaphor, foundation for medieval aesthetics from the writings of John Scotus Eriugena," *Dionysius* 1 (1977): 133, 140–41; on affirmative and negative theology as mutually indispensable moments in the march towards God, and on Richard's own use of both theological methods, see Gaston Salet, "Les chemins de Dieu d'après Richard de Saint-Victor," in *L'homme devant Dieu: mélanges offerts au Père Henri de Lubac* (Paris: Aubier, 1964), pp. 73–88.

29. On the relation of the Neoplatonic philosophy of procession and return to Denys' notion of assent and denial, see *MT* 3, n. 17, and *CH* 1, n. 4.

30. A lost or fictitious treatise.

31. Also lost or fictitious.

32. *MT* 3, pp. 138–39.

33. *MT* 3, p. 139.

34. This is so, fundamentally, because of the opposition of the created nature to knowledge of God. As R. Roques notes, "leur opposition est presque irréductible." Thus, whether using conceptual, affective, or even

symbolic categories, the irreducibility of the opposition between manifestation and source requires denial. Cf. R. Roques, *Structures théologique*, p. 138.

35. *MT* 5, p. 141. The concept of the One beyond all conceptions is expressed elsewhere many times in Denys. Cf. *DN* 1.1, pp. 49–50: "Indeed the inscrutable One is out of the reach of every rational process. Nor can any words come up to the inexpressible Good, this One, this Source of all unity, this supra-existent Being. Mind beyond mind, word beyond speech, it is gathered up by no discourse, by no intuition, by no name." "No intuition, no name" would also seem to preclude "love" which, as we have seen, was a favorite twelfth-century category for "knowing" by "unknowing." But for Denys, love too would have to be denied as a name, word, or intuition of the Inexpressible. See also the discussion of the intrusion of the affective element into the Dionysian corpus of the medieval period in Rorem, *Pseudo-Dionysius*, especially pp. 214–25.

36. *MT* 1.1, p. 135.

37. *MT* 1.3, pp. 136–37. My emphasis.

38. In fact, the opening poem of *The Mystical Theology* beginning with "Trinity!! Higher than any being . . ." and quoted in part above, is a partial outline of Richard's *De arca mystica*. In brief the elements of the outline are the emphasis on Trinity (Richard's final stages of contemplation lead to the Trinity symbolized by the two cherubim), the notion of guiding or leading beyond the unknown (Richard's text is rich in *ducere*/*ductor* and their cognates used to develop the concept of *manaducto* or "guiding hand"), the wisdom of heaven as the goal of the journey (again, symbolized in Richard by the cherubim and explicitly stated as the meaning of the tropological interpretation), the mystic, hidden knowledge in scripture (which Richard's tropological interpretation attempts to mine), and the location of the deepest mysteries hidden in "brilliant darkness of a hidden silence, amid the deepest shadow" (Richard symbolically represents that hidden place upon the ark where God will come to speak and meet the contemplative as hidden in the deepest shadow provided by the outstretched wings of the cherubim). Denys directly refers to the Divinity as "him who has made shadows his hiding place," in *MT* 1.1, p. 136.

39. *MT* 3, p. 159.

40. *De arca* IV.vi, 139D; 267: "angelicos illos excessus in ardua divinae incomprehensibilitatis arcana audeat attentare."

41. Denys' use of angels as symbols in the *Celestial Hierarchy* and *Letter Nine* will be taken up in Chapter 3. There, the nature of symbol and Richard's use of symbol in contemplation provide the appropriate context.

42. The connection between "rays" and "angels" is not apparent until further in this chapter in *The Divine Names*, when the indefinite "they" in the translation is equated with "my book *The Properties and Ranks of the Angels*." That the "they" refers to angels is apparent by Denys' overall description of them and the mention of this book. The book which Denys here refers to is lost or fictitious. See *DN* 4.2, p. 72.

43. *DN* 4.1, p. 72. R. Roques points out the important Dionysian theme that the angelic hierarchies are not only shaped or receptive, but that each also transmits what it receives. Cf. R. Roques, *Structures théologique*, p. 122–23.

44. Cf. *DN* 7.2, p. 107.

45. For Denys, the "gift" is generally divinization (*theōsis*), generally defined as the gift that God bestows on beings endowed with reason and intelligence through their participation in the hierarchies. Cf. *EH* 1.2, p. 197, and *EH* 1.4, p. 198.

46. *DN* 7.2, p. 106.

47. Cf. *De arca* I.xii, 78B. " . . . in quantum unusquisque coelitus accipit, et angelicae sibi similitudinis habitum divinitus superducit."

48. See McGinn, n. 2 above.

49. This is not to be confused with that more famous dialectical idealism of Hegel or the dialectical materialism of Marx involving synthesis. Cf. G. W. F. Hegel, *The Phenomenology of Mind*, trans. F. B. Baile (London: Allen and Unwin, 1931); Karl Marx in *The Marx-Engels Reader*, ed. Robert C. Tucker (New York: W. W. Norton, 1972). Nor should this dialectic be confused with the is/is not dialectic epistemologically refined and applied to nature by Eriugena. Cf. Dermot Moran, *The Philosophy of John Scottus Eriugena*. It is, simply, not an either/or dialectic, as the symbol of the cherubim makes clear.

50. On the nature and use of *coincidentia oppositorum*, see Ewert Cousins, *Bonaventure and the Coincidence of Opposites* (Chicago: Franciscan Herald Press, 1978), especially chaps. 1 and 7. Neither Bonaventure nor Richard of St. Victor used the term *coincidentia oppositorum* in a conscious way. Both C. Jung and M. Eliade, however, have pointed out the unconscious structuring capacity of the coincidence of opposites as it rises, through a variety of symbols, myths, dreams, stories, and rituals, to a conscious level. See C. G. Jung, *Mysterium Coniunctionis*, vol. 14 of the *Collected Works of C. G. Jung*, trans. R. F. C. Hull (New York: Pantheon, 1963); Mircea Eliade, *The Two and the One*, trans. J. M. Cohen (London: Harvill Press, 1965); John Valk, "The Concept of the *Coincidentia Oppositorum* in the Thought of Mircea Eliade," *Religious Studies* 28: 31–41. Nicholas of Cusa employed this paradoxical method as a conscious dialectic in the fourteenth century. See *De docta ignorantia*, in *Nicolai de*

Cusa opera omnia, ed. Ernst Hoffmann and Raymond Klibansky (Leipzig: Meiner, 1932).

51. Reason begins to totter, shake, be corrupted, disturbed, or weakened (*labefactari*) when it seeks to consider the things above itself. Cf. *De arca* IV.iii, 137D.

52. What is "beyond reason," in most cases, is *revelatione.* There is also, however, an affective element to "beyond reason." Though this affective element is not fully developed by Richard in this treatise, it does at times arise, and often in the context of his core metaphor of flight. For instance, Richard says at one point that the cloud of our mind (*mentis nostrae nubila*) must be blown away by divine inspiration or revelation. This mind-cloud is certainly an intellective metaphor. But in order to see God clearly, this cloud must be blown away so that the wings of the heart (*cordis nostri alas*) might see God face to face. This heart-wing is clearly an affective metaphor intended to move "beyond reason" by means of ascension or flight. Cf. *De arca* IV.x, 145B.

53. *De arca* I.xii, 78C; 172–73. "Animadvertere, obsecro, quam apte ex adverso sibi opponunitur, et ex adverso statuuntur in earum videlicet rerum figuram quarum hae rationi consentire, illae rationi contraire videntur. . . . Vide ergo ne forte in illo cherubin qui a dextris stabat, illud contemplationis genus intelligi debeat quod est supra rationem, non tamen praeter rationem. In illo autem qui a sinistris illud quod est supra rationem, et videtur esse praeter rationem." These same assertions, that the first cherubim pertains to things above reason while the second pertains to things above and beyond reason, are reiterated at ibid., IV.xvii, 156B–C, with the additional association of the two cherubim with the unity and diversity within the Trinity: "Secundum hanc itaque distinctionem videte ne forte ad primum cherubin specialiter pertineant ea quae considerantur circa divinae illus summae et simplicis essentiae unitatem; ad secundum autem cherubin ae quae considerantur circa personarum Trinitatem."

54. A few of these pairs of opposites associated with the symbol of the cherubim which have value for this and later chapters include (all references are to *De arca*):

Active/Passive (or Work/Leisure): Richard is a master at depicting the active nature of contemplation and the passive nature of activity, ending his treatise with the words *otiosi otiosis locuti sumus* at V.xix; the active/resting nature of contemplation is always left in paradox, best illustrated as active resting as in "hovering"; Mary was "emptied for contemplation" (*contemplationi vacabat*) at I.i; the summary chapter (I.xii) is for those who are busy (*occupatis*) while the remainder of the treatise is for those persons at leisure *quia otiosi sumus et otiosis loquimur;* the last two contemplations (associated with the two cherubim) are remote from human industry (*remota ab omni humana industria*) at I.xii; contemplation, seemingly the practice of passivity, is seen as the activity which never ends (*negotium*—i.e., not-rest—*quod nullo fine terminatur*) at I.i; the practice of contemplation is seen as an activity: "*et cum ejusmodi industriae usum in promptu habuerimus*" at II.xiv; there is a "natural working" (*naturalis operatio*) within the context of the grace of contemplation at II.xv; the work of contemplation is almost always associated with covering (*hoc opus arcae operculum*) at III.iii, while the rest of contemplation is associated with unveiling, manifesting, or opening (*mirandae tranquillitatis secretum*); work, activity, industry is associated with creation, while rest and tranquility are associated with restoration and glorification at III.xx; Bezeleel forges the cherubim both in working (*operaretur*) and by intuition or contemplation (*intueretur*) at IV.xxii; the cherubim actively assent to their opposite by resting, finding comfort in (*adcuiesco*) their opposite at IV.xix; there is labor and sweat involved in constructing the cherubim, the symbol of contemplative rest, "*Ecce jam quanto labore sudavimus*" at IV.xvi.

Empty/Full: these two categories are rarely explicit in Richard, though the fundamental relation between God's presence and absence on the ark is a relation of empty to full and, I believe, empty/full and presence/absence are played out in the context of the birthing symbolism of the ark and the cherubim. The one explicit use of these opposites is in a brief discussion of Mary and Martha: Mary, who chooses the highest part, chooses to be empty (*vacare*), while Martha is carrying or bears (*gerente*) solicitude and, in a birthing sense, is full, at I.i.

Hidden/Revealed (or Unconcealed): *manifestiora/occultiora* at I.xii; objects of contemplation at all six levels are *spectaculum*, or "manifested things"; Richard's "night work" (*lucubratio*) is associated with *resero, arcanus, reconditus* (reveal, secret, concealed) at I.i and this same night work "derives wisdom from hidden things" (*Ab istis etenim trahitur sapientia de occulto*) at II.viii; *induit* or "put on, clothe, cover" at III.xxii; the wings of the cherubim are often "covering" or "concealing" the propitiatory, the place were God has promised to "manifest" God's self, cf. "*tegant expandientes alas et operientes oraculum*" at IV.i and IV.ix— this is a direct citation of Exodus 25:20; being inside and outside all things, below and above all things, nothing is more secret (*secretius*), withdrawn (*remotius*), hidden (*occultius*) than God, at IV.xvii; the holy of holies itself (the ark, or symbol for the soul according to Richard's symbolic anthropology) that intimate and most secret place (*intimum et secretissimum locum*), at IV.xxiii.

Light/Dark: these opposites are, of course, very closely related to hidden/revealed above—for instance: light which is the wisdom of God both conceals and reveals when at one time it pours a ray of light into the eyes of the mind (*lucis suae radios nunc mentis oculis infundere*) while at another time it obscures by means of withdrawing (*nunc subtrahendo iterum abscondere*) at II.xiii; Richard links light and dark, claiming a metaphor of vision in the midst of the night as in "this night is my illumination" (*haec nox illuminatio mea*) at III.x; human understanding is able to investigate the deepest things, the most secret, the hidden, the obscure, those things enfolded in darkness and to call them out into the light (*penetrare, involuta, perplexa, obscura et in tenebris posita, evolvere, ennodara, illustrare, et in lucem evocare*) at III.xxi; the cherubim's wings are often used to provide a shadow (*adumbratio*) by which our understanding is darkened by comparison to divine things, and by which the wings are said to conceal or protect (*tegere*) the propitiatory and a veil is established between world and God, cf. IV.ix; cloud/fire opposites are also related to this category, as when Moses enters the cloud, when divine light absorbs the mind and mind is lulled to sleep in oblivion so that divine light is equal to human darkness, cf. "*quando humana mens ab illa divini luminis immensitate absorpta, summa sui oblivione sopitur*" at IV.xxii.

Open/Close: *operit/claudit* at I.i.

Presence/Absence: an explicit mention of these opposites is rare in Richard but can be found in the context of a discussion on the hidden (apophatic) nature of God at IV.xvii (*Item si in omni loco est, nihil illo praesentius. Si extra omnem locum est, nihil illo absentius*).

Similar/Dissimilar: see discussion in Chapter 4 on symbols in Richard.

Unity/Diversity: Unity and diversity are the most explicit coincidence of opposites in Richard, the two cherubim symbolically applied to the unity of substance and trinity of persons within the Trinity. The discussion of those things concerning the unity of the supreme and simple divine essence (*circa divinae illus summae et simplicis essentiae unitatem*) and pertaining to the first cherub is found at IV.xvii. Those things concerning the trinity of persons (*circa personarum Trinitatem*) and pertaining to the second cherub are found at IV.xviii. The necessity of maintaining the coincidence of opposites within the trinitarian dialectic of unity and diversity as symbolized by the cherubim (*sic in summis illis et divinis astruamaus substantiae unitatem, ut tamen non evacuemus personarum Trinitatem, et sic confirmemus personarum Trinitatem, ut tamen non dissipemus substantiae unitatem*) is found at IV.xix. The trinitarian image in the soul (mind, Wisdom, love), found as the cherubim, simultaneously balancing the paradox of unity and diversity, gaze back at each other and back upon the propitiatory (soul), the trinitarian image then becoming a springboard for a brief discussion of the Incarnation, is found at IV.xx.

Visible/Invisible: see discussion in Chapters 3 and 4 on symbols.

55. *De arca* III.x, 119D, 120A; 235, 236. "Habet autem hoc ultimum et summum coelum diem suam, habet nimirum et noctem suam. . . . Siquidem fecit Deus lunam et stellas in potestatem noctis, et idcirco *haec nox illuminatio mea* in deliciis meis." My emphasis.

56. Cf. *De arca* I.xii, 78D; 173. "Manifestiora autem sunt rationi consentanea, occultiora autem rationi adversantia."

57. Cf. *De arca* II.xiv, 92A; II.xv, 94A; IV.xx, 161D. The rational principle of similitude and its relation to the dialectic of visible/invisible will be discussed in detail in Chapter 4 on Richard's use of symbol.

58. *De arca* III.i, 108D–109A; 219. "Constat (hoc contemplationis genus) . . . in incorporeis et invisibilibus essentiis utpote spiritibus angelicis, et spiritibus humanis."

Richard also defines what is beyond reason as "that which transcends the smallness of our capacity by the greatness of its incomprehensibility" (*quae capacitatis nostrae exiquitatem incomprehensibilitatis suae magnitudine transcendunt*), IV.ii, 136D. "Incomprehensibility" is itself a favorite term of Richard's (cf. III.iii on the secret of tranquility related to incomprehensibility; III.xvii and III.xxiv on the incomprehensibility of God's absence, gifts, and grace; IV.xii on the magnitude of God's incomprehensibility shown by the remoteness of his vision; IV.xviii on incomprehensibility and symbols, and especially IV.vi on the symbolic and apophatic flight of angels into the secret places of divine incomprehensibility.)

The term "incomprehensibility" certainly has its Dionysian flavor and serves in part, I believe, to undermine the claim of such excellent scholars as G. Dumeige and B. McGinn that the actual effect of Denys on Richard's thought was more by way of illustration than real influence or inspiration. In addition, and more important, B. McGinn himself notes that two of the critical criteria for establishing specifically Dionysian apophatic theology (as opposed to other Western strands including Augustine and Boethius) is a distinction between positive and negative predication, and the use of eminent terminology (i.e., terms prefixed by Latin *super*, indicating that God surpasses all created categories). Cf. McGinn, "Pseudo-Dionysius and the Early Cistercians," p. 216. McGinn's point is that the twelfth century, Richard included, did not meet these two criteria of Dionysian apophatic theology. I believe the body of this book clarifies Richard's positive distinction between positive and negative. In addition Richard does use eminent terminology, and quite often: e.g., III.i and III.ii, *super mundanarum essentiarum*; III.vii, *supercoelestium spectaculorum*; III.x, *supereminens magnitudo Spiritus divini*; III.xxiv, *supercoelestium animorum consona concordia*; IV.i, *Ad supermundana itaque, imo ad supercoelestia hujusmodi operis forma nos provact*; IV.v, *harum novissimarum speculationum supereminentia . . . supercoelestium et divinorum*; IV.vii, *supercoelestium animorum . . . superexcellentium spirituum*; IV.ix, *ex contemplatione creatricis essentiae ejusque supereminentiae*. Richard also uses Latin borrowings from the Greek that are of supereminent importance to Denys' methodology, including *theoriis/theoricos* at III.v, IV.vii, IV.xvi and *anagogicos* at IV.xvi. Richard's positive use of negative and positive predication, his use of terms for the unknowability or incomprehensibility of God, the abundant use of eminent terminology, and explicit use of Dionysian terms of contemplation and ascent place him, I believe, firmly in the Dionysian strand of apophatic theology.

59. An error in the text at III.ii, 109D mistakes *rimarum* for *rimamur*.

60. *De arca* III.x, 119D–120A; 235–36. "Habet autem hoc ultimum et summum coelum diem suam, habet nimirum et noctem suam. . . . Verumtamen haec nox sicut dies illuminabitur, eo quod quilibet inferiorum coelorum dies ab hujus noctis claritate superetur. Siquidem fecit Deus lunam et stellas in potestatem noctis, et idcirco haec nox illuminato mea."

61. But note that darkness "illuminates" is a decidedly positive image arising out of the negative image of darkness. Here, reversing the epigram of Mortley, *Word to Silence*, p. 35, affirmations secrete a "negative transcendent statement."

62. Cf. *De arca* I.xi, 77D.

63. These things are also available through the authority of divine scripture, as Richard notes. Cf. *De arca* III.xv, 124B: "possumus . . . vel ex divinarum Scripturarum auctoritate colligere, vel rationis attestatione probare."

64. *De arca* III.xxi, 130C–D; 251. "Vide quomodo illud humani ingenii acumen soleat profunda investigare, intima quaeque penetrare, involuta, perplexa, obscura et in tenebris posita, evolvere, enodare, illustrare, et in lucem evocare. Intimos, ut ita dicam, latitantis naturae sinus abditosque recessus vivacitatis suae subtilitate quotidie adit, irrumpit atque pertransit, festinans et anhelans semper in ulteriora penetrare, et altiora conscendere."

65. *De arca* III.xiv 123D, 124A; 241, 242. "Quis inquam, in hac adhuc carne positus, animam suam, vel quamlibet spiritualem substantiam in sua puritate vidit, vel etiam videre potuit? Procul dubio in hac parte humanus intellectus caecus est a nativitate it necesse habet quotidie Domino clamare: "Illumina oculos meos" (Ps xii). . . . Quantumcunque ergo in hac consideratione ingenium tuum exercueris, quantumcunque studium tuum continuaveris, quantumcunque in hac parte sensum tuum dilataveris, scientiam tuam ad plenum cubitum extendere non poteris."

66. *De arca* III.xix, 128B; 248. "Recte ergo dicti operis altitudini nulla mensura praescribitur, quia glorificationis nostrae modus, ut dictum est, nullo nostro sensu comprehenditur."

67. "Being" and "goodness" are available to the senses and to human intellect, while glorification is not. Cf. *De arca* III.xix.

68. *De arca* III.xix, 129A; 249. "Tacendo clamat quod omnino indignum ducat de ejus operis nos mensura instruere, ad cujus inchoationem humana infirmitas in hac vita vix potest assurgere."

69. *De arca* III.xix, 126C; 248.

70. Cf. *De arca* III.xxiv, 133D: "qiudquid bonitatis ejus in nobis gratia imprimit, vel reformat."

71. Cf. *De arca* IV.xvi, 155C and 155D. These terms are discussed in the context of the discovery, showing, and implementation of divine love as metaphorically described in the Song of Songs. Thus the inebriation or excess of mind or what is above and beyond mind "shades" into love: it literally "shades" in that Richard uses the spreading or stretching out of the wings of the cherubim to overshadow or conceal (*obumbraculum*) the propitiatory as a metaphor for the meeting of the inebriated mind with divine love. Safely, love and mind meet in shadow. Richard will use much of Book V to continue the discussion of *alienatio* and *excessus mentis*, though no longer in the context of the symbol of the cherubim. Cf. Appendix A.

72. Of course it is possible that one could posit immediate and unmediated illumination as an anthropological category as do, for instance, the analytical philosophers Alvin Plantinga and Nicholas Wolterstorff in their work on "Reformed epistemology." I believe Richard, too, was interested in immediate and unmediated illumination but tended to claim that illumination takes place in the context of categories such as grace, sanctification, and restoration. On evidentialism, foundationalism, and Reformed epistemology and anthropological categories, see Alvin Plantinga and Nicholas Wolterstorff, eds., *Faith and Rationality: Reason and Belief in God* (Notre Dame: University of Notre Dame Press, 1983).

73. On Book V of *De arca mystica*, see Appendix A. *De arca mystica*, I–IV, contain the manner by which the mind and heart might enter the inmost places of hidden secrets (*in illud intimum arcanorum secretarium introeat*, III.xxiii, 163A), while Book V is an account of Richard's own experience and return already burdened by a veil of forgetting (*velum oblivionis*, ibid.).

74. *De arca* III.ii, 111B; 222. "Sed in illa rationem rerum visibilium, in ista essentiarum invisibilium dignitatem aut occultam rimamur, aut propatalam miramur." Migne reads *propalatam*.

75. Richard reiterates that "We are divinely commanded to make two cherubim. By this we are advised to seek two kinds of contemplation in the things that are above reason." (*Duos autem cherubin facere divinitus jubemur, unde in his quae supra rationem sunt, duo contemplationum genera quaerere admonemur.*) *De arca* IV.iii, 136D; 261. Chapter iii then goes on to explain the difference between "above" and "beyond" reason represented by the two cherubim. Essentially, that which is "above" reason requires the mediation of faith, which is supported by Scripture and authentic witnesses or revelation, while reason actually weakens those things formerly held certain by faith in those things which are "beyond" reason. In the context of the relation of the apophatic and cataphatic methods, the point which is beyond every affirmation or denial, that which is both "above" and "beyond" reason, is accessible only to faith. Cf IV.iii.

76. Or what Javelet calls humanity attaining "*ressemblance angélique.*" Cf R. Javelet, "Bonaventure et Richard de St-Victor," p. 83.

77. *De arca* IV.i, 135D; 260. "Constat itaque supra hominem esse, et humanae rationis modum, vel capacitatem excedere, quae ad haec duo novissima contemplationum genera videntur pertinere. Unde oportuit ea ad similitudinis expressionem non tam humana quam angelica effigie repraesentare. Nisi enim humanae ratiocinationis angustias harum speculationum materia excederet, humanae potius quam angelicae similitudinis formam formandi operis exemplum habere operteret. Oportet ergo nos supra nosmetipsos levare, et ad ea quae supra rationem sunt contemplatione ascendere, si ad angelicae similitudinis instar cupimus intelligentiae nostrae volatum formare. Quaeramus itaque quae sint illa quae supra rationem sunt, quae humanae rationis vim ratiocinationisque nostrae modum transcendunt."

78. *De arca* IV.v, 139B; 264. "Profecto si ad horum speculationem sublavatus fueris ultra haec alia ad quae adhuc ascendere habeas ulterius omnino invenire non poteris. Profecto ultra Deum nihil est. . . ."

79. *De arca* IV.v, 139C; 265. "Supra Deum nihil est sed nec esse, vel esse posse, vel cogitari potest. Non est quo scientia altius ascendat, vel altius ascendere valeat. Plenitudo itaque scientiae Deum cognoscere."

80. Cf. *De arca* IV.v, 139B, in which the outermost portions (*extrema*) of our "going-to-be-made-work" (*operis nostri factura*), in which the supreme levels of all knowledge are copied and figuratively expressed (*figuraliter exprimunter*), are named "cherubim."

81. But it is important to maintain that the cherubim do *not* perfectly emulate, even by similitude, the Creator. Cf. IV.viii, 142D: *Sed nec angelus utique in coelo illam Creatoris sui similitudinem perfecte aemulatur.* To emphasize the difference and at the same time balance the apophatic and cataphatic ascent, Richard suggests calling one cherubim "divine

similitude in rational substances" (*divina in rationabilibus substantiis similitudo*) and the other cherubim "multiplex dissimilitude in the same essences of supreme divinity" (*in eisdem essentiis Divinitatis summae multiplex dissimilitudo*). Ibid., 142D. Thus, while one cherubim is explicitly cataphatic, the other apophatic, neither is in full similitude to the creator.

82. The word *abalienatione* indicates separation from or transformation of the essence of. Zinn translates "alienation." Kirchberger translates "abstraction."

83. *Suspensa* as a participle has the sense of "hovering." The important phrase, "dum in ejusmodi cherubin aspectum suspensa stuperet" is translated by Zinn as, "while it is astounded as it is suspended in the viewing of such Cherubim"; and by Kirchberger as, "lying numbed and amazed at the sight of the Cherubim."

84. *De arca* IV.ix, 144B; 272. "Utinam cum tanto studio et desiderio, in eorum aspectum raperemur, et in eorum admiratione, cum tanta animi abalienatione, supra nosmetipsos duceremur, ut interim mens nostra seipsam nesciret, dum in ejusmodi cherubin aspectum suspensa stuperet. . . ."

85. Richard uses other images to indicate this sense of "unknowing" of self and world. Most are associated with flight, either of birds or of the cherubim. Cf. the excellent example at the beginning of IV.x, 145A–B where, with the cherubim, the contemplative spreads the wings of his or her mind (likewise extending the heart by desire) awaiting the breath of inspiration. In like manner, the mind can soar on the wings of its contemplation, thereby rising above itself and flying away. In so flying it flies above all changeability (including self) and with the passionate force of the eagle transcends all passibility. Richard is highly symbolic and evocative, trying numerous images to depict what is both within and beyond images. A second way in which Richard attempts to indicate the sense of "unknowing" is to equate divine understanding (human "unknowing") with love. The concept of love is not well developed in *De arca mystica*; it is much more developed in some of Richard's other writings (cf. *De quator gradibus violentae charitatis*) and by later writers dependent on Richard. He nonetheless does work briefly with the term. As we might expect in a treatise so deeply influenced by the symbolic balance of opposites, Richard intimately links the growth of love to increase in knowledge: "Otherwise the abundance of divine understanding grows in us fruitlessly unless it augments the flame of divine love in us. And so longing ought always to grow in us on account of knowledge and knowledge on account of love." (Alioquin frustra in nobis divinae cognitionis abundantia crescit, nisi divinae in nobis dilectionis flammam augescat. Debet itaque in nobis crescere semper, et ex cognitione dilectio, et nihilominus ex dilectione cognitio.) IV.x, 145D.

86. *De arca* IV.xii, 148D; 278. "et incomprehensibilitatis suae magni-
tudinem visionis elongatione ostendit."

87. These two allegories are complex and interwoven into the overall
discussion on the ark and cherubim. The transition between the allegories
and the discussion of the cherubim always moves from the angels about
to take flight, wings spread, ready to hover, to a discussion of the language
of love based on these allegories. This point is always at a critical juncture
where the "rational" discussion of angels seems to begin to break down.
The allegories and the discussion of the Song of Songs assist in Richard's
effort to "forge" the wings of the cherubim in the soul. The interweaving
of cherubim narration and allegory or Song of Song narration is given
below.

Richard usually picks up the narration on the cherubim at the end of
each of the following chapters.

Book IV.ix: Discussion of Exodus 25:20: "Spreading wings and covering the oracle, let them cover both sides of the propitiatory" (*utrumque
latus propitiatorii tegant expandentes alas et operientes oraculum*). Book
IV.x-xvi are intended to expand on this verse by explaining how the
contemplative might spread his or her own wings.

Book IV.x: Abraham and Elijah as types of "preparation" for the
coming of the Lord. While both wait, one represents patient endurance,
the other labor.

Book IV.xi: Elijah, who runs out to meet the Lord, is presented as an
allegory of seeing God face to face.

Book IV.xii: Abraham and Elijah are used to develop an allegory of
the relation of experience and interpretation. Some experiences "seen by
ecstasy of mind" can be "brought down for human understanding," while
others cannot.

Book IV.xiii: First use of bridal imagery from Song of Songs. Discussion
of the incessant waiting by the soul to receive the bridegroom. Richard
comments, "if you do not wait with straining desire, perhaps our cherubim
have not yet wings."

Book IV.xiv: While waiting, our affections become entangled in the
world, yet our longing will elevate us. In this waiting and listening, there
is "much need for the spreading out of wings."

Book IV.xv: Through the Song of Songs, Richard has access to a second
set of symbols for union of the soul with the transcendent. By emptying
and waiting, the soul is made pure in order to receive the visits of the
Bridegroom in the garden, the hall, the chamber, and the bridal bed.
In the

> *garden* he (the Bridegroom) is heard (*ex hortulo auditur*)
> by memory, by recollection, by showing

hall he is seen (*in vestibulo videtur*)
 by understanding, by wonder, by contemplation
chamber he is kissed (*in thalamo deosculatur*)
 by affection, by love, by devotion
bed he is embraced (*in cubiculo amplexatur*)
 by applause, by delight, for the infusion of his sweetness.

With these the soul will wait gladly, with Abraham and Elijah, at the entrance of her habitation. With these metaphors of union Richard says, "our beaten work begins to make a great deal of progress . . . our cherubim begin to spread out their wings widely and to hover at every hour for flying."

Book IV.xvi: Affective bridal mysticism from Song of Songs used to support the rational discussion of the cherubim at that point where *ratio* no longer suffices to express our union or presence with God. Though the allegory of Abraham and Elijah and the commentary on the Song of Songs seem to be a digression, it is apparent that these chapters are, in fact, used to support or assist in "our beaten work" of forging the cherubim in our hearts: "We must endeavor to love our God intimately and supremely and cling at all hours with supreme longing to the joy of contemplation. . . . This will mean that our cherubim have spread-out wings."

Book IV.xvii: Returns to a discussion exclusively devoted to cherubim and Exodus, starting where IV.ix left off, at 25:21.

Thus at each instance where languages begin to disintegrate and where the cherubim move "beyond" the rational nature in flight, Richard strengthens the wings by digressions on receptivity and love.

88. *De arca* IV.xii, 149A; 279. "Debemus itaque, juxta Abrahae et Eliae exemplum, in ipso habitationis nostrae exitu et velut in ostio Dominicum adventum exspectare."

89. *De arca* IV.xii, 149B. Richard gives several hints that we recognize what is beyond affirmation and denial only from divine revelation or showing (*ex divina revelatione*). Cf. ibid., IV.xxi, 163D. This important aspect of Richard's spiritual anagogy will be discussed in more detail in Chapter 3 on the function of symbol and Chapter 6 on the weaving of the ark and cherubim in the heart of the contemplative.

90. *De arca* IV.xii, 148B; 277.

91. *De arca* IV.xvii, 157C; 291. "Essentialiter ergo est intra omnia et extra omnia; infra omnia et supra omnia." In addition to these spacial components, Richard also wrestles with the relation of apophatic to cataphatic method when he focuses on memory and vision. Cf. *De arca* IV.xxiii, 167C–168A: *reminiscentes non reminiscimur, et non reminiscentes reminiscimur, dum videntes non pervidemus, et aspicientes non per spicimus.*

92. *De arca* IV.xvii, 157C; 291. "Si intra omnia, nihil illo secretius; si extra omnia, nihil illo remotius; si infra omnia, nihil illo occultius; si supra omnia, nihil illo sublimius. Quid ergo illo incomprehensibilius quo nihil secretius, nihil remotius, nihil occultius, nihil sublimius?"

93. *De arca* IV.xvii, 157D; 291–92. "Item si in omni loco est, nihil illo praesentius. Si extra omnem locum est, nihil illo absentius. Sed nunquid eo ipso absentius quo omnium praesentius, et eo ipso praesentius quo omnium absentius cui aliunde et aliunde non est esse omne quod est. Sed si absentissimo nihil est praesentius, si praesentissimo nihil est absentius, quid illo mirabilius, quid illo incomprehensibilius?"

CHAPTER 3

1. These citations, noted by Châtillon in *DS* 13: 602, are found in *In apocalypsim Joannis* cols. 687A, 688AD, 689C, 759A, in Migne, vol. 196. Dumeige, *DS* 3: 325, notes that the version used was that of Eriugena, probably known to Richard through the *Commentariorum hierarchiam coelestem S. Dionysii Areopagite* of Hugh of St. Victor, a long passage from which Richard reproduces without naming Hugh.

2. *In Apoc.* I.1, 686B. "quando oculos ad exteriora et visibilia aperimus, . . . et quia perspicax non est, non penetrat occulta. Quae nihil denique mysticae significationis continet."

3. *In Apoc.*, I.1, 686C. "quando species, vel actio sensui visus foris ostenditur, et intus magna mysticae significationis virtus continetur."

4. On the Hugonian and Augustinian background for Richard's use of the "three eyes," see P. Sicard, *Diagrammes médiévaux et exégèse visuelle, le Libellus de formatione arche de Hugues de saint-Victor*, Bibliotheca Victorina IV (Turnhout: Brepols, 1993), pp. 187–91. While Hugh sometimes speaks of two eyes (*oculus carnis* or *oculus cordis*), his primary pattern is of the three eyes, *oculus carnis, oculus rationis, oculus contemplationis.* As Sicard notes, "L'oeil de la contemplation peut être guéri par la foi" (p. 188). Richard, in *De arca* III.ix, IV.xxi, incorporates and expands on Hugh's system, associating the "eyes" with various levels of contemplation: first and second contemplation use the metaphor of the eye of the flesh (*oculus carnis*), the third uses the eye of reason or the intellectual eye (*oculo rationis/oculus intellectualis*), the fourth uses the eye of understanding (*intelligentiae oculus*), the fifth uses seeing by means of ecstasy of mind (*mentis excessum videndo*), a vision inspired by Augustine's intellectual or mental vision, and the sixth uses the eye of faith (*fidei oculo*). In this last contemplation, Richard shifts Hugh's eye of contemplation which is

healed or reformed or opened by faith to, simply, the "eye of faith." See also Table 1 above, on the Six Kinds of Contemplation.

5. *In Apoc.* I.1, 686D. "animus per Spiritum sanctum illuminatus formalibus rerum visibilium similitudinibus, et imaginibus praesentatis quasi quibusdam figuris et signis ad invisibilium ducitur cognitionem."

6. *In Apoc.* I.1, 686D–687A. "spiritus humanus per internam aspirationem subtiliter ac suaviter tactus nullis mediantibus rerum visibilium figuris sive qualitatibus spiritualiter erigitur ad coelestium contemplationem."

7. *In Apoc.* I.1, 687A. "In sacratissimorum eloqorum praeter radiatas illuminationes quando possible est respiciemus symbolice nobis et anagogice manifestas coelestium animorum."

8. *In Apoc.* I.1, 687B. Note that "contemplating" is *contemplanda*, present participle, and therefore current and ongoing. "Symbolum est collectio formarum visibilium ad invisibilium demonstrationem. Anagoge, ascensio sive elevatio mentis ad superna contemplanda." In his *In hierarchiam coelestem.* 2, *PL,* 175, 941B, Hugh also defines symbol as a collecting of forms for the demonstration of invisible things: "symbolum est collatio formarum visibilium ad invisibilium demonstrationem." Richard thus uses *collectio* indicating a rhetorical recapitulation or in logic a conclusion or inference, while in Hugh, "collecting" translates *collatio*, which itself is used as an almost literal translation of the Greek *symballein.* On the senses and uses of *collatio* at St. Victor in the first half of the twelfth century, see P. Sicard, *Diagrammes médiévaux et exégèse visuelle,* Appendix 2.

9. Cf. ibid., 687B

10. *In Apoc.,* I.1, 687C. (Emphasis mine). "Unum quo formis, et figuris, et similitudinibus rerum occultarum veritas obumbratur. Aliud quo nude et pure sicut est absque integumento exprimitur. Cum itaque formis, et signis, et similitudinibus manifestatur quod occultum est, vel quod manifestum est describitur, symbolica demonstratio est; cum vero pura et nuda revelatione ostenditur, vel plana et aperta ratione docetur, anagogica."

11. Though this work will not treat hierarchy explicitly, hierarchy is inextricably connected with the notion of symbolism in the Dionysian system. On hierarchy, see Chenu, *Nature, Man and Society,* pp. 79–88, who sees positive attributes of hierarchy for Christianity providing direct participation of all things in the divine nature and its negative attribute as introducing intermediaries between god and humanity; cf. also René Roques, *L'univers Dionysien, structure hiérarchique du monde selon pseudo-Denys* (Paris: Aubier, 1954), chap. 1. McGinn, "Pseudo-Dionysius and the Early Cistercians," p. 219, numbers the important

themes associated with hierarchy as "continuity, viz., that all things are bound together and harmoniously inter-related on the chain of being stretching from God to the furthest reaches of matter, and theophany, or the doctrine that all created being has its deepest meaning as a manifestation of God."

12. *The Celestial Hierarchy*, II.5; p. 153 in *Pseudo-Dionysius: The Complete Works*, trans. Colm Luibheid (New York: Paulist Press, 1987).

13. *Similitude* and *dissimilitude* in Richard. But note that Dumeige, *DS* 3: 326, cautions that Richard does not always use the words in the same sense as the Latin translators of Denys. Still, Dumeige, who as we saw in Chapter 2 thinks of Denys' influence on Richard as important but not pervasive or derivative, emphasizes that influence on Richard's symbolic method: "Richard ne retient que la théologie symbolique." Ibid., p. 326.

14. However, these cherubim, as we will see, also transcend this dialectic.

15. Interestingly, Denys also has an image that comes close to Richard's "hovering," and also of interest is the fact that the image arises out of the context of a discussion of motion and stillness in the relation between the Good, the Beautiful, and the One. Denys' image is that of movement in the pattern of a "spiral." Denys applies the movements of circle, straight line, and spiral to the divine intelligences and to the human soul. But he does not link these patterns of movement to the flight patterns of birds as Richard does. Cf. *The Divine Names* IV, 7–9.

16. R. Mortley, *From Word to Silence*, pp. 232–41, presents an excellent discussion of the relation of hidden to revealed in the context of a larger examination of Denys' shift from the logic of noncontradiction to the logic of contradiction.

17. That is the "light" that comes down bestowing every good and perfect gift from the "Father of lights," from James 1:12. Denys had opened the *Celestial Hierarchy* with this verse, allowing him to discuss hierarchy as well as symbol.

18. Cf. *CH* I.2–3; 146.

19. *CH* II.1; 148.

20. *CH* II.2; 149. See also Denys' *Letter IX*, I; 283, on this same theme.

21. This double way of incongruous imagery should be taken in the context of Denys' claim in *The Divine Names* that the very same things are both similar and dissimilar to God. *DN* IX.7–10; 118–119.

22. Cf. *CH* II.3; 149.

23. *CH* II.3; 150.

24. On the anagogical function of symbols in Denys, see Paul Rorem, *Biblical and Liturgical Symbols within the Pseudo-Dionysian Synthesis* (Rome: Pontifical Institute of Medieval Studies, 1984), especially

Chapter 7. Rorem, following and expanding on Roques, examines the terms for "return" (*epistrophe*) and for "uplifting" (*anagoge*), evaluating their relationship and following the sequence of the "upward" movement from its starting point to its goal. Rorem's general thesis is that the "anagogical" dimensions of Denys' biblical hermeneutics and those of his liturgical interpretation are basically the same (p. 99). Rorem concludes that "The uplifting movement (in Dionysian mysticism) begins with perceptible symbols and then, by incorporating the principle of negation into the practice of biblical and liturgical interpretation, moves on to their intelligible meanings. Next comes the negation or abandonment of these conceptions, no matter how lofty, in the final and silent ascent to the ineffable" (p. 132).

25. But we can never be too eager to deny or abandon symbols. In fact, for Denys, symbols are useful and function for all but the very highest, most rare, and fleeting moments of contemplation. For all but these sublime moments, Denys offers profoundly good advice as to the utility of symbols: "We have therefore to run counter to mass prejudice and we must make the holy journey to the heart of the sacred symbols. And we must certainly not disdain them, for they are the descendants and bear the mark of the divine stamps. They are the manifest images of unspeakable and marvelous sights." *Letter IX.* 2; 284.

26. *CH* II.4; 151.

27. *CH*, II.5; 152–53.

28. On the issue that the distinction between affirmative and negative theology corresponds to similar and dissimilar symbolism and that affirmative theology meets with the same problems as similar symbols, see McGinn, *Foundations of Mysticism*, pp. 173–74; Louth, *Denys the Areopagite*, pp. 45–47; Roques, *Structures théologiques*, pp. 141–43: "Du même que le symbolisme dissemblable a dû redresser les illusions du symbolisme ressemblant, il faudra, pareillement, que la démarche négative corrige les représentations intelligibles de la théologie affirmative."

29. In this sense they are similar to Richard's *materialem manuductionem* of the *In Apoc.* I.1, 688A, noted above, in that they provide a "guiding hand" by means of the visible, material world; a guiding hand that at the same time leads beyond the visible, material world. Richard calls his "guiding hand" the *rerum corporalium imagines* through which in sacred scripture "those things which are incorporeal and invisible are figured." He then goes on to quote Denys verbatim, without citation, on the many forms and figures the angels manifest in scripture. Cf. *In Apoc.* I.1; 688B, quoting Denys' *CH* II.15; 182.

30. Roques, *Structures théologiques*, p. 142. "Des images sans ressemblance . . . leur défaillance est déjà pour l'espirit un stimulant qui

l'empeche de s'engourdir ou de s'hypnotiser sur des figurations dont l'enchantement naturel compromettrait peut-être sa montée vers Dieu."

31. Or, put another way, "the very same characteristic is in one way a similarity to be affirmed and in another way a dissimilarity to be negated . . . even the loftiest similarity is ultimately dissimilar to the thearchy and, conversely, even the lowliest dissimilarity is also similar to it in some way. Thus all along the continuum each depiction is simultaneously similar and dissimilar to God." Cf. Rorem, *Biblical and Liturgical Symbols*, p. 92. Denys explicitly states in *The Divine Names* IX.7; 118, that "the very same things are both similar and dissimilar to God."

32. Cf. McGinn, *Foundations of Mysticism*, p. 174.

33. A wider, more complete definition and utilization of symbol will be encountered in Richard's *De arca mystica*, II.xvii. But Richard does combine the ideas of symbol and anagogy in other works, e.g., in the prologue to *In Apocalypsim*, he defines symbol in opposition to anagogy. Anagogy is *elevatio mentis ad superna contemplanda*. Symbol is *collectio formarum visibilium ad invisibilium demonstrationem* (*In Apoc.* I,i, *PL*, 196, 688A). Richard thus uses a method of sensible signs which he names, after Denys, *manuductio materialis* or material guides. R. Roques notes the same distinctions between symbol and anagogy in the work of Hugh of St. Victor. For Hugh, he says, there are two very distinct manifestations of divine revelation: those which copy by forms, figures, and similitudes, and those which are expressed without veils. The first manner is symbolic, the second is anagogical. ("Hugues voit là deux espéces bien distinctes de manifestations ou de révélations divines: celle qui recourt aux formes, figures et ressemblances sensibles, et celle qui s'exprime à découvert et sans voiles. La premiére serait la maniére symbolique; la seconde, la maniére anagogique.") For Denys, on the other hand, one can have authentic symbolism only in and through anagogy. ("Il ne peut y avoir de symbolisme authentique que dans et par l'anagogie.") See R. Roques, *Structures théologiques*, pp. 330, 338ff.

34. Rorem, *Biblical and Liturgical Symbols*, p. 9, puts this relation between the "cold" cognitive ascent and the "warm" spiritual journey nicely: "The ancient and medieval view of scriptural and ritual symbols involved both subtle theories of the cognitive process and the conviction that this process was not just a matter of human will and skill but a spiritual journey through the symbols to God."

35. On Hugh's use of symbol see Chenu, *Nature, Man, and Society*, chaps. 2, 3; Zinn, "Book and Word," pp. 143–69; McGinn, "Pseudo-Dionysius and the Early Cistercians," pp. 217–19; R. Baron, *Science et sagesse chez Hugues de Saint-Victor* (Paris: P. Lethielleux, 1957), pp. 181–83; Baron, *Études sur Hugues de Saint-Victor* (Paris: Desclée de Brouwer,

1964), pp. 133–218; Roques, *Structures théologiques*, pp. 294–364. On the Hugonian use of symbols in revelation and illumination and their anagogic function, see P. Sicard, *Diagrammes médiévaux et exégèse visuelle*, pp. 184–187. M. L. Fuehrer, "The Principle of Similitude in Hugh of Saint Victor's Theory of Divine Illumination," *American Benedictine Review* 30 (March 1979): 80–92, is especially good on the pre-Dionysian sources of symbol. On the Hugonian synthesis of Augustine and Dionysius with regard to symbol, see Chenu, *La théologie au douzième siècle*, Etudes de philosophie médiévale, vol. 45 (Paris: J. Vrin, 1957), chaps. 5, 7, 8, 13; Zinn, "Book and Word," pp. 143–46.

36. *Commentariorum in hierarchiam coelestem S. Dionysii Areopagite*, III, *PL*, 175, 960D. "collatio videlicet, id est coaptatio visibilium formarum ad demonstrationem rei invisibilis propositarum." For other key passages on the symbol as a *collatio* of visible forms for the demonstration of invisible things, see ibid., 940D, 941B, 946AB, 1053C.

37. On the relation of mundane and divine theology, see *In hier.* I.1, 923D–928B. For a discussion of Hugh's use of the terms, see R. Roques, *Structures théologiques*, pp. 297–301. On the works of creation and restoration, see *De sacramentis* I, prol., ii and iii, *PL*, 176, 183A–184C.

38. *In hier.* I.1, 926C. On the relation of the two *simulacra* related to *opus creationis* and *opus restaurationis*, see *De sacramentis* I, prol. chaps. i–iii, 183A–184C and I,6.iv, 266B–267B.

39. That is, following Rom. 1:20ff, they made idols of the manifestations of God in the world.

40. *In hier.* I.1, 923D–925A. "Et praesumpsit, et dixit ut ultra pergeret ad sapientiam summam confidens in sapientia sua, quasi via esse potuisset ad illam. Et ascendit, et elevatus est ut ad alta corde perveniret. Et fecit sibi scalam, speciem creaturae, nitens ad invisibilia Creatoris. . . . Nam illa, quae videbantur, nota erant, et erant alia quae nota non erant, et per ea quae manifesta sunt, putaverunt ire in illa, quae abscondita fuerunt, et corruerunt mente ultra possibilem veritatem in mendacia figmentorum suorum, ubi non est inventum amplius, quod apprehenderent. Ideo stultam fecit Deus sapientiam hujus mundi, quia in illa non potuit inveniri sapientia Dei; . . . Praedicatus est Christus crucifixus, ut humilitate veritas quaereretur. Sed mundus medicum [modicum] despexit, et non potuit verum agnoscere."

41. They end in error which they venerate: "Haec sunt simulacra errorum quae theologia . . . vanitatis eorum, et deceptionis praedicat veneranda." Cf. *In hier.* I.1, 926B. On Latin quotations in text above, see ibid., 925B–926B.

42. The mundane philosophers, on the other hand, are confounded by pride (*superbi*) at the summit of truth. They despise the humility of faith in

the death of the Savior: "humilitatem fidei in morte Salvatoris dispiciunt." Cf. *In heir.* I.1, 926B.

43. *In hier.* I.1, 926C. "Simulacrum naturae erat species hujus mundi. Simulacrum autem gratiae erat humanitas Verbi. Et in utroque Deus monstrabatur, sed non in utroque intelligebatur; quoniam natura quidem specie sua artificem demonstravit, sed contemplantis oculos illuminare non potuit. Humanitas vero Salvatoris et medicina fuit, ut caeci lumen reciperent, et doctrina pariter ut videntes agnoscerent veritatem."

44. *In hier.* I.1, 926D. "Prius ergo illuminavit, postea demonstravit. Natura enim demonstrare potuit, illuminare non potuit."

45. *In hier.* I.1, 926D–927A. "Per simulacra igitur naturae, Creator tantum significabatur; in simulacris vero gratiae praesens Deus ostendebatur, quia illa operatus est ut intelligeretur esse; in istis vero operatus est ut agnosceretur praesens esse. Haec est distantia theologiae hujus mundi ab illa, quae divina nominatur theologia. Impossibile enim est invisibilia, nisi per visibilia demonstrari: et propterea omnis theologia necesse habet visibilibus demonstrationibus uti in invisibilium declaratione. . . . Theologia vero divina opera restaurationis elegit secundum humanitatem Jesu, et sacramenta ejus."

46. R. Roques points out that for Hugh, "sometimes anagogy also designates spiritual interpretation by which the understanding restores a symbol to its highest signification." See *Structures théologiques*, pp. 320–21.

47. The distinction between anagogy and presence is pointed out, though in different terms, by René Roques. Finding a distinction between Denys' hierarchical cosmology as always viewed from an objective point of view and Hugh's hierarchical cosmology emphasizing psychological, moral, practical, and affective points of view, Roques says that "Par là s'explique que Hugues ait voulu séparer plus que ne l'avait fait Denys le signe de sa signification et donner au signe lui-même une valeur en soi, en accusant son 'réalisme propre.' " For Denys, according to Roques, the symbol functions only anagogically. For Hugh it functions anagogically, but also as a signifier of presence in that, psychologically and practically, it participates in its own reality. On the distinction between Denys' and Hugh's hierarchical cosmology, see Roques, *Structures théologiques*, p. 325. On the dual function of symbol in Hugh, see ibid., p. 329.

48. On the idea of visible creatures and forms providing a "guiding hand" (*manuductio*) in the contemplative ascent, see Zinn, "Book and Word," pp. 167ff. See also *De sacramentis* II.VIII.vii on the application and function of symbol as both *similitudo* and *veritas*; that is, it serves the dual function of truth (it is what it is) and guide (it points beyond itself). *De arca mystica* is full of the verb *ducere* and its cognates. They are

used to illustrate the leading or guiding quality of symbols, certain people (most commonly Moses), and the material world. For a comprehensive but by no means exhaustive list: *deducetur*, II.xiii, 90D; *manuductione*, II.xvii, 95D; *perducitur/manuductionem/ducum itineris*, II.xvii, 96A; *conducit*, II.xvii, 96B; *ductus fuit*, III.xiv, 124A; *adducere*, III.xviii, 127D; *adducit*, III.xxi, 131A; *perducere*, IV.v, 139C; *duceremur*, IV.ix, 144B; *obducitur*, IV.ix, 144C; *deducit*, IV.xi, 147C; *introducimus/introducitur*, IV.xii, 148D; *adducuntur*, IV.xvii, 156C; *adducta sunt*, IV.xx, 162D; *educere/traducere/introducere*, IV.xxi, 164B; *adduci*, IV.xxii, 166B; *ducuntur*, IV.xxiii, 166D.

49. *De sacramentis*, I.X.ix, 342A. "Nunc scilicet quando per fidem videmus, videmus per speculum in aenigmate; tunc autem quando videbimus per contemplationem videbimus facie ad faciem."

50. Hugh also uses the distinction between image and thing to discuss the nature of the body and blood of Christ in the Eucharist. The body and blood is an image according to the appearance of bread and wine (*imago est, secundum speciem panis et vini*), it is a thing according to the truth of its substance (*res est secundum substantiae suae veritatem*). Cf. *De sacramentis* II, VIII, vii, 467A.

51. *Didascalicon* V.iii, trans. Taylor, pp. 121–22. As with mundane and divine theology, it is the philosopher who knows only words (the human voice), which, once uttered, perish, while the divine theologian knows things (the voice of God speaking to men), which, once created, subsist.

52. On *integumentum* or *involucrum* as methods of symbolically wrapping or enveloping truth, see Chenu, *Nature, Man, and Society*, pp. 110ff.

53. *De sacramentis* II, I, ix, trans. Deferrari, p. 234.

54. *De sacramentis*, II.VIII.vii, *PL*, 176:486D.

55. Chenu, *Nature, Man, and Society*, p. 103.

56. General discussions of symbol and metaphor in religious language present a complex and sometimes daunting array of methods and theories. For a useful summary of contemporary approaches, see Thomas Fawcett, *The Symbolic Language of Religion* (London: Allen & Unwin, 1972), chaps. 1 and 2. For a good summary of the work of Clifford Geertz, Victor Turner, and Paul Ricoeur, see Caroline Walker Bynum, "The Complexity of Religious Symbols," in *Gender and Religion*, ed. C. Bynum, S. Harrell, P. Richman (Boston: Beacon Press, 1986), pp. 4–11. For an excellent discussion of classical accounts, problems of definition, and theories of metaphor (including substitution, emotive and incremental theories) see Janet Martin Soskice, *Metaphor and Religious Language* (Oxford: Clarendon Press, 1985), chaps. 1–3. For a now classic discussion of the relation of theology and symbol, see Paul Tillich, "Theology and Symbolism," in *Religious Symbolism*, ed. F. Ernest Johnson (New York:

Harper and Brothers, 1955), pp. 107–16. For a good summary from the perspective of the history of religions approach, see Mircea Eliade, "Observations on Religious Symbolism," in *the Two and the One* (London: Harvill Press, 1965), chap. 5. On Ricoeur's explanation of symbol and sign, see Paul Ricoeur, *Interpretation Theory: Discourse and the Surplus of Meaning* (Fort Worth: Texas Christian University Press, 1976), pp. 45–69. On the relation between religious awareness and symbolic expression, see Frederick J. Strong, *Emptiness: A Study of Religious Meaning* (Nashville: Abingdon Press, 1967).

57. Cf. C. Bynum, "The Complexity of Religious Symbols," pp. 2–4. Bynum adopts the term "polysemic symbol" from the work of Victor Turner, in Bynum et al., *Gender and Religion*, p. 10.

58. Cf. Paul Tillich, "Theology and Symbolism." Nipping at the heels of Richard of St. Victor by the mere space of eight short centuries, Tillich points out that "the direct object of theology is not God; the direct object of theology is His manifestation to us, and the expression of this manifestation is the religious symbol" (p. 108). Tillich's famous definition of symbol is as follows: "This is the great function of symbols, to point beyond themselves in the power of that to which they point, to open up levels of reality which otherwise are closed, and to open up levels of the human mind of which we otherwise are not aware" (p. 109).

59. Cf. Grover A. Zinn, "Mandala Symbolism and Use in the Mysticism of Hugh of St. Victor," *History of Religions* 12 (August 1972): 318. On the transformational function of mandala symbolism, see also Jung, "The Symbolism of the Mandala," pp. 91–213; Cousins, *Bonaventure and the Coincidence of Opposites*, chap. 6.

60. Mircea Eliade, *The Two and the One*, pp. 205f.

61. *Sermons et opuscules spirituels inédits*, ed. Châtillon, p. xlvi, n.1. For Châtillon, according to the logic of identity or noncontradiction, *"une chose est ce qu'elle est, et non autre chose,"* and according to the logic of participation, *"une chose est ce qu'elle, mais aussi autre chose."* It is through symbols used according to this "logic of participation" that the medieval period is able to balance its dialectical inclinations and to develop a psychology of transformation in the context of contemplation and the spiritual quest. The concept goes back at least to Eriugena who says, "There is nothing, in visible and corporeal things, that does not signify something incorporeal and invisible" (*Periphyseon* V,3; 865–66, cited in E. Gilson, *Christian Philosophy in the Middle Ages*, p. 120). Gilson adds that this statement "could be the charter of medieval symbolism."

62. Cf. G. Ladner, "Medieval and Modern Understanding of Symbolism: A Comparison," *Speculum* 54 (April 1979): 223–56. According to Ladner, symbols grounded in an analogy of being refer ultimately "to the

coexistence of similarity and dissimilarity between creatures and God," and tend toward metaphorical, analogical, and comparative functions (pp. 225, 227). On the other hand, symbols utilizing an analogy of participation refer to "hierarchical unity" and tend toward participatory and unitive symbolism (p. 227). Comparing the two analogies, Ladner goes on to comment, "as to the related contrast between analogy and participation, it is admittedly one of degree only, since both contain elements of polarity and unity, of similarity and of dissimilarity. Nevertheless, it may be said only of analogy that it requires *polarity* as its extreme limit and only of participation that it requires *unity* as its consummation." Taken as supplementary ideologies, analogy and participation form a kind of coincidence of opposites that is echoed in Richard's own use of the cherubim to symbolize unity and personhood within the Trinity. Ladner provides telling insight into how Richard of St. Victor might employ the dialectical method of the coincidence of opposites even as he "participates" in the relational presence of God. Exploring contemporary notions of symbol, he notes that Jean Piaget and Paul Ricoeur "have already moved in a direction where participation, transformation, and unification have equal standing with mere similarity and opposition." He adds that Ricoeur and Claude Lévi-Strauss have shown "how closely sacrifice is connected, especially in a Christian context, with the metonymic aspect of symbolism, an aspect which in Christianity culminates in the participation of the Church in the real presence of Christ in the Eucharist" (pp. 241, 241, n.93). The space on the ark, between the two Cherubim, is in some sense a eucharistic space: the cherubim oppose while the real presence of Christ coincides. But again, this is not a "Word" for Richard to speak. It is to be eaten, experienced, participated in.

63. Cf. R. Mortley, *From Word to Silence*, pp. 221–41. Mortley's typology is developed in the context of Denys' use of apophatic language, making it particularly applicable to Richard. Mortley traces two principles of logic that in turn have direct application to language. The first is the Aristotelian tradition of the logical principle of noncontradiction. In the second, "The use of contradiction (hidden and manifest; spoken of and unspeakable) strikes a new note in the philosophy of classical antiquity" (p. 237). This second priciple of contradiction is characteristic of philosophical mysticism: "Contradiction arises out of a desire to supersede language, just as the *via negativa* does. Both manoeuvres are examples of speculative philosophy trying to cause language to rise above itself, to move out of its own limits. . . . both techniques are attempts to interfere with the usual structure of language" (pp. 239–40). Thus for Mortley, contradictory logic and contradictory (dissimilar) symbols are an attempt to force symbols to play a different tune, as it were, from the language

that surrounds them. Mortley also draws conclusions about the logic of contradiction that are similar in nature to the symbolism and logic of participation formulated by Châtillon and Ladner. For example, Mortley says, "Contradiction is an attempt to use language; . . . It is designed to force language to include, rather than exclude. . . . Contradiction is holistic in character, forcing us to embrace incompatibilities rather than to choose between them" (p. 240). Both the symbolism of participation and the symbolism of contradiction thus function to integrate and transform, rather than separate and deny.

64. Cf. E. Cousins, "States of Consciousness: Charting the Mystical Path," in *Fires of Desire: Erotic Energies and the Spiritual Quest*, ed. John Shea and Fredrica Halligan (New York: Crossroads, 1992), pp. 126–45; E. Cousins, *Bonaventure and the Coincidence of Opposites*, chaps. 5 and 6; B. McGinn, "Ascension and Introversion in the *Itinerarium mentis in Deum*," in *Bonaventura 1274–1974* (Rome: Grottaferrata, 1974), vol. 3, pp. 535–52; P. Sicard, *Diagrammes médiévaux et exégèse visuelle*, Appendix 6, "Symboles architecturaux, arches et tabernacles." Symbols of the center or introversion are those such as a dwelling place, a house, a castle, or a temple, which are associated with the soul and thus find divinity at the center. Symbols of ascent or extroversion such as a ladder, a mountain, or the passage from earth to heaven move in an exterior and ascending direction symbolizing various levels of being one traverses in the spiritual journey. According to this typology it is quite a simple matter to see Richard's totalizing symbol of the ark and cherubim as effectively employing symbols of the center and of ascent: the ark is a typical centering symbol; the cherubim and their propensity for flight are symbols of ascent.

65. On the symbolism of the sacred ground, cf. M. Eliade, *The Two and the One*, pp. 195–201; on the symbolism of magic flight, see ibid., pp. 211ff., and M. Eliade, *Mythes, rêves et mysteres* (Paris: Gallimard, 1957), pp. 99ff., especially pp. 110ff. The symbolism of sacred ground, related to the symbolism of the center, forces a rediscovery of our rootedness in matter and earth, making available a new spirituality of matter. (Also on this issue, see E. Cousins, "States of Consciousness," pp. 23, 25.) Symbols of magic flight, on the levels of spiritual activity, reveal ideas of liberty and transcendence. In his discussion of the symbolism of magic flight, Eliade has recourse to depth psychology, which "has taught us that a symbol delivers its message and fulfills its function even when its meaning escapes the conscious mind." Cf. *The Two and the One*, p. 211. In *De arca mystica* Richard of St. Victor, consciously or not, employed material or grounded symbols (the ark) and symbols of magic flight (the cherubim).

66. These typologies, of course, by no means exhaust the literature. For a detailed analysis and explication of these and other typologies of symbols, especially as they influence Richard of St. Victor, see S. Chase, "Into the Secret Places of Divine Incomprehensibility: The Symbol of the Cherubim in *De arca mystica* of Richard of St. Victor" (Ph.D. diss., Fordham University, 1994), pp. 129–40.

CHAPTER 4

1. On the flight pattern of birds as "hovering," see *De arca* I.v, 69A and on contemplation as "hovering," *De arca* I.iv, 67D. For full citations, see "Contemplation" and "Hovering" sections in Introduction section of this work.

2. The careful reader will note the shift in symbolic structure of this work from that of Richard's work. Richard, of course, in his consideration of contemplation based on the structure of the ark and cherubim, moves from crown to propitiatory to first cherubim to second cherubim. This work uses the same symbolic structure to weave its chapters, but in a different order. It moves from crown to first cherubim to propitiatory to second cherubim. The shift may reflect something of the difference of method and content of this work from that of Richard's treatise.

3. *De arca* I.i, 63D; 151. "habeat nomen ex re, haec quae dicitur arca sanctificationis."

4. Cf. *De Sacramentis* II.VI, vi–vii, *PL*, 176, 465D–467B, where Hugh points out that sacred symbols not only point beyond themselves but are also "true" in and of themselves. (*Ergo mors Christi vera fuit; et tamen exemplum fuit, et resurrectio ejus vera fuit, et exemplum fuit.*) This "truth" or thing (*res*) is thus believed to be truly and substantially present (*sic res ibi veraciter et substantialiter praesens creditur*). In the context of the Eucharist, Jesus Christ is then both *imago (secundum speciem panis et vini in qua cernitur)* and *res (secundum substantiae suae veritatem)*. See also *De Sacra.* I.IX where *imago* and *res* are associated with faith and contemplation.

5. *De arca* I.i, 63D; 151. "sit dicitur arca sanctificationis vobis."

6. *De arca* I.v, 69B; 159. "Iuxta hoc sane prepositarum similitudinum exemplar contemplationis nostrae volatus multiformiter variatur."

7. Cf. *De arca* I.v, 68D.

8. *De arca* I.xii, 78A; 172. "Duo autem novissima contemplationum genera exprimuntur angelica figura. Et recte quidem illa operis factura non humanam sed angelicam formam habuit quae illa contemplationum genera per similitudinem repraesentare oportuit, quorum materia omnem

humanam rationem excedit." Zinn renders *operis factura* as "material product." I believe that Richard did not intend the cherubim as contemplation to be static, however. The "work" is ongoing; it is always in the process of being accomplished, whether with regard to the "work" of contemplation, the symbolic "form" of the angel, or the general fabrication of the angel on the ark of Moses. Contemplation is, after all, as Richard points out, a work, a labor, a trouble, a pain, an exertion on the order of a bird beating its wings rapidly to stay in one place.

9. *De arca* I.xii, 78C; 173. "rerum figuram quarum hae rationi consentire, illae rationi contraire videntur."

10. *De arca* I.xii, 78B; 172. "Sed in ultimis istis duobus totum pendet ex gratia et omnino longinqua sunt, et valde remota ab omni humana industria, nisi in quantum unusquisque coelitus accipit, et angelicae sibi similitudinis habitum divinitus superducit."

11. Richard, in a later chapter, links the work of the symbol of the cherubim seen in I.xii (that is, the *operis factura*) to the *facientes operationem* or working in "deep waters" (*facientes operationem in aquis multis*). Such "symbol work" presents "wondrous manifestations to those who see marvelous things in the depths . . . [those who explore such wonders] sometimes elicit something hidden, sometimes persuade justice, sometimes dissuade from something unjust. Certainly, they who know how to make things in this way work in deep waters. They are those who see wondrous things in the depths . . . and Wisdom is drawn out from hidden things." *De arca* II.viii, 86B–D; 184–185: "miranda spectacula eorum qui vident mirabilia in profundo . . . aliquando ad eliciendum aliquod occultum, aliquando ad persuadendum justum, aliquando ad dissuadendum aliquod injustum. Isti sane qui noverunt facere hujusmodi operationem in aquis multis, isti, inquam, sunt qui vident mirabilia in profundo . . . et sapientiam trahabat de occulto."

12. *De arca* II.xii, 89A; 190. "Ad hoc itaque genus pertinet quoties per rerum visibilium similitudinem rerum invisibilium qualitatem deprehendimus, quoties per visibilia mundi invisibilia Dei cognoscimus."

13. See Table 1. Contemplations one through three have to do with objects of the natural world, while contemplation four has generally to do with the "objects"—whether psychological, emotional, or rational—arising from the soul.

14. *De arca* II.xii, 89D; 190. "quia invisibilia Dei a creatura mundi per ea quae facta sunt intellecta conspiciuntur." Richard does not cite Romans at this point. The Vulgate reads: "invisibilia enim ipsius a creatura mundi per ea quae facta sunt intellecta conspiciuntur."

15. *De arca* II.xii, 89D–90A; 190 (emphasis mine). "Recte autem haec contemplatio qui ut ad invisibilia ascendat baculo se corporeae similitu-

dinis sustentat, et quadam, ut ita dicam, corporalium proprietatum scala se ad alta sublevat."

16. In fact, as Richard says, not only is physicality integrated into the contemplative ascent, "this very speculation always inclines itself spontaneously to exploring the particular properties of corporeal things so that it may have something from which it might draw a similitude from one thing to another." Ibid., 90D; 190: "Sic nimirum, sic ista speculatio, usque ad indagandas rerum corporearum proprietates, sponte se inclinat, ut habeat unde ex istis ad illa similitudinem trahat."

17. *De arca* II.xii, 90B; 190. "quia contemplantis animus ad invisibilia comprehendenda ex rerum visibilium similitudine non parum adjuvatur."

18. In fact, Richard distinguishes five grades or modes by which the rational principle of similitudes (*similitudinum*—Migne wrongly reads *similtiudinum*—*ratio quaeritur*) is sought and assigned an object in the investigation of invisible things (*in invisibilium investigationem*). The first mode is when a similitude is taken from the manner in which it is itself (*ex eo unde ipsum est*) or, better, from that which it itself is (*ex eo quod ipsum est*). The second and third similitudes draw their similitude from that which something is in itself (*ex eo quod in ipso est*); the fourth and fifth from that which something is through itself (*ex eo quod per ipsum est*). Richard then gives examples of the working of each kind of similitude from scripture. See *De arca* II.xv, 93A–94B. This chapter in Richard also distinguishes between the rational principle of similitude (*similitudinum ratione*) and the grace of similitude (*similitudinis gratia*). Cf. ibid., 93D. This is the first time Richard uses *similitudinis gratia*, placing it in the context of the passage on rain and snow falling from heaven to give life on earth quoted from Isaiah. Richard seems to be implying that similitudes themselves descend from heaven like rain or snow (they fall like grace), giving seed and providing the bread of life. This then is an early indication that even "rational similitudes" are a "grace" from above, a gift. Richard's exemplarism would justify such a gift metaphysically, his theory of contemplation would necessitate such a gift as the broadest context of Wisdom.

19. *De arca* II.xii, 90C; 191. "Habent tamen corporea omnia ad invisibilia bona similitudinem aliquam, sed alia infimam quamdam, et valde longinquam, et pene extraneam. Alia autem viciniorem et manifestiorem. . . ."

20. These include nearness (*viciniorem, propinquiorem*), to approach or draw near (*appropinquare*), to cling or cleave to (*inhaerere*), to graft into (*inserere*), and to bear or give birth to (*gerere*). Cf. *De arca* II.xii, 90A–C. With reference to the latter, Zinn translates *gerunt* as "show," thus maintaining the visual image, but I think it more to the point that

these likenesses, both near and far, actually carry the stamp or image of the invisible. *Gero* in Richard is thus, I think, closer to the idea of "bear, give birth to" so that the likenesses or similitudes (themselves "impregnated" by the *imago Dei*) give birth to "the image of the invisible."

21. *De arca* II.xii, 90C; 191. "Ab ipsis ergo quae ad illa vicinius accedunt, et quae invisibilium imaginem evidentiorem gerunt, debemus itique similitudinem trahere, ut ad ea quae per experientiam non novimus, per ea quae cognovimus intelligentia nostra possit ascendere. . . ."

22. *De arca* II.xiv, 92B.

23. Cf. *De arca* II.xiv, 91D–92A: "est a visibilibus ad invisibilia similitudinem trahere, et ex illorum consideratione ad istorum cognitionem propositae similitudinis assignatione ascendere."

24. Yet we must keep in mind that experience, reason, the body, and nature are all in some sense human constructions and thus only distantly similar to the invisible and the spiritual. The danger, of course, as Paul was warning in Romans 1, is that these human constructions will be taken for the invisible and made Gods. Richard thus warns, "humana instituta ad invisibilia et spiritalia valde lonqinquam, et omnino peregrinam similitudinem habere." Ibid., II.xiv, 92C. Human institutions have only a distant, foreign likeness, and so angelic, dissimilar symbols will be introduced.

25. *De arca* II.xvii, 95D–99A; 199–203.

26. This point is here emphasized to contradict the notion that mysticism in general, and particularly medieval and twelfth-century mysticism, is dualist and Platonist in its denial of the body. Richard, for example, was dualist and Platonist, but he was much more: through imagination guiding reason, the contemplative moves from the natural, visible world to the invisible through the bodily senses: the invisible is simply not accessible without the bodily senses. He is dualist, but more importantly Richard is integrative and intuitive; he empowers body, nature, and senses. For just one of many examples, picked because it is otherwise extremely insightful, of the misapprehension of twelfth-century rationalism and mysticism based on a false assumption of radical dualism, see Tina Stiefel, *The Intellectual Revolution in Twelfth Century Europe* (New York: St. Martin's Press, 1985), especially Chapter 1 on "Intellectual Background."

27. *De arca* II.xvii, 96A. "Dum enim imaginatio rationi rerum visibilium formas repraesentat, et ipsam ex earumdem rerum similitudine ad invisibilium investigationem informat quodammodo illuc eam conducit quo per se ire nescivit." Throughout this passage, cognates of *ducto* abound. *Manuductio*, the leading or guiding hand, as pointed out by Grover Zinn, is a favorite Victorine theological and spiritual term. Other

cognates from this passage alone include *perducitur*, the imagination as *ducem itineris*, and the imagination conducting (*conducit*) reason.

28. *De arca* II.xvii, 96C; 200. "Quoties ergo cognoscendarum rerum, per corporeum sensum, experientiam capere cogitur, toties interior homo noster ducem suum sequi videtur. Absque dubio sensus carnis, sensum cordis in cognoscendis rebus praecedit; quia, nisi prius sensibilia per sensum corporeum animus caperet, omnino non inveniret quid de eis saltem cogitare potuisset."

29. On the concept of spiritual senses, see Karl Rahner, "The Spiritual Senses According to Origen" and "The Doctrine of the Spiritual Senses in the Middle Ages," in Karl Rahner, *Theological Investigations*, vol. 16, trans. David Morland (New York: Crossroad, 1983), pp. 81–103; 104–34.

30. *De arca* III.i, 108D–109A. "in incorporeis et invisibilibus essentiis utpote spiritibus angelicis . . . ad imaginem Dei creata." On the *imago Dei* in Richard of St. Victor, especially in *De arca mystica*, see Ellen M. Ross, "Humans' Creation in God's Image: Richard of St. Victor, Walter Hilton, and Contemporary Theology" (Ph.D. diss., University of Chicago, 1987), pp. 67–85.

31. Concerning the value of the propitiatory as symbol, Richard says, "But the artful work of our propitiatory is rightly brought above all in wood, when, by placing the fantasies of the body under foot, the soul is raised to the heights by the power of the sublime investigation and there 'hovers' in wonder in these things." *De arca* III.ii, 111B; 222: "Sed artificiale illud propitiatorii nostri opus recte quidem lignis omnibus super fertur, quia, calcatis undique corporalium phantasmatum occursibus, sublimis hujus investigationis libramine animus ad summa levatur, et in eorum admiratione suspenditur."

32. The structural aspects of symbol employed by Richard manifest a symbology based on an analogy of being as described above by Châtillon and Ladner in Chapter 3. The so-called process aspects of symbol employ a symbology based on participation and the logic of participation described by Ladner and Mortley, and on centering as described by Cousins and McGinn.

33. *De arca* III.iii, 113A–B; 225. "Primum ergo est in hac considera- tione, ut redeas ad teipsum, intres ad cor tuum, . . . Discute quid sis, . . . Disce ergo ex tuo spiritu cognoscere quid debeas de aliis spiritibus aesti- mare. Haec porta, haec scala, hic introitus, iste ascensus, hac intratur ad intima, hac elevamur ad summa, haec via ad hujus speculationis fastigium, haec fabricandi propitiatorii artificium."

34. The symbol of the sun, in addition to functioning as an image of self-knowledge, also serves as an image of restoration. Cf. *De arca*

III.vii, 117C: "quia mira illic supercoelestium spectaculorum jucunditate reficitur [he is restored or refreshed]."

35. *De arca* III.vii, 117D, 118A; 232, 233. "In loco autem suo sol renascens paulatim ad altiora conscendit quia per sui cognitionem in coelestium contemplationem assurgit. . . . Vides quantum valeat homini plena cognitio sui? Ex hac siquidem proficit ad cognitionem omnium coelestium, terrestrium et infernorum." The subtitle of III.vi also sums up the idea of self as symbol of ascent and understanding of self as *renascens* or restoration: "Quomodo ex speculatione sui spiritualium intelligentia comparatur, seu etiam amissa reparatur." *De arca* III.vi, 116D. Taking *reparare* as prepare anew, repair, restore, renew, Richard teaches, "How from speculation of oneself an understanding of spiritual things is acquired or 'restored' after having been lost."

36. *De arca* III.v, 115B; 228. "et per spiritus tui considerationem in spirituum contemplationem assurgere, et in hunc modum ex spiritualibus spiritualia *comparare*, incipis et tu pariter spiritualis esse."

37. *De arca* III.viii, 118C; 233. "sua quaedam terra, suum habet coelum." Richard uses the image of the soul as microcosm of earth and heaven to elaborate on the triple sense by which the self may be considered. These considerations are: the imaginative (*imaginale*), by which are considered the images and similitudes of visible things; the rational (*rationale*), by which are considered the definition of all visible things and the investigation of invisible things; and the intellectual (*intellectuale*), by means of which are contemplated the spiritual things and even divine things. Cf. ibid., 118D: "In primo itaque coelo continentur omnium visibilium imagines et similitudines. Ad secundum vero pertinent visibilium omnium rationes, diffinitiones et invisibilium investigationes. Ad tertium autem spectant spiritalium ipsorum, etiam divinorum comprehensiones et contemplationes." The fourth contemplation, symbolized by the propitiatory and concerned with the soul or self, is made by means of reason (*in ratione et secundum rationem*). But precisely in that it probes the deep things of the soul, this contemplation has access still to imagination and cognitive or intellective functions which consider visible, invisible, and revealed "spiritual" things. The fifth and sixth contemplations will rely all or in part on grace or showing (*revelatione*). The implication of these considerations for Richard's symbolic theology is that, even at the level of soul, he can continue to speak of symbols in terms of "similitudes."

38. Again, this is made possible through the *imago Dei*. On the soul made in the image and similitude (from Genesis 1:26) of God, cf. *De arca* III.xiii; III.xx–xxiv. In each case the soul still functions, because of the *imago Dei*, as microcosm or symbol, though deformed, of God.

39. *De arca* III.x, 121B; 237. "ex multa consideratione et agnitione spiritus tui subleveris ad cognitionem et contemplationem spiritus angelici et Spiritus divini." From this consideration comes the "abundance of Gold" (*copia auri*) from which the contemplative's propitiatory and angels are forged. Specifically, the "abundance of Gold" with regard to the soul is "the brilliance of the highest Wisdom better able to shine forth . . . than by the creation, restoration, and glorification of the soul." Ibid., 120D. (. . . summae sapientiae claritas poterit tibi melius elucescere . . . quam animae videlicet *creatione, reparatione, glorificatione?*) In speaking of the beginning (*creatione*), advancement (*reparatione*), and consumation (*glorificatione*) of the "building of the ark" and so of the reconstruction of the soul, Richard makes a triple distinction in the spiritual essences of divine gifts. First, the spiritual nature (*spiritalis natura*) is created so that it might be (*sit*); second, it is made just so that it might be good (*bona sit*); third, it is glorified so that it might be blessed (*beata sit*). Thus the soul and the symbols associated with the soul are "through creation started toward the good, through justification expanded into the good, and through glorification consummated in the good." Ibid., III.xi, 121D. (Per creationem itaque ad bonum initiatur, per justificationem in bono dilatatur, per glorificationem in bono consummatur.)

40. That is the Neoplatonic reversal of the procession from the One by means of descending affirmations to the return to the One by means of ascending denials.

41. *De arca* III.x, 119D–120A; 235–236. "Habet autem hoc ultimum et summum coelum diem suam, habet nimirum et noctem suam, et si hoc coelum attendimus, quandiu in hac vita sumus, quid aliud quam noctem habemus vel habere possumus, donec nox in suo cursu iter peregerit, et aurora lucis rutilans noctis tenebras deterserit. . . . Sequidem fecit Deus lunam et stellas in potestatem noctis, et idcerco haec nox illuminatio mea."

42. *De arca* III.xix, 128B; 248. "Sed glorificationis nostrae modum quis sensus hominum capere, quae ratio potest comprehendere?"

43. *De arca* III.xix, 128D–129A; 249. "Hoc est sane quod Scriptura sancta tacite innuit, quae de propitiatorii nostri altitudine omnino nihil dixit, ac si per taciturnitatem ipsam altius clamet . . . Tacendo clamat. . . ." *Innuit* here indicates "to give a nod to, make a sign or symbol to."

44. Another example of Richard's move toward a symbolic method based on the dialectic of hovering stems from the simple consideration of the praise due God the Creator. The dialectic develops from the curious relation between self-knowledge and the knowledge of angels. Richard says, "If you notice how much you exceed the beastly spirit in mental sense you will sing heartily, 'I praise the Lord who gave me understanding' (Ps. 15:7).

If you consider angelic understanding, you will surely profess, 'God, you know my foolishness' (Ps. 68:6)." (Si attendis quantum praecedas sensu spiritum brutum, cantabis praecordialiter: "Benedicam Dominum, qui tribuit mihi intellectum" (Psal. xv). Si cogites intelligentiam angelicam, clamabis profecto: "Deus, tu scis insipientiam meam" (Psal. lxviii). *De arca* III.xiii, 122D). Balanced upon the fulcrum of self-knowledge and symbolized by beast and angel, one is confronted with the paradox of understanding and foolishness.

45. Cf. *De arca* xxii, 131C. "Nec tamen adeo mirum quod pro diversis rebus animus saepe et subito contrariis se qualitatibus induit, sed illud multo mirabilius quod propter unam eamdemque rem contrariis affectibus contrarios affectus superducit."

46. *De arca* III.xxiv, 134D. "corde uno in tanta pluralitate tam multiplicium affectionum."

47. Cf. *De arca* III.xxiv, 136A; 258: "Indeed, we have completed our propitiatory according to the design [*propositum*] set forth in the divine example [*documenti*]." (. . . profecto propitiatorium nostrum juxta propositum divini documenti modum explevimus.)

48. On the subject of the function and location of angels in the bible see *The New Catholic Encyclopedia*, 1966 ed., s.v. "Angel: In the Bible," by T. L. Fallon; *The Interpreter's Dictionary of the Bible*, 1991 ed., s.v. "Angel," by T. H. Gaster, and see especially pp. 131ff. on "Cherubim and Seraphim"; *A Dictionary of the Bible*, 1988 ed., s.v. "Angel," by A. B. Davidson; William George Heidt, *Angelology of the Old Testament: A Study in Biblical Theology* (Washington, D.C.: Catholic University of America Press, 1949); Louth, *Denys the Areopagite*, pp. 33–35.

49. On the subject of angels and cherubim in the patristic tradition, see Jean Daniélou, *Les anges et leur mission* (Chevetogne, Belgium: Editions de Chevetogne, 1953); *Dictionnaire de spiritualité: ascétique et mystique doctrine et histoire*, vol. 1, 1936 ed., s.v. "Anges: la dévotion aux anges," by Joseph Duhr; Denys the Areopagite, *La hiérarchie céleste*, ed. by René Roques (Paris: Les Editions du Cerf, 1958), pp. lvii–lxiii; and Geddes MacGregor, *Angels: Ministers of Grace* (New York: Paragon House, 1988), which contains an excellent bibliography on sources in English, French, and German on the general subject of angels. On the subject of the exegesis of Exodus 25 on the cherubim and the ark of the covenant, see Chapter 1 of this work, especially under the headings "The Greek Patristic Influence" and "The Latin Patristic Influence."

50. On the functions of angels, see Daniélou, MacGregor, Louth, and *Dictionnaire de spiritualité*, "Anges: le role des anges," cited in n.49 above.

51. In Denys the nine choirs appear as three ranks of three orders of beings: in descending order, the first rank includes seraphim, cherubim, thrones; the second rank dominations, powers, authorities; the third rank principalities, archangels, angels. Denys is not original in giving such a list of nine ranks, nor is the order always consistent. On Dante's acknowledgment and support of the Dionysian scheme and his gentle and witty subordination of the celestial scheme of Gregory the Great, see *Paradiso* 28.130–35. On earlier Christian writers naming the nine heavenly beings, see Louth, *Denys the Areopagite*, pp. 36–37; Rorem, *Pseudo-Dionysius*, pp. 73–90.

52. *CH* III.1, 164D; 153.

53. On the important issue of hierarchy in Denys, see René Roques, *L'Univers Dionysien: structure hiérarchique du monde selon le pseudo-Denys* (Paris: Aubier, 1954), who finds an organizing principle in the definition of hierarchy as order, understanding, activity.

54. *CH* IV.ii, 180A–B; 156–57.

55. *CH* VI.ii, 200D; 160. Cf. also VII.ii, 208C–D; 163–64 and IV.ii, 180A; 157. It should be noted that for Denys the seraphim, cherubim, and thrones are entirely equal, they "form a single hierarchy which is truly first and whose members are of equal status" (VI.ii, 201A; 161).

56. Denys the Areopagite, *La hiérarchie céleste*, p. xlix, l. "De ce point de vue, ce qui caractérise essentiellement la première hiérarchie (Séraphins, Chérubins, Trônes), c'est sa proximité *immédiate* du Principe divinisateur. Rien ne l'en sépare. Première par le rang, elle reçoit la première les illuminations théarchiques, dans leur tout premier éclat et selon toute leur vigueur originelle . . . disons que toutes ses relations avec Dieu s'opèrent sans aucune espèce d'intermédiaire: elless sont directes, *immédiates*." (Emphasis mine.)

57. I am thankful to Bernard McGinn for pointing out that the distinction between "disintegration of differences" and "separateness in union" is, especially in Plotinus, not always sharply drawn between Christian and Neoplatonist. Still, as a matter of degree, I believe the distinction holds, especially with regard to the Christian tradition's effort to image metaphors of "union" based on the doctrines of Trinity and the two natures of Christ.

58. *CH* VII.i, 205B; 161. On the etymology for seraphim (*ceux qui brûlent* and *ceux qui chauffent*), see R. Roques, *L'univers Dionysien*, pp. 138–39; Denys the Areopagite, *La hiérarchie céleste*, p. 105, n.5; Louth, *Denys the Areopagite*, pp. 47–48. On other locations of discussion of seraphim within the Dionysian corpus and on explicit biblical appearance of seraphim in Isaiah 6:2–6, see C. Luibheid, *Pseudo-Dionysius:*

Complete Works, p. 161, n.71. On the lack of an affective connotation in Denys' etymology of seraphim and on the mediaval period's accretion of an affective connotation, see P. Rorem, *Pseudo-Dionysius*, pp. 73–83; 237–40.

59. *CH* VII.1, 205B; 161. On the etymology for cherubim (*masse de connaissance* or *effusion de sagesse*), see R. Roques, *L'univers Dionysien*, pp. 140ff. Roques, while emphasizing the equivalence of the orders of cherubim and seraphim, calls the seraphim "perfection in their spiritual ardor" and the cherubim "perfection in fullness of knowledge or Wisdom" (ibid., p. 140). See also Denys the Areopagite, *La hiérarchie céleste*, p. 108f., n.2. On other locations of discussion of cherubim within the Dionysian corpus and explicit biblical references to cherubim, see C. Luibheid, *Pseudo-Dionysius: Complete Works*, p. 161, n.72.

60. *CH* VII.1, 205C; 162.

61. *CH* VII.2, 208C; 163 (emphasis mine).

62. *EP* IX, 1108C; 284.

63. *CH* VII.i, 205B; 161.

64. *CH* IV.ii, n.54, cited above.

65. Cf. R. Roques, *Structures théologiques*, p. 336, on the relation of similar to dissimilar symbols and how the understanding finally "exits" from figures in Hugh.

66. *De sacramentis* I.x.ix, 342D. "Ergo qui per fidem vident, imaginem vident; qui per contemplationem vident, rem vident."

67. *Commentariorum hierarchiam coelestem S. Dionysii Areopagite*, *PL*, 176, 985A. "Ut et ipsae similitudines, quae similiter utrinque proponi videntur, dissimiliter tamen accipiantur; et alliter hic, aliter illic intelligantur." Commenting on the relation between similar and dissimilar symbols in which, according to Hugh, "you received dissimilarity through the very similitude [*similitudinibus ipsis dissimiliter acceptis*], ibid., 984D, R. Roques says, "Whatever may be the nature of symbol, the principle regulation of its interpretation will remain that of dissimilar symbolism: it will be necessary that the understanding reject its immediate and natural sense in order to rigorously maintain that irreducible difference which separates figure from truth." See *Structures théologiques*, p. 341.

68. And according to Hugh, as Grover Zinn has pointed out, this "thing" has always itself been looking in the direction of the one "converted" to and in faith. References in this paragraph are from *De Sacramentis* I.x.ix, *PL*, 176, 341D–344A.

69. Also in Richard's *Expositio difficultatum suborientium in expositione Tabernaculi foederis*, I.ii, *PL*, 196, 213B, the cherubim are said to look back mutually upon each other (*mutuo se respiciant*). Though

Richard notes that their bodies are turned toward the exterior of the tabernacle (*corpore . . . ad exterius tabernaculum versi erant*) while their faces turn toward the ark in their midst (*versis vultibus . . . arca in medio stabat*).

70. *De Sacramentis* I.v.xxvii.

71. Elsewhere Hugh evokes the nature of "thing" (which of course we are designating as the *opus restaurationis* which *est incarnatio Verbi*) in different ways. One motif is "liquefaction" of the soul of the contemplative by the fire of divine love, which is derived from Denys and used in *De arca Noe mystica* (*Libellus de formatione arche*, as originally titled by Hugh and recently edited by P. Sicard, CCCM [Turnhout: Brepols, 1994]): "Contemplation, having liquefied by the fire of divine love [*per ignem divini amoris*] that which is to be reformed, pours it into the die [in monetam] of divine likeness." Cited in Zinn, "*De Gradibus Ascensionum*," p. 75. Richard himself takes up the metaphor of liquefaction in the third level of his *De quatuor gradibus violentae charitatis*. Another motif is that of Christ as the central axis of the mystic ascent and represented in Hugh's two treatises on Noah's ark in mandalic form as the central figure of the cosmic square. See Zinn, "Mandala Symbolism," especially pp. 324; 338–40. Hugh's personality seems to have found the cataphatic power of symbols evocative and fecund; Richard, as explored in Chapter 5, contemplates their apophatic power.

72. *De Sacramentis* Prologue, i. It is important to note that Hugh's work here emphasizes the historical manifestation of Christ and reinforces that historical manifestation by insisting that the work of restoration includes this Word as well as its sacraments: "The work of restoration is the Incarnation of the Word and all its sacraments, both those which have gone before from the beginning of time, and those which come after, even to the end of the world" (p. 3 in Deferrari translation). In Hugh, one way of participating in Christ is through these sacraments.

73. Hugh himself discusses the threefold knowledge of the angels by which they are (1) wise in that they recognize that they have been made similarly to God, (2) discerning in that they recognize by whom they have been made, and (3) understanding in that they recognize with and for what they have been made. Cf. *De Sacramentis* I.v.xiv, p. 81 in Deferrari translation.

74. On Richard's assent to the apophatic power of negation and his insight on the power of revelation to cross the apophatic boundaries of silence to utter a final cataphatic Word, see section titled "Interlude: Image, Thing, and Word" in Chapter 5.

75. *De arca* IV.i, 135B; 259. "Duos quoque cherubin, aureos et productiles facies ex utraque parte oraculi."

76. *De arca* IV.viii, 142A; 269. "Cherubin unus sit in latere uno, et alter in altero."

77. *De arca* IV.ix, 143D; 271. "Utrumque latus propitiatorii tegant, expandentes alas, et operientes oraculum."

78. *De arca* IV.xvii, 156B; 289. "Respiciant se mutuo versis vultibus in propitiatorium."

79. *De arca* IV.xxi, 163B; 300. "Inde loquar ad te desuper propitiatorio, et de medio duorum cherubin."

80. Cf. the chapter heading to *De arca* IV.viii at 141D: "Quod quintum contemplationis genus similitudinum rationem admittit, sextum vero totius similitudinis proprietatem excidit."

81. Cf. *De arca* IV.viii, 143D: "Primus itaque cherubin quas a dextris assistit, quia in ea quae rationi omnino aliena non sunt, oculum contemplationis infigit. Secundus autem cherubin quasi a sinistris figitur, qui illa sola maxime contemplatur, quibus omnis humana ratio contraire videtur."

82. The text in *De arca* IV.viii, 142B; 269 reads, "You were a sign of similitude, full of Wisdom and elegant in the delights of the paradise of God." (Tu signaculum similitudinis, plenus sapientia et decore in deliciis paradisi Dei fuisti.) But the scriptural text actually refers to the "son of man," as the Lord addresses Ezekiel. It does not refer to angelic beings at all.

83. Richard's argument for dissimilarity is based on Ps. 85:8, Isa. 40:17, Exod. 15:11, and Ps. 82:8.

84. *De arca* IV.viii, 142C; 269–270. "Quid igitur aliud ex tam diversis sententiis colligimus, nisi quod veraciter, et absque dubio Auctori nostro, ex aliquo similes, et ex aliquo dissimiles existimus?"

85. Cf. *De arca* IV.viii, 142D, 143B. One cherubim therefore stands for "divine similitude in rational substances" (divina in rationabilibus substantiis similitudo), while the other cherubim stands for "many-faceted dissimilitude in the same essences of supreme Divinity" (in eisdem essentiis Divinitatis summae multiplex dissimilitudo).

86. *De arca* IV.viii, 143A; 270. "qualiscunque similitudinis adaptatio facile accommodatur." "ad quae nulla similitudinis adumbratio se plene coaptat."

87. Cf. *De arca* IV.i, 135B–D. In this short section Richard indicates the symbolic nature of the cherubim themselves by extolling them as a similitude set forth (*proposita similitudine*) in scripture, and alternately as a formula (*formulam*), as representing the very form and manner of our work (*formulam operis nostri formam*), as copied and expressed to us under a form (*exprimitur, imitatur, formam*), and as being proper to represent (*repraesentari*) under an angelic form (*angelica forma*) something great to us. He also says of the cherubim that it is proper to represent

(*repraesentare*) them by an expression of similitude (*similitudinis expressionem*) and by means of an image (*effigie*). And finally, in seeking those things that are above reason, it is necessary to form (*formare*) the flight of our understanding in the image of (*instar*) an angelic similitude (*angelicae similitudinis*). It is also important to recall, as pointed out in Chapter 2 of this work, that the cherubim also represent a hidden knowledge (*secretioris scientiae*) of those things above human reason. In this section, Richard is outlining the function of the cherubim as a symbol or form of symbol against the backdrop of his discussion of apophatic knowledge.

88. *De arca* IV.i, 135C; 259. "sed summos et Deo immediate conjunctos, cherubin vocare solemus. Ad supermundana itaque, imo ad supercoelestia hujusmodi operis forma nos provacat, et ad summorum et divinorum speculationem intelligentiam nostram sub hac propositione invitat."

89. And, for Richard, that which is *supra rationem* is precisely those divine things which through the cherubim he hopes to represent: "Therefore, whatever of this sort [i.e., *supra rationem vero divina*] which transcends the smallness of our capacity by the magnitude of its incomprehensibility ought to be said to be above reason." Cf. *De arca* IV.ii, 136D (Merito ergo ejusmodi quaeque supra rationem esse dicenda sunt, quae capacitatis nostrae exiguitatem incomprehensibilitatis suae magnitudine transcendunt).

90. But not, however, beyond the capacity of symbol. For Richard it is important to maintain the functional quality of symbol in the "regions" beyond reason. This is so that revelation itself can function and is specifically maintained by the flight of angels in contemplation. Angelic similitude allows the smallness of our nature to ascend to the incomprehensible when we ourselves forge the form of angelic similitude through contemplation (cf. ibid., 136D: "Ut ergo in nobis angelicae similitudinis formam qualicunque modo possimus excudere"). To so "forge," we must "hover": suspend our soul in perpetual quickness in wonder of such things (cf. ibid., 136D: "opertet in ejusmodi rerum admiratione animum nostrum jugi celeritate suspendere").

91. Cf. *De arca* IV.xxi, 164B.

92. In this sense Richard collapses the dichotomy in symbol between image (*imago*) and thing (*res*) that we found above in Hugh of St. Victor's symbolic theology. Where earlier, Richard had maintained the dichotomy, now with the symbol of the cherubim "joined immediately to God" he moves closer to the symbolic theology found in Denys. That is, the cherubim in a sense are what they represent. They function both anagogically and as if "seeing face to face." Though the symbols are composed of language and so are prone to the "deficiencies" of language, they come, it seems, from a "place" beyond language. One of these

revelatory "places" is scripture, composed certainly of language, but through which "Moses seems to designate by a mystical description." Cf. *De arca* IV.i, 135B: "Moyses (in his verbis) videtur ex mystica descriptione designare."

93. Cf. *De arca* IV.iv, 138B; 263: "In these twin speculations [i.e., the fifth and sixth symbolized by the cherubim] nothing of the imagination, nothing of phantasy ought to occur, whatever speculation this twin spectacle of this last work sets forth for us, it excludes every property of corporeal similitudes." (In hac gemina speculatione nihil imaginarium, nihil phantasticum debet occurrere, long enim omnem corporeae similitudinis proprietatem excedit quidquid spectaculi tibi haec gemina novissimi operis specula proponit.)

94. Cf. *De arca* IV.v, 139B (*figuraliter exprimuntur*) and 139D (*figura*). Zinn translates by "symbolic figure" and "symbolic expression," respectively (265).

95. Richard is not always precise with his terms that fall within the family of resemblance to "reason." Thus while *scientia* is on the one hand the knowledge beyond which we are not able to ascend, on the other hand it is understanding as *intelligentia* by which we ascend to divine things through dissimilar symbols. At the same time, similitude functions perfectly well for knowledge (*scientam*) of external and corporeal things, acquaintance (*notitiam*) with invisible things, and knowledge (*cognitionem*) of invisible things, but not for an understanding (*intelligentiam*) of divine things. Cf. *De arca* IV.v, 138D.

96. *De arca* IV.v, 139B, 139D; 265. "Si ergo cherubin plenitudo scientiae dicitur, vide quam recte illa exprema operis nostri factura cherubin nominature in qua scientiae omnis summi gradus figuraliter exprimuntur. . . . Recte igitur hujus operis figura cherubin dicitur in qua ad omnis scientiae plenitudinem initiamur."

97. To the "shadow" or "dwelling" only, because "The perfection of this fullness begins in this life, but is consummated in the future life." *De arca* IV.v, 139D. (Hujus plenitudinis perfectio in hac vita inchoatur, sed in futura consumatur.)

98. In moving from IV.v to IV.vi, Richard makes a transition from the "way of knowledge," which we have been discussing, to the "way of the heart" by means of compunction and tears. The former utilizes metaphors of union by knowledge based on John 17:3, the latter utilizes metaphors of sight based on the beatific vision of Matthew 5:8. This transition, the "way of the heart," and the relation of both ways in attaining the secret, difficult to reach places of divine incomprehensibility (*in ardua divinae incomprehensibilitatis arcana*) will be discussed in Chapter 6 of this work.

99. *De arca* IV.vii, 141B; 267. "Et quomodo illam formam exprimere valeam quam videre non valeo?"

100. *De arca* IV.vii, 140D; 267. "Cogita cujus sit excellentiae illius ordinis in se similitudinem per imitationem trahere, qui summae claritati immediate adhaeret, qui facie ad faciem, et sine speculo, et sine aenigmate videt."

101. Cf. *De arca* IV.vi, 140B.

102. *De arca* IV.vii, 141A; 267. "Denique aliud est arcam facere atque aliud est cherubin formare."

103. *De arca* IV.ix, 143D; 271. "nos vel contra mala roborant, vel ad virtutem adjuvant."

104. Cf. *De arca* IV.ix, 144A.

105. This is not the contemplative's doing, but a passive alienation of the soul; and Richard is careful to describe the process with verbs in the passive voice: we may be snatched away (*raperemur*), we may be led (*duceremur*).

106. Cf. *De arca* IV.ix, 144B.

107. Cf. *De arca* IV.ix, 144C.

108. And between God's voice and the people of God who, terrified at the prospect of hearing God's voice directly, beg to hear only the human voice. Cf. Exodus 20:18–19.

109. *De arca* IV.ix, 144C, 144D; 272–73. "Quid ergo mirum, si hujus-modi obumbratione propitiatorii nostri utrumque latus obducitur? Nam quidquid divinum simile, vel divinis dissimile in nobis cernitur, divinorum, uti jam dictum est, comparatione fuscatur. . . . Recte ergo dicti cherubin utrumque propitiatorii nostri latus tegere dicuntur, quia in nobis nihil omnino reperitur, quod summis et divinis non sit vel peregrinum in qual-itate, vel incomparabile ex quantitate."

110. *De arca* IV.xi, 147B; 276. "Summae sapientiae lumen sine aliquo involucro, figurarumve adumbratione, denique non per speculum et in aenigmate, sed in simplici, ut sic dicam, veritate contemplatur."

111. A symbol which functions in a similar way is that of the Celestial Rose used by Dante in Cantos 30–33 of the *Paradiso*. The rose serves to structure Dante's vision of heaven and is essential to his description of the heavenly vision but recedes and dissolves as Dante recounts his vision within the rose of the saints, angels, Bernard, Beatrice, the Virgin, and ultimately his vision of the triune God.

112. Cf. *De arca* IV., 147D.

113. On the inability of reason to bring this exterior vision inward and communicate it to others and therefore the necessity to rely on the "Wis-dom" of admiration, desire, and the loving inflammation of the hovering

soul, see *De arca* IV.xii, 149A: "Assuescimus in contemplationem adducere, et in eorum admiratione animum nostrum suspendere, et pascere, humiliare, et in divinorum desiderium acriter inflammare." Richard also describes this Wisdom of love as the seeking and awaiting with song and sighing of a dove for its mate. Cf. ibid., IV.xiii, 150D: "Colloque protenso foras prospicere, et unici tui adventum cum columbino quodam cantu et gemitu quaerere et exspectare." With the image of the dove Richard maintains the symbolism of flight, birds, and especially of outstretched wings as an image of longing and desire.

114. *De arca* IV.xii, 149B; 279. "Debemus, juxta divinum documentum, cherubin nostrorum alas expandere, et in revelantis gratiae occursum rapidis desideriorum passibus festinare."

115. As noted earlier, Chapters IV.xi–xvi digress from the direct discussion of the cherubim, though I believe they are also concerned with the "forging" of the wings of the Cherubim. The digressions consider Abraham and Elijah as two types of preparation for the coming of the Lord. While both wait patiently, one waits in silence and contemplation and one in labor. The digression also considers bridal imagery from the Song of Songs. Thus the "Beloved" makes a brief appearance in these chapters as the object of the two types of waiting.

116. *De arca* IV.xv, 154A; 286. "Hoc tempore, ut arbitror, illud opus nostrum ductile incipit non mediocriter proficere et consummationi appropinquare, eo quod illi nostri cherubin incipiant alas suas jam latius extendere, et sese jam quasi ad volatum omni hora suspendere."

117. *De arca* IV.xvii, 156A. "Respiciant se, inquit, mutuo versis vultibus in propitiatorium."

118. *De arca* IV.xvii, 156B; 289. "Secundum hanc itaque distinctionem videte ne forte ad primum cherubin specialiter pertineant ea quae considerantur circa divinae illius summae et simplicis essentiae unitatem; ad secundum autem cherubin ea quae considerantur circa personarum Trinitatem."

119. Considering especially a series of coincidental opposites including simplicity and boundlessness, and unity and diversity, which are related through the method of mutual comparison (*mutua collatione*) and are found thus to share a "supreme and simple divine essence." Cf. *De arca* IV.xvii, 157B. This method, Richard claims, is *supra rationem, nec tamen praeter rationem*.

120. Authority, scripture, and revelation make possible both the consideration of the dual nature of Christ and the Trinity of persons. Without revelation and scripture, the Trinity of persons would otherwise be "not only incomprehensible to human reason, but also, you will discover, discordant to human reason" (quae humanae rationi non solum

incomprehensibilia, sed etiam dissona reperies). *De arca*, IV.xviii, 159A. In fact, it is these very attributes that are repugnant to reason by which we are led (*adducuntur*) into contemplation. Cf. IV.xvii, 156C. For more detailed interpretations of Richard's metaphysical and psychological work on the Trinity, see E. Cousins, "The Notion of the Person in the *De Trinitate* of Richard of St. Victor"; G. Salet, *La Trinité*; J. Ribaillier, *De Trinitate: texte critique avec introduction, notes et tables*; A.-M. Ethier, *Le "De Trinitate" de Richard de Saint-Victor* (Ottawa: Publications de l'Institut d'Etudes médiévales d'Ottawa, 1939). Critical editions of *De Trinitate* are found in Salet and Ribaillier.

121. *De arca* IV.xix, 160C, 161B; 296, 297. "et diligenti observatione praecavendum ut sic asseremus ea quae pertinent ad unum, ut non illa destruamus quae pertinent ad alterum. . . . Cherubin itaque cherubin respicit, quando quod unus dicit alius non contradicit. Cherubin cherubin respicit, quando quintum contemplationis genus illa, quae suae considerationis sunt, sic asserit, ut tamen quae alterius sunt, omnino evacuare nolit."

122. Cf. *De arca* IV.xix, 160C.

123. Cf. *De arca* IV.xix, 160B–161C, various locations.

124. *De arca* IV.xix, 160D; 296. "quia contraria assertione multum diversis sententiis, et sibi ipsis oppositis intendunt et acquiescunt."

125. *De arca* IV.xx, 161C. Richard here, somewhat inexplicably, shifts from the word *mutuo* to *invicem* to express reciprocity and mutuality.

126. *De arca* IV.xx, 161D; 297. "Quando novissima duo contemplationum genera in eo quod de sublimibus et divinis concorditer sentiunt, ab illo quae quarto contemplationis generi subjacent, in assertionis suae testimonium rationis similitudinem trahunt."

127. *De arca* IV.xx, 162C; 298–299. "in hac ipsa rationali creatura, si diligenter attendimus, aliquod, ut credimus, summae Trinitatis vestigium invenimus."

128. This exemplarist pattern, so reminiscent of Denys' pattern of procession and return, is recognizable only upon having reached the fifth and sixth levels of contemplation. At these levels, in order to speculate on the divine, the contemplative first moves from consideration of the cherubim to an investigation of rational creatures (*in divinarum rerum speculatione, et investigatione rationalem creaturam attendere*), and only then from rational symbols back into an understanding of divine things (*et inspecta similitudine ad Divinitatis intelligentiam, altius proficere*). Cf. ibid., 162C.

129. Again, we must keep in mind that while these spatial metaphors indicate a hierarchy of ascent and descent, they are also meant to indicate movement inward to the core or center or womb of the holy of holies.

130. *De arca* IV.xx, 161C; 297. "Item unus cherubin alium respicit, quando (quod fieri consuevit) nostra speculatio a penultimo genere incipit, et in novissimum desinit. Vel econtrario ab ultimo incipit, et in penultimum descendit."

131. *De arca* IV.xx, 161D–162; 298. "Quid itaque aliud est cherubin vultus suos in propitiatorium vertere, quam in divinarum rerum speculatione, et investigatione rationalem creaturam attendere, et ex inspecta similitudine ad Divinitatis intelligentiam, altius proficere?"

132. Richard notes that "God reserved the truth of things (*rerum veritatem*), which is the supreme truth, for himself; but he conceded to his image the power of forming images of things at any time." Cf. *De arca* IV.xx, 162B: "In quo et illud invenies valde notabile, quod rerum veritatem, quae summa veritas est, reservavit sibi, rerum vero imagines qualibet hora formandas suae concessit imagini." Richard's *rerum veritatem* echoes Hugh of St. Victor's distinction between *res* and *imago*.

133. *De arca* IV.xx, 162D; 299. "Omnis enim mens sapientiam suam diligit, et idcirco sapientiae suae amor ex utraque procedit. Est enim sapientia a mente sola, amor vero ex mente pariter et sapientia."

134. Cf. *De arca* IV.xx, 162D.

135. While *verso* in the active voice is "turn about, twist around, meditate upon," here in the passive voice it can be translated "to hover."

136. *De arca* IV.xx, 161D, 297. Richard says of the rational but created spirit, that "From that nature in whose created condition we ought not to doubt, vestiges of the divine image have been most violently impressed and most visibly expressed" (ibid., "Ab illa, inquam, natura in cujus conditione divinae imaginis vestigia vehementius impressa, et evidentius expressa, non dubitamus"). This separation between the rational but created spirit and the divine and uncreated Spirit also gives Richard an opportunity to discuss the Incarnation and particularly the two-natures doctrine.

137. *De arca* IV.xx, 162D; 299. "Notandum sane quod tria illa quae in rationali anima consideranda occurrunt, personarum Trinitatem non faciunt."

138. *De arca*, IV.xx, 162D; 299. "Vide ergo quia in his quae pro similitudine adducta sunt in rationali animo ad illam summam Trinitatem major est dissimilitudo quam similitudo."

139. The dissimilarity between the image-Trinity in the soul and the divine Trinity itself (which rejects any complete identification of soul and divinity) is the fulcrum-point which uniquely identifies Richard's form of contemplation as Latin Christian and distances it from Eastern forms of divinization. Whether Richard's form of contemplation may, on the

other hand, be accurately characterized as "angelization" or even, in contemporary vernacular, "humanization," will be discussed in Chapter 6 of this work. Richard's form of contemplation is also characterized by the fact that while it does "make use of pure understanding" (*pura intelligentia utitur*), it is "always concerned with objects or things" (*semper contemplatio est in rebus*). The "highest" object, of course, being the Trinity. Cf. *De arca* I.iii, 67D.

140. *De arca* IV.xx, 162D; 299. "Nec mirum tamen quia secundus cherubin dissimilitudinis latus in propitiatorio nostro vicinius tangit. Latus autem similitudinis quasi e longinquo respicit."

141. This Wisdom is virtue or right action in the world, but it is also, though paradoxically unnamed, Christ. Cf. Chapter 5 of this work.

142. They also, of course, manifest the two natures of Christ, but this is not explicitly stated by Richard. Ambiguity and mystery as symbolized by the cherubim are, at this point, clear, but the identity of mystery is not always so: both Trinity and the Incarnate Christ incorporate mystery and serve as final entry points to the secret places of divine incomprehensibility.

143. Cf. *De arca* IV.xx, 163A.

144. Exodus 25:22a reads in full, "inde praecipiam et loquar ad te supra propitiatorio scilicit ac medio duorum cherubin". Richard focuses on "I will speak to you" by quoting the passage as, "Inde loquar ad te desuper propitiatorio, et de medio duorum cherubin."

145. *De arca* IV.xx, 163A; 299. "Sola sapientia voci humanae incorporatur, et per vocem corporalem egreditur, egressa agnoscitur."

146. Cf. *De arca* IV.vi, 140B.

147. Cf. *De arca* IV.xxi, 164B and IV.xxii, 165A.

148. Cf. *De arca* IV.xxi, 164B. All six kinds of contemplation can be achieved, according to Richard, either in human understanding (allegorized by Bezeleel and symbolized by light and indicating the cataphatic way) or in ecstasy of mind (allegorized by Moses and symbolized by either darkness or light and indicating the apophatic way). This in fact indicates another representation of the cherubim: contemplation according to human understanding and contemplation according to ecstasy of mind.

149. Cf. *De arca* IV.xxii, 165C; 303. "In medium nebulae Moyses ingreditur . . . divini luminis immensitate absorpta."

150. This phrase, "Hanc sublevate animi pacem, obnubilationem et illuminationem," is one of the best summaries of Richard's contemplative method based upon hovering.

151. *De arca* IV.xxii, 165C; 303. "Ita ut mirari valeas, et juste mirari debeas quomodo concordet ibi nubes cum igne, et ignis cum nube: nubes ignorantiae, cum igne [Migne here reads *nube*, but the context obviously calls for *igne*] illuminatae intelligentiae. Ignorantia et oblivio

notorum et expertorum, cum revelatione et intelligentia, prius ignotorum et eousque inexpertorum. Nam uno eodemque tempore humana intelligentia, et ad divina illuminatur, et ad humana obnubilatur. Hanc sublevati animi pacem, obnubilationem et illuminationem Psalmista paucis verbis comprehendit, cum dicit: " 'In pace in idipsum dormiam et requiescam.' "

152. From what we know of Richard's exegetical method in *De arca mystica*, we can guess that the fabric of this clothing, even the very flight of the angel, is Wisdom, the imitation of which leads the soul to the face of God.

153. It may be that Richard is here proposing a form of relating opposites symbolically other than that of hovering. We can, without pushing the shift too dramatically, see Richard as moving from a metaphysical and theological mode of symbolism to a more psychological mode. On the metaphysical level Richard may find it more precise to speak of the relation between the angels as "hovering." But on the psychological level, in Chapter xxii, Richard begins to speak of the relation between light and dark, fire and cloud, ignorance and understanding as one of harmony or concord (*concordet*). This is so especially on the psychological level of the relation of the soul to the divine. Thus divine light (*divini luminis*) is in harmony with the sleep and oblivion of self (*summa sui oblivione sopitur*), the cloud of ignorance (*nubes ignorantiae*) is in harmony with the cloud of illuminated understanding (*nube illuminatae intelligentiae*), and the ignorance and forgetting of things known and experienced (*ignorantia et oblivio notorum et expertorum*) is in harmony with revelation and understanding of things previously unknown and unexperienced (*revelatione et intelligentia prius ignotorum et eousque inexpertoram*). "Harmony," at certain times and in explaining certain functions, is a good description of the relation of the cherubim. But is not the best. It tends to collapse the difference between the cherubim, and that, for theological as well as psychological reasons, is clearly not Richard's overall intent.

154. *De arca* IV.xxii, 164D; 302. "Ut aliquid in his perspicacius et limpidius cernere possit, ipsa mens humana semetipsam excedit, et in abalienationem transit apte quidem eadem ipsa non tam humana effigie quam angelica forma mystice exprimere oportuit."

155. They are at this point receiving a deeper and deeper awareness of the transcendent things to which they are immediately attached. They are the means of a sublime consideration (*sublimi consideratione*) by which the contemplative "hovers in wonder at the excellency of unity and Trinity." (Cf. *De arca* IV.xxi, 163: "in summae unitatis et Trinitatis admiratione suspenditur.") The cherubim hover, just as they provide a model of hovering. As receptors they absorb, in a sense, all dialectics of

coincidence of opposites and focus the opposites onto that space wherein God will speak.

156. Note that "seeing" does not satisfy longing: the cherubim of Chapter xix are always *looking* (*respiciant*)—in fact that is, along with flying, ontologically what they are. In Chapter xxi, it is even more apparent that, for the contemplative, "seeing" is akin to wandering, because the God that such "seeing" accomplishes is as absent as he is present. Thus *oculo intellegentiae* and *per mentis excessum saepe videndo* do not satisfy longing: God is not in the *mutuo respicit* of the cherubim, but rather between them in God's own revelation.

157. The image of the cherubim as "receptors" and "transmitters" is of course another way of speaking of the cherubim as participants in the angelic hierarchy. As the hierarchical beings closest to God, they both receive and transmit the Divine rays of emanation in their "purest" form.

158. *De arca* IV.xxiii, 168D; 307. "Quod unus ex sola Domini vocatione, alter ex propria deliberatione ad secretum illud divinae revelationis alloquium subintrabat."

159. *De arca* I.xii, 78D. "otiosi sumus et otiosis loquimur."

160. In a similar way, as I suggested above, the cherubim symbolize the different paths of Moses and Bezeleel. One symbolizes entry into the secret place of God by means of the call of God (*vocatione Domini*), the other symbolizes entry into that same secret place by means of deliberation and work (*propria deliberatione*). Yet the cherubim, again, gaze through those different paths to the one secret place of God's revelation.

161. *De arca* IV.xxiii, 168C; 307. "et idem nihilominus sit illum se in nebulam, istum se intra velum ingerere."

162. *De arca* IV.xxiii, 168C. "ad secretum illud divinae revelationis alloquium subintrabat."

163. In contemplations one through three, using symbols drawn from nature, Richard is primarily interested in the *similitude* of the symbol to God. In contemplation four, using symbols drawn from or evoking the soul, Richard is primarily interested in the *imago* of God in the symbol.

164. See Table 2.

165. This concept is explicit in Richard's *De Trinitate* (cf. especially *De Trinitate* III. xiv, xv, xix, xx) and forms the basis for the very presence of the Holy Spirit. On *caritas* among equals, cf. *De Trinitate* III. vii, xxi, xxiv, xxv, and Ewert Cousins, "Theology of Interpersonal Relations," pp. 68–70.

166. I am indebted to Professor Ewert Cousins for pointing out and giving concrete expression to the journey symbol in Richard and in other spiritual writers.

CHAPTER 5

1. On this "phenomenal veil" and the possibility of accessing truth, beauty, and the "God who is" behind the veil, see Erazim Kohák, *The Embers and the Stars: A Philosophical Inquiry into the Moral Sense of Nature* (Chicago: University of Chicago Press, 1984), pp. 179–218.

2. For an excellent discussion of the "necessary intervention of divinity" between "separating" images such as the cherubim, see Sanford Budick, *The Dividing Muse: Images of Sacred Disjunction in Milton's Poetry* (New Haven: Yale University Press, 1985), especially Appendix B, "The Logos Medium of Bonaventure's *Itinerarium*," pp. 154–65.

3. See especially the discussion of the Latin patristic allegorical interpretation of the ark and cherubim in Chapter 1 of this work.

4. See *De arca* I.i, 63C.

5. This preliminary presupposition serves to ground the question of Christological absence. Certain Christological aspects *are* absent in Richard's work, such as the incarnate Christ, the "humility of the word," the humanity of Christ, Christ as exemplar or mediator, and Christ as logos. Others, as we will see, make brief appearances, then retreat. These latter include the restorative or redemptive work of Christ, Christ as cocreator, the crucified Christ, and the glorified and sanctifying Christ. As we shall also see, Christ is in some manner manifest, though not as name but rather as an existential process of sanctification equated with Wisdom. Robert Javelet has noted Richard's emphasis on God rather than Christ. Javelet says, "dans le '*De IV gradibus violentae caritatis*,' le Christ est plus manifeste . . . mais le discours du Benjamin major est axé sur Dieu, plus que sur le Christ." See R. Javelet, "Saint Bonaventure et Richard de Saint-Victor," p. 65; see also R. Javelet, "Sens et réalité ultime," p. 236: "Dans la spiritualité de Richard, surtout dans les *Benjamin*, le rôle du Christ pourrait sembler inexistant." These statements are true but in need of intense refining. Javelet himself, in fact, refines his first thesis, stating by the end of his article (p. 95) that while Bonaventure focuses on Christ as exemplar or mediator (*exemplaire, médiateur*), Richard focuses on the glorified Christ (*la consommation*).

6. It is important to take Richard at his own word, that he is not interested in an allegorical interpretation of the ark and cherubim as Christ. But, and this is an important "but," the twelfth-century context of his denial that is discussed below, and the very obvious hints that some form of Christology is just below the surface trying to assert itself regardless of Richard's stated intention, indicate that there is more to Richard's assertive denial than he can, or is willing to, speak.

7. The best English translation of *Itinerarium* is in Bonaventure, *The Soul's Journey into God, The Tree of Life, The Life of St. Francis*, trans. Ewert Cousins (New York: Paulist Press, 1978), p. 54. Cousin's explanation for breaking text into "sense lines," is found on p. 46. All quotations in English are cited from this edition and are hereafter designated *SJG*. Quotations and references in Latin are given according to the standard text of the *Itinerarium* in *Doctoris Seraphici S. Bonaventurae opera omnia*, 10 vols. (Quaraccchi: Collegium S. Bonaventurae, 1882–1902), vol. 5 (1891), pp. 295–313, and are designated *Itin*.

8. The most explicit similarity is that of the symbolic structure of both works. Richard, using the ark and cherubim, describes six kinds of contemplation leading to God. Bonaventure, using the six wings of the seraph, describes six levels of illumination by which the soul passes into God. On Bonaventure's similar and parallel use of cherubim in *Itinerarium*, see *SJG* 5.1, p. 94:

> By these Cherubim we understand
> the two modes or stages
> of contemplating the invisible and eternal things of God:
> one is concerned with the essential attributes of God
> and the other with those proper to the Persons.

The first cherub's gaze is thus fixed on being itself (*ipsum esse*), viewing God's essential attributes in Chapter 5 of *Itinerarium*. The second cherub looks upon the good itself (*ipsum bonum*), contemplating the emanations in Chapter 6. Cf. *SJG* 5.1, p. 94; 6.1, p. 102. On the cherubim turning toward the mercy seat and seeing Christ, see *SJG* 6.4, p. 106:

> The Fact that they [Cherubim] faced each other,
> *with their faces turned toward the Mercy Seat,*
> is not without a mystical meaning,
> . . . .
> the superwonderful union of God and man
> in the unity of the Person of Christ.

See also *SJG* 6.5, pp. 106–7; 6.6, pp. 107–8. Bonaventure tends to associate the humanity of Christ with the first cherubim and union/persons within the Trinity and Christ as a duality of natures with the second cherubim. Richard, on the other hand, associates union within the Trinity with the first cherubim and persons within the Trinity with the second, while neither nature of Christ is explicitly associated with either cherubim. The best comparison to date of Richard and Bonaventure's work in *De arca mystica* and *Itinerarium*, is found in R. Javelet, "Saint Bonaventure et Richard de Saint-Victor." Javelet's conclusion (pp. 95–96) is that Bonaventure focuses on exemplarity, as the means of contemplative ascent, while Richard focuses on symbolism using imagination, contemplation, and grace as the means of ascent. But, importantly, Javelet's final assessment is that "Les différences ne doivent nous masquer les innombrables similitudes dans le schéma même des ces traités."

9. *Itin*, Prologue, 3: "Via autem non est nisi per ardentissimum amorem Crucifixi."

10. *SJG* VII.1,2,6; pp. 110–12, 115–16.

11. Cousins, *Bonaventure and the Coincidence of Opposites*, p. 131. See also the whole of Chapter 5 of this work on the notion of Christ the Center in Bonaventure's thought, and Zachary Hayes, O.F.M., *The Hidden Center: Spirituality and Speculative Christology in St. Bonaventure* (New York: Paulist Press, 1981).

12. The presence of Christ the mediator in the *Itinerarium* is noted also by R. Javelet, who claims that while Richard starts with the sense world, Bonaventure starts with the supreme exemplar, which is Christ. He finds in addition that in Bonaventure the propitiatory represents Christ the mediator (*Itinerarium* 7.2) while in Richard the propitiatory represents purified human reason. Cf. R. Javelet, "St. Bonaventure et Richard de Saint-Victor," pp. 86, 89. It may be argued that in Richard the cherubim, serving as mediators to transcendent divinity, circumvent the necessary mediation of Christ. But this tendency in Richard is constantly "corrected" by the fact that the cherubim look beyond themselves. They are fullness of Wisdom, but never Wisdom itself.

13. *Itin*, 7.2 (quoted in English above): "Ad quod propitiatorium qui aspicit plena conversione vultus, aspiciendo eum in cruce suspensum . . . ; pascha, hoc est transitum, cum eo facit . . . et cum Christo requiescat in tumulo."

14. Cf. *De arca* IV.xviii–xx. The coincidence of Christology and Trinity based on their mutual incomprehensibility is discussed below.

15. Recall that, in Richard, the door, gate, ladder is the self, that is, entering one's heart (*intres ad cor tuum*) and learning to understand one's spirit (*disce ergo ex tuo spiritu cognoscere*). Cf. Chapter 4 of this work and *De arca* III.iii, 113A–B.

16. G. Zinn, "Mandala Symbolism," p. 327, discusses Christ as mediator, way, and goal in the mandalic schema of Hugh of St. Victor. Cousins also discusses the function of Christ in the mandala symbolism of Bonaventure (*Bonaventure and the Coincidence of Opposites*, chap. 6, "Mandala Symbolism"). Richard's symbolic depiction of the cherubim and ark has obvious mandalic qualities.

17. For a more definitive survey of the twelfth-century Christological climate, see works cited elsewhere by Châtillon, Baron, Javelet, de Lubac, Roques, Zinn, McGinn, Cousins, Dumeige, and Salet. See especially S. Chase, "Secret Places of Divine Incomprehensibility," Appendix A.

Note also Chapter 1 of the present work which points out Christological patterns in early exegesis of Exodus 25, all of which Richard knew.

18. On Denys' Christology see McGinn, *Foundations*, pp. 180–82, who notes that "the issue is not about the orthodoxy of Dionysius's Christology (though some have suspected him of Monophysite tendencies), nor is it about failure to mention Jesus the Christ—he appears often in the corpus. The issue is rather how central Jesus' theandric activity is to the process of return." See also J. Pelikan, "Odyssey of Dionysian Spirituality," pp. 15–17, 19–21; P. Rorem, "Uplifting Spirituality," p. 144; R. Roques, *L'univers Dionysien*, pp. 305–29; R. Roques, *Structures théologiques*, pp. 235–36; V. Lossky, *The Mystical Theology of the Eastern Church* (New York: St. Vladimir's Seminary Press, 1976) pp. 39, 139, 220f.

19. Cf. *DN* 1.1, p. 49, "we must not dare to resort to words or conceptions concerning the hidden divinity which transcends being, apart from what the sacred scriptures have divinely revealed." See also *DN* 1.2, p. 50.

20. *CH* 15.9, p. 191. These words are in fact the final words of the *Celestial Hierarchy*.

21. Cf. *DN* 2.7, p. 64, "the Son and the Spirit are divine offshoots, the flowing and transcendent lights of divinity"; and *DN* 2.10, p. 65, "The divinity of Jesus is the fulfilling cause of all."

22. From McGinn, *Foundations*, p. 395, n. 260, citations include *DN* 1.4, 2.10; *CH* 4.4; *EH* 3.III.11–13, 5.III.5; *Ep.* 3.

23. *Ep.* 4, pp. 264–65.

24. *Ep.* 9.1, p. 283; 9.2, p. 284.

25. Cf. Chapter 2 of the present work.

26. *EH* 2.III.6–7, pp. 207–8.

27. *EH* 4.III.4–12, pp. 228–32. Of interest to Richard is the fact that this rite is explained in the symbolic context of the seraphim and the altar (4.II, p. 224; 4.III.6, p. 229) and that in the oil "Jesus came down among us to make us holy" (4.III.10, p. 231).

28. *EH* 3. See also *Letter Nine* concerning the nourishment and completion afforded by the table of Christ, and especially in the context of Richard's contemplation leading to the "rest" of consummation, how Denys says, "we must think of the leading to the table as the rest from numerous labors. . . . It is Jesus himself who gladdens them and leads them to the table, who serves them, who grants them everlasting rest, who bestows and pours out on them the fullness in beauty" (*Ep.* 9.5, pp. 287–88).

29. See McGinn, *Foundations*, p. 181, citing *EH* 1.2, p. 197.

30. R. Roques notes that although Denys does not exclude the Incarnation, or the cross, or the earthly role of the humanity of the Word,

he focuses more clearly on the divinity of the Word and his (Johanine) illuminating presence within the hierarchies. Cf. *Structures théologique*, pp. 303–4.

31. Cf. *EH* 7.I.2, p. 250, and *Ep.* 8.1, p. 271, which propose the life of Jesus for our imitation.

32. *CH* 7.2, p. 163 (emphasis mine). See also *CH* 7.4, p. 164.

33. Roques, *Structures théologiques*, p. 363–64: "Il a plus volontiers décrit la divinisation de l'intelligence comme une expérience intime. . . . Ces points de vue ont amené Hugues à marquer d'un trait pratique et affectif toutes les notions essentielles du système dionysien."

34. *De Sacramentis*, Prologue 2, *PL*, 176, 183B: "The work of restoration is the incarnation of the Word. . . . Indeed, the incarnate word is our king."

35. Human history inclines one, naturally, to conceive of the restoration "following" the Incarnation. This is not precisely true in the Victorine mind. For Richard and Hugh, sacred history is, as it might seem to our human sense of history, paradoxical, yet not improbable. For a Victorine, the restoration precedes in time the redemptive Incarnation which is its cause. Or perhaps more helpfully, *on est sauvé avant la venue du Christ par la venue du Christ*. Thus in this section on Hugh's view of the relation of Christ to the work of salvation, I am careful to use words describing the relation such as "linked" and "accomplished" rather than "follows." On salvation history in general and the relation of the Incarnation to the restoration in Hugh, see G. Zinn, "History and Contemplation," pp. 267ff.

36. Cf. *De Sacramentis*, I.X.viii.

37. Hugh makes a distinction between the humanity of the Word (*humanitas Verbi*) which initiates images of grace (*In hier.* I.1, 926B) and the humility of the crucified (*humilitatis crucifixis*) which initiates divine theology (*In hier.* I.1, 926C). Mundane philosophy has neither the ark of Wisdom nor humility, divine theology can arrive at humility only through the humanity of Christ. Divine theology, the highest Wisdom, thus requires the flesh of the eternal word in the humanity of Jesus (*carnem Verbi aeterni in Jesu humanitate*). Richard echoes this notion in *De arca* I.i in the context of a discussion of Mary sitting silently at the feet of Christ. There he says that "the highest Wisdom of God is concealed in the flesh" (*summam Dei sapientiam in carne latitantem*). Richard's *In hier.* I.1, 926D, states that through the simulacrum of nature God is understood to be (*ut intelligeretur esse*), while through the simulacrum of grace God is known to be present (*ut agnosreretur praesens esse*). It is the grace of this "presence" in the form of the flesh of the eternal Word that is the very core of the work of restoration and sanctification.

Richard could not have been unaware of this sense of presence and participation.

38. *De arca Noe*, ed. Sicard, II, VII, pp. 87–89. "Omnis Scriptura divina unus liber est, et ille unus liber Christus est, quia omnis Scriptura divina de Christo loquitur, et omnis Scriptura divina in Christo impletur." Cited in de Lubac, *Exégèse médiévale*, vol. 1, p. 322, as *De arca Noe mor.* I.II, c.viii (*PL*, 176, 642C). See also R. Roques, *Structures théologiques*, pp. 375–77, on the twelfth-century notion of Christ alone being the exegete of scripture.

39. *De sacramentis*, Deferrari, II.1.xii, p. 250. Thus according to Christ's humanity Richard would have no need of mentioning him, but according to his divinity he could not avoid it in the construction or contemplation of the ark. This point creates a conflict with Denys, who, with regard to the divinity of Christ, speaks of hiddenness and cautions silence.

40. Ibid., xiii, p. 250.

41. Ibid., xii, p. 249. Here presence and "union" are synonymous, thus making Christ as mediator a requirement for God's presence and speaking on the ark.

42. Ibid., II.IV.xvii, p. 278.

43. Ibid., II.VIII.i, p. 304.

44. Ibid., II.VII.xii, 471B.

45. This is based on Richard's reading of John 14:6, "ego sum via et veritas et vita, nemo venit ad Patrem nisi per me."

46. *De praeparatione anime ad contemplationem (Benjamin Minor)*, *PL*, 196, c. LXXVII, 55D: "Illi soli ut arbitror, sine errore currunt, illi soli sine impedimento perveniunt, qui Christum sequuntur, qui a veritate ducuntur. Quisquis ad alta properas, securus eas, si te praecedit veritas: nam sine ipsa frustra laboras. Tam non vul fallere, quam non valet veritas falli. Christum ergo sequere, si non vis errare."

47. Cf. *Liber de Verbo incarnato*, *PL*, 196, IX–XV, pp. 1004B–1010D. Chapter VIII of this same work links Christ to different moments of salvation history.

48. On the gospel commentaries, see *Liber exceptionum*, II.XI–XIV, pp. 439–517.

49. Cf. *De quatuor gradibus violentae caritatis*, *PL*, 196, 1207A–1224D. For instance, Richard says (1222C–1223A), "Haec est forma humilitatis Christi. . . . In tertio itaque gradu anima in Deum glorificatur, in quarto propter Deum humiliatur. In tertio gradu conformatur divinae claritati, in quarto ver conformatur Christianae humilitati. . . . In tertio itaque gradu quodammodo mortificatur in Deum, in quarto quasi resuscitatur in Christum. Qui igitur in quarto gradu est, veraciter dicere potest:

'Vivo autem jam non ego, vivit vero in me Christus' (Gal II)." As noted elsewhere, the best that can generally be done in dating Richard's works is to develop a chronology. Of the works mentioned in this chapter, *L. except.* would seem to be earliest, written early in the period 1153–62 (Châtillon, *L. except.*, ed., p. 81), followed probably by the two *Benjamins* (first *Minor* then *Major*) late in the same period, followed by *Liber de Verbo* around 1162 (Châtillon, *DS* 13: 607), followed "probably" by *De Trinitate* and *De quatuor gradibus*, both later and mature works after the period 1162 (see Dumeige, *Richard de S. Victor*, pp. 100–101, on *De quatuor* and Ribaillier, *De Trinitate*, pp. 11–13; Châtillon also makes a case for *De Trinitate* being written before 1162, cf. *DS* 13: 609).

50. *De Trinitate* III.IX, *PL*, 196, 921C: "Ecce quomodo natura humana atque divina videntur se mutuo, et quasi ex opposito respicere, alterutra alteri veluti per contrarium respondere. Sic invicem respicere habent, et mutuo respondere debent."

51. *De Trinitate*, III.II, *PL*, 196, 916D: "Ubi autem totius bonitatis plenitudo est, vera et summa charitas deese non potest."

52. On the notion of charity and on the notion of shared love for a third person in *De Trinitate*, see E. Cousins, "Theology of Interpersonal Relations." On the notion of the good and charity (*bonitas, caritas*) in Richard and the Christian tradition, see G. Salet, *La Trinité*, pp. 477–80.

53. For a complete survey of all such Christological references/ omissions, see S. Chase, "Secret Places of Divine Incomprehensibility," Appendix E, pp. 306–7.

54. Cf. *De arca* I.i, 64C–65A: "quicunque sanati sunt ab initio per sapientiam saniti sunt . . . neminem posse placere Deo nisi fuerit sapientia cum eo. . . . Purgatur autem per sapientiam. . . . Ipsa utique est quae emundat, ipsa quae sanctificat, ut per assiduam veritatis contemplationem."

55. This association is, of course, based in part on two notions: (1) that all scripture "speaks" of Christ and yet the Old Testament must, by its very nature, "speak" in silence, and (2) that in the Old Testament Wisdom itself is present with and assists in creation and is itself the "way" of the wise.

56. Cf. *De arca* III.x, 120D. Richard does refer opaquely here to Christ: the highest Wisdom, he says, shines forth in "his express image and in his most excellent work" (*in expressa illius imagine, quam in excellentissimo ejus opere*) of creation, restoration, and glorification. But the context is that of the work symbolized by the propitiatory, not the work of Christ. Zinn's translation of "image of that One and in His most excellent work" (p. 237) is a bit too Christocentric.

57. *De arca* III.xi, 121C; 238. "Primo spiritalis natura creatur ut sit. Secundo justificatur ut bona sit. Tertio glorificatur ut beata sit. Per

creationem itaque ad bonum initiatur, per justificationem in bono dilatatur, per glorificationem in bono consummatur."

58. *De arca* IV.xviii, 158D–159A; 293–94. "Multa in hunc modum, et pene innumera circa personarum Trinitatem invenies, quae humanae rationi non solum incomprehensibilia, sed etiam dissona reperies . . . multa ejusmodi in Verbi incarnatione circa substantiarum unionem."

59. This *ordo* of incomprehensibility and sublimity is found at *De arca* IV.xviii, 160A.

60. Described, for instance, as *mutua collatione, seipsos mutuo respicere, mutuo concordiae consensu, respiciant se cherubin mutuo, mutuum respectum, cherubin cherubin respicit, se mutuo respiciunt.* See *De arca* IV.xix, 160C–161C.

61. *De arca* IV.xix, 161B; 297. "Verumtamen juxta mutuum respectum profitemur, quia solus Filius veraciter incarnatus est."

62. R. Javelet also notes that Richard does not terminate the sixth degree of contemplation in exemplaristic meditation on Christ, as does Bonaventure, but that Richard comes close in associating the mystery of the Trinity with the mystery of the Incarnation. Cf. R. Javelet, "Bonaventure et Richard de Saint-Victor," p. 89.

63. *De arca* IV.xx, 162D–163A; 299. "Si tibi mirum sit quomodo solus Filius (Patris videlicet sapientia) incarnatus sit, quomodo in carne ad nos venit, et tamen a Patre non recessit, perpende quod et in imaginaria Trinitate sola mentis sapientia voci humanae incorporatur, et per vocem corporalem egreditur."

64. Cf. *De arca* IV.xx, 162A: "that true thing, of which God is the highest truth, God reserved to God's self" (quod rerum veritatem, quae summa veritas est, reservavit sibi).

65. *De arca* IV.xxi, 163B; 300. "Illud quoque non negligendum, nec sine diligenti consideratione praetereundum, quod Dominica voce promittitur, cum ad Moysen dicitur: 'Inde loquar ad te desuper propitiatorio videlicet, et de medio duorum cherubin.' "

66. Cf. *Itin.* Prologue, 3, "ut transeat ad pacem per ecstaticos excessus sapientiae christianae. Via autem non est nisi per ardentissimum amorem Crucifixi." *De arca mystica*, a treatise on the "fullness of knowledge," does not treat in a comprehensive way the notion or language of love. Later work, in which Richard had no hesitation in mentioning Christ, would deal comprehensively with love. For Richard, only in the context of love and the burning love of Christ may the name of the flesh of the eternal Word be spoken.

67. This birth signifies Richard of St. Victor as a wise old man: his theurgy is silence.

68. *De arca* IV.xviii, 159D; 294. "Vide quam multis in locis idem Christi corpus quotidie consecratur et habetur."

69. Hugh makes this distinction between "image" and "thing" based on the distinction between faith and contemplation, but he also makes an elaborate distinction in his sacramental theology between the "image" and "thing" present within the elements of the Eucharist. See especially *De sacramentis* II.VIII.i–xiii. This latter distinction may very well be a factor in Richard's not naming Christ in this tropological treatise, but the evidence based on eucharistic theology internal to *De arca mystica* is very slim. See only *De arca* IV.xviii. And yet, the cherubim may themselves be the phenomenological bracket that removes the veil of "image." Cf. E. Kohák, *The Embers and the Stars*, pp. 179–95.

70. Cf. *De sacramentis* I.X.ix. On the property of words or symbols or images to cover (*involucra verborum*) the truth or thing, see *De sacramentis* II.I.ix.

71. *Didascalicon* VI.vi, p. 146, trans. J. Taylor.

72. *De arca* IV.xx, 162B; 298. "In quo et illud invenies valde notabile, quod rerum veritatem, quae summa veritas est, reservavit sibi, rerum vero imagines qualibet hora formandas suae concessit emagini."

73. *De arca* IV.xx, 162A.

74. This is not a turn into "self" and away from "world." It is a turn to the "natural" as opposed to the "artificial," a turn to the "person" as opposed to the "construct," and as such a turn to inward is a turn to "other." So Augustine in *Of True Religion*, as Rome crumbled, counseled "Noli foras ire, in te redi, in interiore homine habitat veritas." (Do not go outside yourself, turn within—truth dwells in the inner man.) And so Edmund Husserl, at the end of the *Cartesian Meditations,* quoted Augustine to the same effect, and received much criticism for turning to solipsism. On metaphors of the inward turn and on the inward turn as a strategy against solipsism, see E. Kohák, *The Embers and the Stars*, pp. 205–18.

75. After all, Exodus 25 does not speak of an encounter with the "image" of God (as the *imago Dei*, no more than an image and thus an encounter with the self), but rather an encounter with God. In promising to speak with us, God promises to be with us—the kind of "being" that symbol and language as image are incapable of making present, though they may provide excellent echoes.

76. Letter Four, 1072B; 264–65.

77. Letter Three, 1069B; 264.

78. And knowable only by *revelatio*, that is, revelation, showing (as translated by Zinn), or unveiling. And again, the cherubim both weave and rend the veil.

79. Including also *revelatio*.

80. But the complete fullness of that participation is always reserved for the future. Even the humanity of Christ is something we cannot fully identify with, and it cannot be fully spoken since, as Richard says in *De Trinitate*, "Christus ascendit corpore, nos ascendimus mente." Since it is thus only in the future that he will return in body and in flesh (*futura est, veniet ipse corporaliter in ea carne*), even the word of Christ's flesh must be spoken with caution and only in anticipation of the future. Cf. *De Trinitate*, Prologue, 889D.

81. *De Trinitate* VI.xiv, *PL*, 196, 978D. "Nam ad hujus ignis immissionem, animus humanus omnem nigredinem, frigiditatem, duritiem paulatim deponit, et totus in ejus a quo inflammatur similitudinem transit."

82. Significantly, by the end of Bonaventure's *Itinerarium*, it is also "fire" by which the contemplative is restored. The fire is, explicitly, God, and it is Christ who enkindles it. Cf. *SJG* 7.6, p. 115: "But if you wish to know how these things come about, ask grace, not instruction, . . . not light but the fire. . . . *This fire is God*, and his furnace is in Jerusalem; and *Christ enkindles it* in the heat of his burning passion." (Si autem quaeras, quomodo haec fiant, interroga gratiam, non doctrinam; . . . non lucem, sed ignem. . . . Qui quidem ignis Deus est, et huius caminus est in Ierusalem, et Christus hunc accendit in fervore suae ardentissimae passionis. *Itin*, 7.6.)

83. Related to the Old Testament dilemma of God's "speaking" not yet being spoken is B. Smalley's comparison of scripture to the bread and body of Christ which "leads to an analogy of mystical interpretation of scripture and the consecration of the host." Richard equates bread and body in the ark: his interpretation of scripture (*opus hominis*) is that of the consecration of the host on the propitiatory (*opus Dei*) which of course he cannot as yet fully perform and so must leave, in part, unspoken. See B. Smalley, *Bible in the Middle Ages*, pp. 91–92.

CHAPTER 6

1. A caution: the neologism, "angelization," does not imply dissociation from what is human. As in the adage, "divinization equals humanization and humanization equals divinization," the term "angelization" is meant to imply both the activity and effort of the human person and the gratuitous gift of grace. Richard of St. Victor attaches the cherubim firmly to the ark, the journey into incomprehensibility is always a journey through the created world and the self, and I have tried to express his contemplative

method as "grounded flight." "Angelization" is thus a word that expresses the dialectic of hovering; it is that median point between humanity and divinity which, requiring them both to dwell as they are, is nonetheless a new creature of their joint creation.

2. *De arca* IV.iv, 140C. "in se coelestium et pennatorum animalium figuram transformet, et humanus animus in eorum se imaginem transfiguret?"

3. For instance, the discussion of the function of symbols in Chapter 3 touches on their anagogic or what might be termed, according to Richard's project of angelization, angelic use. Much of Chapter 4 deals with the process of "angelization" in the context of the various uses and function of the symbol of the cherubim in *De arca mystica*. And Chapter 4 in particular initiates the idea of angelization by defining it provisionally as (1) the ability to see the paradox/mystery in the very core of God (what we might now call the trinitarian structure of God's incomprehensibility) and (2) the capacity to dwell in the "consciousness of the presence of God" while maintaining the fullness of this paradox.

4. *De arca* IV.vi, 140C. "angelicos illos excessus in ardua divinae incomprehensibilitatis arcana audeat attentare." It is important to remember that incomprehensibility, mystery, or wonder are available and indeed are aspects of the very fabric of contemplation at every level. The "heaven" of mystery could thus emerge in contemplation of the created world, of the self, or of the divine.

5. *Excudo*, in reference to birds, may mean "to hatch." The reference to the first instance of this usage is to Cicero, whom Richard may have known. The usage is, at any rate, extremely applicable to Richard's project: that the process of fabricating the cherubim could be given both a birthing and an aviary connotation in one stroke is not only appropriate, it is masterful.

6. Cf. *De arca* V.i, 169B; 309. "Behold: In this work we who accept the office of Bezeleel, as it were, take pains to give instruction back to you for the zealous pursuit of contemplation and to exert ourselves with great force in making this ark." (Ecce nos in hoc opere quasi Beseleel officium suscepimus qui te ad contemplationis studium instructionem reddere et quasi in arcae operatione desudare curavimus.)

7. Exodus 25:18 tells Moses, "Duos quoque cherubin aureos et productiles facies." The material and the manner by which the cherubim must be made, that is *aureos et productiles*, has been variously translated by Zinn as "gold and beaten work," by NIV as "hammered gold," by RSV as "of gold, of hammered work." I would also point out the nuances of producing into existence, bringing light to knowledge, and bringing up

into maturity present in the verb *produco*, so that a sense of nurturing into being and knowledge is also involved. Thus perhaps "the gold that nurtures one into well-being" is a possible translation. In any case, it is on the basis of this *aureos et productiles* that Richard attempts to weave the cherubim in the soul of the contemplative.

8. These word groupings in the contexts of apophatic theology and the symbolic function of the cherubim are also noted in Chapters 2 and 4 above.

9. *De arca* IV.i, 135B–D; 259–60. "Libet sane huic descriptioni vehementer intendere, et doctrinae nostrae regulam ex proposita similitudine sumere, et juxta descriptionis hujus formulam operis nostri formam, vel modum excudere. . . . Vere aliquid magnum, vere aliquid praeclarum, aliquid utique supermundanum, et omnino aliquid plus quam humanum esse debuit, quod sub angelica nobis forma repraesentari oportuit. . . . Unde oportuit ea ad similitudis expresssionem non tam humana quam angelica effigie repraesentare . . . si ad angelicae similitudinis instar cupimus intelligentiae nostrae volatum formare."

10. *De arca* IV.ii, 136D; 261. "Ut ergo in nobis angelicae similitudinis formam qualicunque modo possimus excudere, oportet in ejusmodi rerum admiratione animum nostrum jugi celeritate suspendere, et ad sublimes et vere angelicos volatus contemplationis nostrae pennas assuescere."

11. *De arca* IV.xiii, 150D; 281. "Sed forte adhuc nostri cherubin alas non habent, vel si habent, expansas nondum habent. Nondum fortassis opus nostrum ad plenum formavimus, necdum formam illam angelicam ex integro, juxta Dominicam sententiam, consummavimus."

12. *De arca* IV.xii, 149A; 279. "Haec sane illa et digna satis materia unde excudenda est angelica forma, pennataque animalia. Ex hac nobis materia cherubin formamus, quando fidei nostrae arcana quae vel ipsi per revelationem didicimus, vel a theologicis viris accepimus, assuescimus in contemplationem adducere, et in eorum admiratione animum nostrum suspendere, et pascere, humiliare, et in divinorum desiderium acriter inflammare."

13. The importance of waiting for the gift of flight (i.e., revelation) is emphasized in the allegorical digressions on Abraham and Elijah waiting at the entrance to their tents and on the Beloved of the Song of Songs waiting in her bridal chamber. Both allegories are given in the context of the cherubim spreading their wings and are intented to further strengthen and forge the wings of the cherubim. The allegories also illustrate the necessity of awaiting the "breath" of God to give flight. Cf. *De arca* IV.x–xvi.

14. *De arca* IV.xv, 154A; 286. "Sub hoc tempore, ut arbitror, illud opus nostrum ductile incipit non mediocriter proficere et consummationi

approprinquare, eo quod illi nostri cherubin incipiant alas suas jam latius extendere, et sese jam quasi ad volatum omni hora suspendere."

15. *De arca* IV.vii, 141A. "Denique aliud est arcam facere atque aliud est cherubin formare."

16. *De arca* IV.xiv, 151D.

17. *De arca* IV.xiv, 152C.

18. As we have seen, Bonaventure, one hundred years later, would not hesitate to speak this Word: "Nam et Cherubin hoc designant, quae se mutuo aspiciebant. Nec hoc vacat a mysterio, quod respiciebant *se versis vultibus in propitiatorium.* . . . Ad quod propitiatorium qui aspicit plena conversione vultus, aspiciendo eum (Christus) in cruce suspensum" (*Itin,* 6.4, 6.2). "For the cherubim who look back upon each other also symbolize this. That they looked back upon each other with their faces turned toward the propitiatory is not void of mystical meaning. . . . Whoever looks back in full conversion toward the mercy seat, their face beholds Christ hanging on the cross."

19. Cf. *De arca* I.xii and IV.viii where the right hand, extended and open, represents the first cherubim, while the left hand, hidden in the vestments and clothing, represents the second. See also *De arca* III.xxii where Richard discusses the will of the rational soul, its manifold affections, and the ordering of affections in virtue. Here the soul clothes itself (*induit se*—emphasizing the meaning of putting on clothing rather than covering) in a variety of affections, presumably hiding rather than revealing virtue.

20. *De arca* IV.xxiii, 167A.

21. Cf. *De arca* IV.xxiii, 168C.

22. This *operis factura* is in important relation to the metaphor of putting on angelic clothing: it is the "name" of the "stuff" of the process of constructing the cherubim. Zinn translates *operis factura* (and elsewhere *materialem facturam,* cf. I.xi, 77B) as "material product," which I believe is too static. *Factura,* a future active participle modifying *operis,* has more the sense of "an about to be done" or "going to be done" thing. This "about to be done" thing has an aspect of always nearing but never quite reaching completion in this life, and is dependent, finally, on the gift of grace for consummation. The cherubim are an "about to be done work" both with regard to the metaphorical work of formation and fabrication of the angels and the "work" of contemplation. Richard's tropological work is, after all, a labor, a trouble, an exertion (*opera*) on the order of a bird beating its wings so fast that it stays motionless: in fact, *operis* here is also in "hovering" complementarity to *otiosus* (leisure). Richard also uses the phrase *operis factura* earlier in the chapter (cf. *De arca* I.xii, 78A) to indicate that the nature of this ongoing work is "beyond all human

reason," though it begins in reason. Thus again, the "about to be done work" is always dynamic, never static, and always "hovering" between mutually affirming and denying coincidental opposites. (Other complementary opposites besides *operis/otiosus* and *rationi consentanae/rationi adversantia* in this chapter alone include *oculto/apertum* and the symbol of the two cherubim themselves). See also *De arca* IV.v, 139B, where the most extreme portions (*extremes*) of "our work which we are about to do" (*operis nostri factura*) are figuratively expressed (*figuraliter exprimunter*) by the name "cherubim."

23. *De arca* I.xii, 78B; 172. "Sed in ultimis istis duobus totum pendet ex gratia et omnino longinqua sunt, et valde remota ab omni humana industria, nisi in quantum unusquisque coelitus accipit, et angelicae sibi similitudinis habitum divinitus superducit. Et forte non sine causa haec novissima operis factura angelicaque figura cherubin nomen accipit."

24. *De arca* IV.vi, 139D.

25. *De arca* IV.vi, 140B,C; 266–67. "Absque dubio et sine omni contradictione non est leve vel facile humanum animum, angelicam formam induere, et insuper mundanum quemdam et vere plusquam humanum habitum transire, spiritales pennas accipere, et se ad summa levare. O quoties necesse est, aurum suum in ignem mittere et iterum extrahere, et nunc in hoc, nunc in illud latus vertere crebrisque ictibus undique tundere, antequam angelicam formam excudat cherubinque producat! . . . Cert prius necesse est assuescat in coelestibus cum coelicolis ambulare, et ad terrena negotia exteriorumque curam (nisi pro solo obedientiae debito charistatisve officio) nunquam descendere antequam angelicos illos excessus in ardua divinae incomprehensibilitatis arcana audeat attentare."

26. Richard gives a hint of this process of constructing the internal icon in a sermon edited by Châtillon which begins, "The Lord has sanctified his temple. The temple of the Lord, according to the tropological sense, is the soul" (Sanctificavit Dominus tabernaculum suum. Tabernaculum Domini secundum sensum tropologicum est anima). See Châtillon, ed., *Liber exceptionem*, X, sermo secundus, pp. 377–79, and Chapter 1 of this work for a translation. Richard comes to *De arca mystica* having done literal exegesis of temple texts (*In visionem Ezechielis*) as well as some allegorical and tropological interpretations of temple texts (some sermons, *Expositio difficultum suborientium in expositione tabernaculi*). Thus the foundation has been laid for a shift from the construction of the temple exteriorly to construction of the temple in the soul made possible by the allegorical equation of temple with soul. For a possible precedent for the internal icon as an interior construction of the tabernacle in the human soul, see Hebrews 9–10, which also hints at possible eucharistic implications for Richard's internal construction. *In visionem Ezechielis* is

based on the "literal" description of the temple of Solomon as shown to Ezechiel by "a man whose appearance shone like bronze, with a linen cord and measuring reed in his hand" (Ezechiel 40:3). *De arca mystica* is based on the words of God to Moses and is tropological. The man "with the cord and measuring reed" is a nascent twelfth-century scientist, a quantifier of the external world. Nonetheless, says Richard, "the highest *sententia* is expressed by the interior altar." *In visionem*, 589A. This highest knowledge, represented by the cherubim in *De arca mystica*, is "present" in the soul, and thus an "internal icon" is available to represent the potential for constant participation in God's presence. On the representation of physical as well as internal or spiritual space in Hugh of St. Victor, see P. Sicard, *Diagrammes médiévaux et exégèse visuelle* (Appendix 3), pp. 263–64.

27. Hugh of St. Victor mentions an ark of counsel (*arcam consilii*) in *De arca Noe morali* ii (*PL*, 176, 635A, cited in J. Taylor, *Didasc.* p. 221) and in *Didascalicon* V.ix, pp. 132–33, where the construction and inhabiting of the *arca sapientiae* in the soul are treated. In the *Didascalicon* passage, Hugh notes that prayer asks, performance goes seeking, and contemplation finds. As expanded and delineated by Richard, the ark and cherubim constructed in the soul provide the space for asking, seeking, finding.

28. *De arca* IV.xxi, 163C; 300. "Cogita quam magnum sit, vel quale omni hora cum opus fuerit Deum consideret, et in qualibet necessitate, cum oportuerit divinum consilium quaerere et accipere, et tunc animadvertere poteris quam sit necessarium vel utile hos tres novissimos speculationum modos familiares habere: *Inde,* inquit, *loquar ad te.*"

29. The standard Victorine pattern of "enlightenment" into divine incomprehensibility is that of purgation, illumination, and union. "Awakening" is sometimes interjected as the first step. J. Châtillon classes the three primary processions of the Victorine spiritual life as purification, reformation, and ascension. All of these describe the process of "angelization," especially reformation, which Châtillon describes as both a journey and a transformation of consciousness. See Châtillon, *Sermons et opuscules spirituels*, pp. lxiii–lxvii. G. Zinn quotes Hugh of St. Victor on the pattern of the ark built in the heart leading to restoration, reformation, and transformation, in "Mandala Symbolism," pp. 334–35.

30. Cf. *De arca* I.x, 76B.

31. *De arca* I.x, 76B,C,D. Immediately after this chapter in which Richard has used the wings of angels as symbols of transformation, he has us (the "You" of I.i) look at the materials and symbols of the ark in order to reinforce the notion of angelic imitation: "If, however, we look at the figure and the material of these six handmade works which

we are about to make. . . ." (Si autem ad figuram et materialem facturam respicimus, ex illis utique sex manufactis operibus. . . .) His use of the same word, *respicimus*, that he uses for the cherubim themselves as they look at the ark and across the propitiatory at each other, reinforces our own "looking" in imitation of the cherubim.

32. *De arca* III.v, 115B; 228. "Cum enim incipis spiritualibus theoriis insistere, et per spiritus tui considerationem in spirituum contemplationem assurgere, et in hunc modum ex spiritualibus spiritualia comparare, incipis et tu pariter spiritualis esse. . . ." This passage is one of the few instances of the use of the Dionysian word *theoriis* for contemplation.

33. The word is also used at III.v, 115D, where Richard asks about the nature of this link: "By what art can I liken myself to this gold?" (Qua arte, quaeso, aurum mihi comparo?) See also P. Sicard, *Diagrammes médiévaux et exégèse visuelle*, pp. 261–62, for a note on the lexicography of *collatio* at St. Victor in the first half of the twelfth century.

34. *De arca*, III.i, 108D–109A; 219. "Constat itaque hoc contemplationis genus in incorporeis et invisibilibus essentiis utpote spiritibus angelicis et spiritibus humanis."

35. *De arca* III.vi, 116D, 117A; 231. "Nescit omnino, nescit quid de spiritu angelico, quid de Spiritu divino sentire debeat qui spiritum suum prius non cogitat. . . . Prius redi ad te quam rimari praesumas quae sunt supra te."

36. *De arca* III.viii, 118B; 233. "Si ergo cupis evolare usque ad secundum, seu etiam usque ad tertium coelum. . . . Si ergo et tu scrutari paras profunda Dei, scrutare pruis profunda spiritus tui."

37. *De arca* III.x, 121B; 237. "ex multa consideratione et agnitione spiritus tui subleveris ad cognitionem et contemplationem spiritus angelici et Spiritus divini."

38. *De arca* IV.i, 135C; 259. "Vere aliquid magnum, vere aliquid praeclarum, aliquid utique supermundanum, et omnino aliquid plus quam humanum esse debuit, quod sub angelica nobis formare praesentari oportuit."

39. *De arca* IV.vi, 140C; 267. "Sed quis digne describat qua arte, quave sollicitudine opus sit, donec in se coelestium et pennatorum animalium figuram transformet, et humanus animus in eorum se imaginem transfiguret?"

40. *De arca* I.i, 63D.

41. Cf. *De arca*, I.i, 65A.

42. *De arca* I.i, 64C; 152. "Haec enim sunt quae coinquinant hominem. Purgatur autem per sapientiam quando fortior superveniens vincit malitiam utpote attingens a fine usque ad finem fortiter, et disponens omnia suaviter (Sap. viii). Et hoc ipsum sic purgari est, ut arbitror, sanctificari."

43. *De arca* I.i, 64C, quoting Wisdom 9:19: "quicunque sanati sunt per sapientiam sanati sunt."

44. The relation of human activity to grace is of course carefully explored by Richard and personified in different and subtle ways by Bezeleel, who actually forges the material of the cherubim; Aaron, who puts on the priestly vestments (angelic clothing) to penetrate the veil of the holy space where the cherubim dwell; and Moses, who climbs the mountain entering the cloud to receive directly the revelation for the pattern of cherubim construction. Indeed, Richard speculates that it may be the same to enter the temple sanctuary as it is to enter the high point of the soul, the same to climb the mountain as to enter the veil, the same to put on angelic clothing as it is to put on priestly vestments (cf. IV.xii, xxi, xxiii). The contemplative, as instructed by Richard, has access to all three personifications and any number of metaphors of divine presence; the important element, however, is the *grace* of contemplation.

45. Cf. *De arca* II.xiii on ignorance and concupiscence described as chains which in purification are smashed to pieces and shattered. See also much of Book III, which uses the metaphor of cleansing and purifying the gold of the propitiatory as the work of purification: III.xiii notes how the essence of contemplation is to encourage one away from vices and toward the good while III.xxiii especially focuses on making the affections of the soul into virtues by setting them in order by means of discretion and fixing them on the good. In Book IV, IV.v–vi describes purification symbolically as the forming and work to be done (*aureos et productiles facies*) in the construction of the cherubim and signifies the shift from the work in gold on the propitiatory to the work in gold on the cherubim by switching from metaphors of union through "knowing" to metaphors of "seeing" by means of a purified heart; IV.vi speaks of compunction and contrition purifying the soul; IV.ix–xvi discusses how knowledge of self and love of God strengthens against evil and assists in formation of virtue; and in a direct reference to the spreading of the cherubim's wings over the propitiatory, IV.ix notes how "love and approbation of the world is covered over [*obducitur*] by contemplation of spiritual creatures."

46. See *De arca* IV.xxii, 166B cited above.

47. Verbs Richard uses to describe the process of purgation and restoration have generally to do with preparation: *comparare*—to prepare or get ready; *addiscere*—to learn in addition; *adducere*—to influence or lead to a new state of mind; *laborare*—to work in the sense of preparation; *recupero*—to regain, recover. See mostly Book III.

48. *Didascalicon* I.v, p. 62, trans. J. Taylor.

49. The "work of contemplation," as pointed out elsewhere and even

more particularly in this context, is a primary example of the core metaphor of "hovering." Richard's playful juxtaposition of *otiosus* and *operis* in describing contemplation indicate that he himself was very aware of this hovering nature of contemplation in which absolute rest is the eternal ground of motion.

50. *De arca* IV.vii, 140D; 267. "Cogita, obsecro, cujus sit excellentiae illius ordinis in se similitudinem per imitationem trahere, qui summae claritati immediate adhaeret, qui facie ad faciem, et sine speculo, et sine aenigmate videt."

51. *De arca* V.iv, 173D; 315. "Supra humanam naturam est, procul dubio pennas habere ad alta volare."

52. *De arca* V.iv, "Quis mihi dabit pennas sicut columbae, et volabo et requiescam?"

53. *De arca* I.i, 65A; 152. "Summam Dei sapientiam in carne latitantem quam oculis carnis videre non poterat."

54. With at least one instance of their location in *De arca mystica*, these verbs include: *imitari* (IV.i, IV.vii), *excudere* (IV.i, IV.ii, IV.vi, IV.vii, IV.xiv), *repraesentare* (IV.i), *formare* (IV.vii, IV.ix, IV.xiii), *producere* (IV.i, IV.vi), *comparare* (III.v), *exprimere* (IV.i), *fabricare* (IV.xxii), *transformare* (IV.iv), *transfigurare* (IV.iv).

VISIO

1. Also from Kohák's book. As to style, content, and vision, I recommend it highly. The quotations are from his final chapter, "*Credo.*"

2. "*Ignus Deus est,*" says Bonaventure. *Itinerarium mentis in Deum*, 7.6.

3. *De arca* V.xiv, 186D: "et hanc nostram naturam exsultationis suae applusum juxta angelicae similitudinis tripudia formare." This short passage bears a striking resemblance to a section of Hugh of St. Victor's *In hierarchiam celestem* (*PL* 175, 946B). Hugh notes how the mental eye is too weak to receive the full light of God without being blinded; that light is thus sifted by "*similitudines et formas,*" proposed "*secundum naturam nostram.*"

4. "Cherub looks back upon cherub." Cf. *De arca* IV.xix, 161B. In the same chapter, Richard writes, *respiciant se cherubim mutuo* and *cherubin ce mutuo respiciunt.*

5. Thus, I believe, preparing the way for the life and breath of Francis of Assisi, who through the stigmata was transported beyond the faltering nature of symbol, becoming Bonaventure's vision and model for speaking and naming the *res* of the *carnem aeterni Verbi* between the two cherubim.

6. I believe there is a real element of birthing in Richard's interpretation of the ark and cherubim. We recall from Chapter 1 the Marian interpretation of the ark and cherubim. The symbols themselves are recognizable as the shape of a womb. This "womb" is the birthing place of the presence of God in the form of the *loquar ad te*, the place of continuous birth of the flesh of the Word in the soul of the contemplative, and the continuous birthing place of the contemplative herself in the sense that in the course of active progress in virtue and of contemplation one dies to self and is reborn many times. The ark and cherubim are a womb of many births.

7. For explication and justification of what might be called a "hermeneutic of participation," see "Methodology" in Introduction of this work.

8. *De arca.* I.iv, 67D. "Contemplatio est libera mentis perspicacia in sapientiae spectacula cum admiratione suspensa."

9. See Appendix A, on Book V of *De arca mystica*.

APPENDICES

1. *De arca* V.xix, 192C; 343. "Melius in hoc nos illorum peritia instruit, quos ad scientiae hujus plenitudinem non tam aliena doctrina quam propria experientia provexit."

2. "Experience" itself is a starting point or foundation in the construction of much of Richard's spiritual theology. On the book of experience (*liber experientiae*) in the twelfth-century, on human and angelic anthropology and their mutual relation through experience, on Richard's "method of human experience," on Victorine spirituality and theology starting with experience, on the relation of tropology to experience, and on the relation of experience and self-knowledge, see S. Chase, "Into the Secret Places of Divine Incomprehensibility," Appendix D: "The Notion of Experience in Richard of St. Victor," pp. 295–97. In a beautiful and evocative chapter, Richard summarizes his discussion of human experience and its relation to self-knowledge by claiming that, "*Nihil recte aestimat qui seipsum ignorat*," III.vi; 116D. Elsewhere on the relation of self-knowledge to fullness of knowledge Richard concludes that "the soul which is attempting to rise to the height of knowledge must make self-knowledge its first and chief concern. . . . The high peak of knowledge is perfect self-knowledge"; see *Benjamin Minor*, LXXV, 54 (*Animus qui ad scientiae altitudinem nititur ascendere, primum et principale sit ei studium seipsum cognoscere. . . . Magna altitudo scientae seipsum perfecte cognovisse*).

3. *De arca* V.xix, 192C; 343: "And so to the summary of our material which we touched upon with succinct brevity in the first book, we have added. . . ." (Ad illam itaque materiae nostrae summam quam in primo libro succincta brevitate perstrinximus . . . adjecimus).

4. Cf. J. Châtillon, "Les trois modes de la contemplation selon Richard de Saint-Victor," pp. 3–26. For a table giving the three modes of contemplation and the relation of the modes to human effort and grace and the causes of each mode, see G. Zinn, "Personification Allegory and Visions of Light," p. 203. For tables on the six kinds of contemplation and on the relation of contemplation to thinking and meditation, see Tables 1 and 2 of this work.

5. For the best all-round focus on the question of love (*caritas*) in Richard that does not fail to elucidate the intellectual (*sapientia*) aspect as well, see Dumeige, *L'idée chrétienne de l'amour.* Dumeige concludes that Richard was able to "synthesize" affect and reason. For an excellent investigation of the theme of love in Richard, see E. Cousins, "Notion of the Person," pp. 76–80. Leclercq, *Histoire de la spiritualité chrétienne* II, focuses on the importance of love in Richard's spirituality on pp. 289–94. On union language that encompasses both "love" and "knowledge," see B. McGinn, "Love, Knowledge, and Unio Mystica," pp. 61–64. J. Châtillon, in "Les trois modes de la contemplation," pp. 3–26, concludes that in Richard love and knowledge mutually assist in the assent to God. For a comparison of Thomas Gallus and Richard on the issue of affect and intellect, see R. Javelet, "Thomas Gallus ou les Ecritures dans une dialectique mystique," pp. 99–110, and R. Javelet, "Thomas Gallus et Richard de Saint-Victor, Mystiques," pp. 206–33. For a bibliography on the notion of "charity" in Richard, see G. Zinn, *Richard of St. Victor,* p. 47, n.25.

6. Cf. *De arca* V.iv, 172D–173D.

7. Cf. *De arca* V.v, 174A–D.

8. *De arca* V.xiii, 183B. "Angelus sane nuntius dicitur."

9. *De arca* V.viii, 177B: "alter angelico ducatu supra communem humanae possibilitatis statum, mentis alienatione levatur."

10. *De arca* V.xii and V.viv: "in illud divinitatis arcanum totum intrare . . . et mirabili transfiguratione spiritus ille ab humano videatur in divinum deficcere . . . dum in coelestibus tota suspenditur, dum angelicis spectaculis tota immergitur."

11. *De arca* V.xiii, 183C-D: "ad aeternorum cognitionem illuminamur, per quem ad eorum desiderium inflammamur . . . animum humanum ad omnem veritatem inducere . . . qui coelestium et aeternorum cognitionem pariter et amorem."

12. *De arca* V.xiii, 183D: "Quid ergo mirum si talis nuntius oppressam

animam a concupiscientiae suae nexibus absolvit, ab ignorantiae suae tenebris evolvit." Denys' discussion of the angelic order of the thrones can be found in his *Celestial Hierarchy*, 7, pp. 161–66. An example of the use of angelic thrones as a model and symbol of discernment can be found in a slightly later contemporary of Richard, Alan of Lille (d. 1203). Alan says that the thrones are those with the knowledge of discerning or judging between good and evil (*discernendi vel iudicandi scientiam habeant inter bonum et malum*). Cf. *Hierarchia Alani*, pp. 231–32 in *Alain de Lille: Textes Inédits*, ed. M-T. d'Alverny.

13. On the higher order's undiluted reception of the original enlightenment in Denys, see *Celestial Hierarchy*, 4.2, p. 157; 6.2, p. 160; 7.1, p. 161.

14. Cf. *De arca* V.vi, 173C: "anima sancta tunc veraciter, quasi fumus et per desertum ascendit." Richard is here drawing out a metaphor from the Song of Songs 8:5: "Who is this coming up from the desert leaning on her lover?" (quae est ista quae ascendit de deserto deliciis affluens et nixa super dilectum suum).

15. On the consummation of virtues as charity and longing for the celestial bridegroom, see *De arca* V.vi, 175C: "consummatio virtutum est charitas . . . affectum suum, in coelestis sponsi desiderium accendit."

16. Cf. the discussion on the phenomenological veil removed by gift in E. Kohák, *The Embers and the Stars*, pp. 187ff.

BIBLIOGRAPHY

PRIMARY SOURCES
EDITIONS AND TRANSLATIONS

1. By Richard of St. Victor

The Latin texts of the majority of Richard's work are found in J.-P. Migne, editor, *Richardi a Sancto Victore Opera Omnia*, in *Patrologiae latinae* (hereafter *PL*), volume 196, Paris, 1855. Works by Richard of St. Victor consulted in Migne, other critical editions, and translations include:

Richard of St. Victor. *In apocalypsim Joannis*. In *PL*, 196: 683–886.

———. *(De arca mystica): De gratia contemplationis, seu Benjamin Maior*. In *PL*, 196: 63–192.

———. *Expositio difficultatum suborientium in expositione Tabernaculi feoderis*. In *PL*, 196: 211–222.

———. *Liber exceptionum*. Critical text with introduction, notes and tables by Jean Châtillon. Paris: J. Vrin, 1958.

———. *Mysticae adnotationes in Psalmos*. In *PL*, 196: 263–400.

———. *Nonnullae allegoriae Tabernaculi foederis*. In *PL*, 196: 192–201.

———. *De praeparatione animi ad contemplationem, liber dictus Benjamin Minor*. In *PL*, 196: 1–80.

———. *De quatuor gradibus violentae charitatis*. In *PL*, 196: 1207–25.

———. *Richard de Saint-Victor: opuscules théologiques*, Textes philosophiques de moyen age, 15. Critical text, introduction, notes and tables by J. Ribaillier. Paris: J. Vrin, 1967.

———. *Richard de Saint-Victor: sermons et opuscules spirituels inédits*, vol. 1: *L'édit d'Alexandre ou les trois processions*. Critical Latin text, introduction, and notes by Jean Châtillon and William-Joseph Tulloch, translation (French) by Joseph Barthélmy. Paris: Desclée de Brouwer, 1949.

———. *Richard of St. Victor: The Twelve Patriarchs, The Mystical Ark, Book Three of the Trinity*. Translation and introduction by Grover A. Zinn. Classics of Western Spirituality. New York: Paulist Press, 1979.

243

––––––. *Richard of St. Victor: Selected Writings on Contemplation.* Translation by Clare Kirchberger. London: Faber and Faber, 1957.

––––––. *De Trinitate: texte critique avec introduction, notes et tables.* Edited by Jean Ribaillier. Paris: J. Vrin, 1958.

––––––. *La Trinité.* Edited, introduction, and notes by Gaston Salet. Sources Chrétiennes, 63. Paris: Editions du Cerf, 1959.

––––––. *De Verbo incarnato.* In *PL,* 196: 995–1011.

––––––. *In visionem Ezechielis.* In *PL,* 196: 527–601.

2. Other Primary Texts and Critical Editions

Alan of Lille. *De sex alis cherubim.* In *PL,* 210: 269–280.

––––––. *Hierarchia Alani.* In *Alain de Lille: textes inédits avec un introduction sur sa vie et ses oeuvres.* Études de philosophie médiévale, 52, par Marie Thérèse d'Alverny, pp. 223–35. Paris: J. Vrin, 1965.

Augustine. *De doctrina Christiana, libri IV.* Corpus Christianorum, Series Latina, Volume 32. Turnholt: Brepols, 1962.

––––––. *Quaestiones in Heptateuchum.* Corpus Christianorum, Latin Series, Volume 32. Turnholt: Brepols, 1975.

Bede the Venerable. *De tabernaculo.* In *Bedae Venerabilis Opera,* Pars II, 2A. Opera Exegetica Corpus Christianorum, Latin Series, Volume 119A, edited by D. Hurst, O.S.B., pp. 1–139. Turnholt: Brepols, 1964.

––––––. *De templo.* In *Bedae Venerabilis Opera,* Pars II, 2A, pp. 141–234.

Biblia sacra iuxta vulgatam versionem. Adiuvantibus Bonifatio Fischer O.S.B., Iohanne Gribomont O.S.B., H. F. D. Sparks, W. Thiele; recensuit et brevi apparatu instruxit Robertus Weber O.S.B. Editio tertia emendata. Stuttgart: Deutsche Bibelgesellschaft, 1983.

Biblical Interpretation in the Early Church. Translated and edited by Karlfried Froehlich. Sources of Early Christian Thought. Philadelphia: Fortress Press, 1984.

Bonaventure. *Bonaventure: The Soul's Journey into God, The Tree of Life, The Life of St. Francis.* Translated by Ewert Cousins. New York: Paulist Press, 1978.

––––––. *Itinerarium mentis in Deum.* In *Doctoris seraphici S. Bonaventurae opera omnia,* 10 vols. Quaracchi: Collegium S. Bonaventurae, 1882–1902, vol. 5, pp. 295–313.

Clement of Alexandria. *The Writings of Clement of Alexandria.* Translated by William Wilson in Ante-Nicene Christian Library. Edinburgh, 1869.

Damascene, John. *Homélies sur la Nativité et la Dormition.* Translation (French) by Pierre Voulet. Sources Chrétiennes, 80. Paris: Editions du Cerf, 1963.

Denys the Areopagite. *Dionysius the Areopagite: The Divine Names and the Mystical Theology*. Translated by C. E. Rolt. London: SPCK, 1940.

———. *La hiérarchie céleste*. Introduction by René Roques, critcal text by Gunter Heil, translation (French) by Maurice de Gandillac. Sources Chrétiennes, 58. Paris: Editions du Cerf, 1958.

———. *Pseudo-Dionysius: The Complete Works*. Translated by Colm Luibheid with forward, notes, and translation collaboration by Paul Rorem. CWS. New York: Paulist Press, 1987.

Eriugena, Johannes Scotus. *De divisione naturae (Periphyseon)*. Edited by I. P. Sheldon-Williams with Ludwig Bieler. Scriptores Latini Hiberniae, volumes 7, 9, 11. Dublin: Dublin Institute for Advanced Studies, 1968–81.

———. *Expositiones in ierarchiam coelestem S. Dionysii*. Edited by Jeanne Barbet. Corpus Christianorum, Continuatio Mediaeualis, no. 31. Turnholt: Brepols, 1975.

Gregory the Great. *XL homiliarum in Evangelia*, Liber II, Homil. XXV. In *PL*, 76: 1188–96.

Hugh of Fouilloy. *Aviarium*. In *The Medieval Book of Birds*, edited, translated, and with commentary by Willene B. Clark. Binghamton, N.Y.: Medieval & Renaissance texts & studies, 1992.

Hugh of St. Victor. *De arca Noe morali*. In *PL*, 176:617–80.

———. *De arca Noe mystica*. In *PL*, 176:681–704.

———. *Commentariorum hierarchiam coelestem S. Dionysii Areopagite*. In *PL*, 175:923–1154.

———. *Didascalicon de studio legendi*. In *PL*, 176:770–812; ed. C. H. Buttimer, *Hugonis de Sancto Victore Didascalicon de studio legendi*.

———. *The Didascalicon* of Hugh of St. Victor, translation with introduction and notes by Jerome Taylor. New York: Columbia University Press, 1961.

———. *Hugh of St. Victor on the Sacraments of the Christian Faith (De Sacramentis)*, translation by Roy J. Deferrari. Mediaeval Academy of America 58. Cambridge, Mass.: Mediaeval Academy of America, 1951.

———. *Hugh of St. Victor: Selected Spiritual Writings*, translated by a religious of C.S.M.V., with an introduction by Aelred Squire, O.P. London: Faber and Faber, 1962.

———. *De sacramentis Christianae fidei*. In *PL*, 176:173–618.

———. *Six opuscules spirituels*. Introduction, critical text, translation (French), and notes by Roger Baron. Sources Chrétiennes, 155. Paris: Editions du Cerf, 1969.

Isidore of Seville. *Mysticorum expositiones sacramentorum, seu quaestiones in vetus testamentum, In Exodum*, chapter XXV. In *PL*, 83:287–322.

Liber ordinis Sancti Victoris Parisiensis. Edited by Lucas Jocqué and Ludovicus Milis. Corpus Christianorum Continuatio Mediaeualis, no. 61. Turnholt: Brepols, 1984.

Nicholas of Cusa. *De docta ignorantia*. In *Nicolai de Cusa opera omnia*. Edited by Ernst Hoffmann and Raymond Klibansky. Leipzig: Meiner, 1932.

Origen. *Homélies sur les Nombres*. Translation and introduction by André Mehat. Sources Chrétiennes 29. Paris: Editions du Cerf, 1957.

Rabanus Maurus. *Allegoriae in sacram Scripturam*. In *PL*, 112:849–1088.

SECONDARY SOURCES
STUDIES

Almond, Philip C. *Mystical Experience and Religious Doctrine: An Investigation of the Study of Mysticism in World Religions*. New York: Mouton, 1982.

Armstrong, A. H., ed. *Plotinus*. New York: Collier Books, 1962.

Aumann, Jordan. *Christian Spirituality in the Catholic Tradition*. New York: Sheed and Ward, 1985.

Baron, Roger. *Études sur Hugues de Saint-Victor*. Paris: Desclée de Brouwer, 1964.

———. *Science et sagesse chez Hugues de Saint-Victor*. Paris: P. Lethielleux, 1957.

Battles, Ford Lewis. "Hugo of Saint-Victor as a Moral Allegorist." *Church History* 18 (1949): 220–40.

Bautier, Rober-Henri. "Les origines et les premiers développements de l'abbaye Saint-Victor de Paris." In *L'abbaye Parisienne de Saint-Victor au moyen age: communications présentées au XIIIe colloque d'humanisme médiéval de Paris (1986–1988)*, edited by Jean Longére. Bibliotheca Victorina I. Turnhout: Brepols, 1991.

Beierwaltes, Werner. "*Negati Affirmatio*: Or the World as Metaphor, foundation for medieval aesthetics from the writings of John Scotus Eriugena." *Dionysius* 1 (1977): 127–59.

Bennett, Judith M. "Medievalism and Feminism." *Speculum* 68, 2 (1993): 309–31.

Benson, R. L. and Constable, G. *Renaissance and Renewal in the Twelfth Century*. Oxford: Clarendon Press; Cambridge: Harvard University Press, 1982.

Berndt, Rainer. *André de Saint-Victor (d. 1175), exégète et théologien*. Bibliotheca Victorina II. Turnhout: Brepols, 1991.

Bernstein, Richard J. *Beyond Objectivism and Relativism: Science, Hermeneutics, Praxis.* Oxford: Basil Blackwell, 1983.

Bonnard, Fourier. *Histoire de l'abbaye Royale et de l'ordre des Chanoines Réguliers de St-Victor de Paris.* Volume 1, première période (1113–1500). Paris, 1907.

Bowman, Leonard, ed. *"Itinerarium": The Idea of Journey.* Salzburg: Institut fur Anglistik und Amerikanistik, Universitat Salzburg, 1983.

Budick, Sanford. *The Dividing Muse: Images of Sacred Disjunction in Milton's Poetry.* New Haven: Yale University Press, 1985.

Burrell, David C. *Analogy and Philosophical Language.* New Haven: Yale University Press, 1973.

Burton-Christie, Douglas. *The Word in the Desert: Scripture and the Quest for Holiness in Early Christian Monasticism.* New York: Oxford University Press, 1993.

Butler, Cuthbert. *Western Mysticism: The Teaching of Saints Augustine, Gregory and Bernard on Contemplation and the Contemplative Life.* London: Constable, 1951.

Bynum, Caroline Walker. *Docere Verbo et Exemplo: An Aspect of Twelfth-Century Spirituality.* Missoula: Scholars Press, 1979.

———. *Jesus as Mother: Studies in the Spirituality of the High Middle Ages.* Berkeley: University of California Press, 1982.

———; Harrell, Stevan; Richman, Paula, eds. *Gender and Religion.* Boston: Beacon Press, 1986.

Cantor, Norman F. *Inventing the Middle Ages: The Lives, Works, and Ideas of the Great Medievalists of the Twentieth Century.* New York: Quill, William Morrow, 1991.

Caputo, John D. *Radical Hermeneutics: Repetition, Deconstruction, and the Hermeneutic Project.* Bloomington: Indiana University Press, 1987.

Cassirer, Ernst. *Philosophy of Symbolic Forms.* 3 volumes. Translated by Ralph Manheim. New Haven: Yale University Press, 1953.

Chase, Steven. "Into the Secret Places of Divine Incomprehensibility: The Symbol of the Cherubim in *De arca mystica* of Richard of St. Victor." Ph.D. Dissertation, Fordham University, 1994.

Châtillon, Jean. "La Bible dans les écoles du XIIe siècle." In *Le moyen age et la Bible.* Paris: Beauchesne, 1984.

———. "Contemplation, action et prédication d'après un sermon inédit de Richard de Saint-Victor en l'honneur de saint Grégoire-le-Grand." In *L'homme devant Dieu: mélanges offerts au Père Henri de Lubac,* pp. 89–98. Paris: Aubier, 1963.

———. "La culture de l'ecole de Saint-Victor au 12e siècle." In *Entretiens sur la renaissance du 12e siècle,* edited by M. de Gandillac and

E. Jeaneau, pp. 147–60. DCCI de Cerisy-la-Salle, no. 9. Paris: Mouton, 1968.

———. "De Guillaume de Champeaux à Thomas Gallus: chronique d'histoire littéraire et doctrinale de l'Ecole de Saint-Victor." *Revue du moyen âge latin* 8 (1952): 139–62, 247–73.

———. *Le mouvement canonial au moyen âge, réforme de l'église, spiritualité et culture*. Bibliotheca Victorina III, études réunies par P. Sicard. Turnhout: Brepols, 1992.

———. "Richard de Saint-Victor." In *Dictionnaire de spiritualité: ascétique et mystique, doctrine et histoire* 13: 593–654. Paris: Beauchesne, 1988.

———. *Théologie, spiritualité, et métaphysique dans l'oeuvre oratoire d'Achard de Saint-Victor: etudes d'histoire doctrinale précédées d'un essai sur la vie et l'oeuvre d'Achard*. Études de philosophie médiévale, no. 58. Paris: J. Vrin, 1969.

———. "Les trois modes de la contemplation selon Richard de Saint-Victor." *Bulletin de littérature ecclésiastique* 41 (1940): 3–26.

Chenu, M.-D. "Un essai de méthode théologique au XIIe siècle." *Revue des sciences, philosophiques et théologiques* 24 (1935): 258–67.

———. *La théologie au douzième siècle*. Études de philosophie médiévale, no. 45. Paris: J. Vrin, 1957. Translated as *Nature, Man and Society in the Twelfth Century: Essays on the New Theological Perspectives in the Latin West*, by Jerome Taylor and L. K. Little. Chicago: University of Chicago Press, 1968.

Clark, Mary T. "The Trinity in Latin Christianity." In *Christian Spirituality: Origins to Twelfth Century*. Volume 16 of *World Spirituality: An Encyclopedic History of the Religious Quest*, ed. McGinn et al. pp. 276–90.

Constable, Giles. "The Popularity of Twelfth-Century Spiritual Writers in the Late Middle Ages." In *Religious Life and Thought*, pp. 5–26. London: Variorum Reprints, 1979.

———. "Twelfth-Century Spirituality and the Late Middle Ages." In *Religious Life and Thought*, pp. 27–59. London: Variorum Reprints, 1979.

Cooke, Bernard J. *The Distancing God: The Ambiguity of Symbols in History and Theology*. Minneapolis: Fortress Press, 1990.

Copleston, Frederick, S.J. *A History of Philosophy*. Volume 2, *Mediaeval Philosophy, Part I, Augustine to Bonaventure*. New York: Image Books, 1962.

Cousins, Ewert. *Bonaventure and the Coincidence of Opposites*. Chicago: Franciscan Herald Press, 1978.

———. "Fecundity and the Trinity: An Appendix to Chapter Three of *The*

Great Chain of Being." In *Jacob's Ladder and the Tree of Life*, edited by M. Kuntz and P. Kuntz, pp. 73–82. New York: Peter Lang, 1987.

———. "Francis of Assisi and Bonaventure: Mysticism and Theological Interpretation." In *The Other Side of God: A Polarity in World Religions*, edited by Peter Berger, pp. 74–103. Garden City: Doubleday, 1981.

———. "The Notion of the Person in the *De Trinitate* of Richard of St. Victor." Ph.D. dissertation, Fordham University, 1966.

———. "States of Consciousness: Charting the Mystical Path." In *Fires of Desire: Erotic Energies and the Spiritual Quest*, edited by John Shea and Fredrica Halligan, pp. 126–45. New York: Crossroad, 1992.

———. "A Theology of Interpersonal Relations." *Thought* 45 (1970): 56–82.

———, general ed. *World Spirituality: An Encyclopedic History of the Religious Quest.* Volume 15: *Classical Mediterranean Spirituality: Egyptian, Greek, Roman*, edited by A. H. Armstrong. New York: Crossroad, 1986. Volume 16: *Christian Spirituality I: Origins to the Twelfth Century*, edited by Bernard McGinn, John Meyendorff, with Jean Leclercq. New York: Crossroad, 1985. Volume 17: *Christian Spirituality II: High Middle Ages and Reformation*, edited by Jill Raitt with Bernard McGinn and John Meyendorff. New York: Crossroad, 1987. Volume 18: *Christian Spirituality III: Post-Reformation and Modern*, edited by Louis Dupré and Don E. Saliers with John Meyendorff. New York: Crossroad, 1989.

Coward, Harold and Terence Penelham. *Mystics and Scholars: The Calgary Conference on Mysticism, 1976.* Waterloo, Ontario: Wilfrid Laurier University Press, 1977.

Cox, Michael. *Handbook of Christian Spirituality.* New York: Harper and Row, 1985.

Crouzel, Henri. "Spiritual Exegesis." In *Encyclopedia of Theology: The Concise Sacramentum Mundi*, pp. 126–33. Edited by Karl Rahner. New York: Seabury, 1975.

Daniélou, Jean, S.J. *Les anges et leur mission d'après les pères de l'église.* Chevetogne, Belgium: Editions de Chevetogne, 1953.

Davidson, A. B. "Angel." In *A Dictionary of the Bible*, 1988 edition, pp. 93–97.

Dawson, Christopher. *Religion and the Rise of Western Culture.* New York: Doubleday, 1950.

Dickinson, J. C. *The Origins of the Austin Canons and Their Introduction into England.* London: SPCK, 1950.

Dondaine, H. F. *Le corpus Dionysien de l'université de Paris au XIIIe siècle.* Rome: Edizioni de Sturia e Litteratura, 1953.

Dronke, Peter. *A History of Twelfth-Century Western Philosophy*. Cambridge: Cambridge University Press, 1988.

———. *Women Writers of the Middle Ages: A Critical Study of Texts from Perpetua (203) to Marguerite Porete (1310)*. New York: Cambridge University Press, 1984.

Duhr, Joseph. "Anges." In *Dictionnaire de spiritualité: ascétique et mystique doctrine et histoire*. Volume 1, 1936 edition, pp. 580–625.

Dumeige, Gervais. *Richard de Saint-Victor et l'idée chrétienne de l'amour*. Paris: Presses Universitaires de France, 1952.

Ebner, Joseph. *Die Erkenntnislehre Richards von Saint Viktor*. Beiträge zur Geschichte der Philosophie und Theologie des Mittelalters, Band 19, heft 4. Münster, 1917.

Elder, Rozanne E., ed. *The Spirituality of Western Christendom*. Kalamazoo: Cistercian Publications, 1976.

Eliade, Mircea. *Mythes, rêves et mysteres*. Paris: Gallimard, 1957.

———. *The Two and the One*. Translated by J. M. Cohen. London: Harvill Press, 1965.

Ethier, A.-M. *Le "De Trinitate" de Richard de Saint-Victor*. Ottawa: Publications de l'institut d'etudes médiévales d'Ottawa, 1939.

Evans, Gillian R. "The Borrowed Meaning: Grammar, Logic and the Problem of Theological Language in Twelfth-Century Schools." *Downside Review* 96 (1978): 165–75.

———. *Old Arts and New Theology: The Beginnings of Theology as an Academic Discipline*. Oxford: Clarendon Press, 1980.

———. "Similitudes and Signification Theory in the Twelfth Century." *Downside Review* 101 (1983): 306–11.

Fairweather, Eugene R., ed. *A Scholastic Miscellany: Anselm to Ockham*. The Library of Christian Classics. Philadelphia: The Westminster Press, 1966.

Fallon, T. L.; Michl, J.; Bialas, A. A.; Tsuji, S. "Angels." In *The New Catholic Encyclopedia*. Volume 1, 1966 edition, pp. 507–19.

Fawcett, Thomas. *The Symbolic Language of Religion*. London: George Allen & Unwin, 1968.

Fiorenza, Elisabeth Schüssler. *Bread Not Stone: The Challenge of Feminist Biblical Interpretation*. New York: Beacon, 1985.

Forest, A.; van Steenberghen, F.; de Gandillac, M. *Le mouvement doctrinal du XIe au XVIe siècle*. Histoire de l'Eglise dupuis les origines jusqu'a nos jours, no. 13. Paris: Bloud & Gay, 1951.

Forman, Robert K. C. *The Problem of Pure Consciousness: Mysticism and Philosophy*. New York: Oxford University Press, 1990.

Fuehrer, M. L. "The Principle of Similitude in Hugh of Saint Victor's

Theory of Divine Illumination." *American Benedictine Review* 30 (March 1979): 80–92.

Gadamer, Hans-Georg. *Truth and Method*. Second revised edition. Translated and revised by Joel Weinsheimer and Donald G. Marshall. New York: Crossroad, 1989.

———. *Philosophical Hermeneutics*. Translated by David E. Linge. Berkeley: University of California Press, 1976.

Gannon, Thomas M. and George Traub. *The Desert and the City: An Interpretation of the History of Christian Spirituality*. New York: Macmillan, 1969.

Gaster, T. H. "Angel." In *The Interpreter's Dictionary of the Bible*, 1991 edition, pp. 128–34.

Gersh, Stephen. *From Iamblichus to Eriugena: An Investigation of the Prehistory and Evolution of the Pseudo-Dionysian Tradition*. Leiden: E. J. Brill, 1978.

Ghellinck, J. de. *Le movement théologique du XIIe*. Second Edition. Museum Lessianum Section Historique, no. 10. Bruges: Editions "de Temple," 1948.

Gibson, Margaret. "The Study of the *Timaeus* in the Eleventh and Twelfth Centuries." *Pensiamento* 25 (1969): 183–94.

Gilson, Etienne. *History of Christian Philosophy in the Middle Ages*. New York: Random House, 1955.

———. *The Mystical Theology of St. Bernard*. Kalamazoo: Cistercian Publications, 1990.

Goodman, Nelson. *Languages of Art: An Approach to a Theory of Symbols*. Indianapolis: Hackett, 1976.

Grant, Robert, with David Tracy. *A Short History of the Interpretation of the Bible*. Philadelphia: Fortress Press, 1984.

Guimet, Fernand. "*Caritas ordinata et amor discretus* dans la théologie trinitaire de Richard de Saint-Victor." *Revue du moyen âge latin* 4 (1948): 225–36.

Hadot, Pierre. "Neoplatonist Spirituality: Plotinus and Porphyry." In *Classical Mediterranean Spirituality: Egyptian, Greek, Roman*. Volume 15 of *World Spirituality: An Encyclopedic History of the Religious Quest*, pp. 230–49. New York: Crossroad, 1989.

Hanning, Robert W. *The Individual in Twelfth Century Romance*. New Haven: Yale University Press, 1977.

Hanson, Bradley C. *Modern Christian Spirituality: Methodological and Historical Essays*. Atlanta: Scholars Press, 1990.

Happold, F. C. *Mysticism: A Study and an Anthology*. Baltimore: Penguin, 1970.

Haran, M. "The Ark and Cherubim: Their Symbolic Significance in Biblical Ritual." *Israel Exploration Journal* 9 (1959): 30–38, 89–94.

Häring, N. M. "John Scottus in Twelfth-Century Angelology." In *The Mind of Eriugena*, edited by John J. O'Meara and Ludwig Beiler, pp. 158–69. Dublin: Irish University Press, 1973

Hayes, Zachary O.F.M. *The Hidden Center: Spirituality and Speculative Christology in St. Bonaventure*. New York: Paulist Press, 1981.

Healy, Patrick J. "The Mysticism of the School of St. Victor." *Church History* 1 (1932): 211–21.

Hegel, G. W. F. *The Phenomenology of Mind*. Translated by F. B. Baile. London: Allen and Unwin, 1931.

Heidegger, Martin. *Basic Writings*. Edited by David Farrell Krell. New York: Harper & Row, 1977.

———. *On the Way to Language*. Translated by Peter D. Hertz. New York: Harper & Row, 1971.

———. *Poetry, Language, Thought*. Translated by Albert Hofstadter. New York: Harper & Row, 1971.

———. *The Question Concerning Technology and Other Essays*. Translated by William Lovitt. New York: Harper & Row, 1977.

Heidt, William George. *Angelology of the Old Testament: A Study in Biblical Theology*. Washington, D.C.: Catholic University of America Press, 1949.

Hellmann, Wayne. "The Seraph in the Legends of Thomas of Celano and St. Bonaventure: The Victorine Transition." In *Bonaventuriana I*. Edited by Chevero Blanco. Rome: Edizioni Antonianum, 1988.

Holmes, Urban T. *A History of Christian Spirituality: An Analytical Introduction*. New York: Seabury, 1980.

Houston, Jean. *The Hero and the Goddess:* The Odyssey *as Mystery and Initiation*. New York: Balantine Books, 1992.

Hügel, Friedrich von. *The Mystical Element of Religion as Studied in Saint Catherine of Genoa and Her Friends*. 2 Volumes. London: J. M. Dent & Sons, 1923.

Hugonin, Mgr. "Notice sur Richard de Saint-Victor." In *Richardi a Sancto Victore Opera Omnia, PL*, 196, xiii–xxxii.

Huizinga, Johan. *The Waning of the Middle Ages: A Study of the Forms of Life, Thought, and Art in France and the Netherlands in the XIVth and XVth Centuries*. New York: St. Martin's Press, 1969 [1924].

Inge, William. *The Awakening of the Soul*. London: A. R. Mowbray, 1959.

———. *Christian Mysticism*. London: Methuen, 1921.

———. *Mysticism in Religion*. Chicago: University of Chicago Press, 1948.

———. *The Platonic Tradition in English Religious Thought.* New York: Longmans, Green, 1926.

James, William. *The Varieties of Religious Experience.* New York: Longmans, Green, 1902.

Javelet, Robert. "La dignité de l'homme dans la pensée du XIIe siècle." In *De dignitate hominis: Festschrift für Carlos-Josaphat Pinto de Oliveira,* edited by Holderegger et al., pp. 39–87. Fribourg: Institut de Théologie Moral, 1987.

———. *Images et ressemblance au douzieme siècle de Saint Anselme à Alain de Lille.* 2 volumes. Paris: Letouzey et Ane, 1967.

———. "Saint Bonaventure et Richard de Saint-Victor." In *Bonaventuriana: Miscellanea in onore di Jacques Guy Bougerol O.F.M.,* edited by Francisco de Asis Chavero Blanco, pp. 63–96. Rome: Edizioni Antonianum, 1988.

———. "Sens et réalité ultime selon Richard de Saint-Victor." *Ultimate Reality and Meaning* 5–6 (1982–83): 221–43.

———. "Thomas Gallus ou les Ecritures dans une dialectique mystique." In *L'homme devant Dieu: mélanges offerts au Père Henri de Lubac,* pp. 99–110. Paris: Aubier, 1963.

———. "Thomas Gallus et Richard de Saint-Victor, mystiques." *Recherches de théologie ancienne et mediévale* 29/30 (1962/1963): 206–33/88–121.

Jeauneau, Edouard. "Le renouveau érigènien du XIIe siècle." In *Eriugena Redivivus,* edited by W. Beierwaltes, pp. 26–46. Heidelberg, 1987.

Jocqué, Lucas and Milis, Ludovicus, eds. *Liber ordinis Sancti Victoris Parisiensis.* Corpus Christianorum, Continuatio Mediaeualis, no. 61. Turnholt: Brepols, 1984.

Johnston, William. *The Inner Eye of Love: Mysticism and Religion.* San Francisco: Harper & Row, 1987

———. *The Still Point.* New York: Harper & Row, 1971.

Jones, Cheslyn, Geoffrey Wainwright, and Edward Yarnold, eds. *The Study of Spirituality.* New York: Oxford University Press, 1987.

Jones, Rufus. *Studies in Mystical Religion.* London: Macmillan, 1909.

———. *New Studies in Mystical Religion.* New York: Macmillan, 1927.

Jung, C. G. *Mysterium Coniunctionis.* In *Collected Works of C. G. Jung,* Volume 14, translated by R. F. C. Hull. New York: Pantheon, 1963.

———. *Psyche & Symbol: A Selection from the Writings of C. G. Jung.* Translated by Cary Baynes and R. F. C. Hull, edited by Violet S. de Laszlo. New York: Doubleday Anchor Books, 1958.

———. "The Symbolism of the Mandala." In *Collected Works of C. G. Jung,* Volume 12, *Psychology and Alchemy,* translated by R. F. C. Hull, pp. 91–213.

Kagan, Harvey D. "Christian Apophatic and Kataphatic Mysticisms." *Theological Studies* 39 (1978): 399–26.

Katz, Steven, ed. *Mysticism and Philosophical Analysis.* London: Sheldon, 1978.

———, ed. *Mysticism and Religious Traditions.* New York: Oxford University Press, 1983.

Kirk, K. E. *The Vision of God: The Christian Doctrine of the Summum Bonum.* Wilton, Conn.: Morehouse, 1931.

Knowles, David, O.S.B. *The Evolution of Medieval Thought.* New York: Vintage Books, 1962.

———. "The Influence of Pseudo-Dionysius on Western Mysticism." In *Christian Spirituality: Essays in Honor of Gordon Rupp*, edited by Peter Brooks, pp. 81–94. London: SCM Press, 1975.

Kohák, Erazim. *The Embers and the Stars: A Philosophical Inquiry into the Moral Sense of Nature.* Chicago: University of Chicago Press, 1984.

Kuntz, Marion Leathers, and Paul Grimley Kuntz, eds. *Jacob's Ladder and the Tree of Life: Concepts of Hierarchy and the Great Chain of Being.* New York: Peter Lang, 1987.

Ladner, Gerhart B. *Images and Ideas in the Middle Ages: Selected Studies in History and Art.* Storia E Letteratura Raccolta Di Studi E Testi, 156. Rome: Edizioni Di Storia E Letteratura, 1983.

———. "Medieval and Modern Understanding of Symbolism: A Comparison." *Speculum: A Journal of Medieval Studies* 54 (April 1979): 223–56.

Lambert, Malcolm. *Medieval Heresy: Popular Movements from Bogomil to Hus.* New York: Holmes & Meier, 1977.

Lash, Nicholas. *Easter in Ordinary: Reflections on Human Experience and the Knowledge of God.* Charlottesville: University Press of Virginia, 1988, rpt. Notre Dame: University of Notre Dame Press, 1990.

Leclercq, Jean. "Aspects spirituels de la symbolique du livre au XIIe siècle." In *L'homme devant Dieu: Mélanges offerts au Père Henri de Lubac*, pp. 64–72. Paris: Aubier, 1964.

———. "Influence and Noninfluence of Dionysius in the Western Middle Ages." In *Pseudo-Dionysius: The Complete Works*, translated by Colm Luibheid, pp. 25–32. New York: Paulist Press, 1987.

———. *The Love of Learning and the Desire for God: A Study of Monastic Culture.* Translated by Catharine Misrahi. New York: Fordham University Press, 1961.

———. *Monks and Love in Twelfth-Century France: Psycho-Historical Essays.* Oxford: Clarendon Press, 1979.

———. *Otia Monastica: Études sur le vocabulaire de la contemplation au moyen age.* Studia anselmiana philosophica theologica; fasc. 51. Rome: Orbis Catholicus, 1963.

———. "Ways of Prayer and Contemplation, II. Western." In *Christian Spirituality: Origins to Twelfth Century.* Volume 16 of *World Spirituality: An Encyclopedic History of the Religious Quest,* ed. McGinn et al., pp. 415–26.

———. Vandenbroucke, Francois; Bouyer, Louis. *Histoire de la spiritualité Chrétienne* II: *La spiritualité de moyen âge.* Paris: Aubier, 1961.

Levante, E. R. de, ed. *The Hexaglot Bible of the Old Testaments,* Volume 1. New York: Funk and Wagnalls, 1901.

Lilla, R. C. *Clement of Alexandria: A Study in Christian Platonism and Gnosticism.* Oxford: Oxford University Press, 1971.

Lindbeck, George A. *The Nature of Doctrine: Religion and Theology in a Postliberal Age.* Philadelphia: The Westminster Press, 1984.

Longère, Jean. *L'abbaye Parisienne de Saint-Victor au moyen âge: Communications présentées au XIIIe colloque d'humanisme médiéval de Paris (1986–1988).* Biblioteca Victorina I. Turnhout: Brepols, 1991.

Lonergan, Bernard. *Doctrinal Pluralism.* Milwaukee: Marquette University Press, 1971.

Lossky, Vladimir. *The Mystical Theology of the Eastern Church.* New York: St. Vladimir's Seminary Press, 1976.

———. *The Vision of God.* Translated by Asheleigh Moorhouse. London: The Faith Press, 1963.

Louth, Andrew. *Denys the Areopagite.* Wilton, Conn.: Morehouse-Barlow, 1989.

———. *The Origins of the Christian Mystical Tradition.* Oxford: Clarendon Press, 1981.

Loewe, Raphael. "The Medieval History of the Latin Vulgage." In *The Cambridge History of the Bible: The West From the Fathers to the Reformation,* edited by G. W. H. Lampe, pp. 102–54. Cambridge: Cambridge University Press, 1969.

Lubac, Henri de. *Exégèse médiévale: Les quatre sens de l'Ecriture.* Théologie: Études Publiées sous la direction de la faculté de théologie S.J. de Lyon-Fourviére, no. 42. 4 volumes. Paris: Aubier, 1954–64.

MacGregor, Geddes. *Angels: Ministers of Grace.* New York: Paragon House, 1988.

Masiello, R. J. "Reason and Faith in Richard of St. Victor and St. Thomas." *The New Scholasticism* 48 (1974): 233–42.

Marx, Karl. *The Marx-Engels Reader.* Edited by Robert C. Tucker. New York: W. W. Norton, 1972.

McFague, Sallie. *Metaphorical Theology: Models of God in Religious Language*. London: SCM Press, 1983.

McGinn, Bernard. "Ascension and Introversion in the *Itinerarium Mentis in Deum*." In *Bonaventura 1274–1974*, vol. 3, pp. 535–52. Rome: Grottaferrata, 1974.

———. *The Foundations of Mysticism*, Volume 1 of *The Presence of God: A History of Western Christian Mysticism*. New York: Crossroad, 1991.

———. "Love, Knowledge, and *Unio Mystica* in the Western Christian Tradition." In *Mystical Union and Monotheistic Faith: An Ecumenical Dialogue*, edited by Moshe Idel and Bernard McGinn, pp. 59–86. New York: Macmillan, 1989.

———. "The Negative Element in the Anthropology of John the Scot." In *Jean Scot Erigène et l'histoire de la philosophie*, pp. 315–25. Paris: Centre national de la recherche scientifique, 1977.

———. "Pseudo-Dionysius and the Early Cistercians." In *One Yet Two: Monastic Tradition East and West*, pp. 201–7. Kalamazoo: Cistercian Publications, 1976.

——— and John Meyendorff, eds. *Christian Spirituality: Origins to the Twelfth Century*. Volume 16 of *World Spirituality*, ed. McGinn et al. New York: Crossroad, 1986.

Moran, Dermot. *The Philosophy of John Scottus Eriugena: A Study of Idealism in the Middle Ages*. Cambridge: Cambridge University Press, 1989.

Morris, Colin. *The Discovery of the Individual: 1050–1200*. London: SPCK, 1972.

Morrison, Karl Frederick. *Tradition and Authority in the Western Church, 300–1140*. Princeton: Princeton University, 1969.

Mortley, Raoul. *From Word to Silence: The Way of Negation, Christian and Greek*. Bonn: Hanstein, 1986

O'Meara, John J. *Eriugena*. Oxford: Clarendon Press, 1988.

Ortony, Andrew, ed. *Metaphor and Thought*. Cambridge: Cambridge University Press, 1979.

Otto, Rudolf. *The Idea of the Holy*. New York: Oxford University Press, 1958.

———. *Mysticism East and West*. Translated by Bertha L. Bracey and Richenda C. Payne. New York: Macmillan, 1932.

Ouy, Gilbert, et al. *Le catalogue de la bibliothèque de l'abbaye de Saint-Victor de Paris de Claude de Grandru 1514*. Introduction by Gilbert Ouy and Veronika Gerz-von Buren, text and index by Veronika Gerz-von Buren, Raymonde Hubschmid, and Catherine Regnier, concordances by Gilbert Ouy. Paris: CNRS, 1988.

Palmer, Richard E. *Hermeneutics: Interpretation Theory in Schleiermacher, Dilthey, Heidegger, and Gadamer.* Evanston: Northwestern University Press, 1969.

Paré, G.; Bunet, A.; Tremblay, P. *La renaissance du XIIe siècle: les écoles et l'enseignement.* Publications de l'institut d'études médiévales d'Ottowa, 3. Paris: J. Vrin, 1933.

Pelikan, Jaroslav. *The Christian Tradition.* 5 Volumes. Chicago: Univeristy of Chicago Press, 1971–83.

———. "The Odyssey of Dionysian Spirituality." In *Pseudo-Dionysius: The Complete Works,* translated by Colm Luibheid, CWS, pp. 11–24. New York: Paulist Press, 1987.

Plantinga, Alvin, and Wolterstorff, Nicholas, eds. *Faith and Rationality: Reason and Belief in God.* Notre Dame: University of Notre Dame Press, 1983.

Rahner, Karl. "The Doctrine of the Spiritual Senses in the Middle Ages." In Karl Rahner, *Theological Investigations.* Volume 16, translated by David Morland, pp. 104–34. New York: Crossroad, 1983.

———. "The Spiritual Senses According to Origen." In Karl Rahner, *Theological Investigations.* Volume 16, translated by David Morland, pp. 81–103. New York: Crossroad, 1983.

Régnon, Théodore de. *Etudes de théologie positive sur la Sainte Trinité.* Four volumes. Paris: Retaux, 1892–1898.

Revel-Neher, Elisabeth. *L'arche d'alliance dans l'art Juif et Chrétien du second au dixième siècles: le signe de la recontre.* Paris: Association Des Amis Des Études Archéologiques, 1984.

Ricoeur, Paul. *Hermeneutics and the Human Sciences: Essays on Language, Action and Interpretation.* Edited, translated, and introduced by John B. Thompson. Cambridge: Cambridge University Press, 1981.

———. *Interpretation Theory: Discourse and the Surplus of Meaning.* Fort Worth: Texas Christian University Press, 1976.

———. *La métaphore vive.* Paris: Seuil, 1975. Translated by Robert Czerny et al. as *The Rule of Metaphor.* Toronto: University of Toronto Press, 1977.

———. "The Symbol Gives Rise to Thought." In *Ways of Understanding Religion,* edited by Walter Capps. New York: Macmillan, 1972.

Riehm, Eduardo C. Aug. *De natura et notione symbolica cheruborum.* Basileae et Ludoviciburgi, 1864.

Robilliard, J. A. "Les six genres de contemplation chez Richard de Saint-Victor et leur origine platonicienne." *Revue des sciences philosophiques et théologiques* 28 (1939): 229–33.

Robinson, I. S. *The Papacy, 1073–1198: Continuity and Innovation.* Cambridge: Cambridge University Press, 1990.

Roques, René; Chevallier, Philippe; Weisweiler, Henri; Dumeige, Gervais. "Denys L'Aréopagite (Le pseudo-)." In *Dictionnaire de spiritualité: ascétique et mystique, doctrine et histoire* 3: 244–429. Paris: Beauchesne, 1957.

———. *Structures théologique: de la Gnose à Richard de Saint-Victor. Essais et analyses critiques.* Bibliothèque de l'Ecole des Hautes Études: Section des sciences religieuses, 72. Paris: Presses Universitaires de France, 1962.

———. *L'univers Dionysien, structure hiérarchique du monde selon pseudo- Denys.* Paris: Aubier, 1954.

Rorem, Paul. *Biblical and Liturgical Symbols within the Pseudo-Dionysian Synthesis.* Toronto: Pontifical Institute of Mediaeval Studies, 1984.

———. *Pseudo-Dionysius: A Commentary on the Texts and an Introduction to Their Influence.* New York: Oxford University Press, 1993.

———. "The Uplifting Spirituality of Pseudo-Dionysius." In *Christian Spirituality: Origins to Twelfth Century.* Volume 16 of *World Spirituality,* ed. McGinn et al., pp. 132–51. New York: Crossroad, 1989.

Ross, Ellen M. "Humans Creation in God's Image: Richard of St. Victor, Walter Hilton, and Contemporary Theology." Ph.D. Dissertation, University of Chicago, 1987.

Sacks, Sheldon, ed. *On Metaphor.* Chicago: University of Chicago Press, 1979.

Saffrey, H. D. "Neoplatonist Spirituality: From Iamblichus to Proclus and Damascius." In *Classical Mediterranean Spirituality: Egyptian, Greek, Roman.* Volume 15 of *World Spirituality,* pp. 250–58. New York: Crossroad, 1989.

Salet, Gaston, S.J. "Les chemins de Dieu d'après Richard de Saint-Victor." In *L'homme devant Dieu: Mélanges offerts au Père Henri de Lubac,* pp. 73–88. Paris: Aubier, 1963.

Seleman, Stephen J. "Richard of Saint Victor and the Mystical Life." *Cistercian Studies* 16 (1980–81): 301–10.

Sheldrake, Philip. *Spirituality and History: Questions of Interpretation and Method.* New York: Crossroard, 1992.

Sicard, Patrice. *Diagrammes médiévaux et exégèse visuelle, le Libellus de formatione arche de Hugues de Saint-Victor.* Bibliotheca Victorina IV. Turnhout: Brepols, 1993.

Smalley, Beryl. *The Study of the Bible in the Middle Ages.* Notre Dame: University of Notre Dame Press, 1978.

Soskice, Janet Martin. *Metaphor and Religious Language.* Oxford: Clarendon Press, 1985.

Southern, Richard William. *The Making of the Middle Ages.* New Haven: Yale University Press, 1953.

———. *Western Society and the Church in the Middle Ages.* New York: Penguin, 1970.

Stace, W. T. *Mysticism and Philosophy.* Philadelphia: Lippincott, 1960.

———. *The Teachings of the Mystics.* New York: New American Library, 1960.

Steinmetz, David, D. "The Superiority of Pre-Critical Exegesis." *Theology Today* 37 (1980): 27–38.

Stiefel, Tina. *The Intellectual Revolution in Twelfth Century Europe.* New York: St. Martin's Press, 1985.

Strong, Frederick J. *Emptiness: A Study of Religious Meaning.* Nashville: Abingdon Press, 1967.

Szarmach, Paul E., ed. *An Introduction to the Medieval Mystics of Europe.* Albany: SUNY Press, 1984.

Thiselton, Anthony C. *The Two Horizons: New Testament Hermeneutics and Philosophical Description with Special Reference to Heidegger, Bultmann, Gadamer and Wittgenstein.* Exeter: The Paternoster Press, 1980.

Tillich, Paul. "Theology and Symbolism." In *Religious Symbolism*, edited by F. Ernest Johnson, pp. 107–16. New York: Harper and Brothers, 1955.

Tomasic, Thomas Michael. "The Logical Function of Metaphor and Oppositional Coincidence in the Pseudo-Dionysius and Johannes Scottus Eriugena." *Journal of Religion* 68 (1968): 361–76.

Toulouse, Jean de. *Liber antiquitatum sancti Victoris.* In *Richardi a Sancto Victore Opera Omnia, PL,* 196: ix–xiv.

Tracy, David. *The Analogical Imagination: Christian Theology and the Culture of Pluralism.* New York: Crossroad, 1981.

———. *Plurality and Ambiguity: Hermeneutics, Religion and Hope.* San Francisco: Harper & Row, 1987.

Tucci, Giuseppe. *The Theory and Practice of the Mandala.* Translation by Alan Houghton Brodrick. London: Rider, 1967.

Tugwell, Simon, O.P. *Albert and Thomas: Selected Writings.* Translated, introduced, and edited by Simon Tugwell. CWS. New York: Paulist Press, 1989.

Turney, Sr. Lillian. "The Symbolism of the Temple in *Itinerarium in mentis deum* of Bonaventure." Ph.D. dissertation, Fordham University, 1968.

Underhill, Evelyn. *Mysticism: A Study in the Nature and Development of Man's Spiritual Consciousness.* London: Methuen, 1911.

———. *The Mystic Way: A Psychological Study in Christian Origins.* London: J. M. Dent, 1914.

———. *The Essentials of Mysticism and Other Essays.* London: J. M. Dent, 1920.

Valk, John. "The Concept of the *Coincidentia Oppositorum* in the Thought of Mircea Eliade." *Religious Studies* 28 (1991): 31–41.

Van Zwieten, J. W. M. "Jewish Exegesis within Christian Bounds: Richard of St. Victor's *De Emmanuele* and Victorine Hermeneutics." *Bijdragen* 48 (1987): 327–35.

Wakefield, Gordon S., ed. *The Westminster Dictionary of Christian Spirituality*. Philadelphia: Westminster, 1983.

Walker, G. S. M. "Richard of St. Victor: An Early Scottish Theologian?" *Scottish Journal of Theology* 11 (1958): 37–52.

Wasselynck, René. "La présence des Moralia de S. Grégoire le Grand dans les ouvrages de morale du XIIe siècle." In *Recherches de théologie ancienne et médiévale* 35/36 (1968/1969): 197–240/31–45.

Zaehner, R. C. *Mysticism, Sacred and Profane*. New York: Oxford University Press, 1961.

———. *Zen, Drugs, and Mysticism*. New York: Vantage, 1974.

Zinn, Grover A. "Book and Word: The Victorine Background of Bonaventure's Use of Symbols." In *S. Bonaventura 1274–1974*. Volume 2: 143–69. Rome: Grottaferrata, 1973.

———. "*De Gradibus Ascensionum*: The Stages of Contemplative Ascent in Two Treatises on Noah's Ark by Hugh of St Victor." In *Studies in Medieval Culture*, V, edited by Sommerfeldt et al., pp. 61–79. Kalamazoo: The Medieval Institute, 1975.

———. "History and Contemplation: The Dimensions of the Restoration of Man in Two Treatises on the Ark of Noah by Hugh of St. Victor." Ph.D. dissertation, Duke University, 1969.

———. "History and Interpretation: 'Hebrew Truth,' Judaism, and the Victorine Exegetical Tradition." In *Jews and Christians: Exploring the Past, Present, and Future*, edited by James H. Charlesworth, pp. 100-123. New York: Crossroad, 1990

———. "Mandala Symbolism and Use in the Mysticism of Hugh of St. Victor." *History of Religions* 12 (August 1972): 317–41.

———. "Personification Allegory and Visions of Light in Richard of St. Victor's Teaching on Contemplation." *University of Toronto Quarterly* 46 (1977): 190–214.

———. "Sound, Silence, and Word in the Spirituality of Gregory the Great." In *Grégoire le Grand*, edited by Jacques Fontaine et al., pp. 367–75. Paris: CNRS, 1986.

———. "Suger, Theology, and the Pseudo-Dionysian Tradition." In *Abbot Suger and Saint-Denis*, edited by Paula Lieber Gerson, pp. 33–40. New York: Metropolitan Museum of Art, 1986.

Index to Biblical Citations
in De Arca Mystica

The order of Biblical Books follows that of *Biblia Sacra Vul2ata* including Apocrypha. Citations from Psalms are given in Vulgate form. Arabic numerals indicate Biblical Book and Chapter, upper case Roman numerals indicate Book from *De arca mystical* lower case Roman numerals indicate Chapter.

Genesis		*III Kings (I Kings, RSV)*	
1.27	IV.viii	10.1–3	V.xii
3.19	V.xiv	10.4–5	V.xii
13.14–15	V.ii	19.13	IV.x
18.1	IV.x	19.14	IV.x
18.1–2	V.viii		
18.33	IV.xii	*IV Kings (II Kings. RSV)*	
41.1–8	V.i	3.15	V.xvii
Exodus		*Job*	
3.14	IV.xxii	5.6	II.x
13.21	V.xv	19.4	III.xiii
15.11	IV.viii	27.6	III.v
23.16–18	V.ii	30.7	V.xiv
25.9	IV.vii		
25.19	IV.viii	*Psalms*	
25.20	IV.ix, IV.xvii	4.7	IV.viii
25.18–20	IV.i	4.9	IV.xxii
25.22	IV.xxi	5.5	III.ix
25.40	IV.xxii	8.2	II.i
29.37	I.i	8.4	III.ix
		10.5	II.ix
Leviticus		12.4	III.xiv
11.44	I.i	15.7	III.xiii
		17.29	V.xv
Deuteronomy		18.10	II.x
32.11	V.iii	31.11	V.xviii
34.1	V.ii	33.9	I.i, III.xix, IV.xiv

35.7	II.viii	144.3	IV.xvii
35.9	IV.xvii	144.9	II.ix
38.6–7	IV.viii	144.13	II.i
39.18	V.xiv		
40.10	II.xvii	*Proverbs*	
41.4	II.xvii	7.4	III.iii
45.11	I.ii		
48.11–12	II.ii	*Ecclesiastes*	
49.23	V.xviii	1.1	II.i
50.9	I.ii	1.5	III.vi
54.7	I.x, V.iv	1.6	III.vii
54.14–16	II.xvii	1.5–6	III.vi
56.4	V.xiii	3.11	II.ii
56.4–5	V.xiii	7.3	III.xv
57.9	III.ix	9.12	I.x
63.3	III.v		
63.7	II.ii	*Canticles*	
63.7,8	V.iv	2.10	IV.xiii
67.5	V.xviii	2.13–14	IV.xiii
68.6	III.xiii	3.6	V.v
72.1	I.ii	5.1	IV.xvi
72.25	III.xiii	5.2	IV.xiii
75.6	II.ii	5.3	IV.xiii
76.3	V.xvi	5.6	IV.xiii
76.7	III.v	5.10	II.xv
78.9	III.xvi	5.15	II.xv
80.14–15	III.xvi	6.9	V.v, V.ix, V.x
82.2	IV.viii	8.5	V.v, V.xiv, V.xv
85.1	V.xiv		
85.8	IV.viii	*Wisdom*	
91.5	II.vi	2.6	III.xv
103.24	II.vi, II.viii	3.7	I.v
106.26	I.v	7.17–20	II.vii
112.3	II.i	7.21	II.vii
113.4	V.xiv	7.30	I.i
115.11	V.ii	8.1	I.i, II.viii
118.18	III.ix	9.19	I.i
118.62	III.ix		
118.81	V.xii	*Sirach*	
118.99–100	III.v	10.9	V.xiv
126.2	II.xvii	24.20	II.xv
131.8	I.i	24.27	II.xv
132.2	II.xv		
138.9	I.x	*Isaiah*	
142.5	II.vi	1.9	III.xvi
		4.5–6	IV.ix

7.9 — II.x
9.7 — III.xxiii
22.13 — III.xv
28.10 — V.xvi
28.10, 13 — IV.xii, IV.xiv
38.3 — III.ix
40.6 — V.xvi
40.17 — IV.viii
40.31 — V.iv
48.22 — V.xiv
55.10 — II.xv
56.12 — III.xv
60.4 — I.v
60.8 — V.ii
64.4 — III.iii

Jeremiah
2.10 — V.iii
17.9 — III.viii
31.21 — V.iii

Lamentations
1.7 — I.ii

Baruch
3.11 — III.xiii

Ezekiel
1.6 — I.x
1.14 — I.v
1.16 — II.xv
28.12–13 — IV.viii
40.26 — II.vi

Daniel
2.1 — V.i

Habakkuk
2.1 — V.iii
3.11 — I.v

Matthew
5.8 — IV.vi
5.16 — III.iii
5.45 — II.ix
17.1–8 — V.ii

17.4 — I.v
23.26 — III.iii

Luke
1.52 — III.xxiii
10.42 — I.i
15.17 — V.viii
24.26 — I.ii

John
1.9 — II.xiii, III.xiii
3.8 — III.xvii
3.20–21 — V.viii
15.5 — III.xvi
15.15 — IV.xvi
17.3 — IV.v
17.5 — I.ii

Acts
5.19–20 — III.xiii
9.17–18 — III.v
12.6–7 — V.xii
12.3–10 — V.xiii
12.11 — V.viii, V.xiii

Romans
1.20 — II.xii, II.xvi
1.21 — II.ii
9.16 — III.xvi, V.xv

I Corinthians
2.9 — III.iv
2.10 — III.viii
4.4 — III.v
4.7 — III.iii
6.17 — V.xiii
12.3 — III.xvi
12.4, 8–10 — III.xxiv
12.11 — III.xvi
13.12 — V.xiv
15.32 — III.xv
15.40–41 — I.x

II Corinthians
1.12 — III.xix
3.18 — IV.vii, IV.xi, V.ix

4.7 III.v 3.5 I.x
10.17 III.iii
12.2 I.x, IV.ix, V.xix *II Timothy*
12.6 III.iii 4.8 II.xxiv

Galatians *James*
5.22 III.xxiv 1.17 IV.xvii, IV.xviii

Ephesians *I Peter*
2.20 II.xv 1.12 I.ii
  3.15 II.vii
Philippians
1.23 I.x *I John*
2.7–9 I.ii 2.27 V.xiii
2.15 III.xvi
3.20 I.x, II.xiii *Revelation*
  1.10 V.xii
Colossians 3.20 IV.xi
2.9 IV.xviii 14.2 II.xv, III.xxiv

GENERAL INDEX

Aaron, 91

absence: balanced by presence, 37, 46–47; within mysticism, 28–29

affections into virtues, 123–24

allegorical exegesis: on Abraham and Elijah, 45–46; of Greek Christian writers, 14–16; Latin patristic influence on, 16–19; *Liber exceptionum* and, 21–27; and revelation, 233n13; ridicule of, 11–13; within cherubim narration, 188–89n87; within Victorine interpretation, 4–8

anagogy: defining, 50–51; of dissimilar symbols, 54; presence vs., 196n47; symbol vs., 194n33

angelic hierarchy, 71, 179n43

angelic clothing: as humanity of Christ, 112; as metaphor, 119–21, 127, 234n22; soul's adornment of, 88–89; tropological interpretation of, 37

angelic form, 121–26

angelic spirituality, 70–75

angelization: angelic form metaphor for, 121–26; in apophatic Christological context, 141; ark/cherubim and, 134; defining use of, 231n1; process of, 116–19, 126–28, 232n3; seraphim as part of, 140; within context of contemplation, 130. *See also* sanctification

angels: in celestial hierarchy, 290n50; cherubim function as, 93–96, 130;

functions of, 208n50; imagery of, 139–40; knowledge of, 211n73; in Patristic tradition 208n48; in Scripture, 208n49; used as dissimilar symbols, 79; vision as *opus restaurationis est incarnatio Verbi,* 111. *See also* the cherubim

Anselm of Canterbury, 104

apophatic Christology, 98, 100–104, 111–14, 141

apophatic language, 44, 199–200n63

apophatic method: Dionysian use of, 31–37; in theology, 30–33, 193n28; used in contemplation, 91–93; used in *De arca mystic,* 37–47

De arca mystica (Richard of St. Victor): absence of Christ within, 100; angelic clothing metaphor for, 119–20; apophatic Christology within, 104–9; cataphatic/apophatic methodology within, 37–47; function/use of symbol in, 61–70; grounded cherubim position in, 10; *imago Dei* doctrine of, 68, 70, 85, 92; influence of Hugh upon, 142–43; *Liber exceptionum* foundation for, 21–27; six kinds of contemplation in, 148–50; symbol of cherubim in, 75–91; thinking, meditation, contemplation in, 151; as tropological exegesis of Exodus 25, 130–31; tropological investigate proposed in, 2–4; use of tropology in, 6–8

De arca Noe (Hugh of St. Victor), 144

265

arca sanctificationis vobis (ark of sanctification for you), 2–3, 63, 104, 116, 124

the ark of Moses: angelization and, 134; as ark of sanctification, 2–3, 63, 104; Augustine's reflection on, 16; compared to Virgin Mary, 15–16; crown of, 19, 122; first symbolic interpretation of, 14; Incarnation and, 19; as journey to God symbol, 96; law/grace associated with, 16–17; pulled up toward cherubim, 12–13; symbols within, 64

Augustine, 16, 26–27

Baron, R., 145
Bezeleel, 89
bird flight patterns, 62–64, 93, 201n1
bodily visions, 49
Bonaventure, 98–100
Book V (*De arca mystica*), 137–41

cataphatic method: and the dialectic of presence and absence, 37–47; used by Denys the Areopagite, 31–32; used in Dionysian synthesis, 33–37
cataphatic symbols, 64–67
Celestial Hierarchy (Denys the Areopagite), 29–30, 48, 55, 71–72, 102, 143
charity (*caritas*): as consummation of virtues, 140–41, 242n15; theology of, 105; Wisdom as, 123; within Book V, 138
Châtillon, Jean, 4–8, 143–46
Chenu, M. D., 58
the cherubim: angelization and, 134; angels function as, 93–96, 130; as ascension and flight symbol, 8; as bordering God's dwelling, 33, 35–37; *coincidentia oppositorum* of, 37–39, 94–96, 180–83n54; compared to Virgin Mary, 15–16; contemplation symbolized by, 36, 42–44, 61–70, 77–78, 172n3; *De*

arca mystica use of, 75–91; divine participation actualized in, 28; formation of, 116–19; as fullness of knowledge, 15, 19, 94; hovering as image of, 12–13, 84, 132–33; incomprehensibility symbolism of, 107–8; as journey to God symbol, 96; "literal" exposition of, 9–10; "mystical transformation" symbolized by, 29; sanctification through, 2, 104; as symbol of Christ and God mysticism, 73–75; as symbols of the Trinity, 15, 82–83, 133; wings of, 44–47, 59, 80–82, 236n31; Wisdom signified by, 72–73, 87–88, 90–91; as womb of Wisdom, 15–16, 42, 59, 94–95, 240n6
Christ: as center of anagogic theology, 100–104, 114; cherubim as symbol of, 73–75; divinity vs. humility of, 112–13, 127, 226n37, 231n80; mediatory nature of, 98–100, 224n12, 224n16; rejection of ark/cherubim as, 26; restoration by, 103; as Wisdom, 73, 108. *See also* divinity; God
Christian mysticism, 28–29, 204n26
Christology: apophatic, 98, 100–104, 111–14; slippage between Trinity and, 135–36; within *Itinerarium mentis in Deum,* 98–100; within Richard's work, 104–9
Clement of Alexandria, 14
coincidentia oppositorum (coincidence of opposites): cherubim symbol of, 37–39, 94–96, 180–83n54; described, 131; dialectic use of, 37–40; hovering as metaphor for, 61, 64, 95; nature and use of, 179n50; within symbols, 51–52; within Trinity/the Incarnation, 83–84
Collationes in Hexaemeron (Bonaventure), 99

Commentariorum hierarchiam coelestem s. Dionysii (Hugh of St. Victor), 30, 146
contemplation: able to see the thing (*rem videre*), 109–11; anagogic use of, 91–93; angelization within context of, 130; at center of ark/cherubim, 121; as beyond metaphors, 117–18; cataphatic symbols of, 64–67, 91–93; preliminary definitions of, xix–xx; dropping dissimilar symbols during, 53; hidden within spreading wings, 80–82; highest levels of, 42; methods used for, 89–91; six wings/kinds of, 122, 148–50, 152–53n6, 223–24n8; spiritual ascent through, 49–50; symbolized by cherubim, 36, 42–44, 61–70, 76–77, 172n3; veil lifted during, 108; within wings of the cherubim, 47
corporeal similitudes, 66
Le Corpus Dionysien de l'université de Paris (Dondaine), 145
Cousins, Ewert, xxi–xxiii, 99, 145

Denys the Areopagite: anagogic theory of symbols by, 51–55, 193n25; angelology of, 71–74; cataphatic/apophatic theology in, 30–33; contribution to apophatic Christology, 101–2; possible influence of, 28–30, 145–47; on types of visions, 48–51; Wisdom of, 111
Didascalicon (Hugh of St. Victor), 142, 144
Dionysian synthesis: contemporary commentary on, 30–33; hierarchy/symbolism in, 191–92n11; medieval treatment of, 28–29; use of apophatic theology in, 33–37
dissimilar symbols: angels as, 79; cherubim function as, 78, 87,

95–96; displayed as similar, 74; distinction between similar and, 31–32, 53–55. *See also* symbols
divine love, 101, 185n71. *See also* charity (*caritas*)
Divine Names (Denys the Areopagite), 36, 53, 102
Divine Scripture: cherubim associated with, 19; interpretation based on literal foundation, 11; three manners of interpreting, 25–26; tropological interpretation of, 3, 6–7; use of incongruous imagery by, 52–53
divine theology (*divina theologia*), 55, 145
divinity: described, 112; from *in medio*, 132; silence concerning the, 101; unity of, 83. *See also* Christ
Dondaine, H. F., 145
Doran, D., 145
Dumeige, G., 29–30, 144

Eriugena, 29–30, 47, 145
excessus mentis, 42, 137–141
excudere, 116–18
Exodus 25: contemplative attributes in, 95; *De arca mystica*, review of, xxiv–xxv, 75–76, 130–31; Greek Christian writers on, 14; interpreted tropologically, 119; Latin Patristic tradition and, 16–21; metaphors within, 126–27; symbolism used in, 92
Ezekiel, 5, 10–11

"face to face," 58, 74
first cherubim, 62, 148, 224n19. *See also* the cherubim
fullness of knowledge: cherubim symbol of, 3, 15, 19, 44, 72, 94; defining, 78; search for, 26–27; testimony to nature of, 105. *See also* Wisdom (*sapientia*)

Gilson, Etienne, 29

glorification, 41
God: boundaries of speech by, 95; cherubim/ark symbol of paths to, 96; Moses/Aaron's path to, 91; presence of, 45; voice of, 90–91, 108–9, 113–14. *See also* Christ; *loquar ad te* (I will speak to you)
God's dwelling, 33, 35–37
grace: associated with the ark, 16–17; breath of aspired, 95; of God's work, 25; images of, 55; relation of human activity to, 238n44; sanctification through, 2, 22–23, 104; symbols of, 203n18; through wings of cherubim, 46
gratia contemplationis (grace of contemplation), 75
Greek patristic tradition, 14–16, 165n58
Gregory the Great, 5, 17–18, 26–27, 163n52
"guiding hand" (*manuductio*), 57, 66, 178n38, 193n29, 196–97n48

healing, 3–4
Hebrews 9, 21
hidden/concealed things, 39–42, 46, 50
hidden knowledge (*secretioris scientiae*), 94
hierarchy: angelic, 71, 179n43; divinity and, 72
Hippolytus, 14
historia (historical interpretation): pulled toward tropological, 13; Richard's use of, 8–13; within Victorine interpretation, 4–8
Holy Spirit, 86, 113
hovering: above the propitiatory, 88–91; applied to symbol function, 70; cherubim as image of, 12–13, 84, 132–33; as *coincidentia oppositorum* metaphor, 61, 64, 95; as contemplation metaphor, 61–62; gaze of opposites which are, 105; preliminary definitions of,

xx-xviii, presence/absence within, 29; spirituality within, 4; synthesis and, 6
Hugh of St. Victor: on angelization, 125; Christology of, 102–4; influence of, 4–5; relationship between Richard and, 142–46; use of symbol by, 55–58, 74–75; on work of restoration, 2–3
humanity of Christ, 112–13, 127, 226n37, 231n80. *See also* Christ as human spirit, 122–26

image: of cherubim, 116–19; of flight, 8, 131–32; symbolism of, 74; thing vs., 109–11, 197n50, 230n69
images of nature (*simulacrum naturae*), 55–57
imago Dei doctrine, 68, 70, 85, 92
imitation of Wisdom, 79–80, 113, 121, 127–28
In apocalypsim Joannis (Richard of St. Victor), 30, 48–51, 54
Incarnation, ark as, 19; cherubim as, 17–18; oppositional content within, 83; and restoration, 103–4, 154–55n7, 226n35; the Trinity linked to, 106–7; as work of divine love, 101
incomprehensibility, 107–8, 120–21, 128, 134–36, 183–84n58
industry (*industria*), 162–63n51
"internal icon" metaphor, 95
the invisible, 64–66
In visionem Ezechielis (Richard of St. Victor), 9, 10–12, 55
Isidore of Seville, 18

Jerome, 26–27

Kirchberger, C., 30, 144
knowledge: of angels, 211n73; love and, 241n5. *See also* fullness of knowledge; Wisdom (*sapientia*)

Ladner, G., 145

Latin Patristic tradition, 16–19
Leclercq, J., 144–45
leisure (*otium*), 162–63n51
Libellus de formatione arche (Hugh of St. Victor), 144
Liber exceptionum (Richard of St. Victor), 6, 9, 10, 21–27, 104
literal exegesis. *See historia* (historical interpretation)
looking back (*respicit*), 74–75
loquar ad te (I will speak to you), 88–91, 112, 119, 121, 128, 134, 240n6
love: charity as final degree of, 105; divine, 185n71; imagery of, 138–39; Incarnation as work of divine, 101; knowledge and, 167n79, 241n5
Lubac, Henri de, 7

McGinn, Bernard, 28, 31, 37
manifestiora (manifested things), 39
metaphors: of angelic clothing, 119–21, 127, 225n22; of angelic form, 121–26; of angelization, 126–28; contemplation as beyond, 117–18; hovering as, 61–62, 64; "internal icon," 95; positive/negative, 39–40; within angel symbolism, 72
mind (*mens*), 86
Mortley, R., 32, 145
Moses: burning bush vision of, 49; contemplative method used by, 89; entering God's dwelling, 35; path to God used by, 91
mundane theology (*mundana theologia*), 55, 145, 158n23
mutual gazing (*videntur se mutuo*), 105
mutuo se respiciant (mutual looking back), 75, 211–12n69
Mystical Theology (Denys the Areopagite), 33–34, 54–55
mystical transformation, 29
mysticism, 28–29, 204n26

negative theology, 30–33, 54–55, 177n28, 193n28
negative to positive theology, 28–30
New Testament, 20. *See also* Divine Scripture
Nonnullai allegoriae tabernaculi foederis (Richard of St. Victor), 6–7

occultiora (hidden or concealed things), 39–42, 46
operis factura (work about to be done), 127
opus conditionis (work of foundation), 2, 5, 55
opus nostrum ductile (our beaten work), 118
opus restaurationis (the work of restoration): as angelization image, 127; angel's vision as, 111; ark/cherubim and, 21, 75; described, 2–3; distinctions of, 55; grace of, 25; humility of Christ in, 57; as reality of moral life, 5
Origen, 14–15
Ottoviano, C., 143–44

patterns of bird flight and thinking, 62–64, 93, 201n1
Philo of Alexandria, 14
plenitudo scientiae (fullness of knowledge), 3, 15, 19, 26–27, 44, 105
positive theology, 28–30, 55, 177n28
presence: anagogy vs., 196n47; balanced with absence, 37, 46–47; cherubim provided continuity of, 95–96; of God, 45; within mysticism, 28–29. *See also* God
propitiatory: as Christ surrogate, 106; hovering above the, 88–91; spreading wings concealing, 80–82; symbolism of, 96, 205n31; two cherubim facing the, 85–86
"psychology of symbol," 67–68
purification, 124–26, 238n45

rem videre (to see the thing), 74, 109–11, 197n50, 230n69
revelation (*revelationem*), 79, 180n52, 230n78, 226n13
Revel-Neher, Elisabeth, 15–16
Richard of St. Victor: as apophatic mystic, 37; Christology within works of, 104–9; Denys possible influence on, 29–30, 145–47; interest in tropological sense, 2–4, 6–8; methodology used by, 151–52n2; as mystic, 29; relationship between Hugh and, 142–46; response to negative/positive theology, 30–33; use of literal exegesis by, 8–13; use of symbols by, 58–60; use of Victorine exegesis by, 4–8
Romans 1:20, 64, 92
Roques, R., 31, 72, 103, 145
Rorem, P., 31

De Sacramentis (Hugh of St. Victor), 3, 142–44
"sacred psychology," 160–61n39
sanctification: ark of, 2, 2–3, 63, 124; defining, 2–3; through grace, 2, 22–23. *See also* angelization
scriptures. *See* Divine Scripture
second cherubim, 62, 148, 234n19. *See also* the cherubim
the seraphim, 72, 140, 210n59
setim wood, 14, 122
Sicard, P., 144
similar symbols: cherubim function as, 87, 95–96; displayed as dissimilar, 74; distinction between dissimilar and, 31–32, 53. *See also* symbols
similitudinis gratia (symbols of grace), 203n18
similitudinum ratione (rational principle of similitudes), 39, 66, 203n18
simulacrum naturae (image of nature), 55–57

six wings of contemplation 122, 223–24n8
Smalley, B., 4–5
Solomon, 27
Song of Songs, 45–46
the soul: in angelic form, 79, 88–89; charity which consumes, 105; church equated with, 23–25; evolution into angelic form, 118; symbols of the, 69–70; Trinity within, 85–86
spirituality: built upon literal foundation, 11–13; Richard's synthesis of, 4, 8, 240n2
spiritual transformation, 121–26
spiritual visions, 49
symbols: adaptation within visions of, 81–82; anagogic theory of, 51–55, 193n25; anagogy vs., 194n33; cataphatic, 64–67; of cherubim, 8; defining, 48–51, 198n58; function and use of, 55–58; Hugh's vs. Richard's use of, 58; modern vs. medieval use of, 198–99n62; patterns forming a, 62–64, 93; process aspects of, 205n32; the propitiatory as, 96, 205n31; Richard's use of, 91–93; soul mysticism and, 67–70; twelfth-century use of, 58–60; used in *De arca mystica*, 61–70. *See also* dissimilar symbols; similar symbols

Taylor, Jerome, 144
temple of Solomon: the position of the cherubim on, 10; vision shown to Ezekiel of, 10–11
"theophanies" (*theophanias*), 50
Toulouse, Jean de, 143
De Trinitate (Richard of St. Victor), 105
the Trinity: apophatic/cataphatic elements of, 34–36; assertions/denials within, 31; cherubim as symbols of, 15, 82–83, 133; image vs. divine, 86–87; the Incarnation

linked to, 106–7; slippage between Christology and, 135–36; within the soul, 85–86

tropological exegesis: defining, 5; pulled toward literal, 13; Richard's use of, 6–8; types of, 160n38; used in *Liber exceptionum*, 23–25; of Wisdom, 121–26; of the Word, 133–34

turned away (*aversus*), 74–75

twin gaze, 82–88. *See also* the cherubim

unity of divinity, 83

the veil: lifted during contemplation, 108; passing through, 90–91; revelation and, 230n78

via et ostium (road and door to the Father), 100

Victorine exegesis: integration within, 131; Richard of St. Victor's use of, 4–8;

Virgin Mary, 15–16

virtues, 123–24, 140, 242n15

visions: function of symbols in, 81–82; types of, 49–50

voice (human), 108–9, 112, 114, 197n51

voice of the Lord, 90–91, 108–9, 113–14. *See also loquar ad te* (I will speak to you)

wings of the cherubim, 44–47, 59, 80–82, 236n31. *See also* the cherubim

Wisdom (*sapientia*): charity as, 123; cherubim signifying, 72–73, 87–88, 90–91; cherubim as womb of, 15–16, 42, 59, 94–95; Christ as, 73, 108; as Christ surrogate, 106; of Denys the Areophagite, 111; healing sanctification through, 3–4; Hugh of St. Victor on, 56; imitation taking form of, 79–80, 113, 121, 127–28; metaphor of clothing as imitation of, 121; Richard's uncovering of, 19, 26–27; as the son, 86; tropological exegesis on, 121–26. *See also* fullness of knowledge

"the Wisdom of the trinity," 15

the Word: ark/cherubim as birthing agent of, 16; as constant prayer, 130; human voice of, 108; made present, 59–60; memory of the promised, 91; and restoration, 103–4, 154–155n7, 226n35; tropology and, 133–34

Zinn, G., 145

About the Author

Steven Chase is Assistant Professor of Spirituality and Historical Theology at the Graduate Theological Union, Berkeley, California and a Fellow at the Center of Theological Inquiry, Princeton, New Jersey. He is currently translating medieval Latin texts by authors speculating on the subject of "Angelic Spirituality."